TIGER & BUNNY 4

ART BY **MIZUKI SAKAKIBARA**

PLANNING / ORIGINAL STORY **SUNRISE**

ORIGINAL SCRIPT **Masafumi Nishida**

ORIGINAL CHARACTER AND HERO DESIGN **Masakazu Katsura**

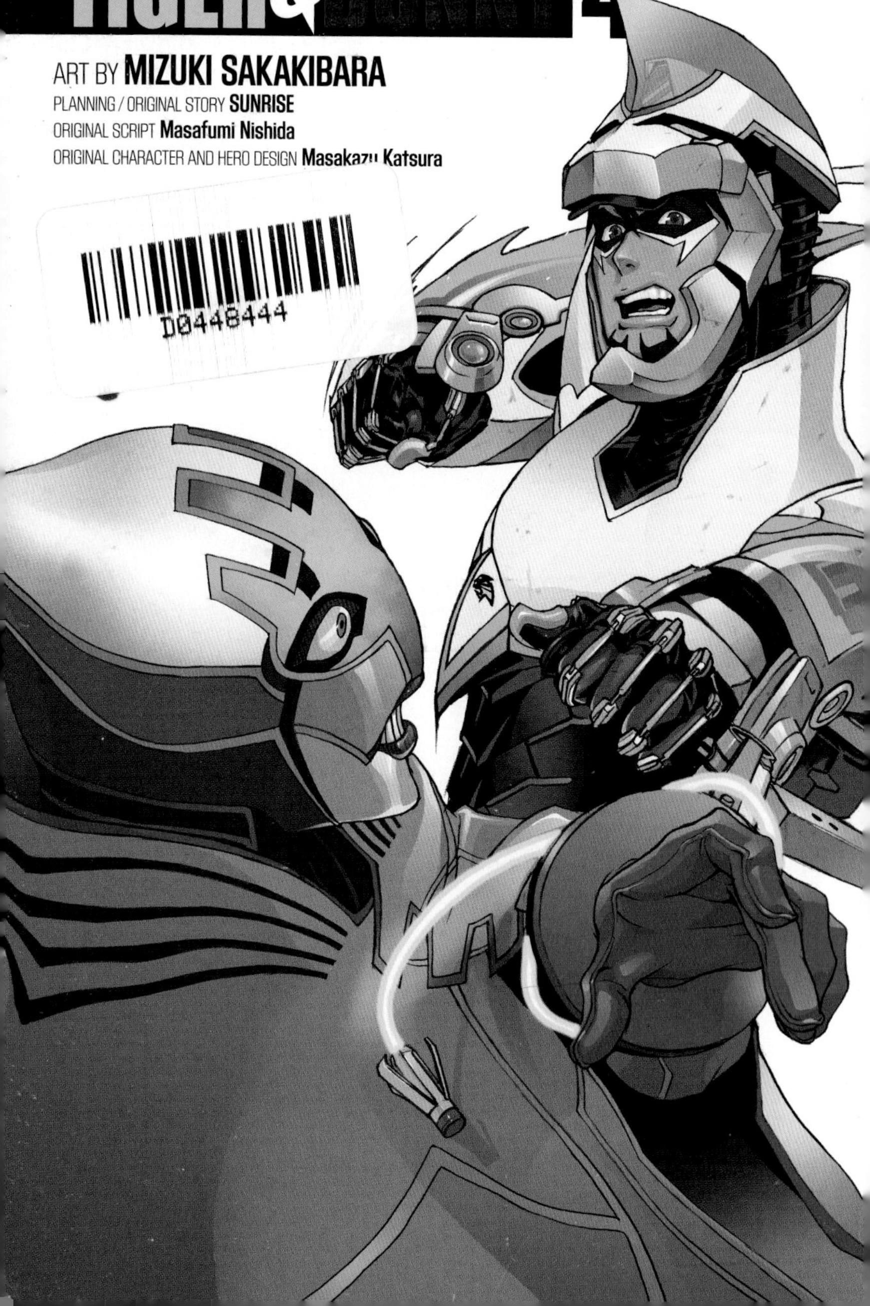

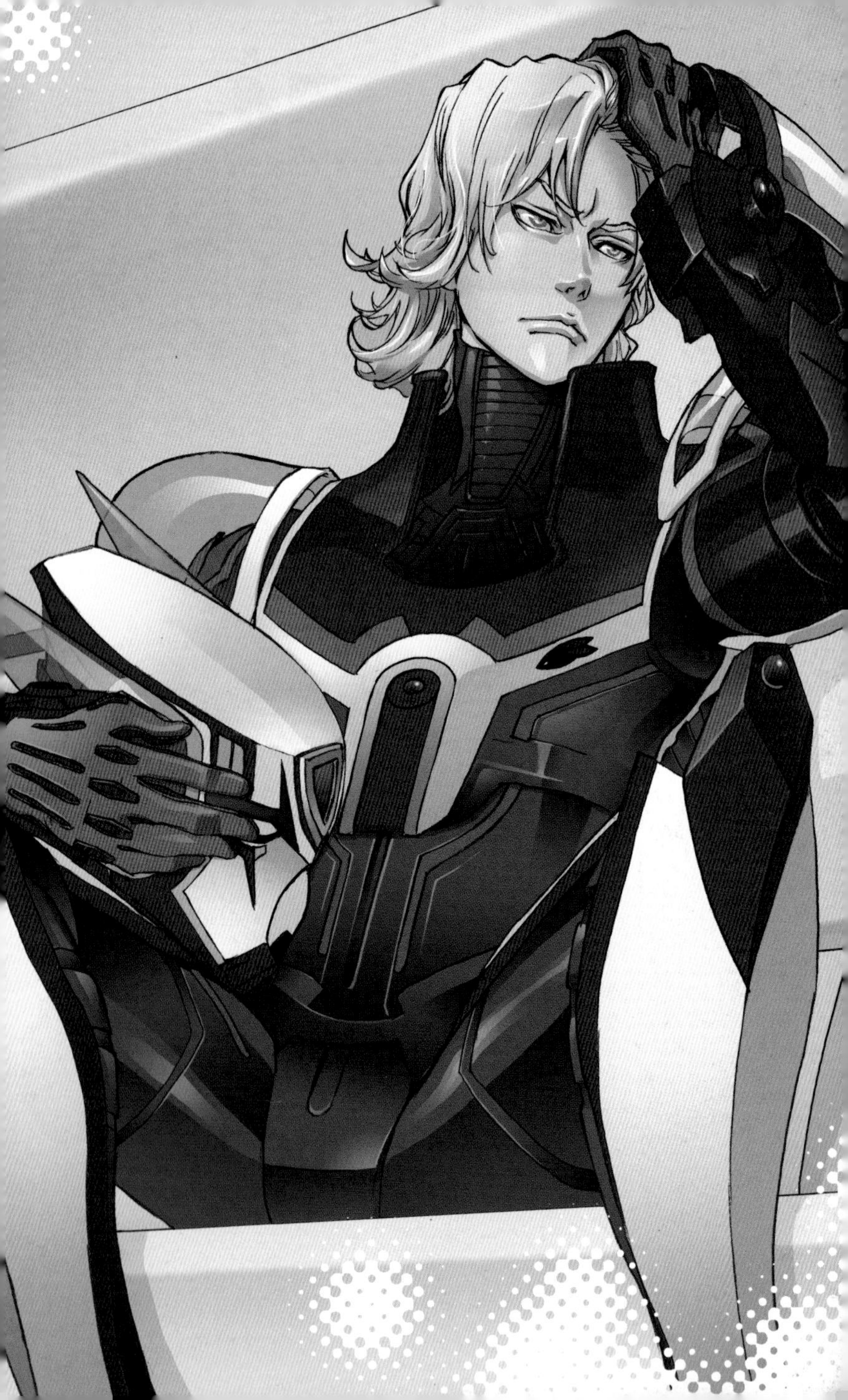

CONTENTS

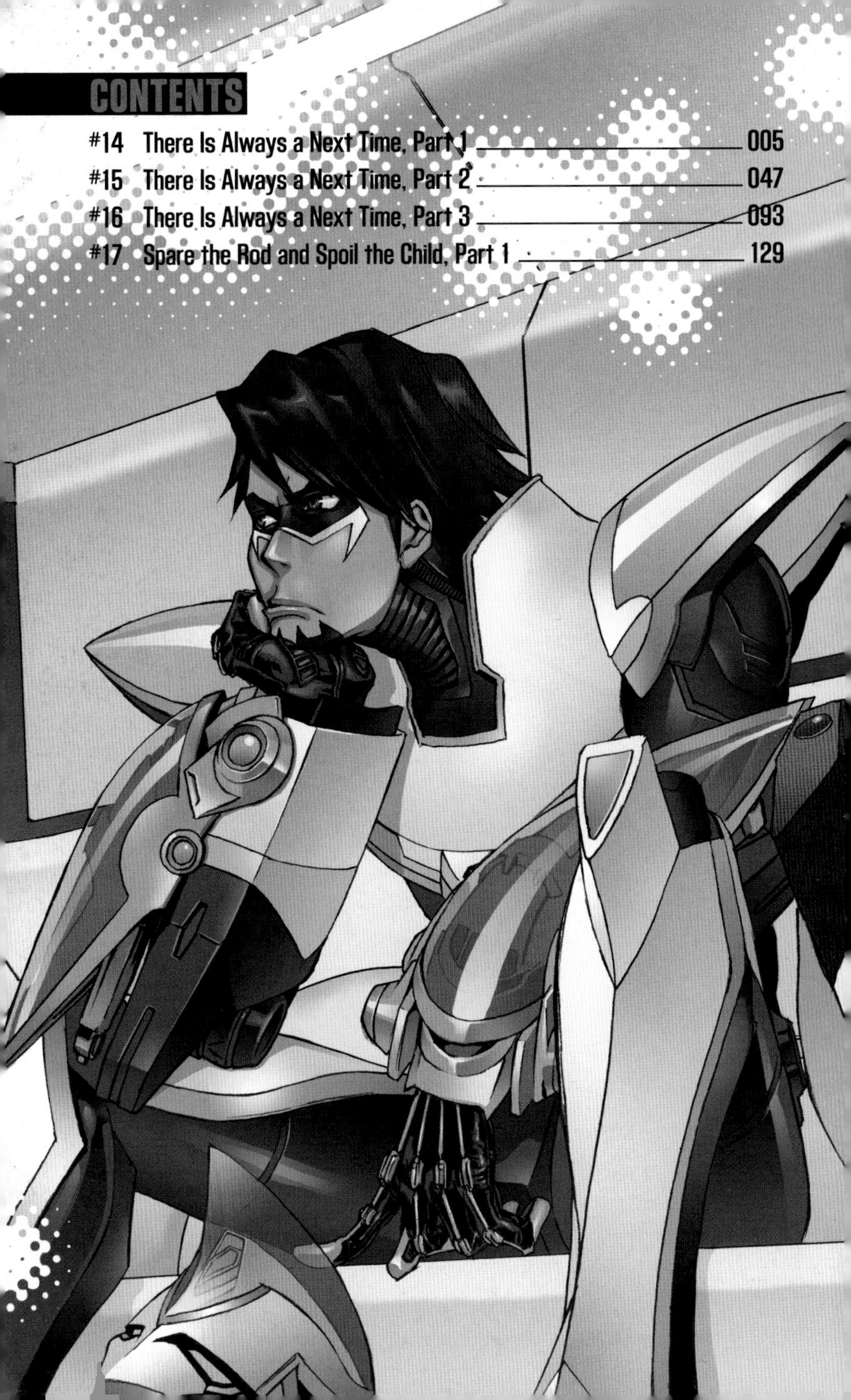

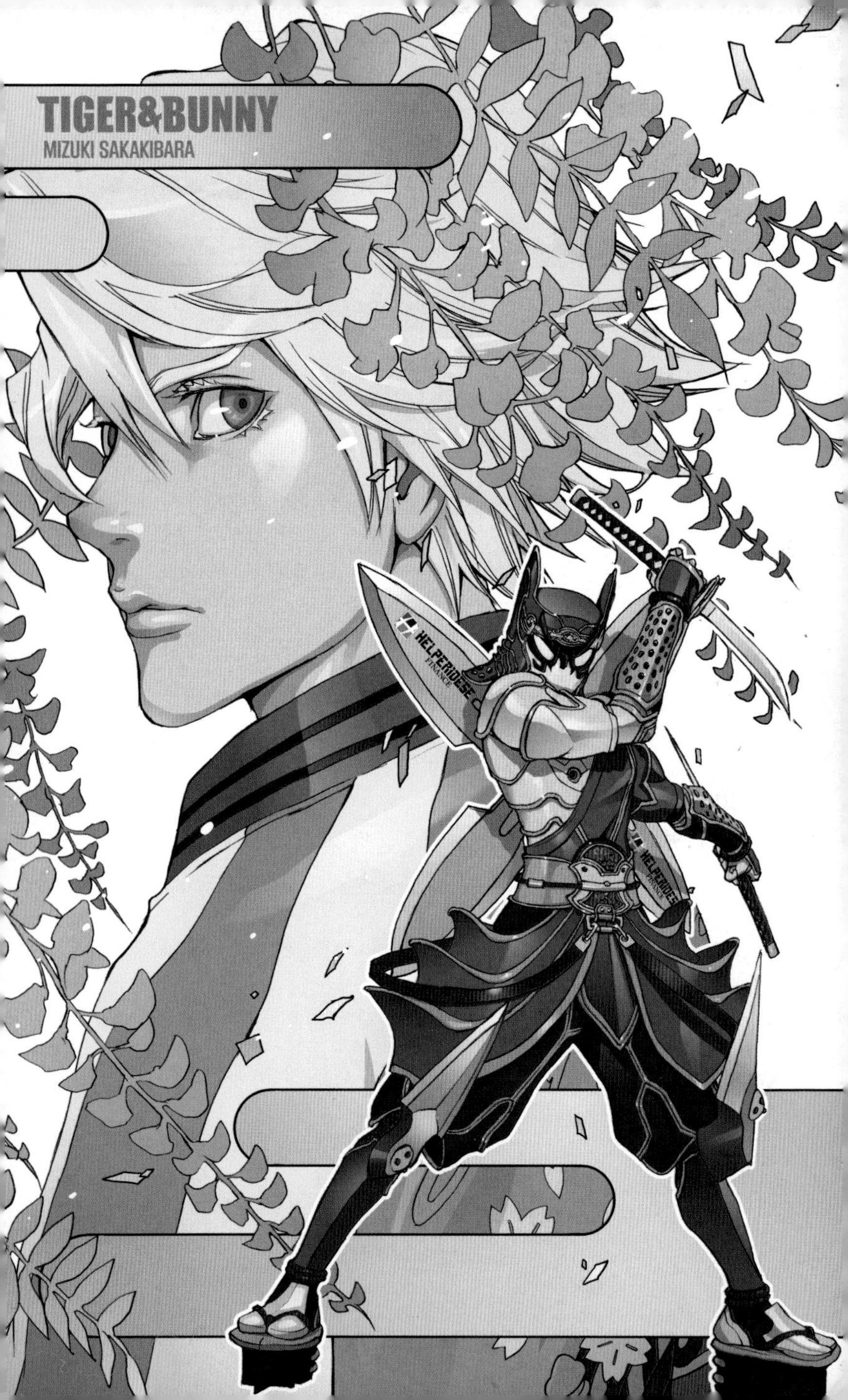
TIGER&BUNNY
MIZUKI SAKAKIBARA
HELPERIDESE
FINANCE

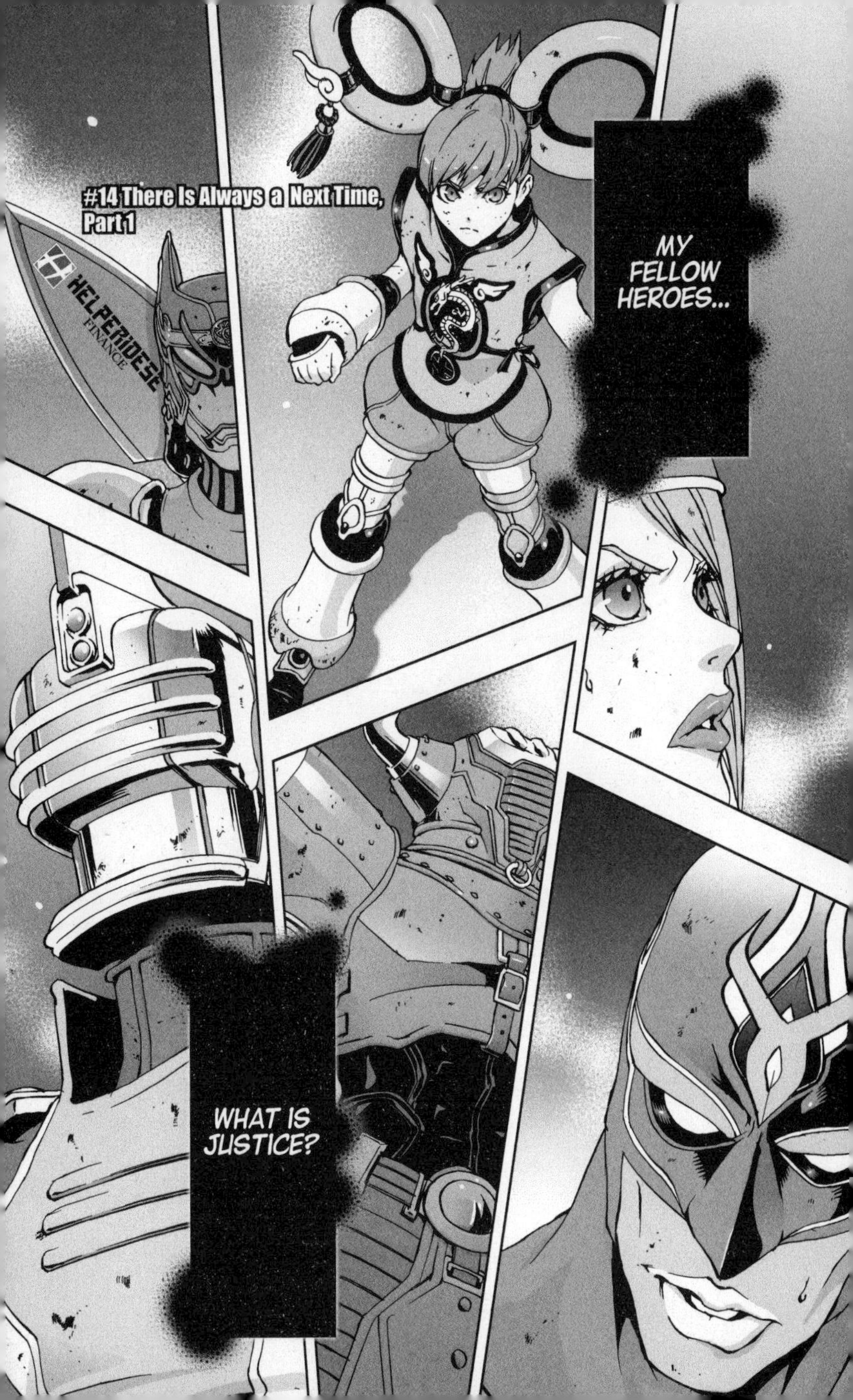
MY FELLOW HEROES...
#14 There Is Always a Next Time, Part 1
HELPERIDESE FINANCE
WHAT IS JUSTICE?

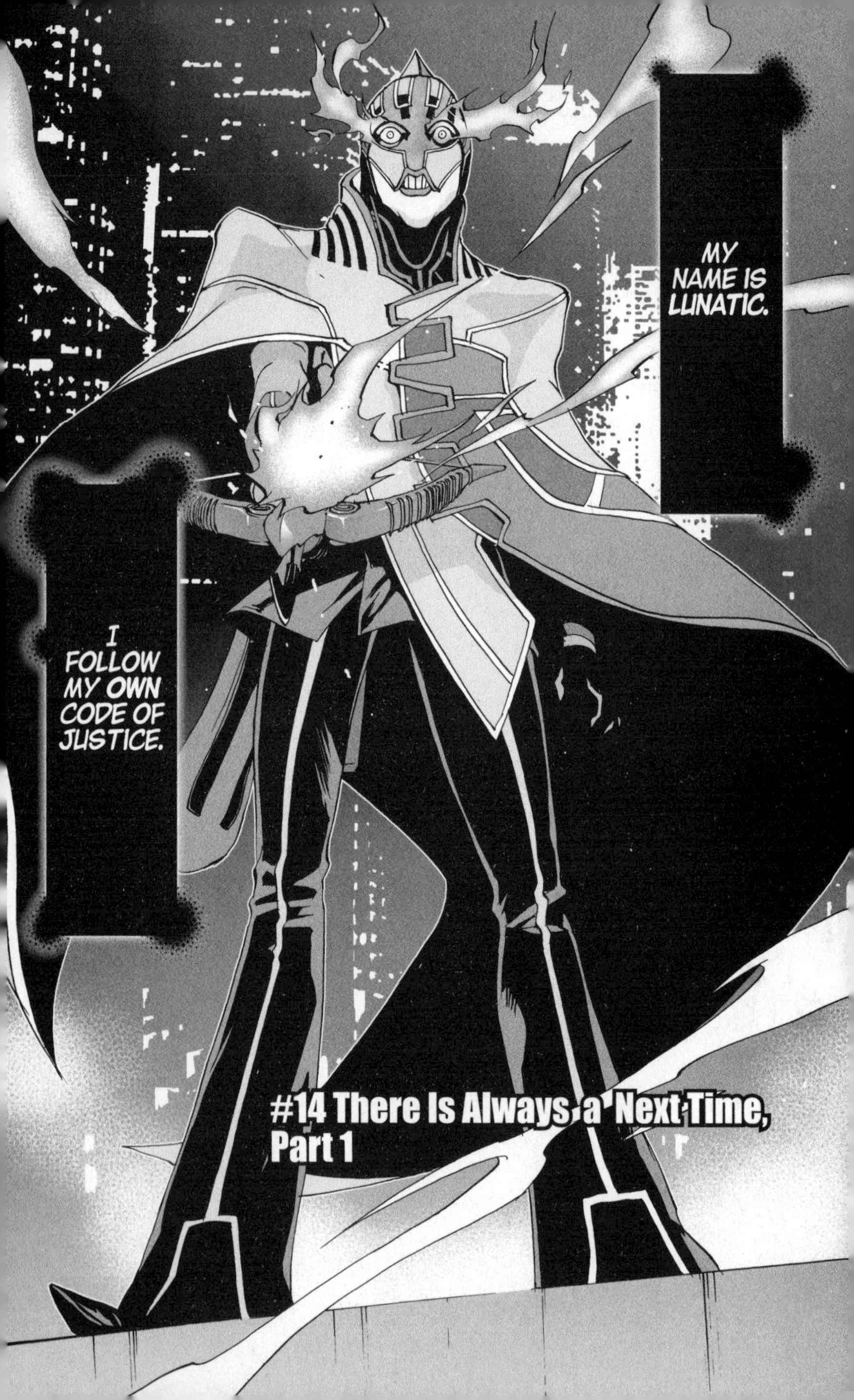
MY NAME IS LUNATIC.
I FOLLOW MY OWN CODE OF JUSTICE.

#14 There Is Always a Next Time, Part 1

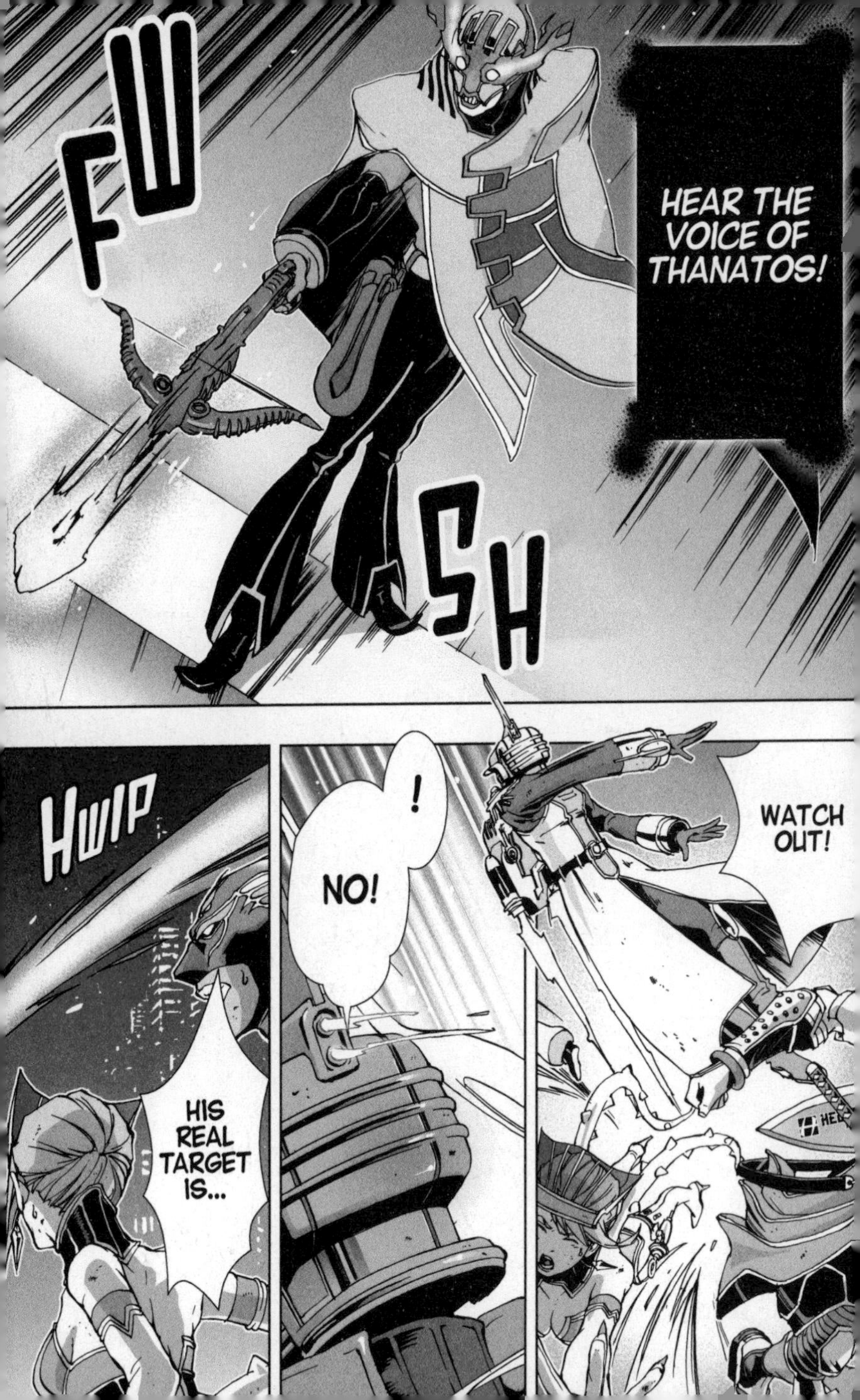
HEAR THE VOICE OF THANATOS!
FW
SH
WATCH OUT!
!
NO!
HWIP
HIS REAL TARGET IS...

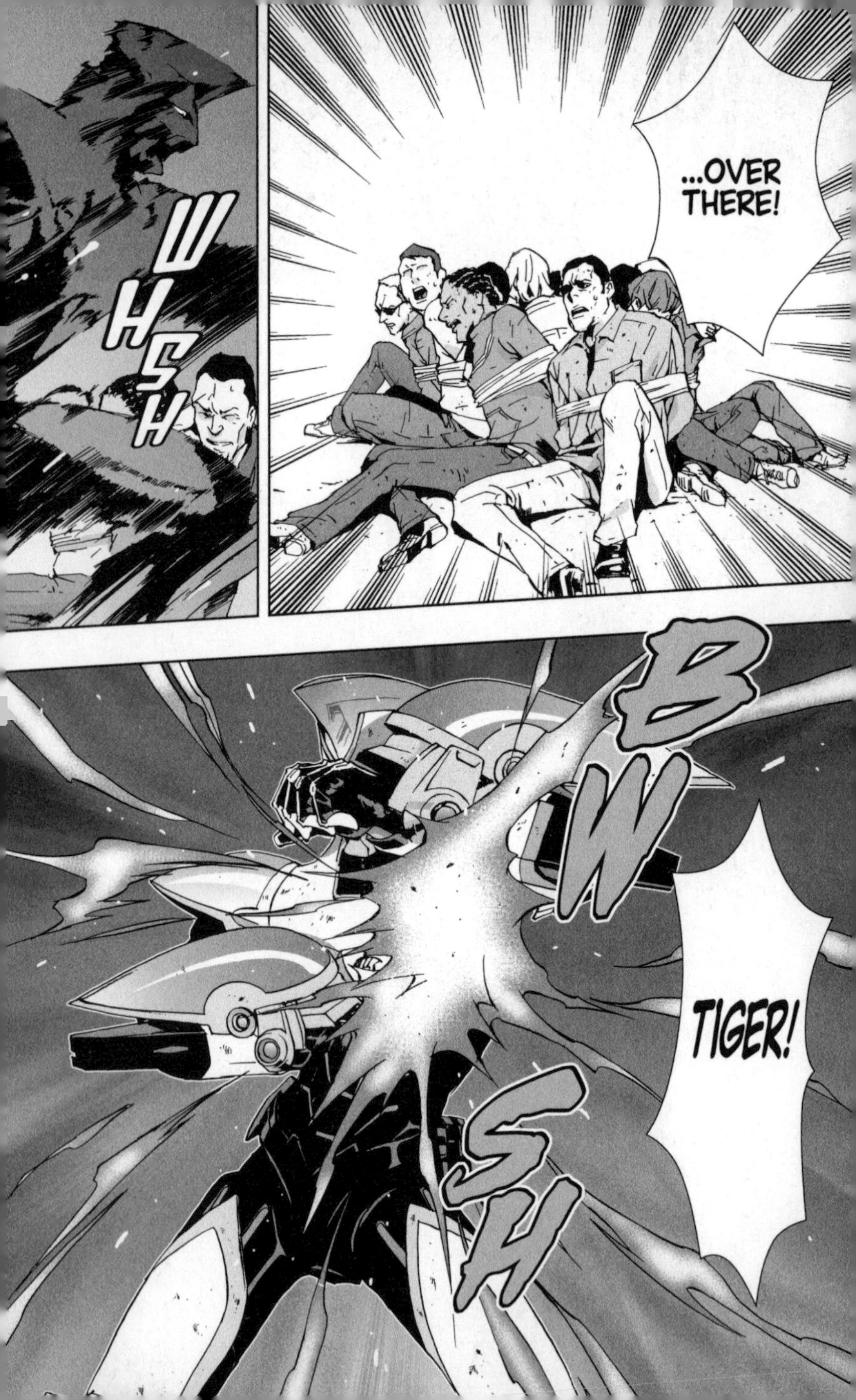
...OVER THERE!
WHSH
BWSH
TIGER!

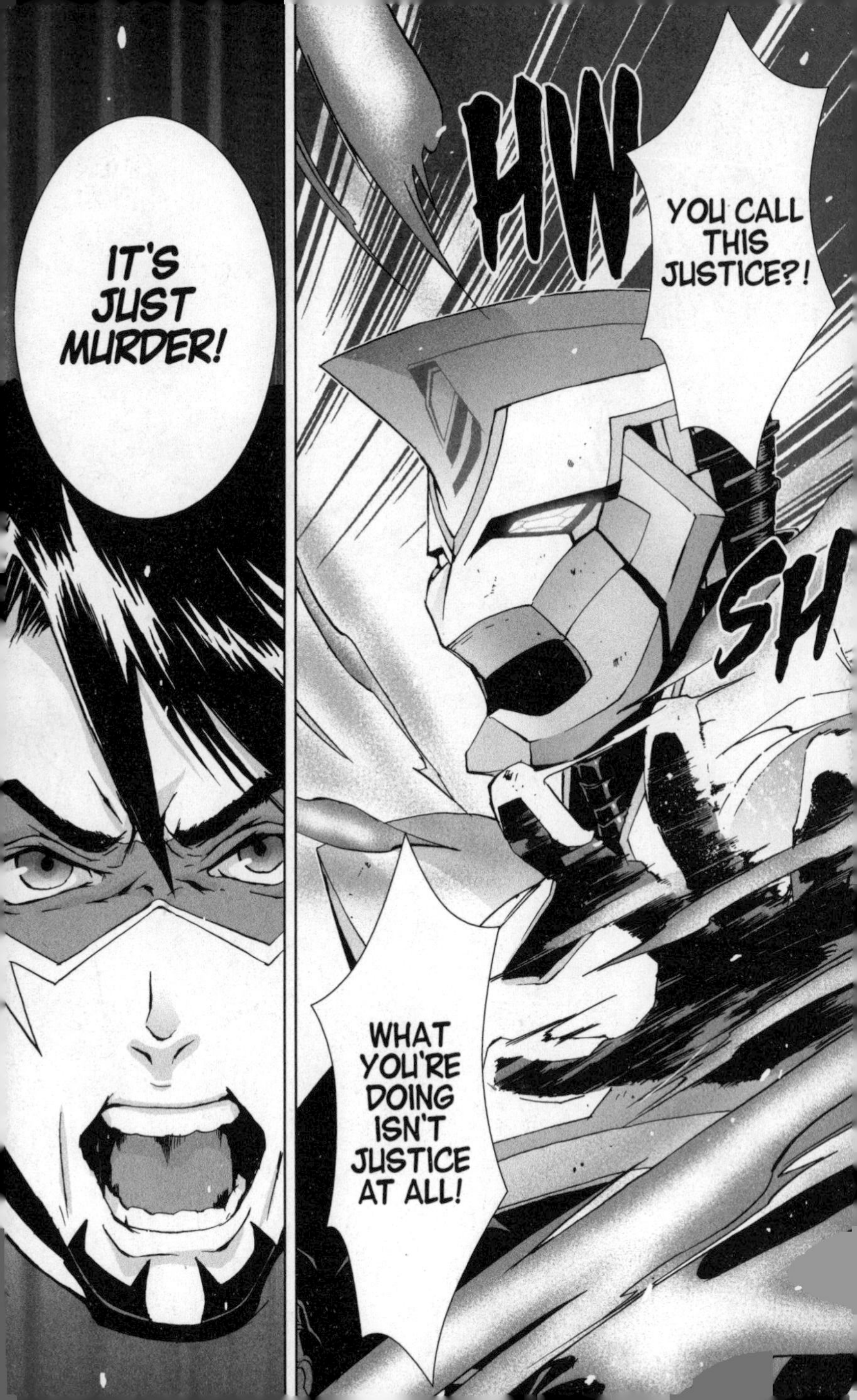
YOU CALL THIS JUSTICE?!
HW
SH
WHAT YOU'RE DOING ISN'T JUSTICE AT ALL!
IT'S JUST MURDER!

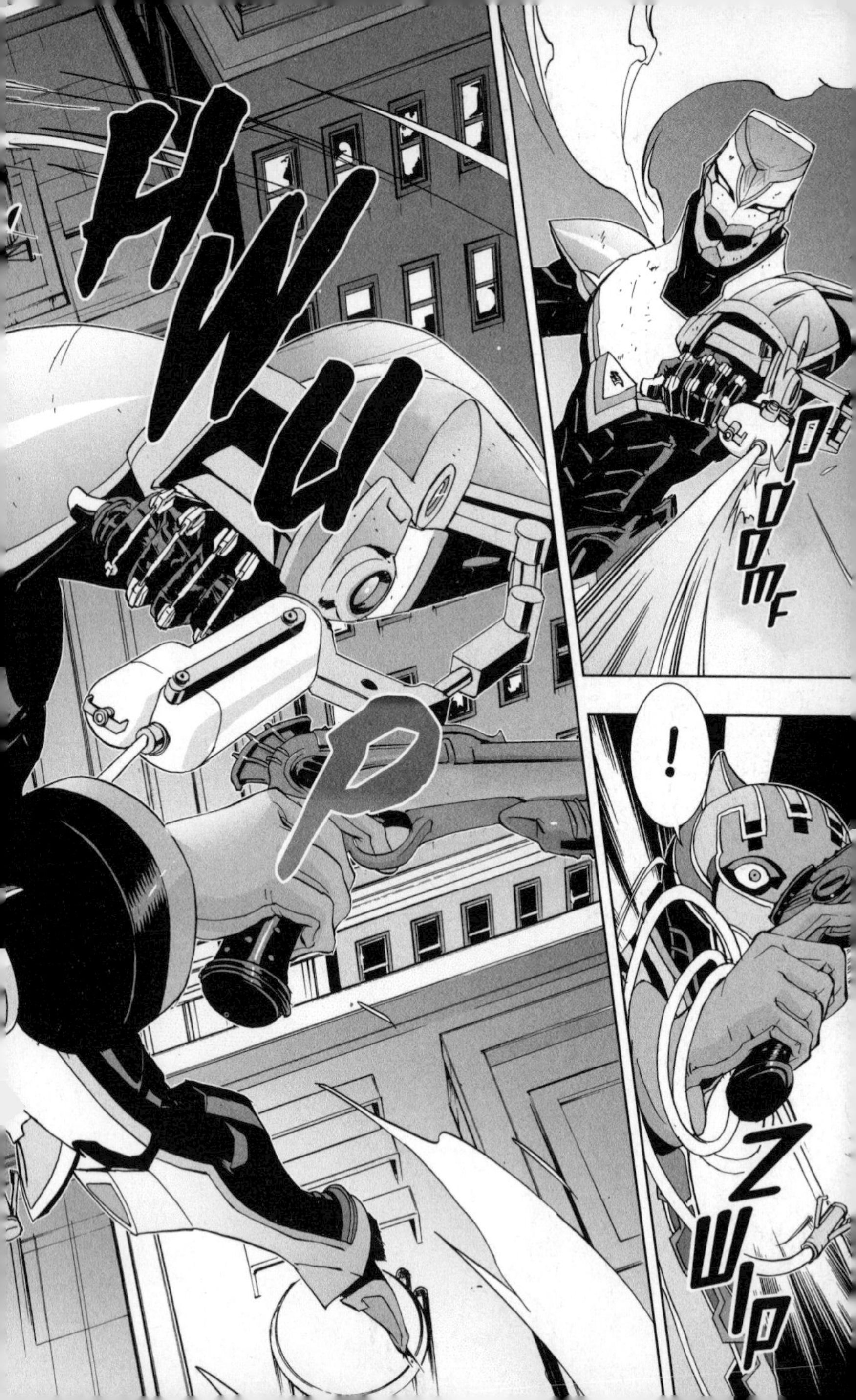
POOMF
!
ZWIP
FWUP

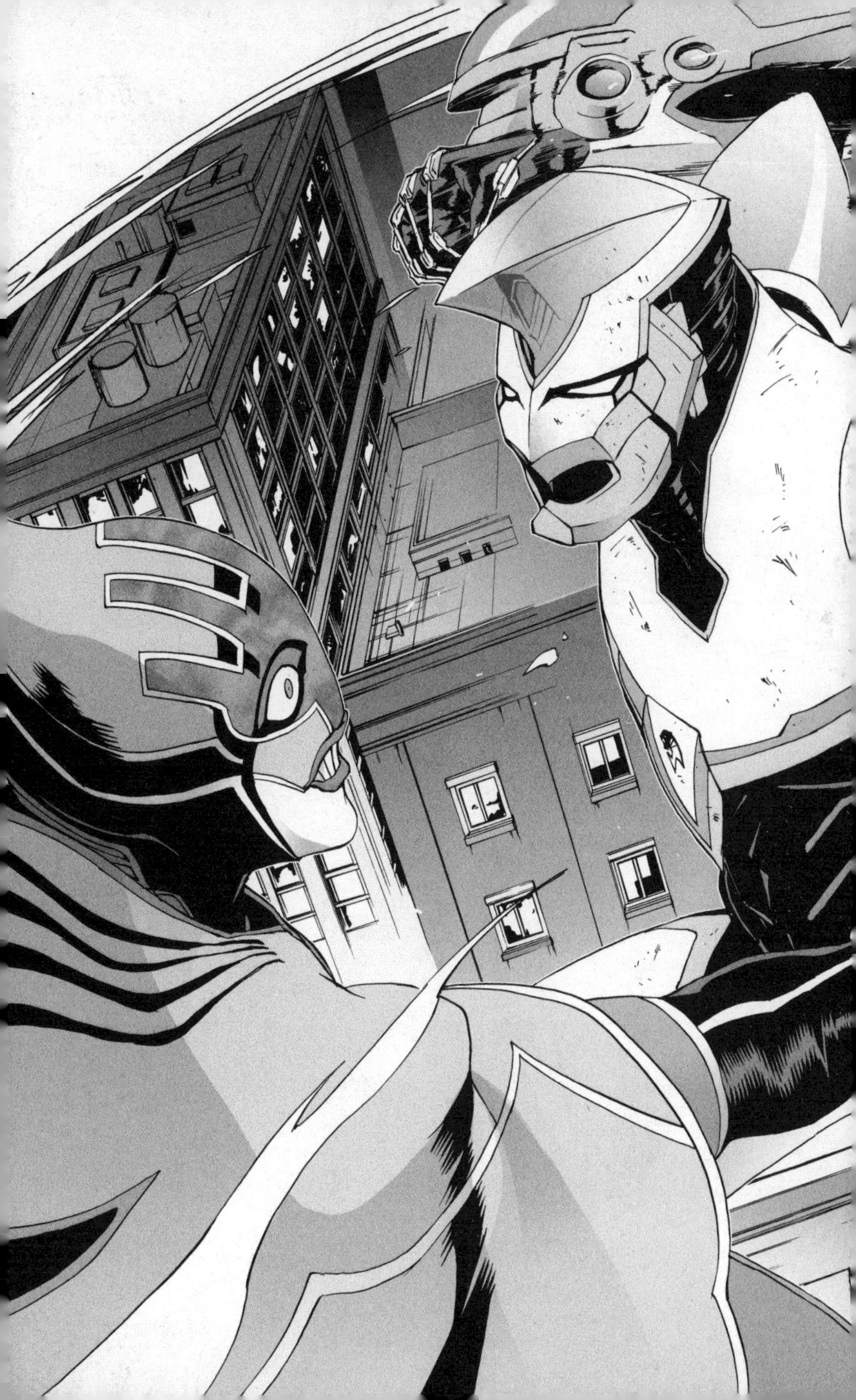

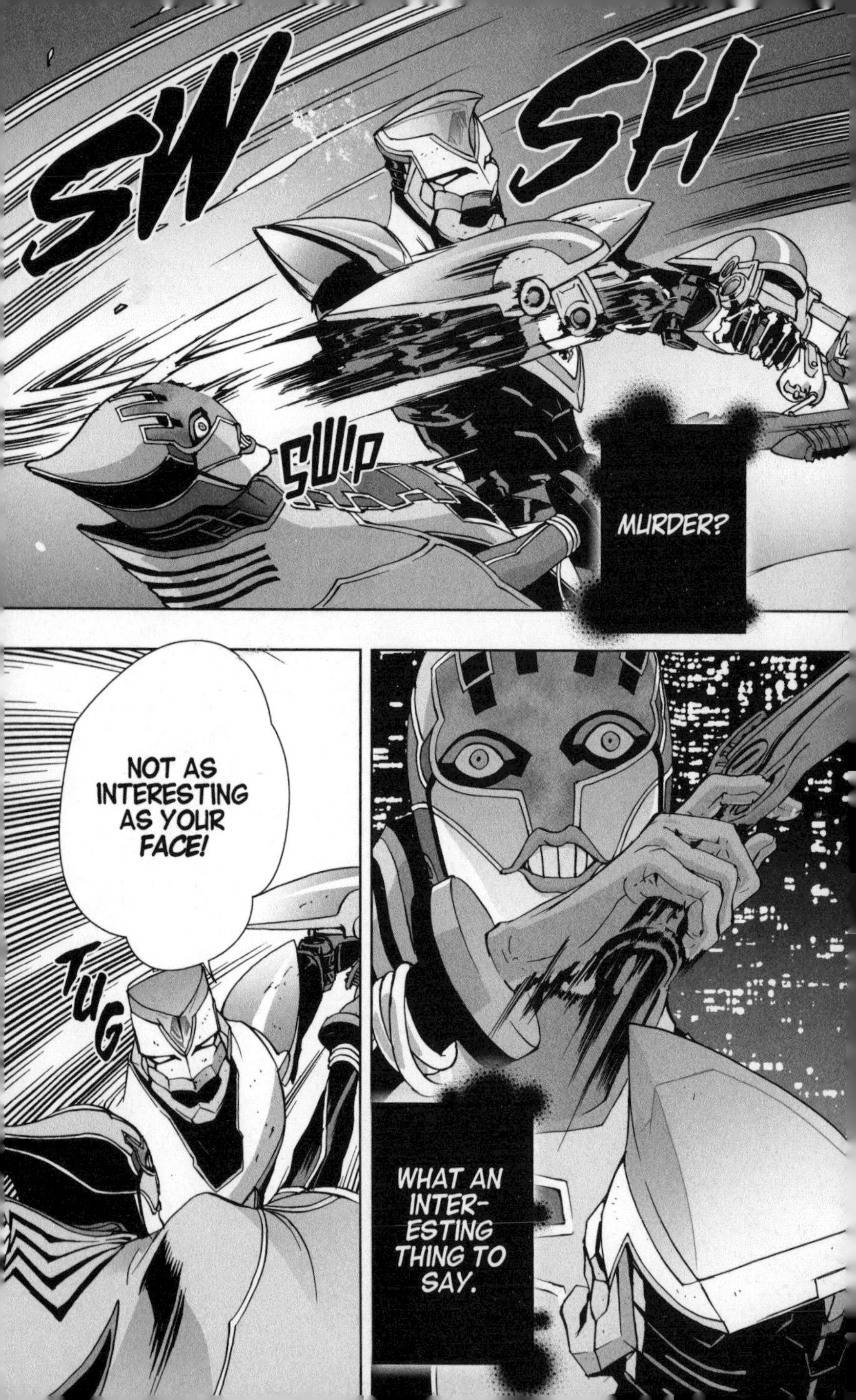
SW SH
MURDER?
SWIP
WHAT AN INTER-ESTING THING TO SAY.
NOT AS INTERESTING AS YOUR FACE!
TUG

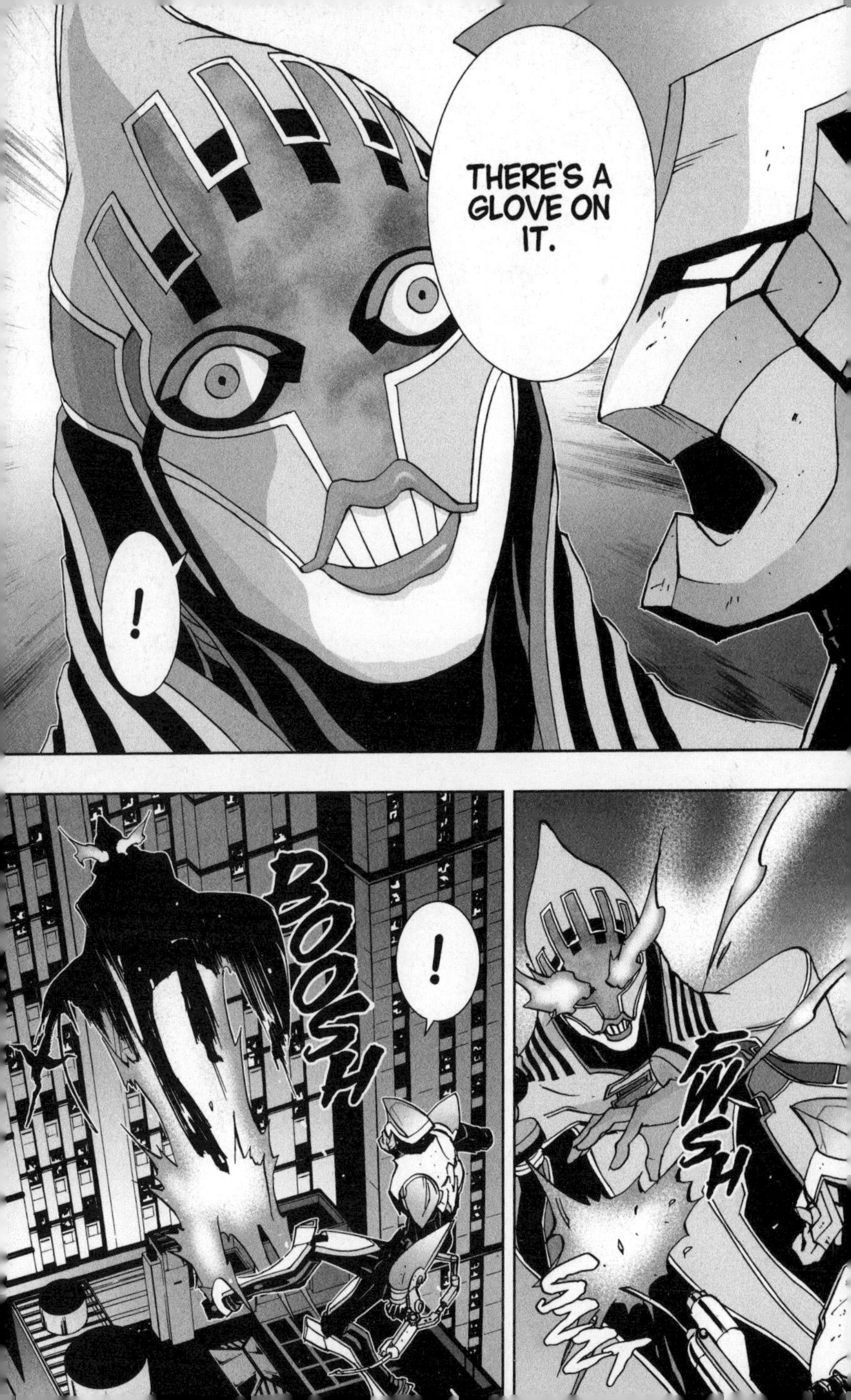
THERE'S A GLOVE ON IT.
!
FWSH
!
BOOSH

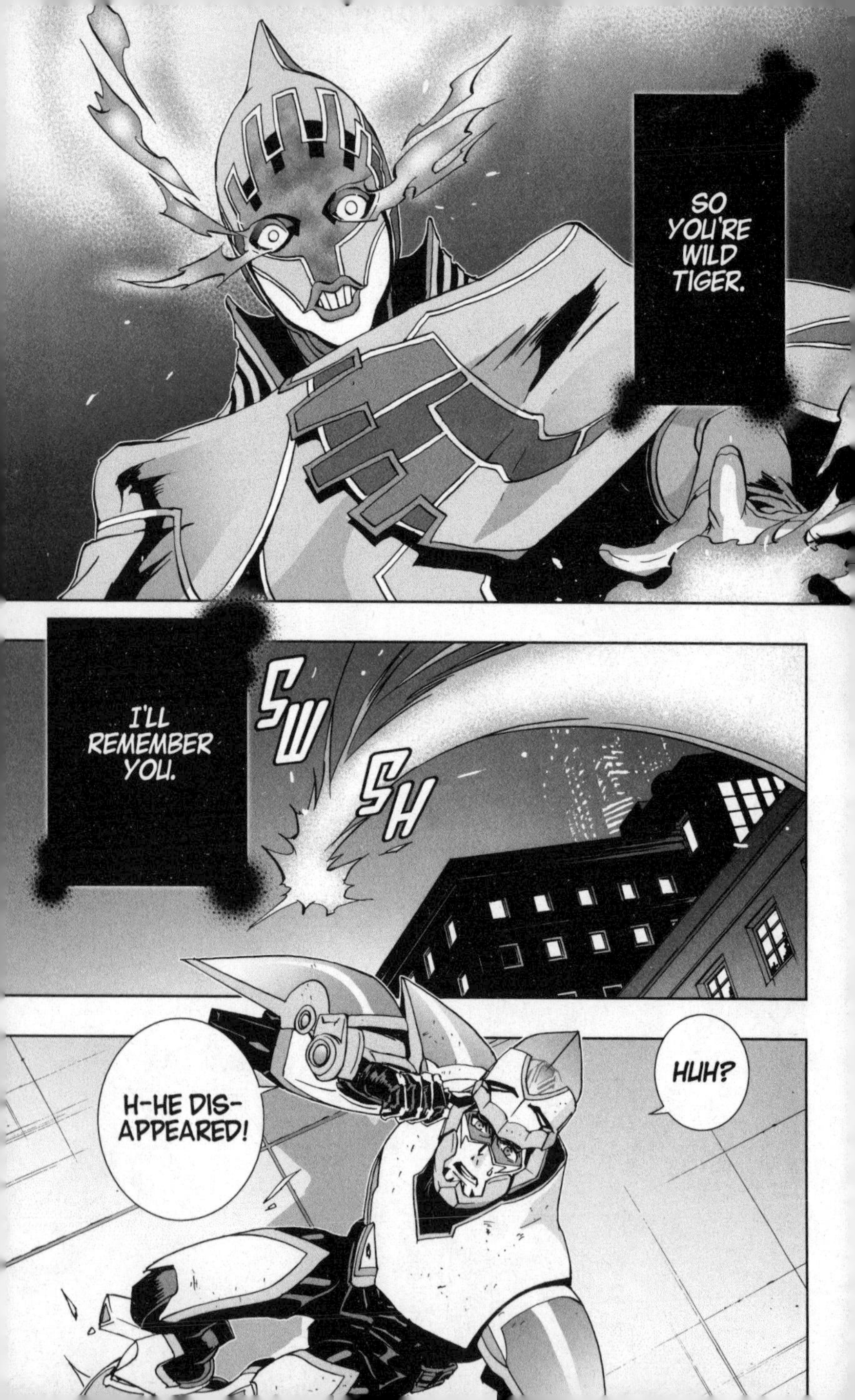
SO YOU'RE WILD TIGER.
I'LL REMEMBER YOU.
SWSH
HUH?
H-HE DIS-APPEARED!

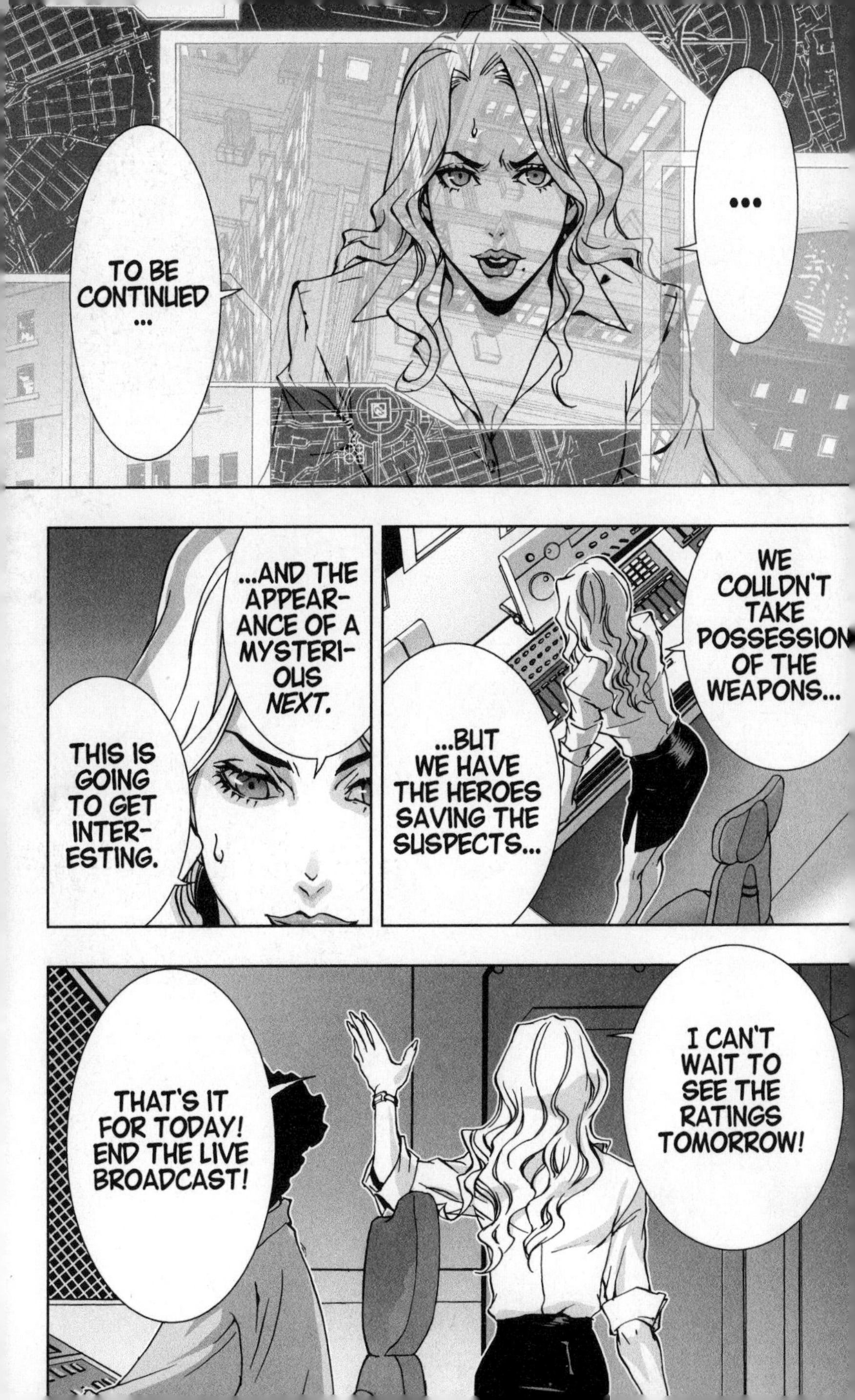
...
TO BE CONTINUED ...
WE COULDN'T TAKE POSSESSION OF THE WEAPONS...
...BUT WE HAVE THE HEROES SAVING THE SUSPECTS...
...AND THE APPEARANCE OF A MYSTERIOUS *NEXT.*
THIS IS GOING TO GET INTERESTING.
I CAN'T WAIT TO SEE THE RATINGS TOMORROW!
THAT'S IT FOR TODAY! END THE LIVE BROADCAST!

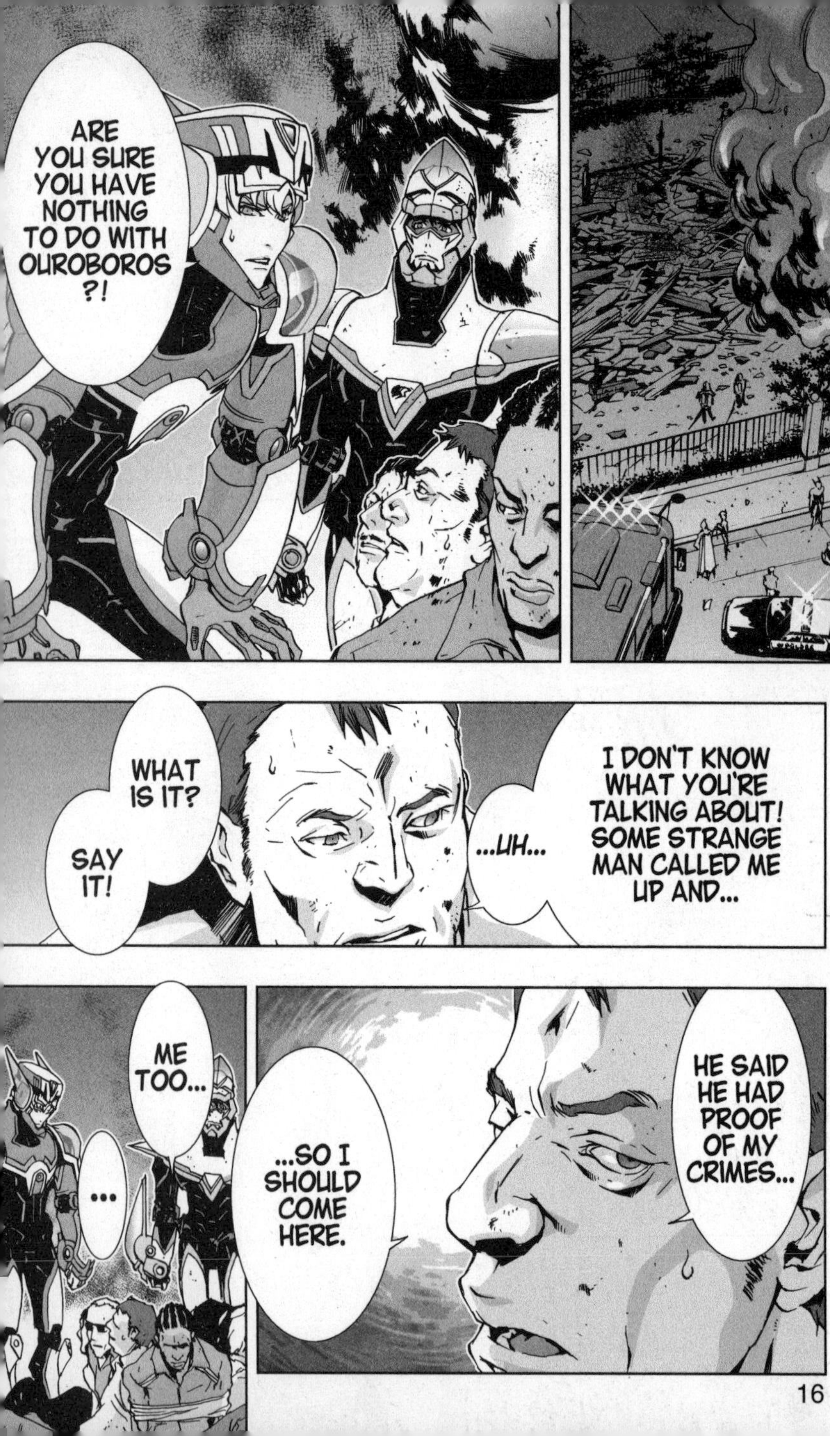
ARE YOU SURE YOU HAVE NOTHING TO DO WITH OUROBOROS ?!
I DON'T KNOW WHAT YOU'RE TALKING ABOUT! SOME STRANGE MAN CALLED ME UP AND...
...UH...
WHAT IS IT?
SAY IT!
HE SAID HE HAD PROOF OF MY CRIMES...
...SO I SHOULD COME HERE.
ME TOO...
...

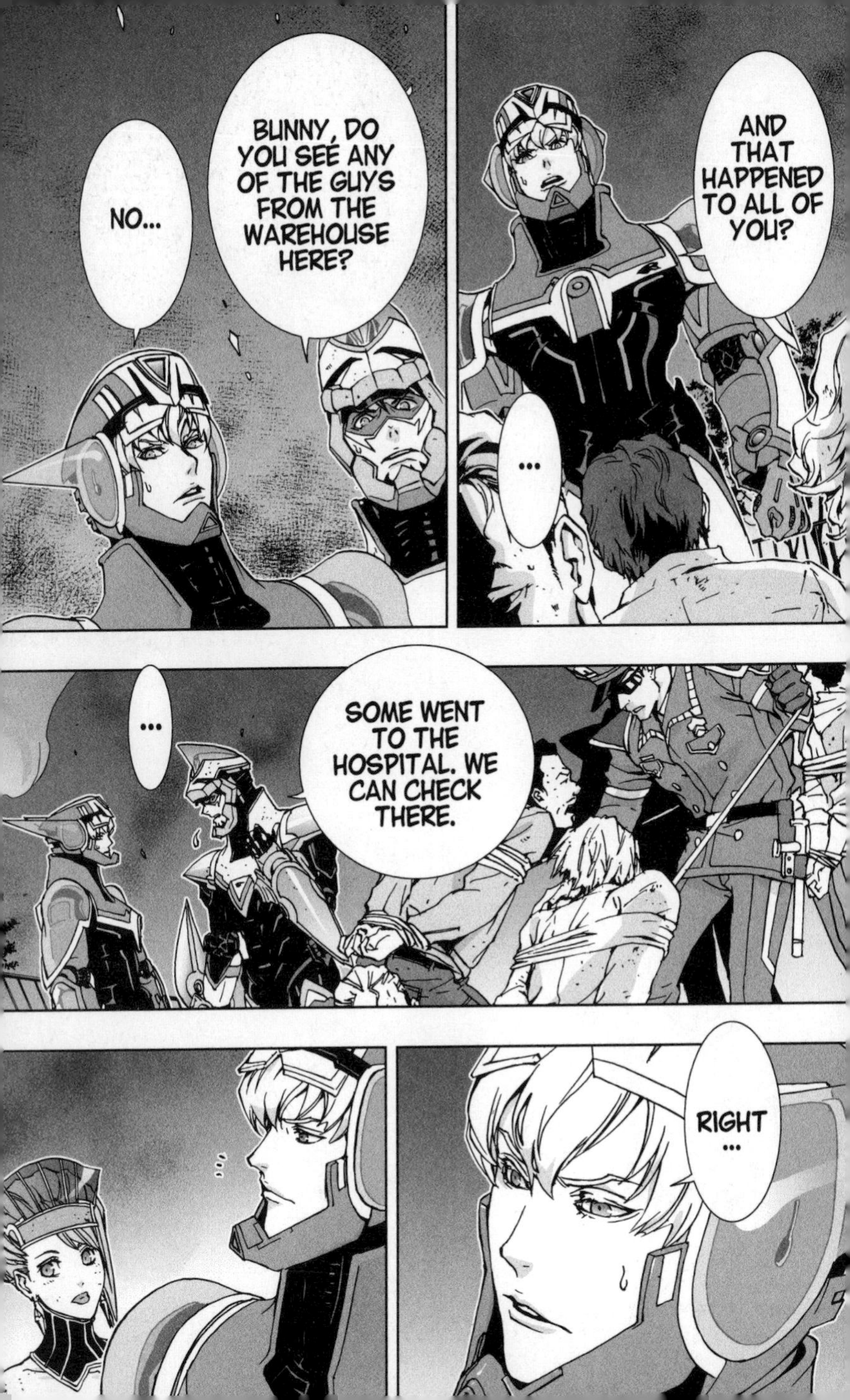
AND THAT HAPPENED TO ALL OF YOU?
...
BUNNY, DO YOU SEE ANY OF THE GUYS FROM THE WAREHOUSE HERE?
NO...
SOME WENT TO THE HOSPITAL. WE CAN CHECK THERE.
...
RIGHT ...

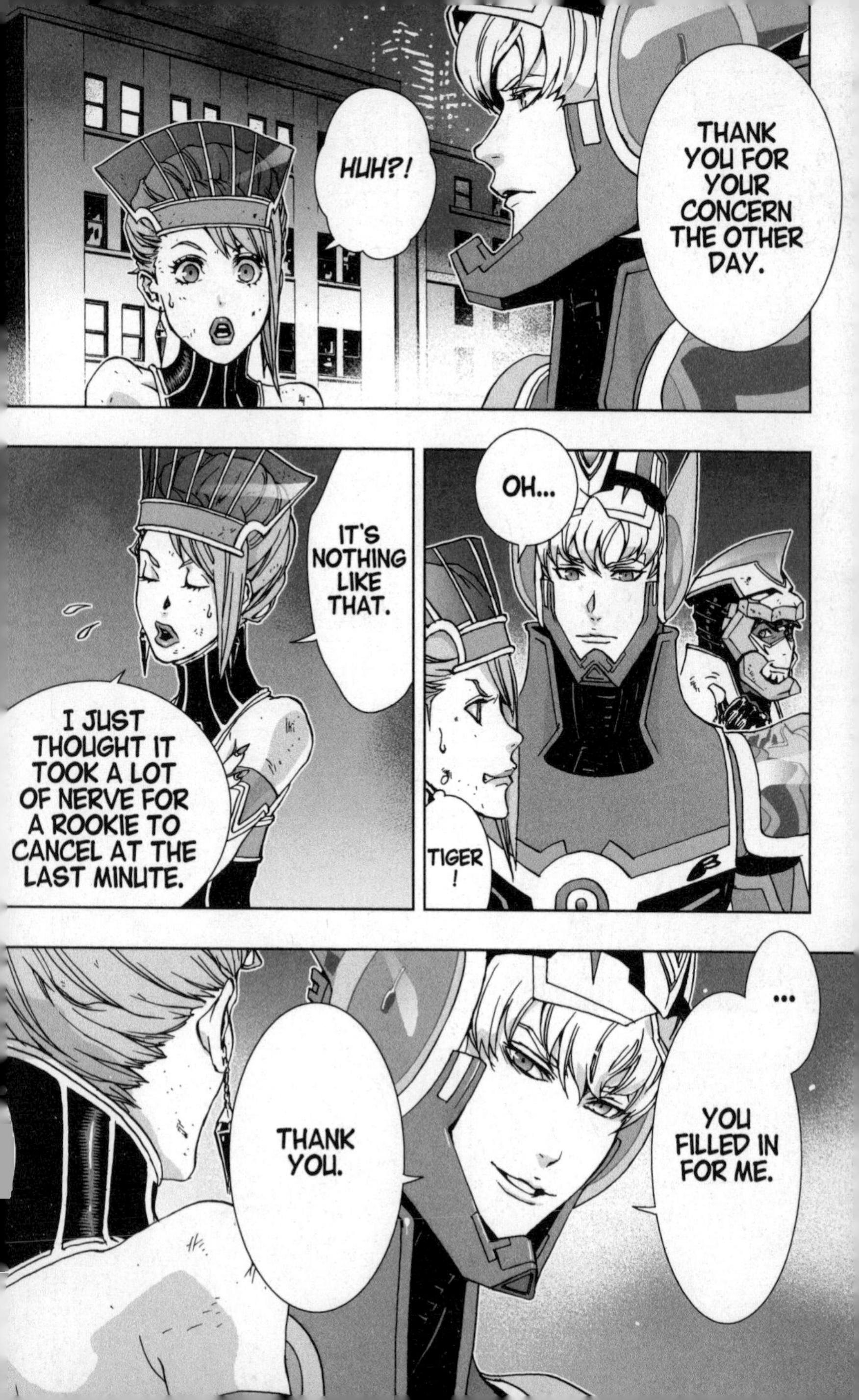
THANK YOU FOR YOUR CONCERN THE OTHER DAY.
HUH?!
OH...
TIGER!
IT'S NOTHING LIKE THAT.
I JUST THOUGHT IT TOOK A LOT OF NERVE FOR A ROOKIE TO CANCEL AT THE LAST MINUTE.
...
YOU FILLED IN FOR ME.
THANK YOU.

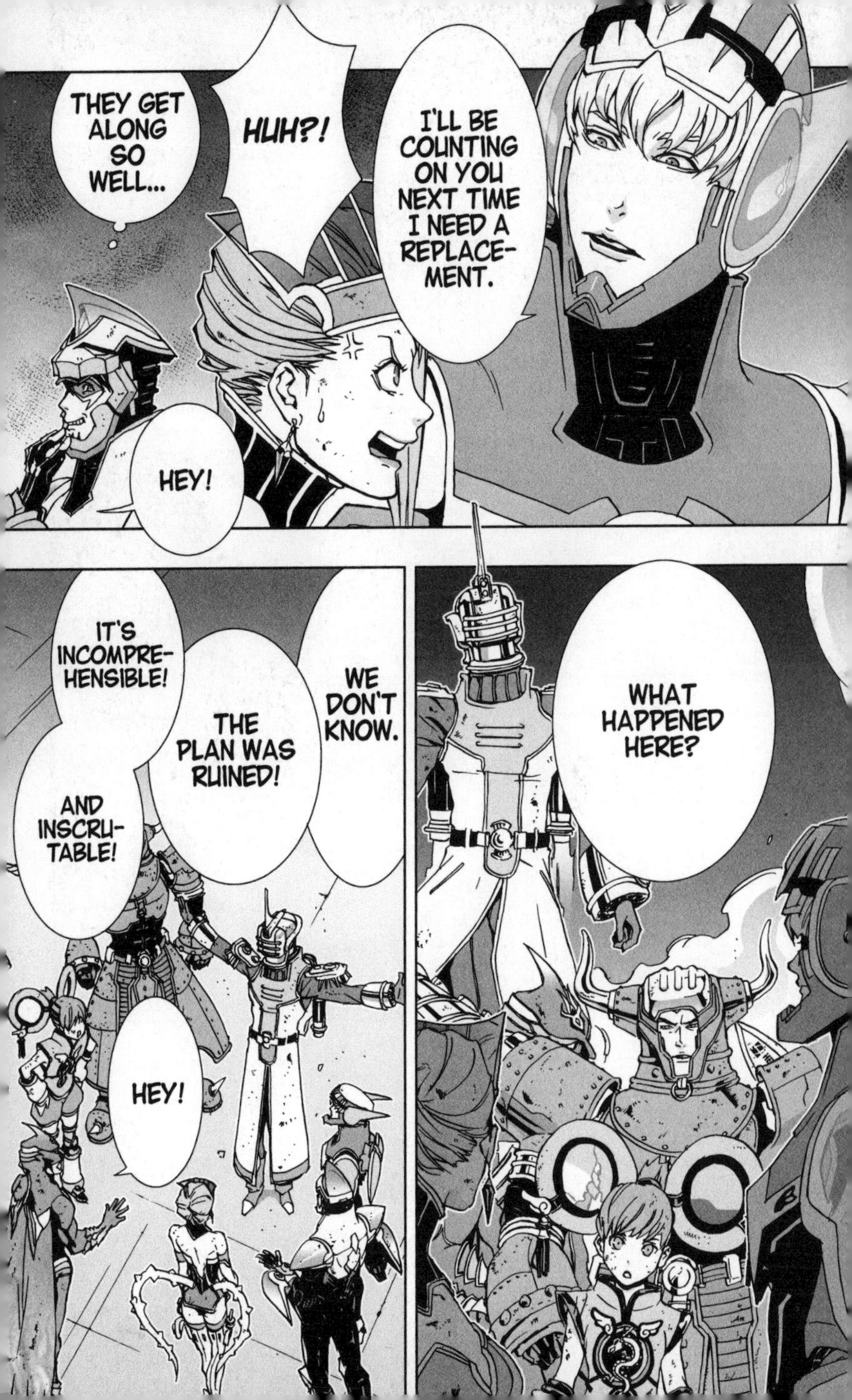
I'LL BE COUNTING ON YOU NEXT TIME I NEED A REPLACEMENT.
HUH?!
THEY GET ALONG SO WELL...
HEY!
WHAT HAPPENED HERE?
WE DON'T KNOW.
THE PLAN WAS RUINED!
IT'S INCOMPREHENSIBLE!
AND INSCRUTABLE!
HEY!

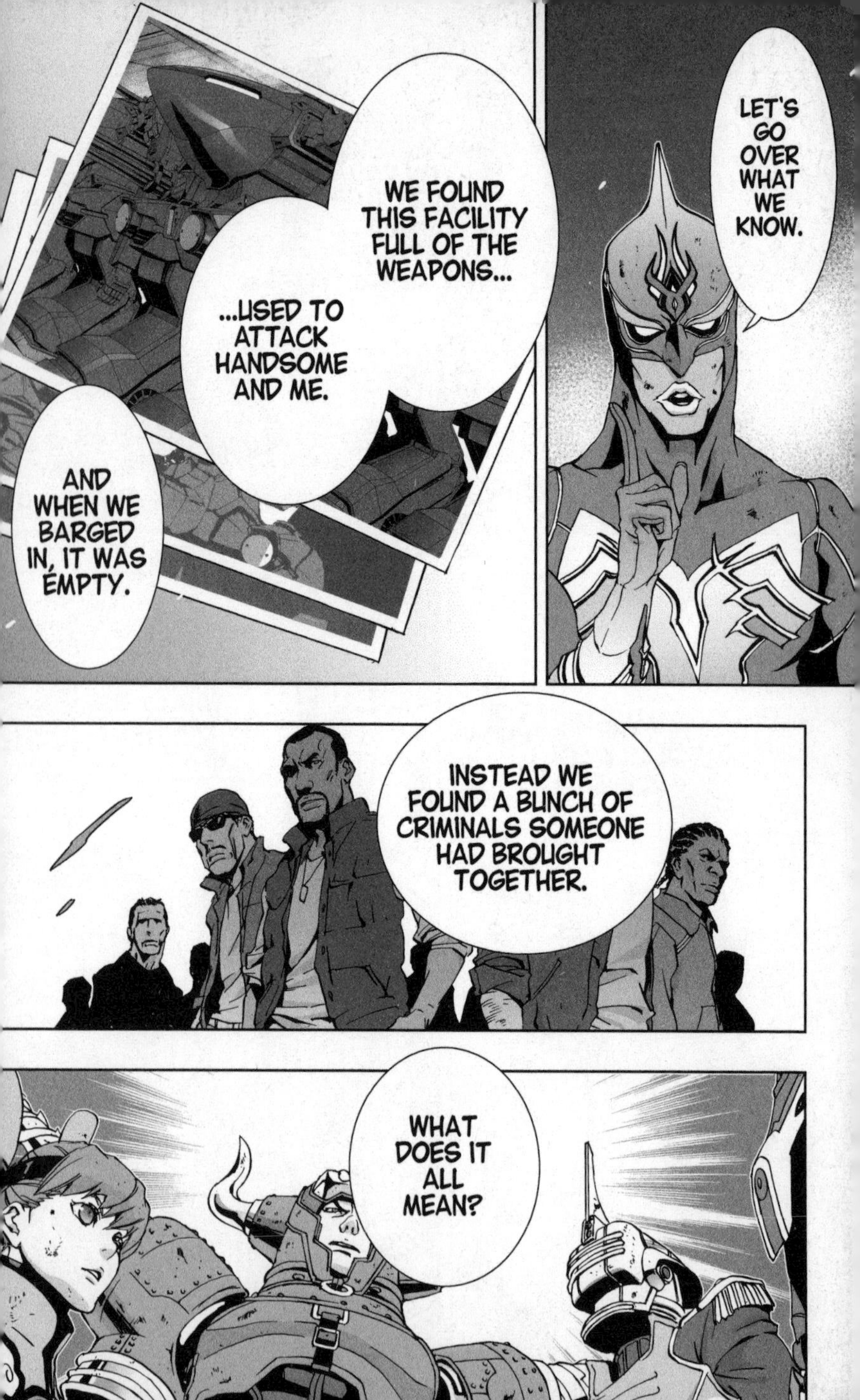
LET'S GO OVER WHAT WE KNOW.
WE FOUND THIS FACILITY FULL OF THE WEAPONS...
...USED TO ATTACK HANDSOME AND ME.
AND WHEN WE BARGED IN, IT WAS EMPTY.
INSTEAD WE FOUND A BUNCH OF CRIMINALS SOMEONE HAD BROUGHT TOGETHER.
WHAT DOES IT ALL MEAN?

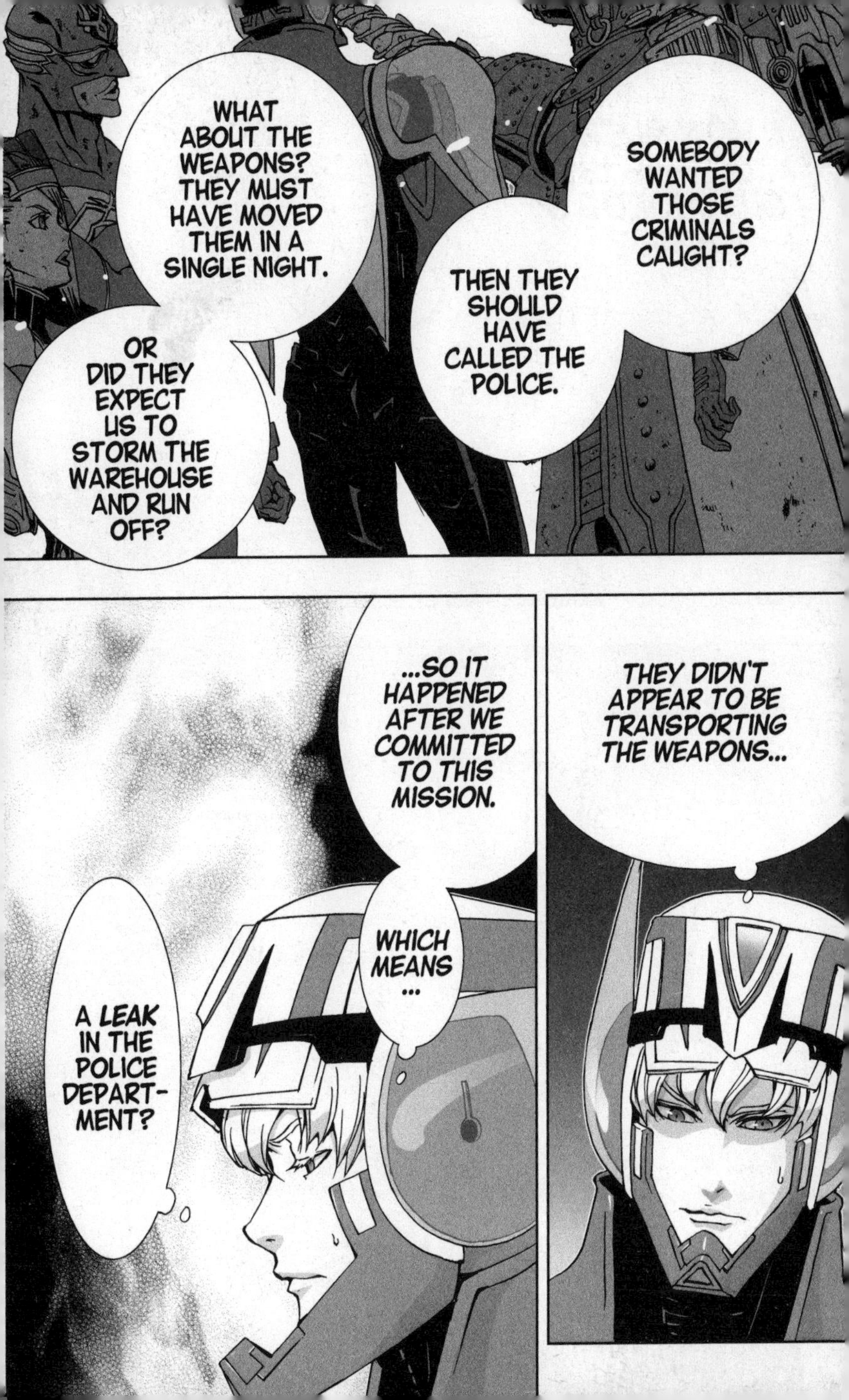
SOMEBODY WANTED THOSE CRIMINALS CAUGHT?
THEN THEY SHOULD HAVE CALLED THE POLICE.
WHAT ABOUT THE WEAPONS? THEY MUST HAVE MOVED THEM IN A SINGLE NIGHT.
OR DID THEY EXPECT US TO STORM THE WAREHOUSE AND RUN OFF?
THEY DIDN'T APPEAR TO BE TRANSPORTING THE WEAPONS...
...SO IT HAPPENED AFTER WE COMMITTED TO THIS MISSION.
WHICH MEANS...
A LEAK IN THE POLICE DEPARTMENT?

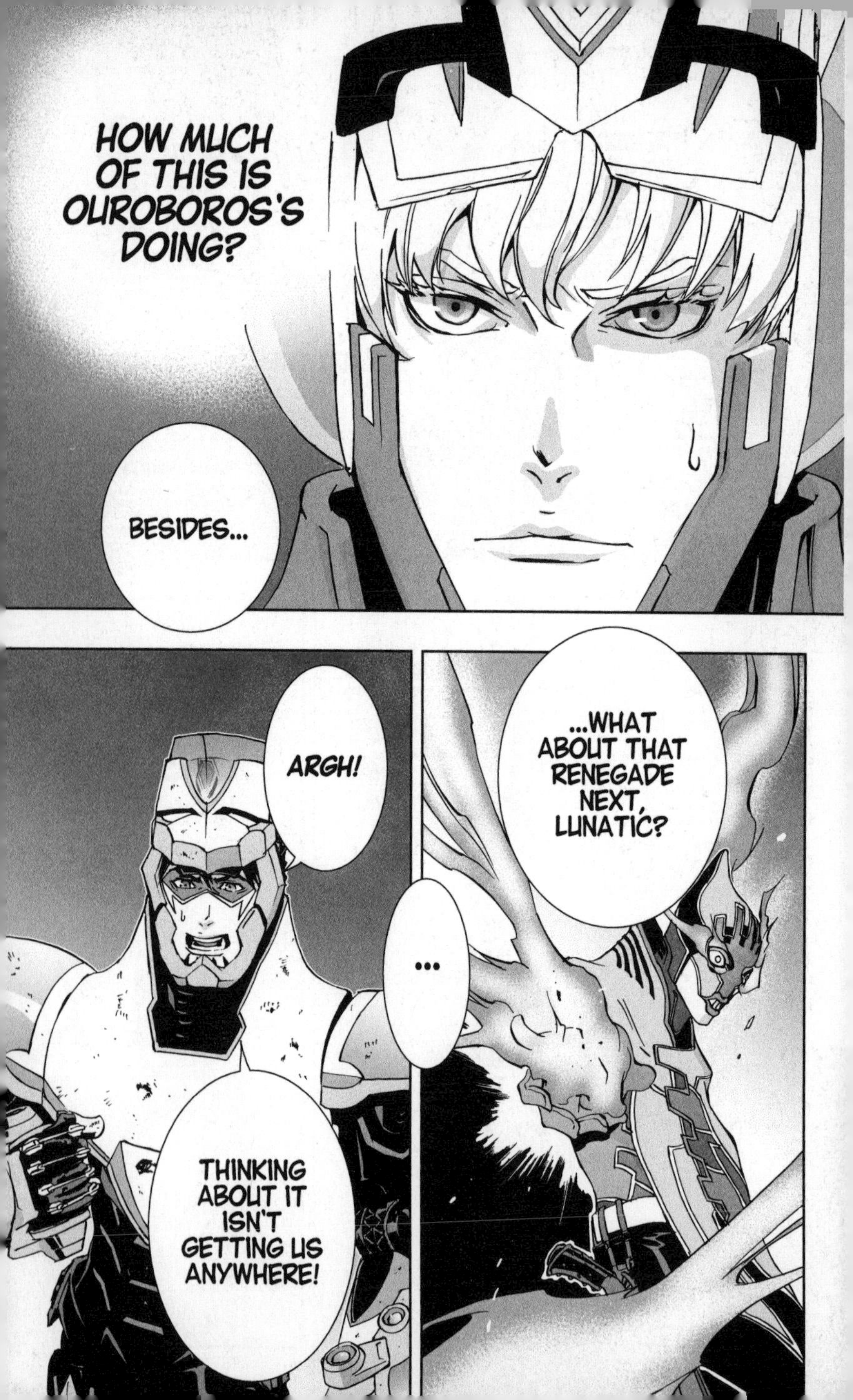
HOW MUCH OF THIS IS OUROBOROS'S DOING?
BESIDES...
...WHAT ABOUT THAT RENEGADE NEXT, LUNATIC?
...
ARGH!
THINKING ABOUT IT ISN'T GETTING US ANYWHERE!

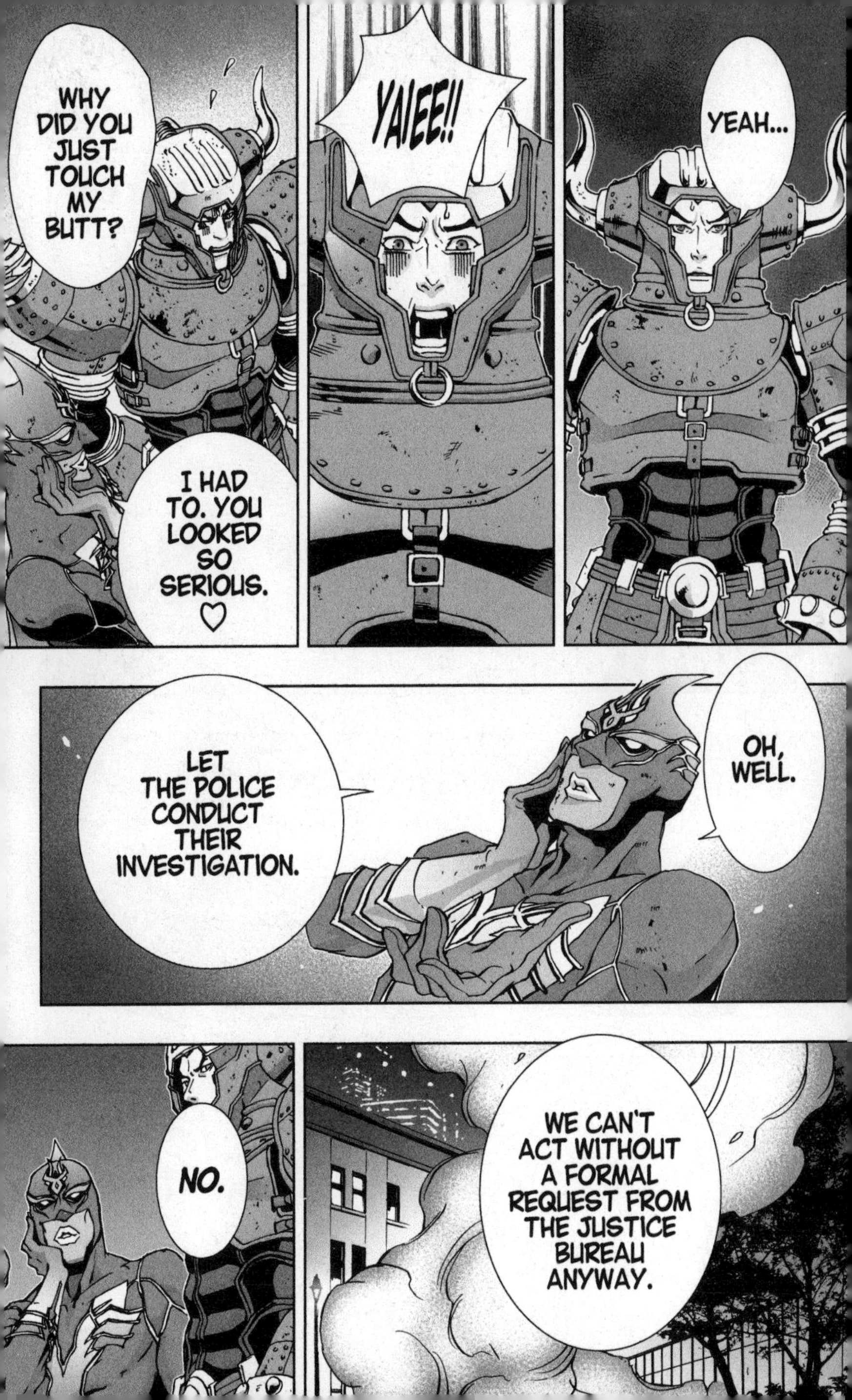
YEAH...
YAIEE!!
WHY DID YOU JUST TOUCH MY BUTT?
I HAD TO. YOU LOOKED SO SERIOUS. ♡
OH, WELL.
LET THE POLICE CONDUCT THEIR INVESTIGATION.
WE CAN'T ACT WITHOUT A FORMAL REQUEST FROM THE JUSTICE BUREAU ANYWAY.
NO.

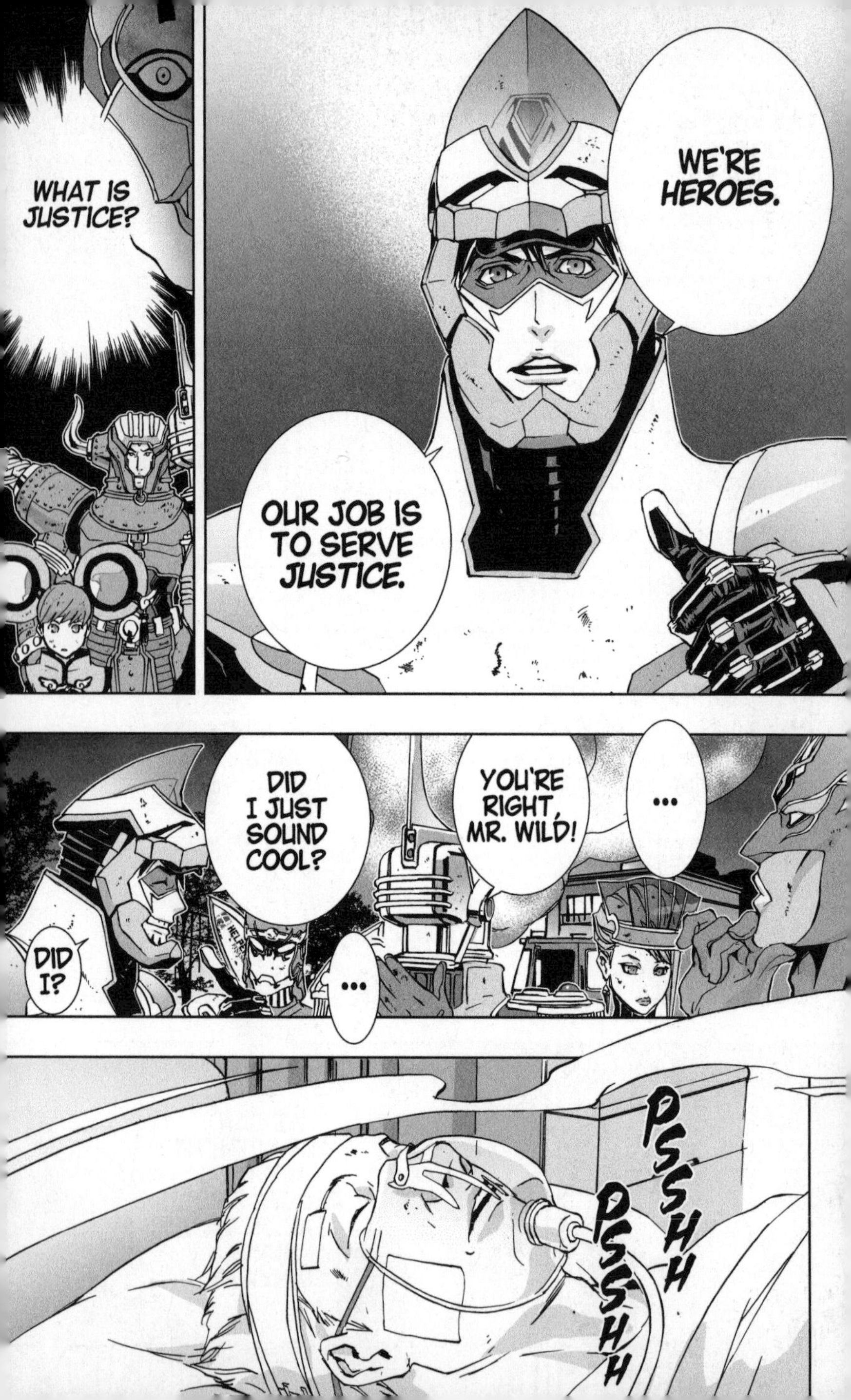
WE'RE HEROES.
OUR JOB IS TO SERVE JUSTICE.
WHAT IS JUSTICE?
...
YOU'RE RIGHT, MR. WILD!
DID I JUST SOUND COOL?
...
DID I?
PSSHH
PSSHH

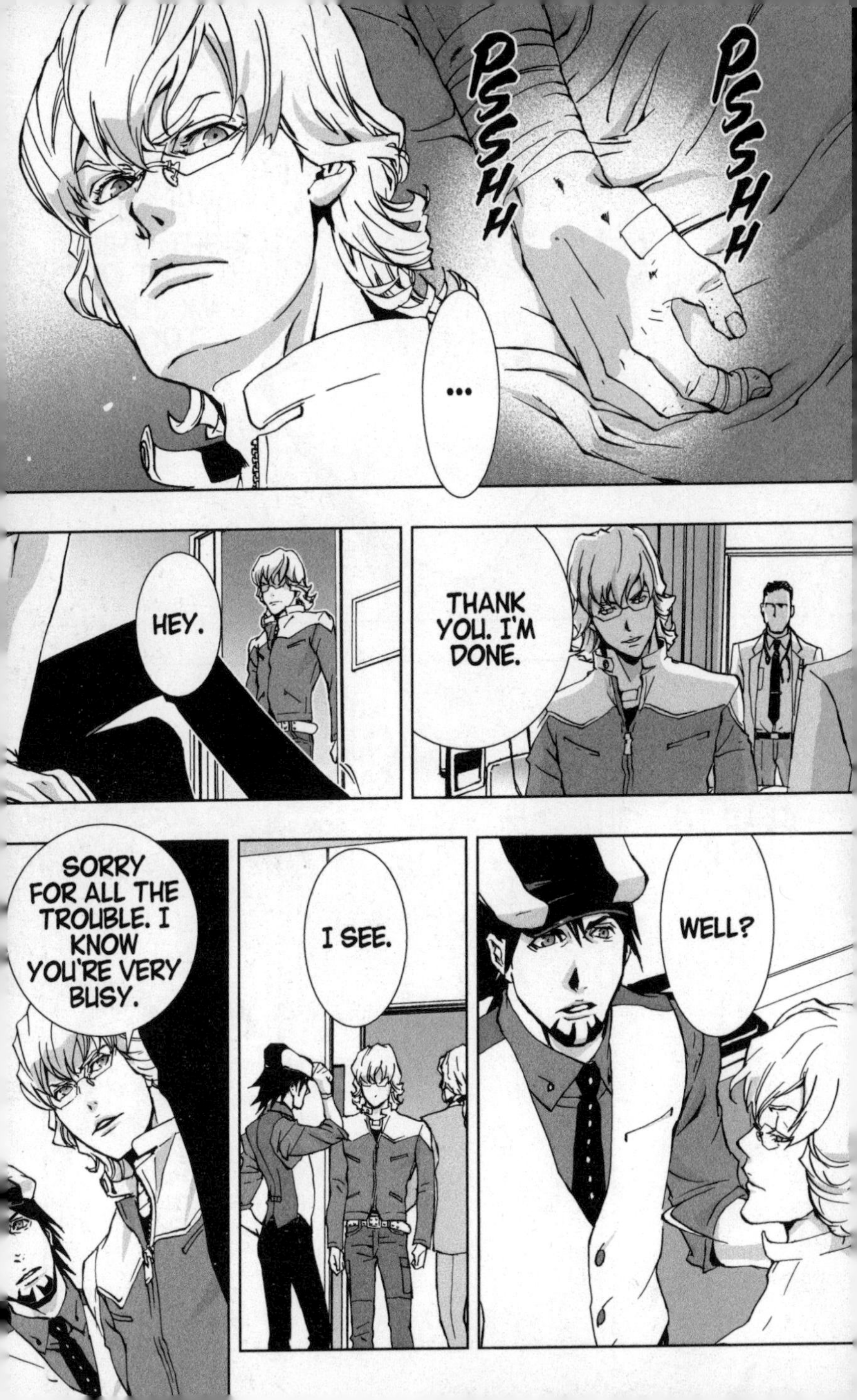
PSSHH
PSSHH
...
THANK YOU. I'M DONE.
HEY.
WELL?
I SEE.
SORRY FOR ALL THE TROUBLE. I KNOW YOU'RE VERY BUSY.

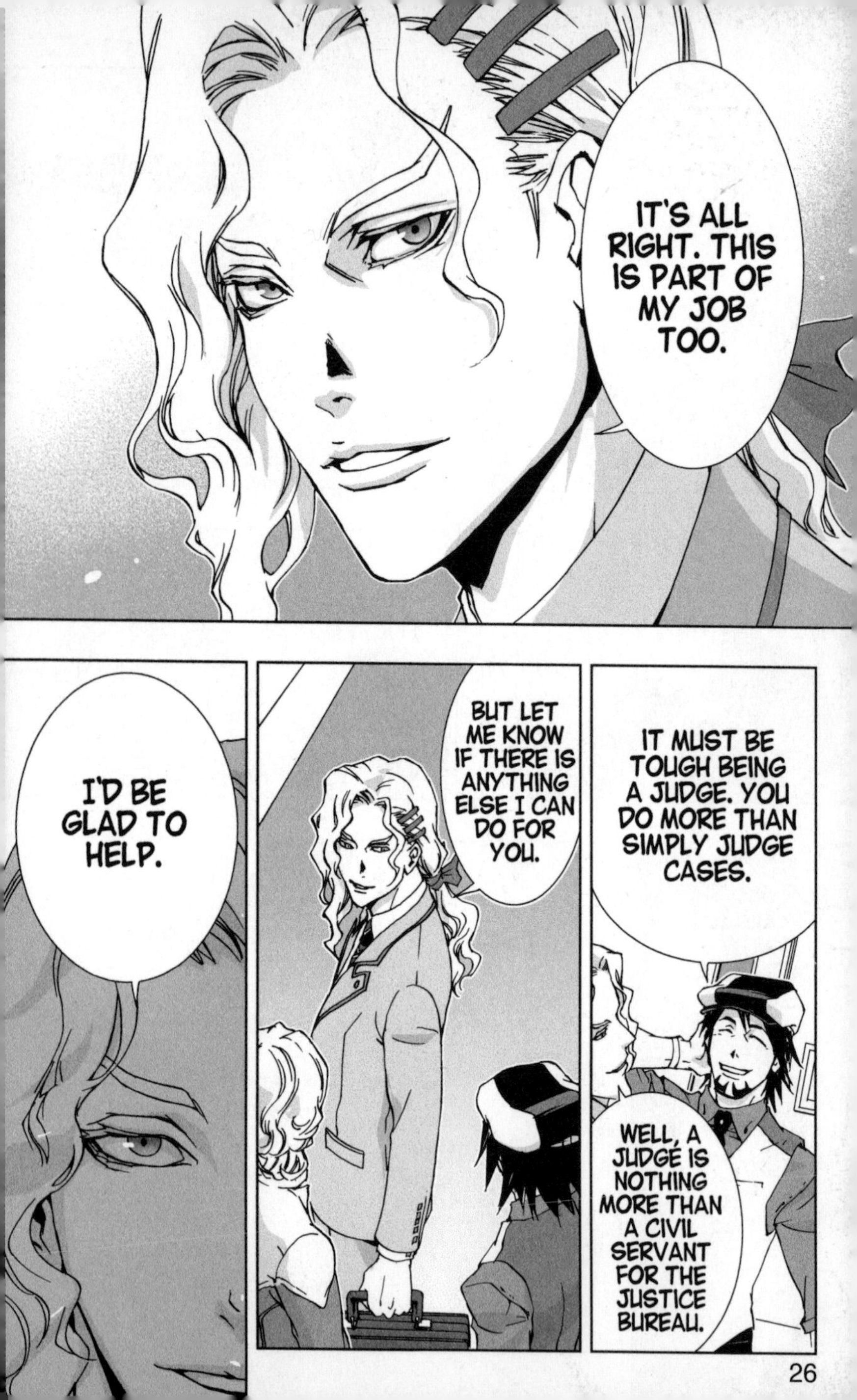
IT'S ALL RIGHT. THIS IS PART OF MY JOB TOO.
IT MUST BE TOUGH BEING A JUDGE. YOU DO MORE THAN SIMPLY JUDGE CASES.
WELL, A JUDGE IS NOTHING MORE THAN A CIVIL SERVANT FOR THE JUSTICE BUREAU.
BUT LET ME KNOW IF THERE IS ANYTHING ELSE I CAN DO FOR YOU.
I'D BE GLAD TO HELP.

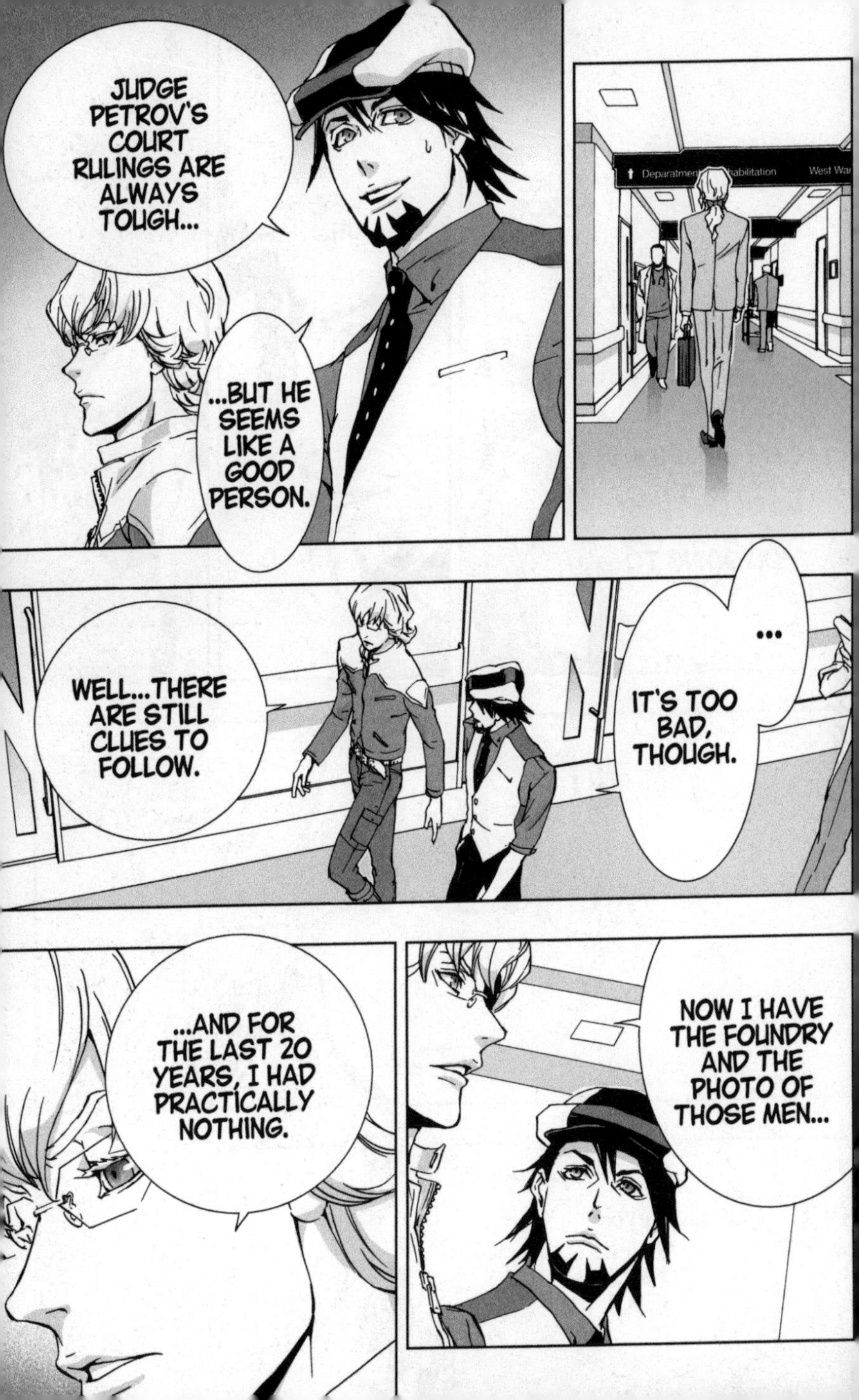
Deparatmen habilitation West War
JUDGE PETROV'S COURT RULINGS ARE ALWAYS TOUGH...
...BUT HE SEEMS LIKE A GOOD PERSON.
... IT'S TOO BAD, THOUGH.
WELL...THERE ARE STILL CLUES TO FOLLOW.
NOW I HAVE THE FOUNDRY AND THE PHOTO OF THOSE MEN...
...AND FOR THE LAST 20 YEARS, I HAD PRACTICALLY NOTHING.

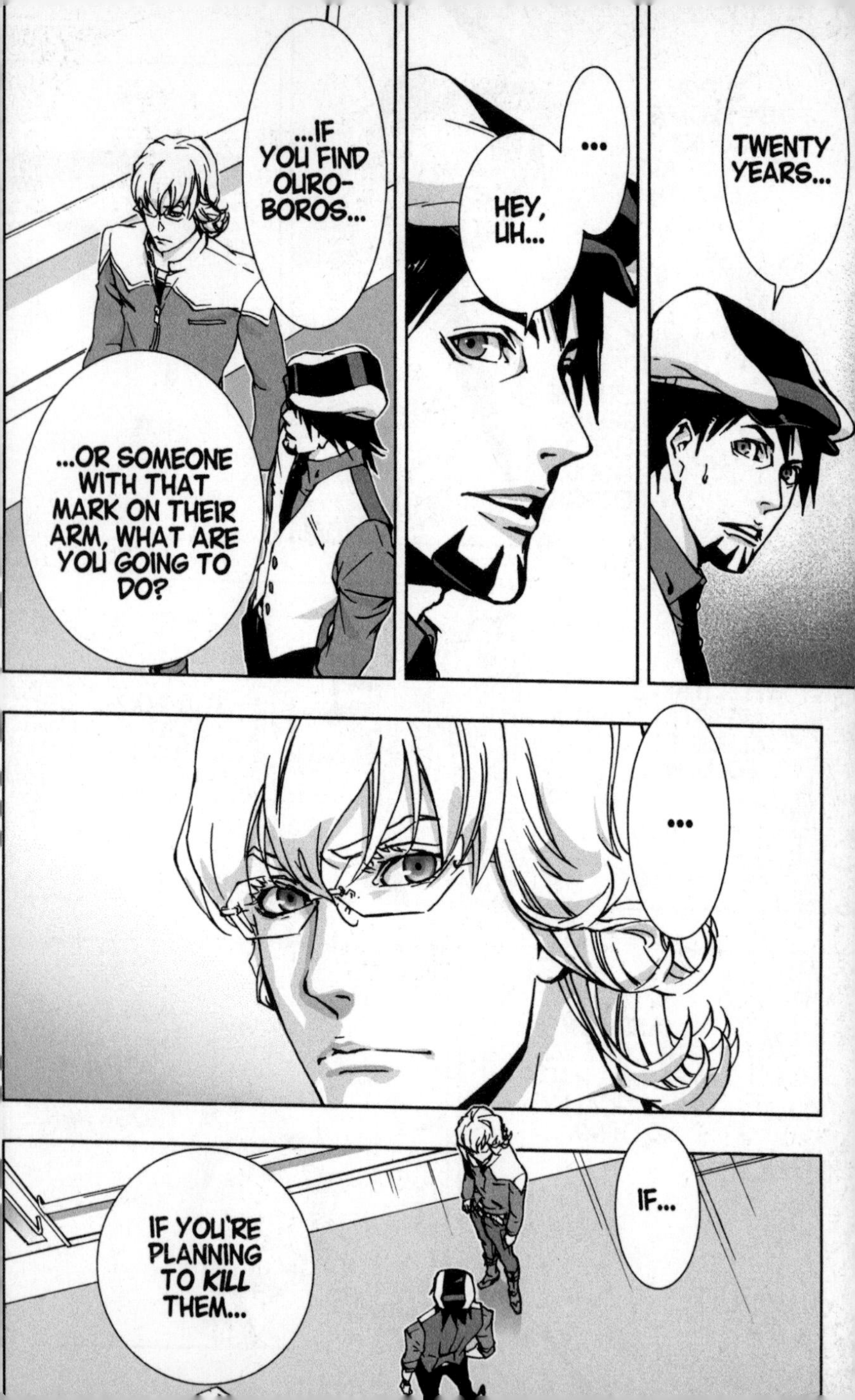
TWENTY YEARS...
...
HEY, UH...
...IF YOU FIND OURO-BOROS...
...OR SOMEONE WITH THAT MARK ON THEIR ARM, WHAT ARE YOU GOING TO DO?
...
IF...
IF YOU'RE PLANNING TO *KILL* THEM...

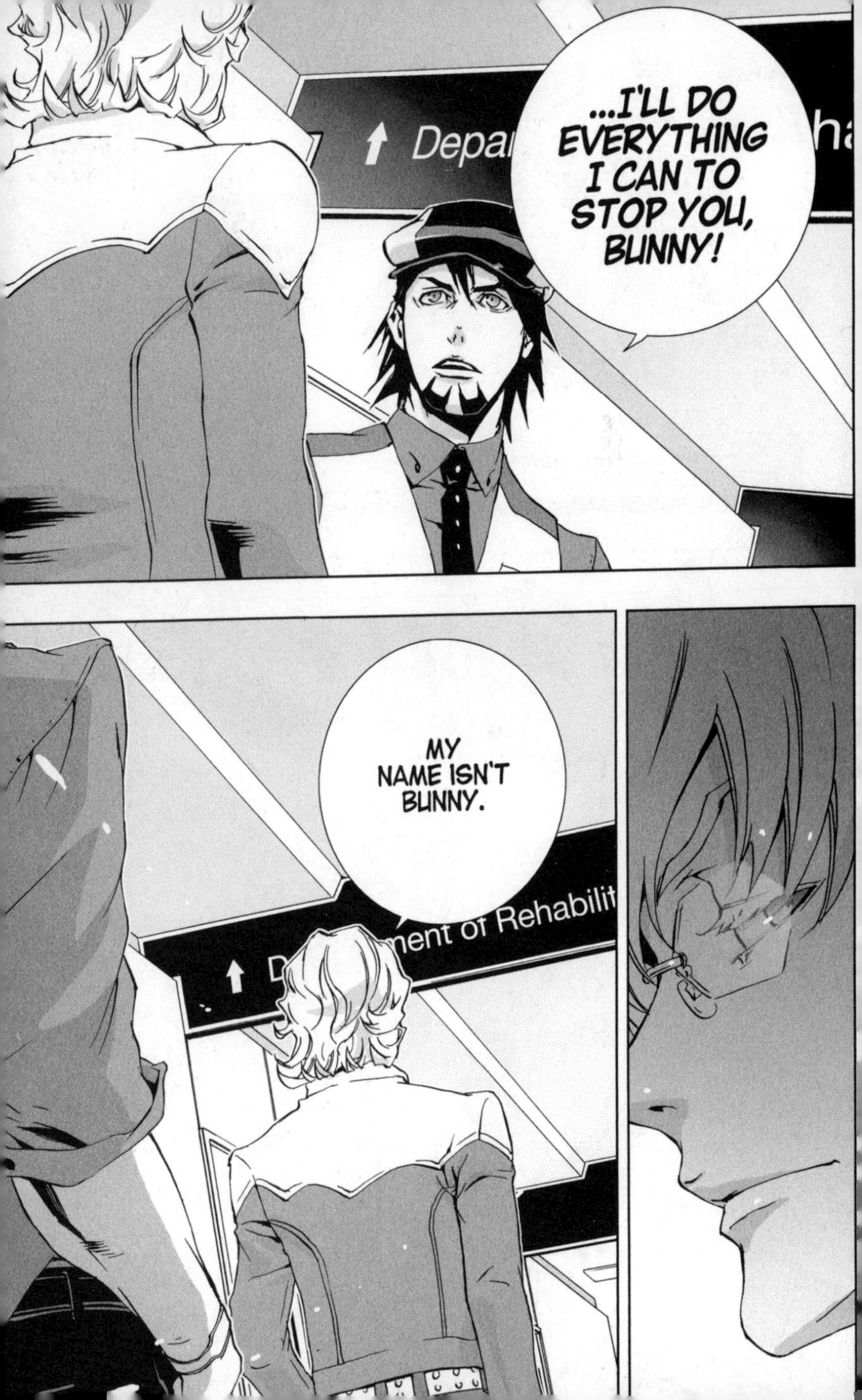
...I'LL DO EVERYTHING I CAN TO STOP YOU, BUNNY!
MY NAME ISN'T BUNNY.

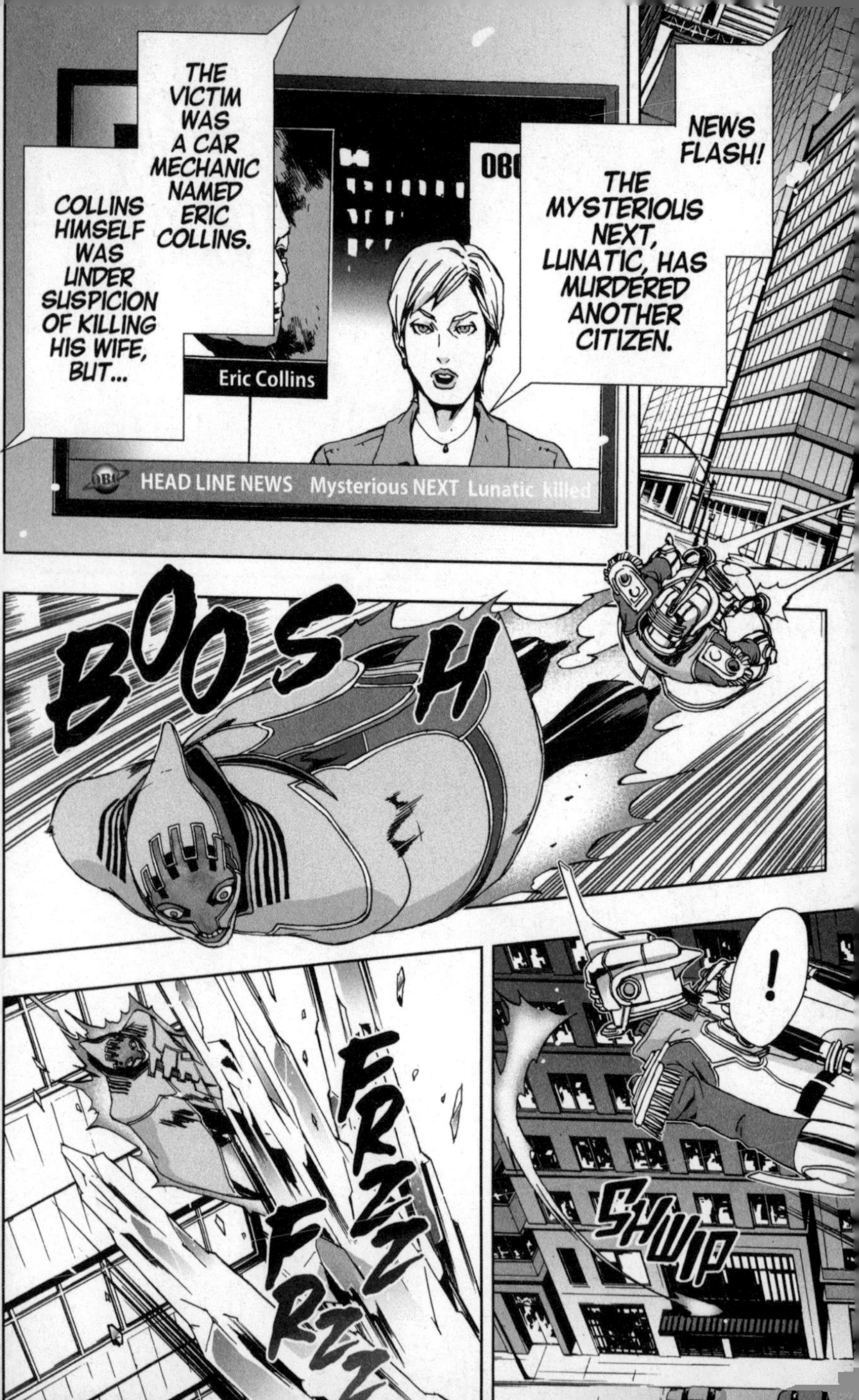
NEWS FLASH! THE MYSTERIOUS NEXT, LUNATIC, HAS MURDERED ANOTHER CITIZEN.
THE VICTIM WAS A CAR MECHANIC NAMED ERIC COLLINS.
COLLINS HIMSELF WAS UNDER SUSPICION OF KILLING HIS WIFE, BUT...
OBC
Eric Collins
HEAD LINE NEWS Mysterious NEXT Lunatic killed
BOOSH
!
SHWIP
FRZZ
FRZZ

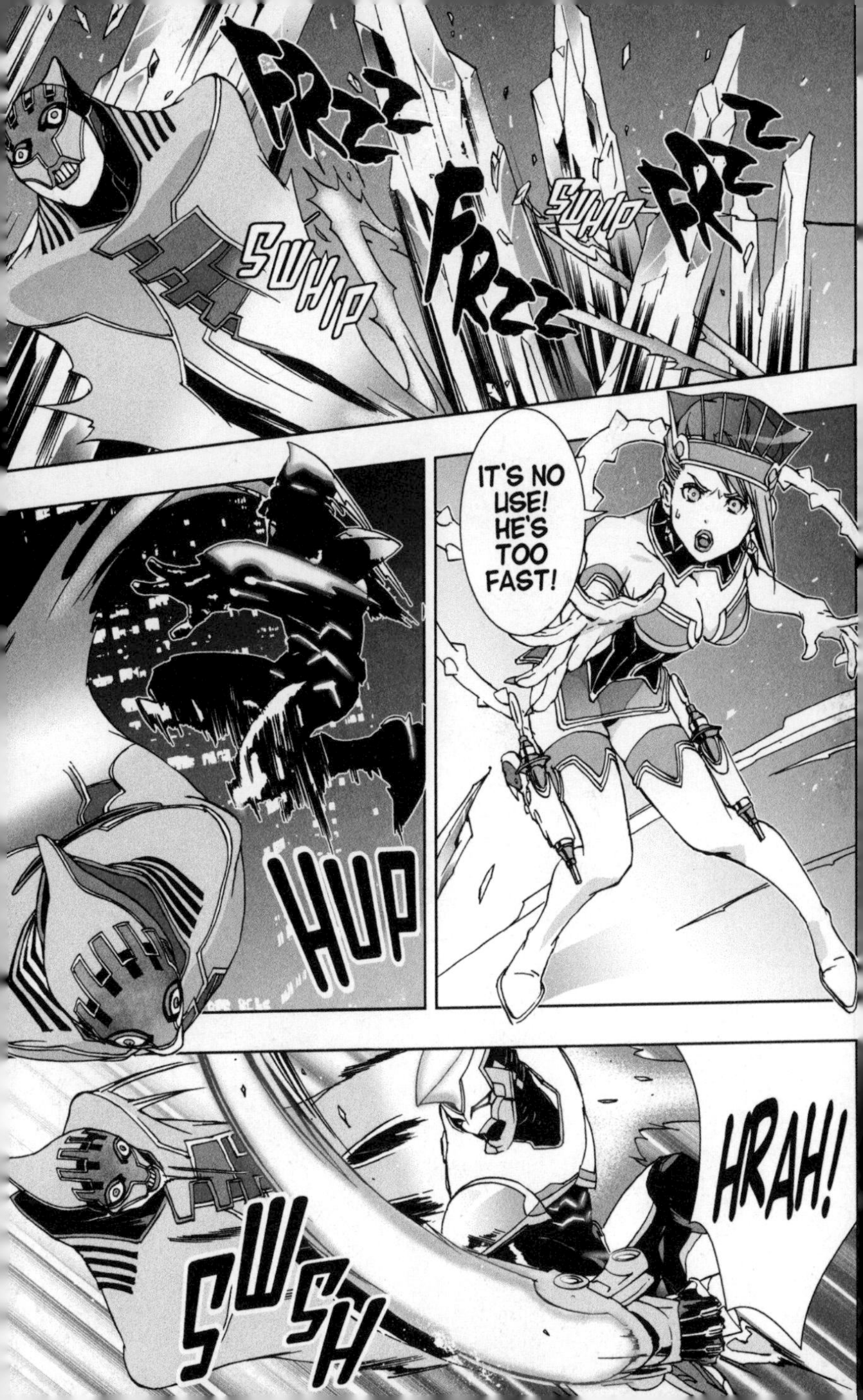
FRZZ
SWHIP
FRZZ
SWHIP
FRZZ
IT'S NO USE! HE'S TOO FAST!
HUP
HRAH!
SWSH

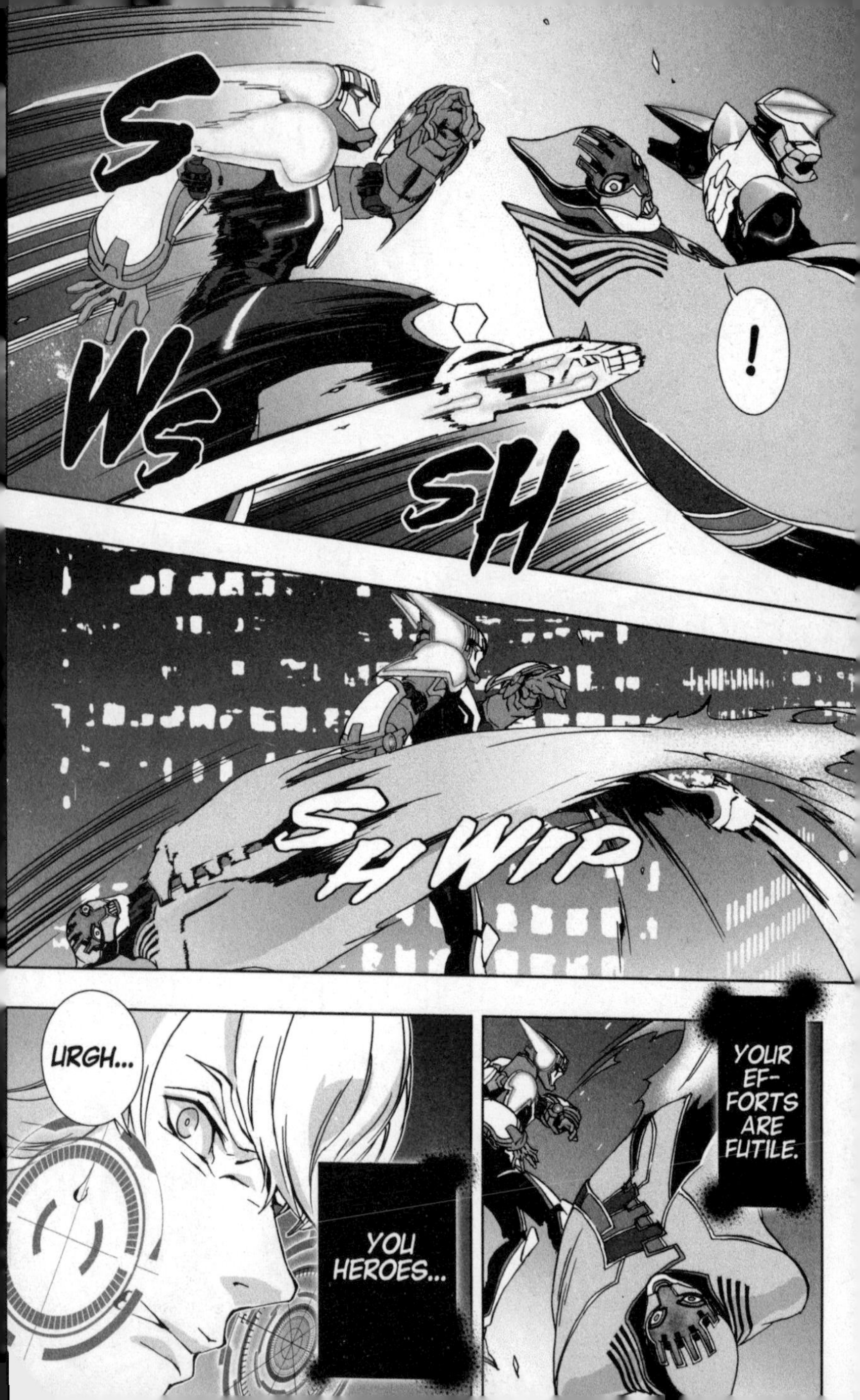

SWSSH
!
SHWIP
YOUR EF-FORTS ARE FUTILE.
URGH...
YOU HEROES...

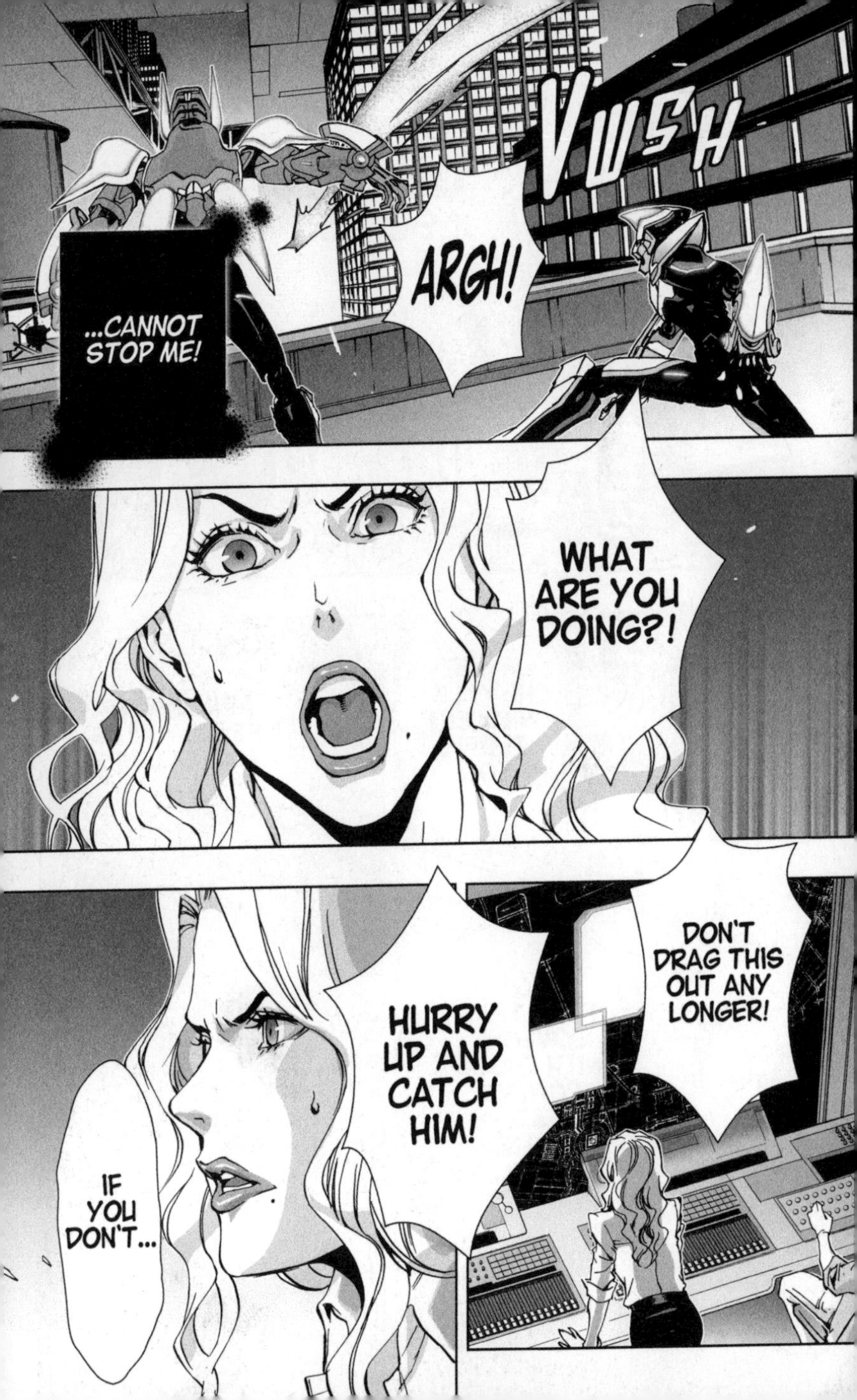
VWSH
ARGH!
...CANNOT STOP ME!
WHAT ARE YOU DOING?!
DON'T DRAG THIS OUT ANY LONGER!
HURRY UP AND CATCH HIM!
IF YOU DON'T...

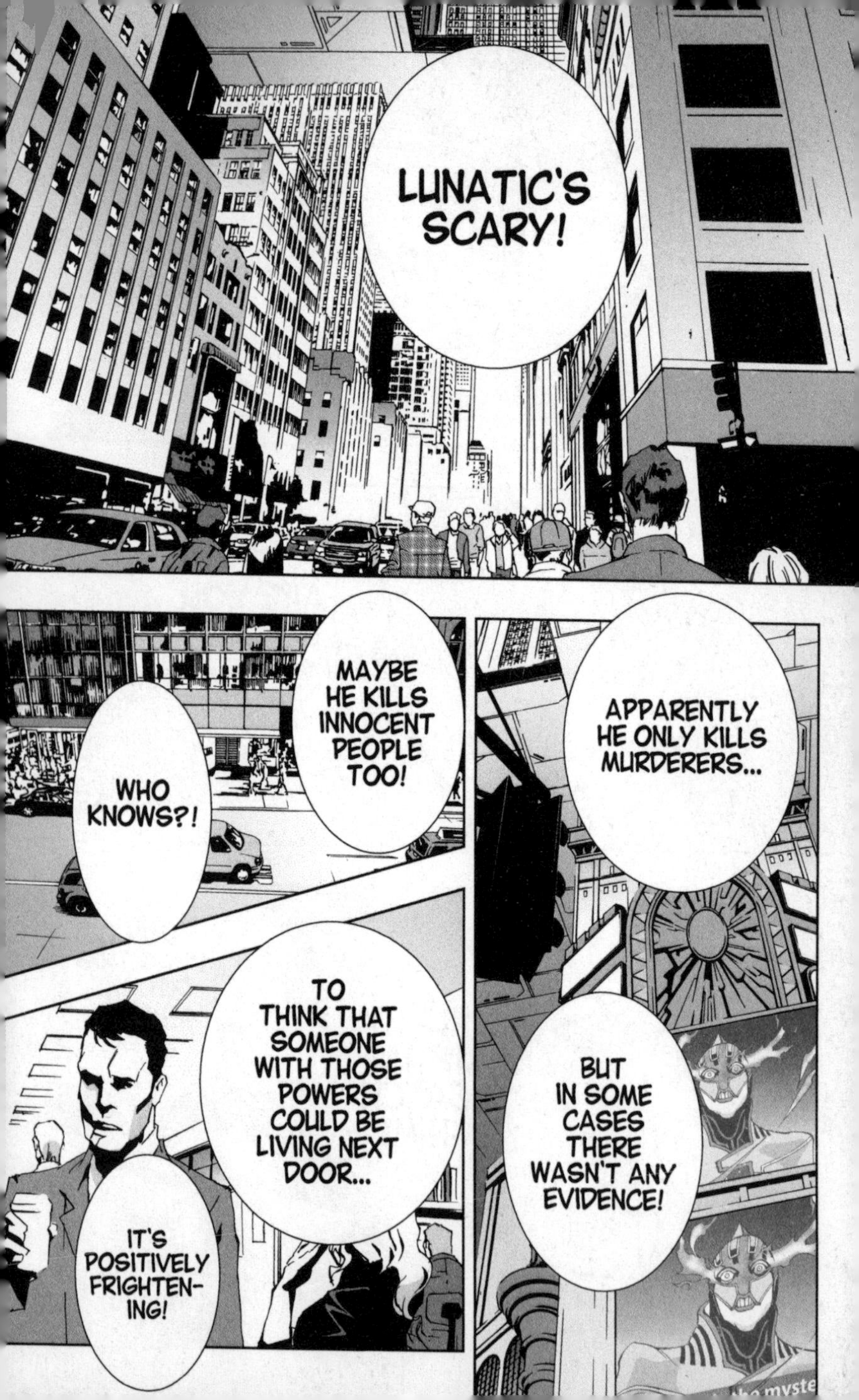
LUNATIC'S SCARY!
APPARENTLY HE ONLY KILLS MURDERERS...
BUT IN SOME CASES THERE WASN'T ANY EVIDENCE!
MAYBE HE KILLS INNOCENT PEOPLE TOO!
WHO KNOWS?!
TO THINK THAT SOMEONE WITH THOSE POWERS COULD BE LIVING NEXT DOOR...
IT'S POSITIVELY FRIGHTEN-ING!

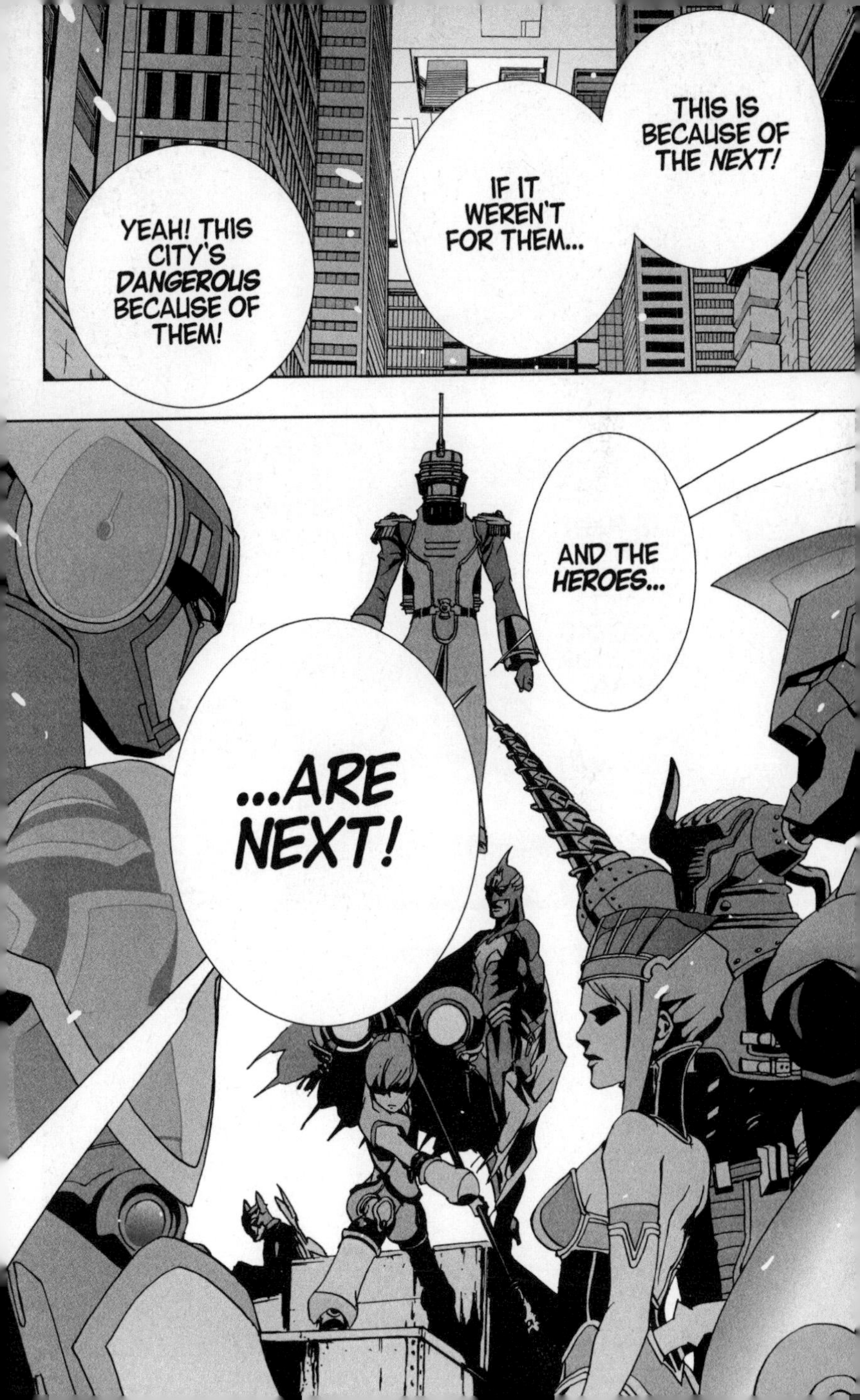
THIS IS BECAUSE OF THE NEXT!
IF IT WEREN'T FOR THEM...
YEAH! THIS CITY'S DANGEROUS BECAUSE OF THEM!
AND THE HEROES...
...ARE NEXT!

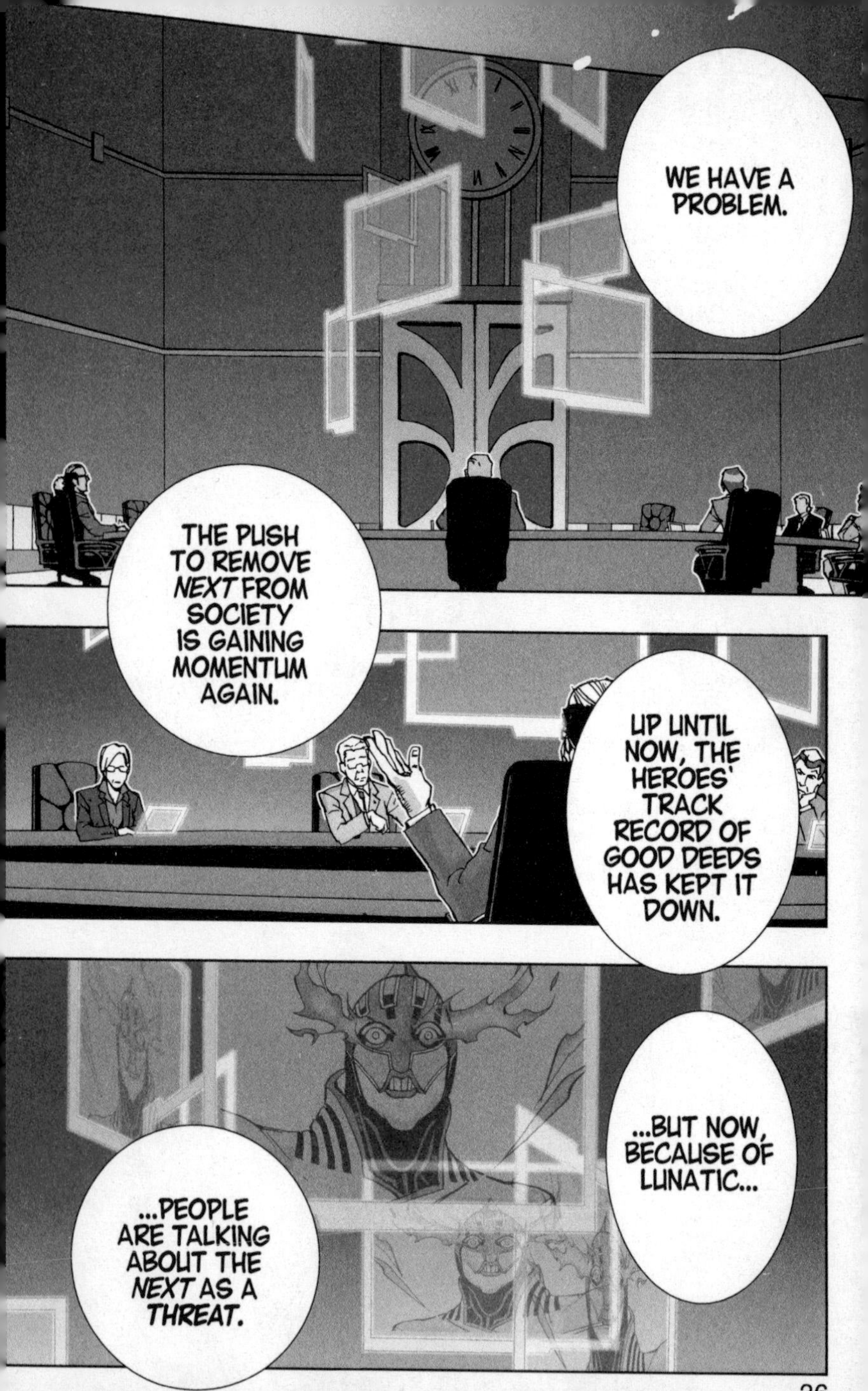
WE HAVE A PROBLEM.
THE PUSH TO REMOVE *NEXT* FROM SOCIETY IS GAINING MOMENTUM AGAIN.
UP UNTIL NOW, THE HEROES' TRACK RECORD OF GOOD DEEDS HAS KEPT IT DOWN.
...BUT NOW, BECAUSE OF LUNATIC...
...PEOPLE ARE TALKING ABOUT THE *NEXT* AS A *THREAT*.

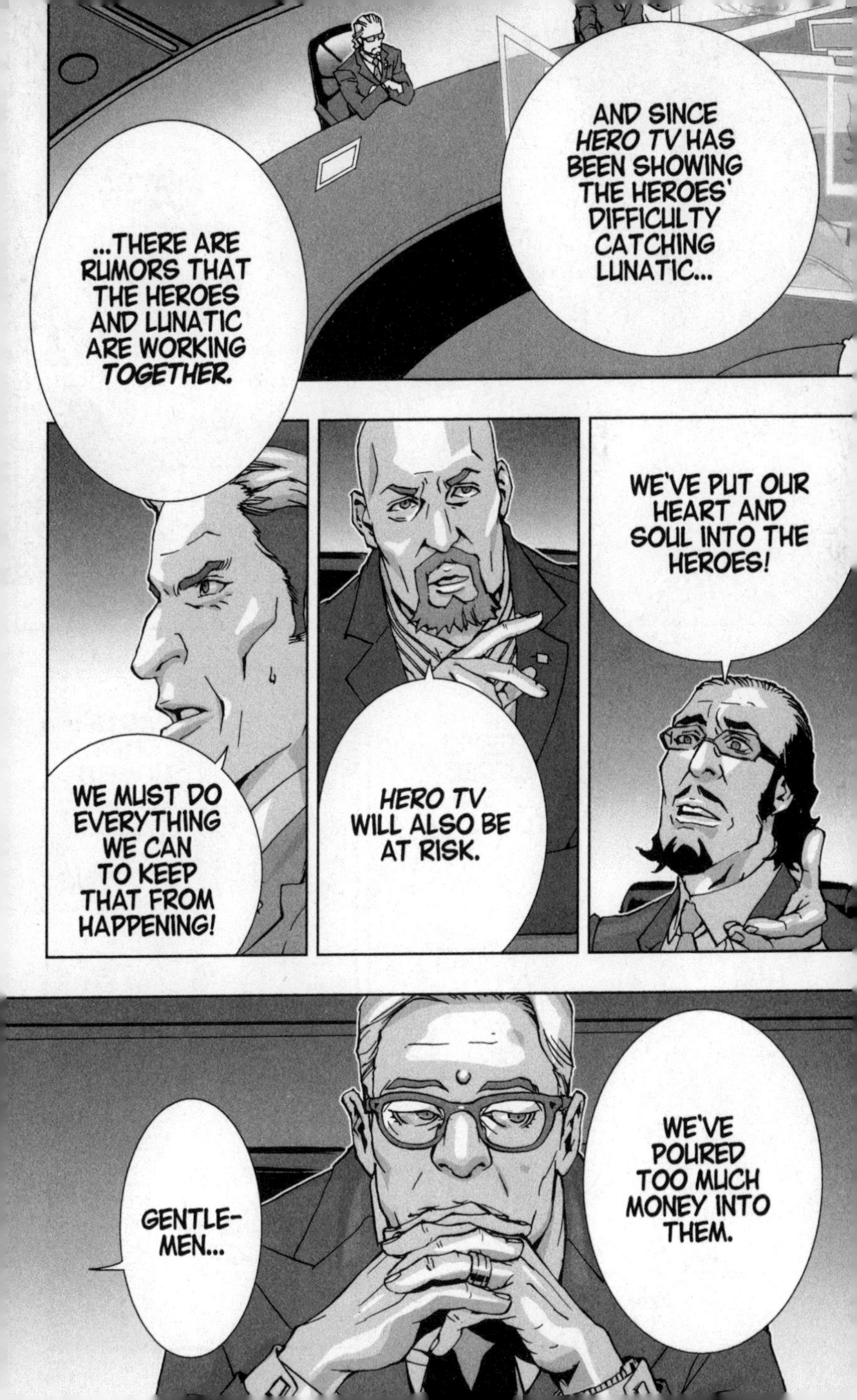
AND SINCE HERO TV HAS BEEN SHOWING THE HEROES' DIFFICULTY CATCHING LUNATIC...
...THERE ARE RUMORS THAT THE HEROES AND LUNATIC ARE WORKING TOGETHER.
WE'VE PUT OUR HEART AND SOUL INTO THE HEROES!
HERO TV WILL ALSO BE AT RISK.
WE MUST DO EVERYTHING WE CAN TO KEEP THAT FROM HAPPENING!
WE'VE POURED TOO MUCH MONEY INTO THEM.
GENTLE-
MEN...

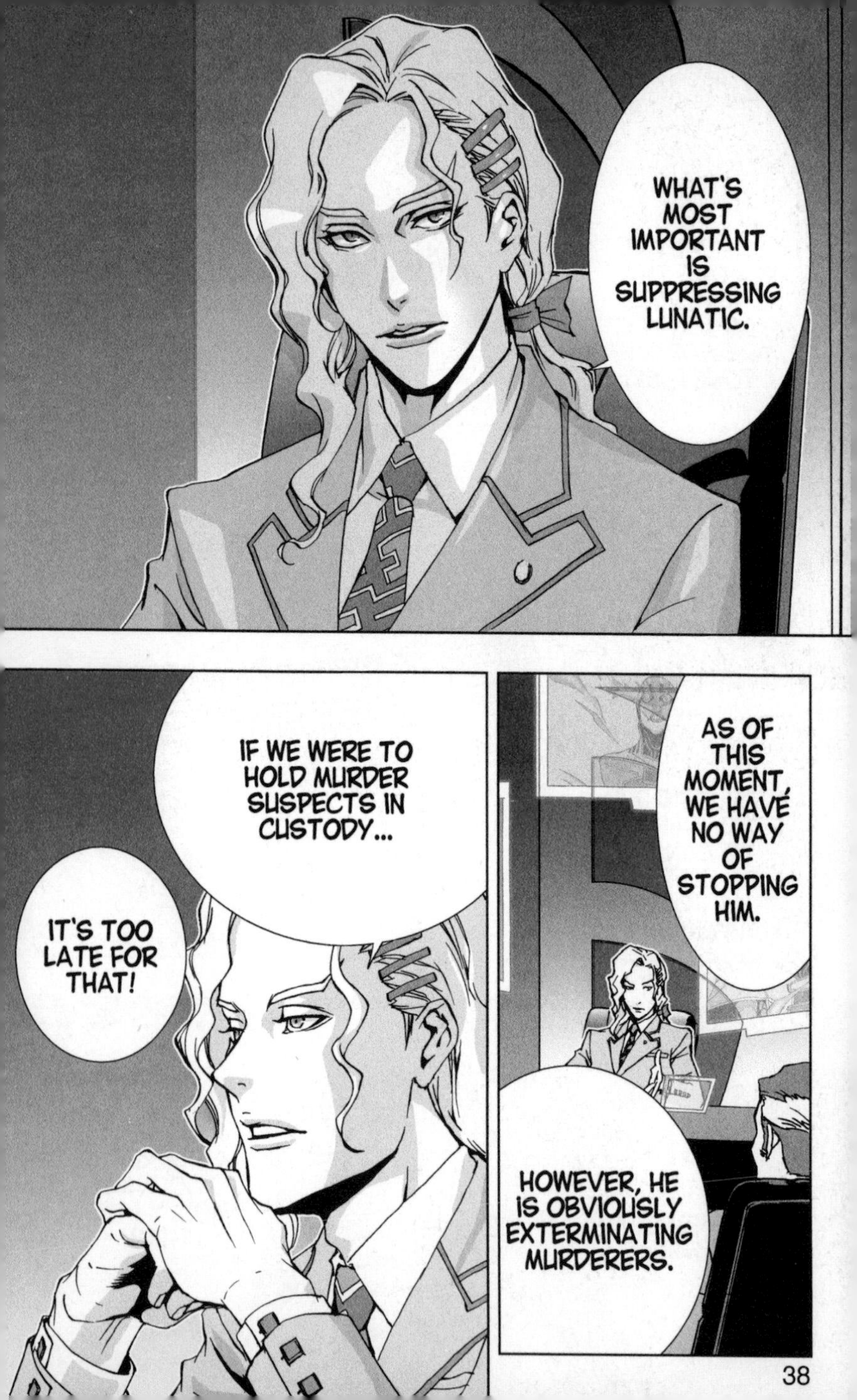
WHAT'S MOST IMPORTANT IS SUPPRESSING LUNATIC.
AS OF THIS MOMENT, WE HAVE NO WAY OF STOPPING HIM.
HOWEVER, HE IS OBVIOUSLY EXTERMINATING MURDERERS.
IF WE WERE TO HOLD MURDER SUSPECTS IN CUSTODY...
IT'S TOO LATE FOR THAT!

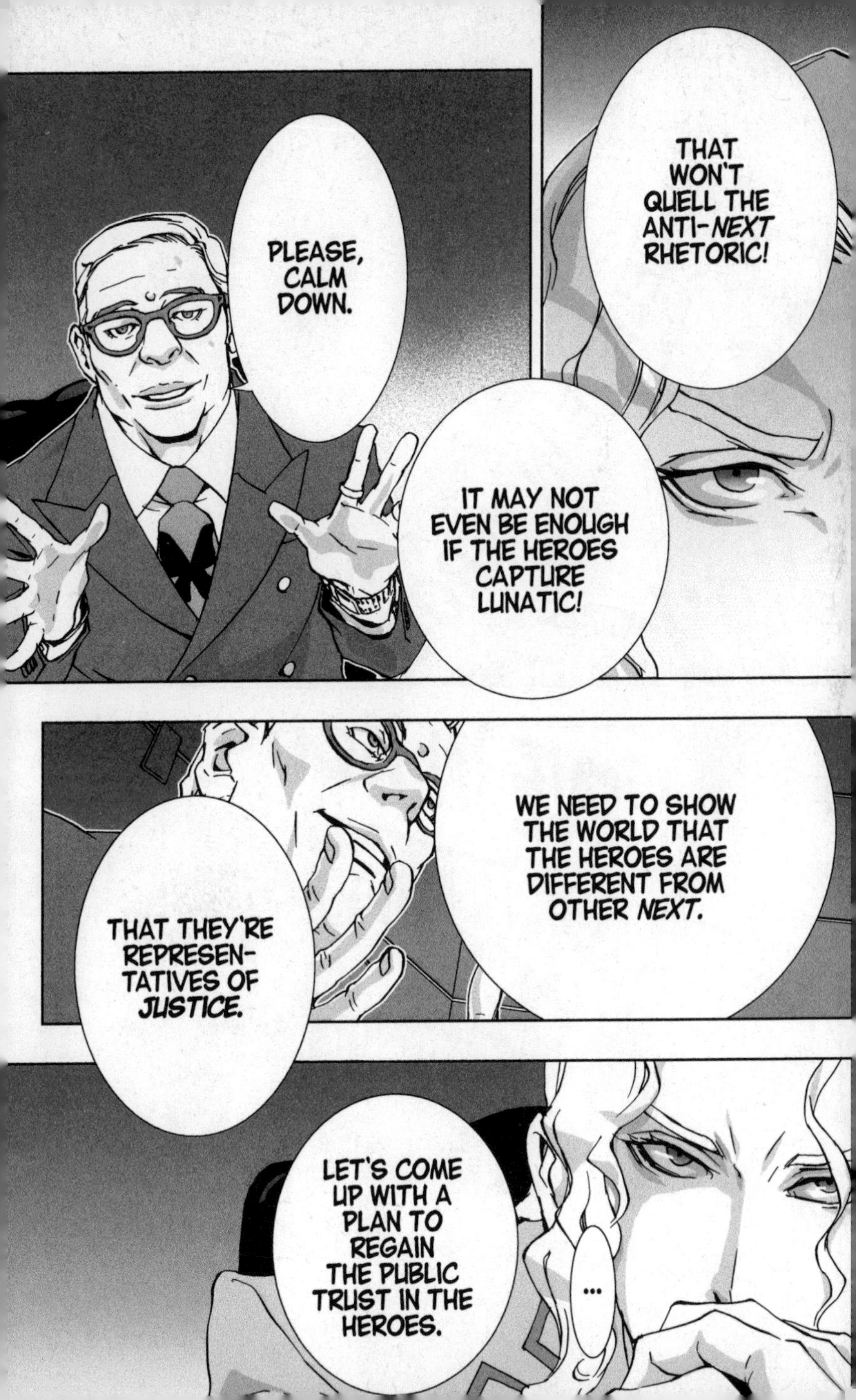
THAT WON'T QUELL THE ANTI-*NEXT* RHETORIC!
IT MAY NOT EVEN BE ENOUGH IF THE HEROES CAPTURE LUNATIC!
PLEASE, CALM DOWN.
WE NEED TO SHOW THE WORLD THAT THE HEROES ARE DIFFERENT FROM OTHER *NEXT*.
THAT THEY'RE REPRESEN-TATIVES OF JUSTICE.
LET'S COME UP WITH A PLAN TO REGAIN THE PUBLIC TRUST IN THE HEROES.
...

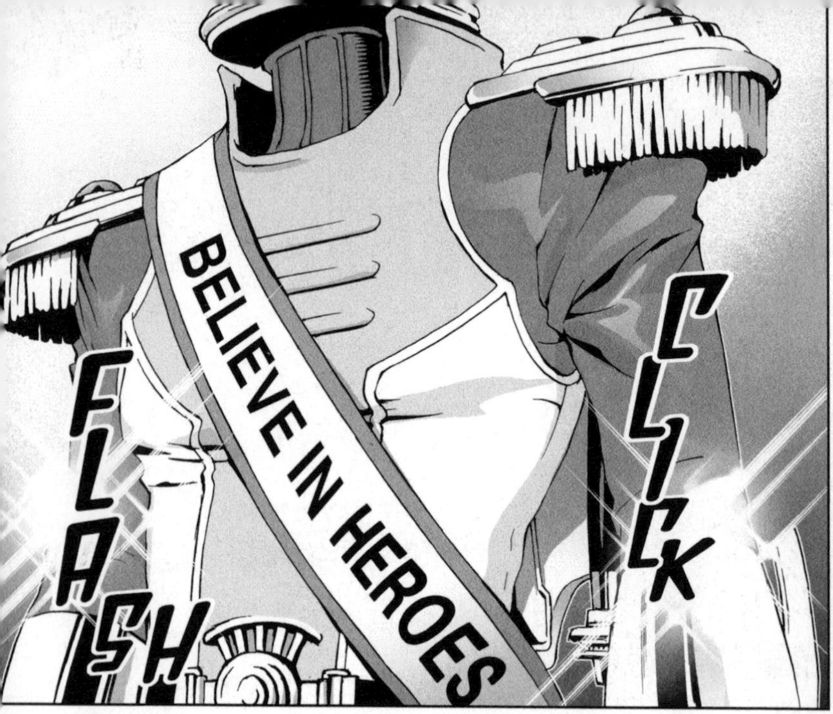
CLICK
BELIEVE IN HEROES
FLASH

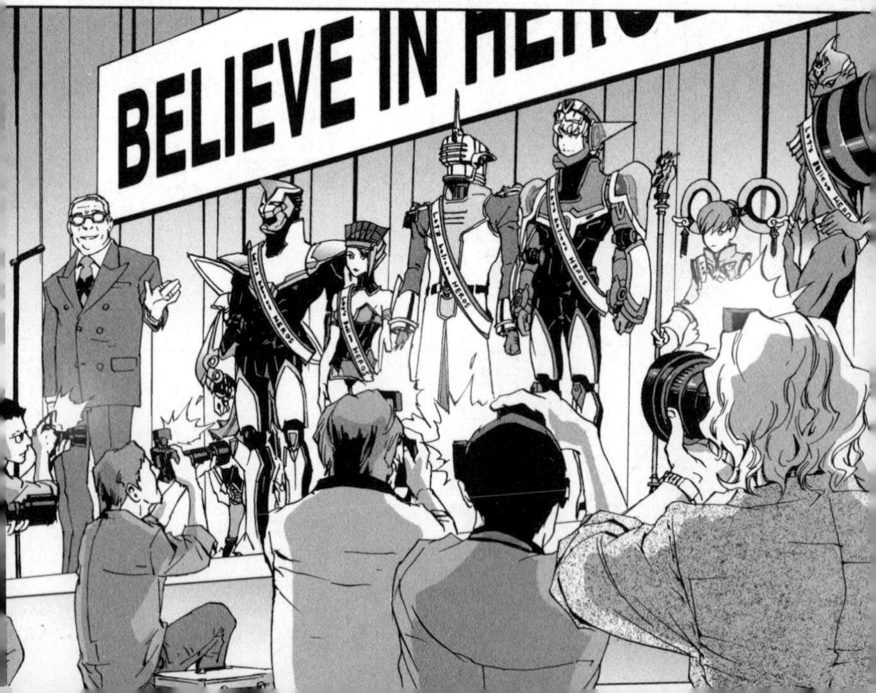
BELIEVE IN HER

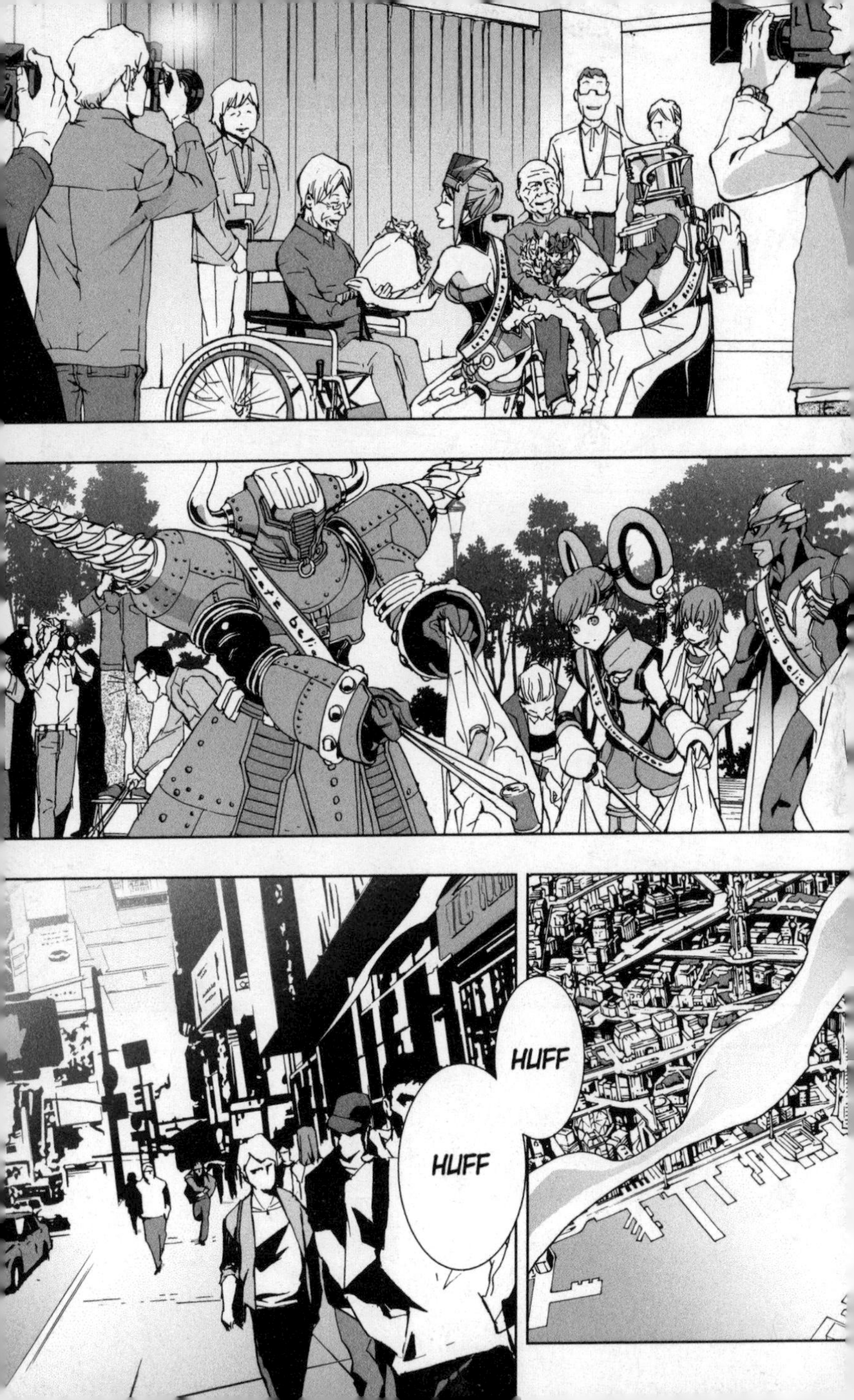
HUFF
HUFF

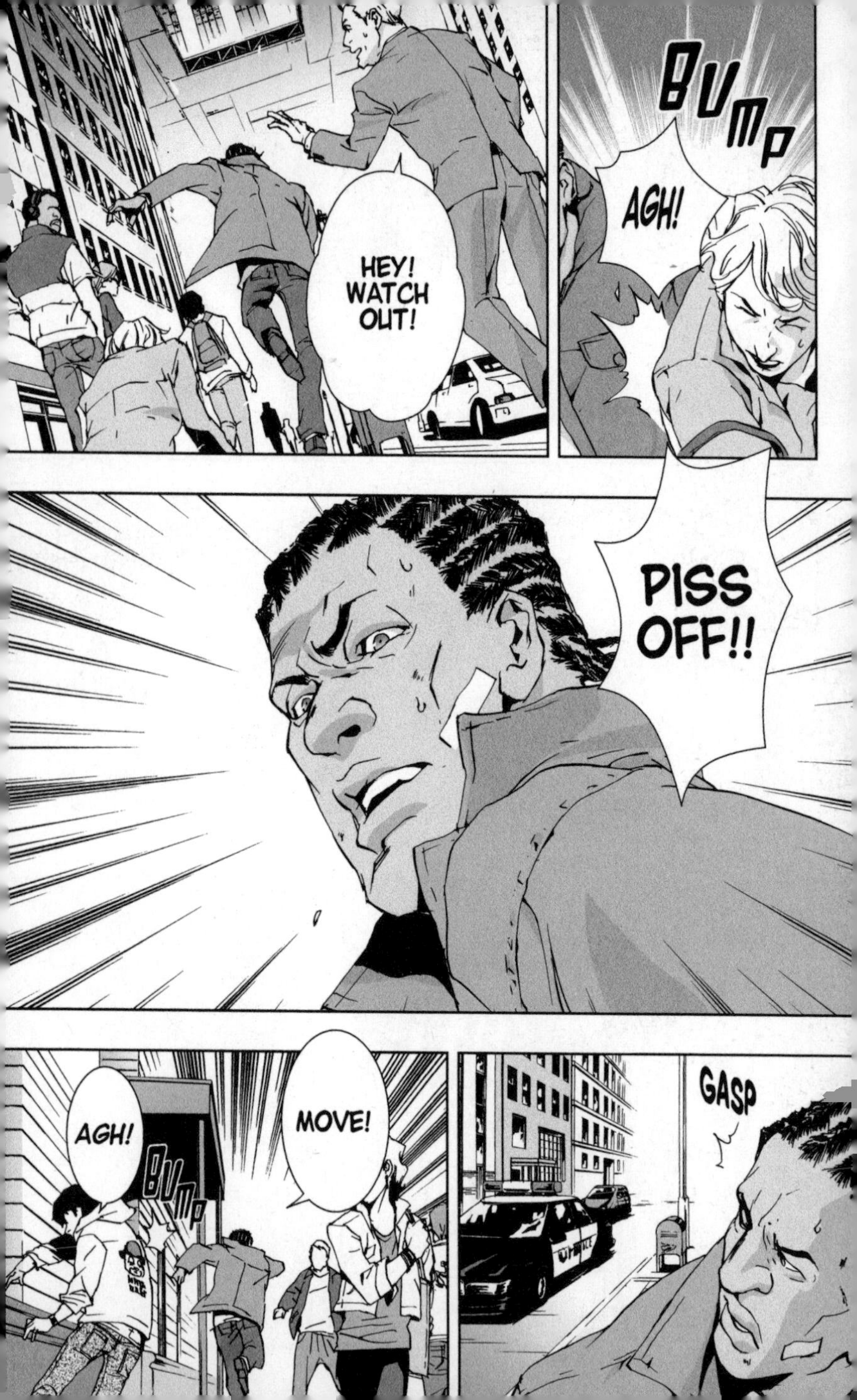
BUMP
AGH!
HEY! WATCH OUT!
PISS OFF!!
GASP
MOVE!
AGH!
BUMP

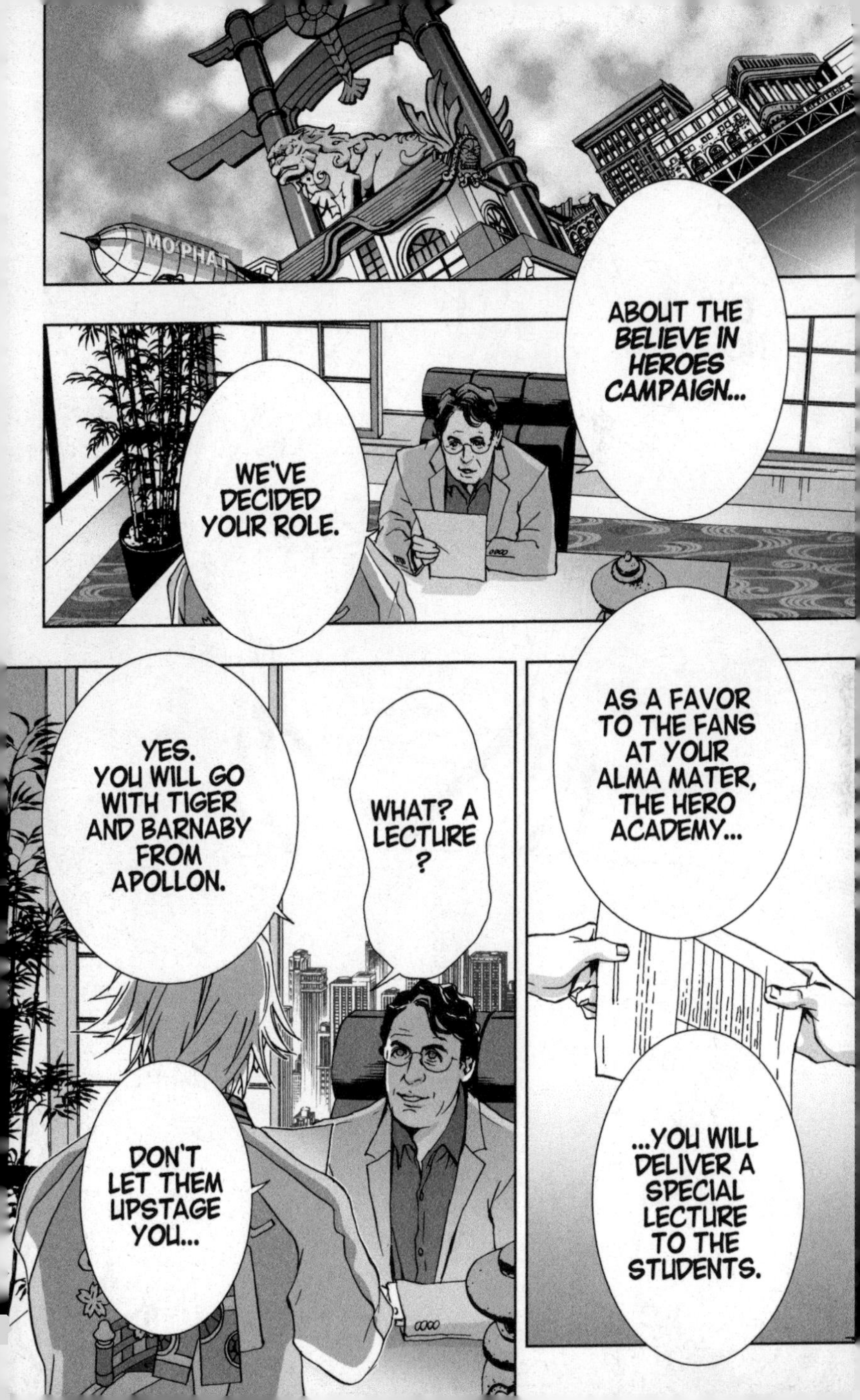
ABOUT THE BELIEVE IN HEROES CAMPAIGN...
WE'VE DECIDED YOUR ROLE.
AS A FAVOR TO THE FANS AT YOUR ALMA MATER, THE HERO ACADEMY...
...YOU WILL DELIVER A SPECIAL LECTURE TO THE STUDENTS.
WHAT? A LECTURE?
YES. YOU WILL GO WITH TIGER AND BARNABY FROM APOLLON.
DON'T LET THEM UPSTAGE YOU...

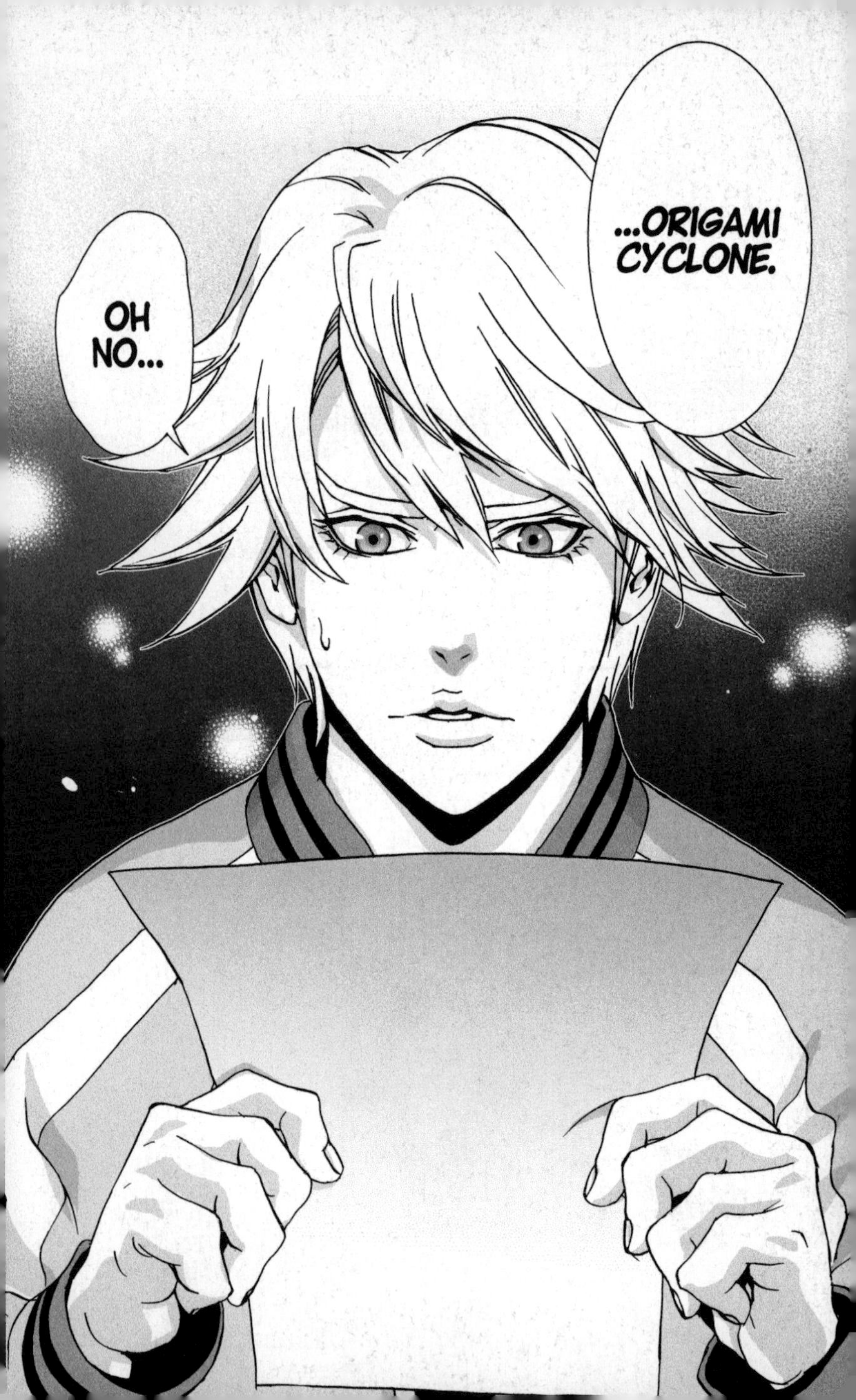
...ORIGAMI CYCLONE.
OH NO...

TIGER&BUNNY

TIGER & BUNNY

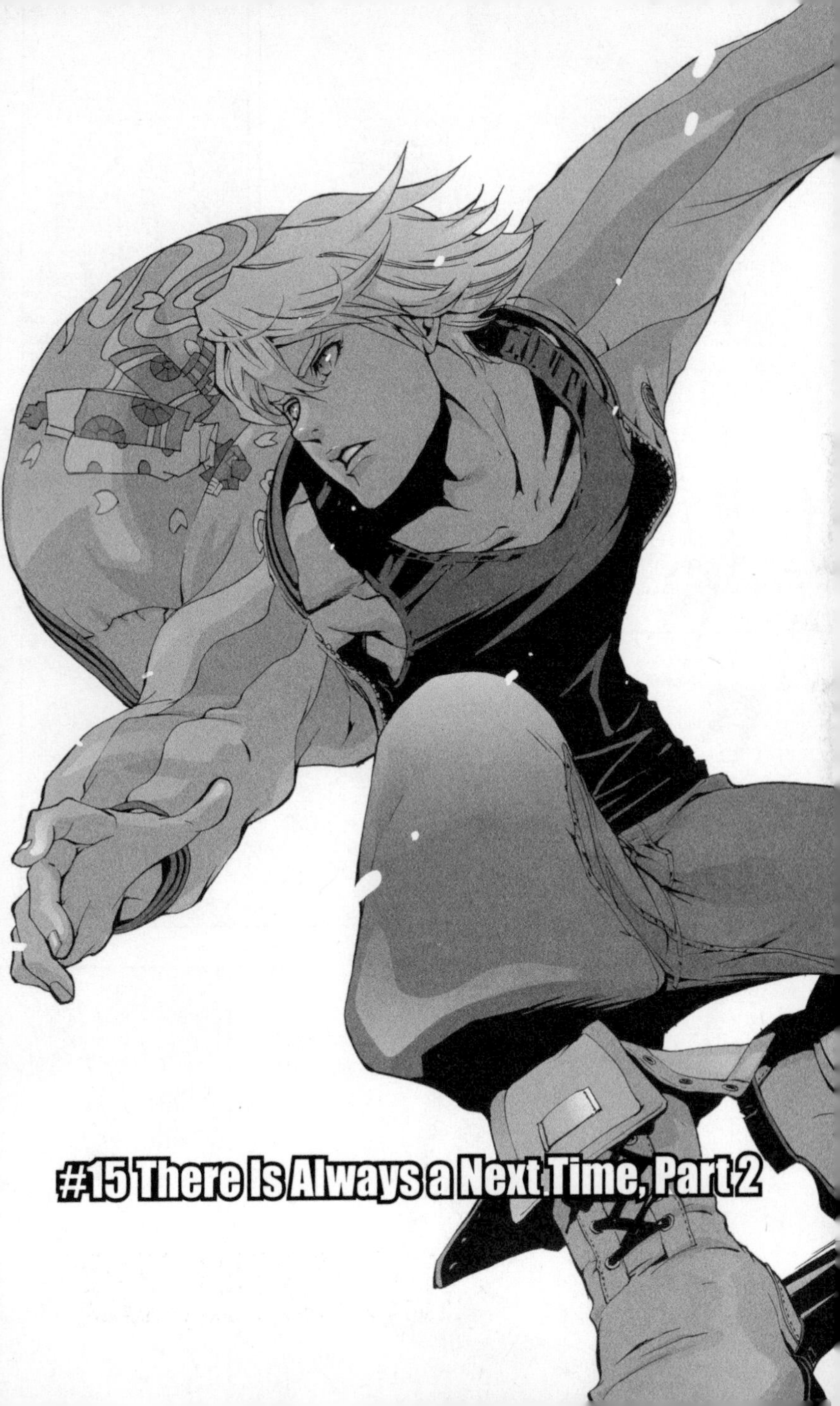

#15 There Is Always a Next Time, Part 2

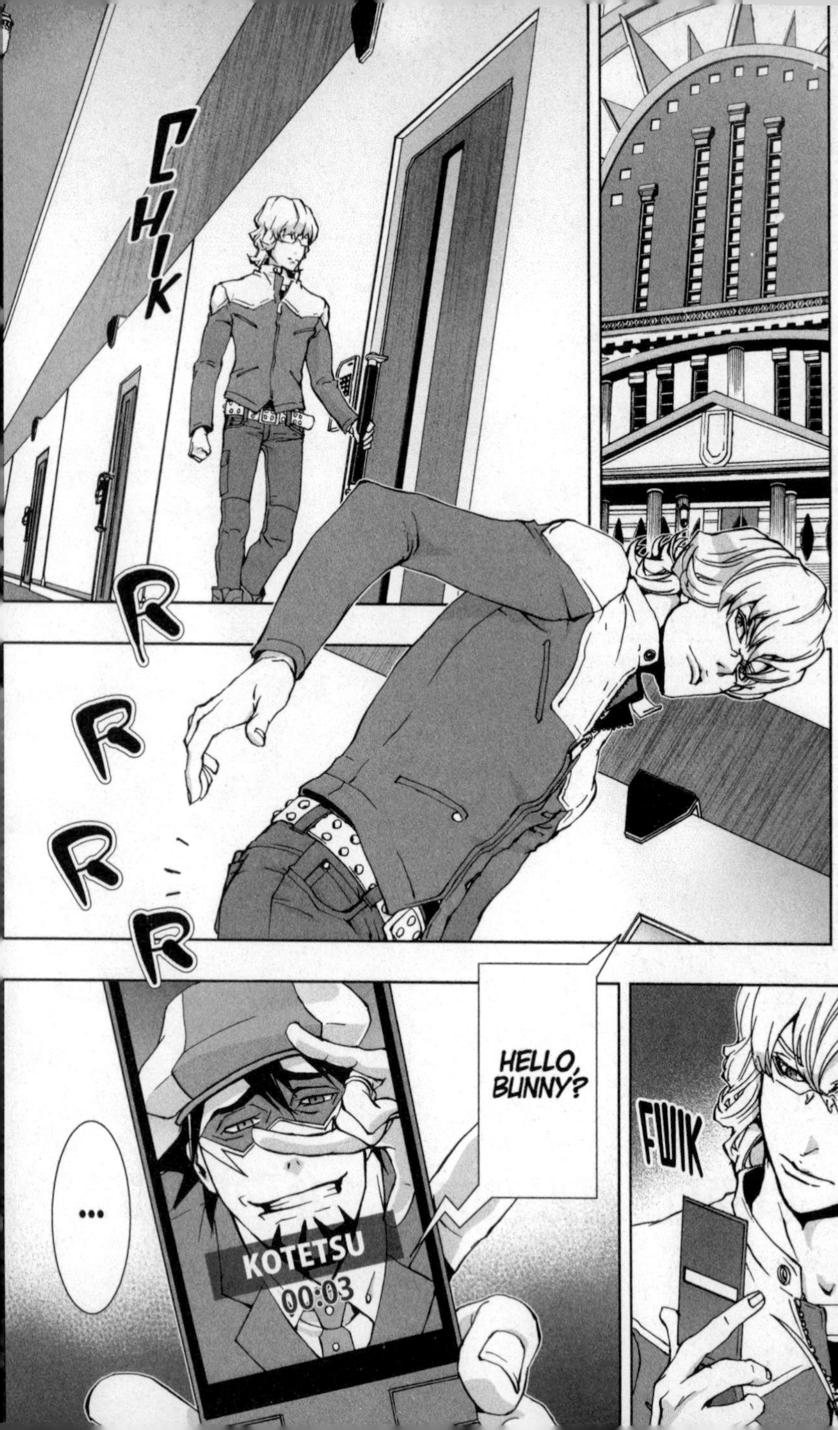
CHIK
RRRR
FWIK
HELLO, BUNNY?
...
KOTETSU
00:03

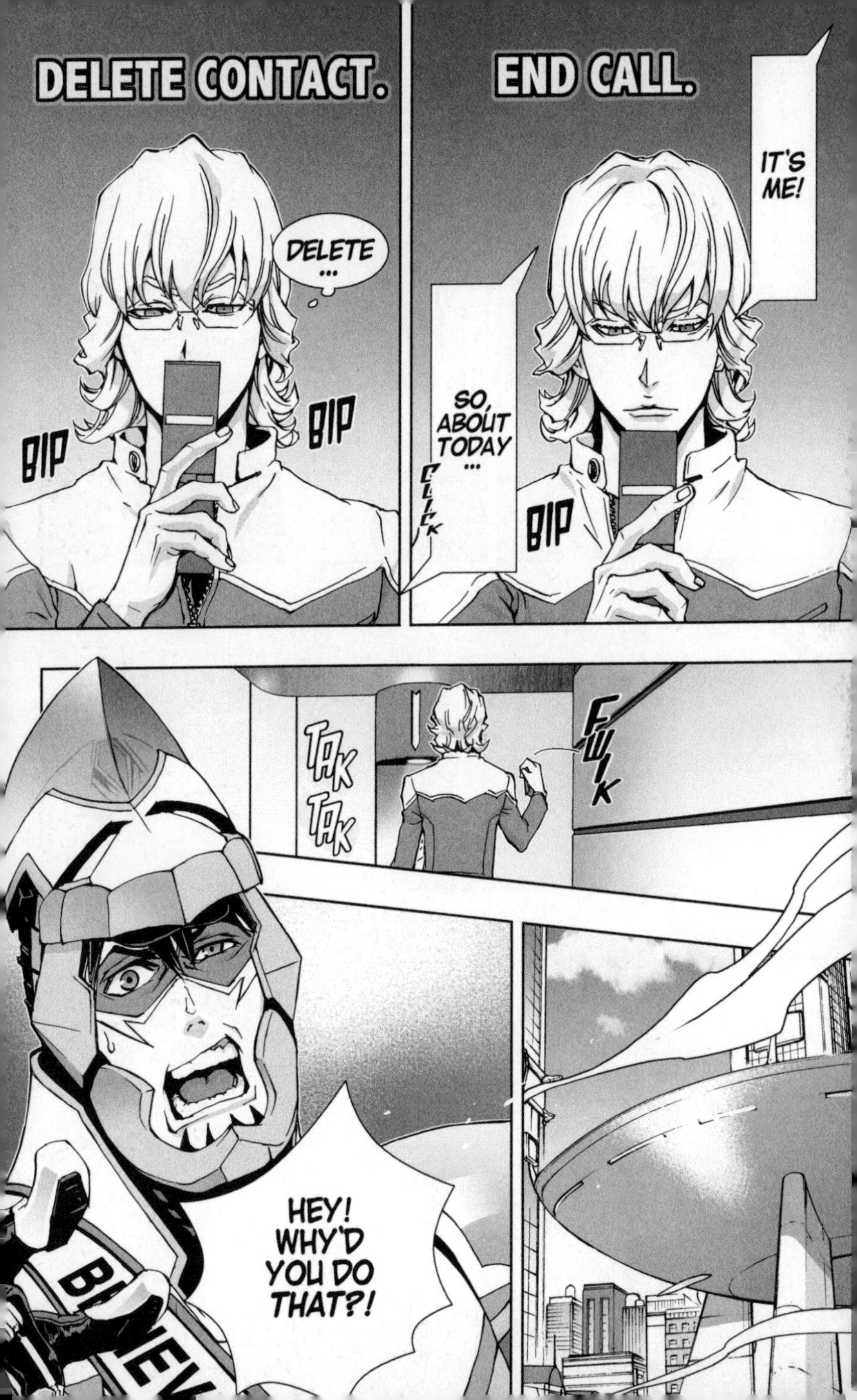
END CALL.
IT'S ME!
SO, ABOUT TODAY ...
CLICK
BIP
DELETE CONTACT.
DELETE ...
BIP
BIP
TAK TAK
FWIK
HEY! WHY'D YOU DO THAT?!

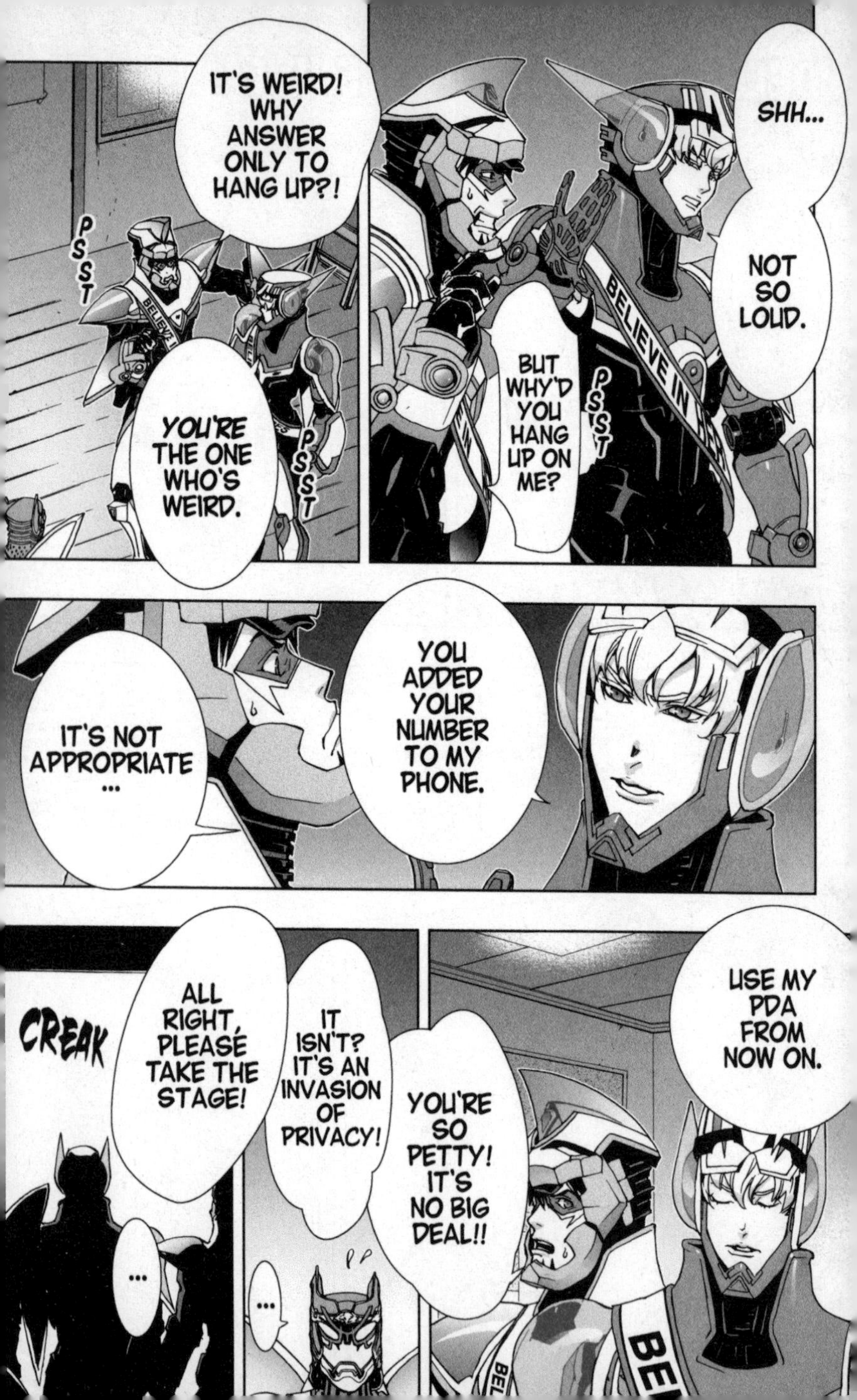
SHH...
NOT SO LOUD.
PSST
BUT WHY'D YOU HANG UP ON ME?
IT'S WEIRD! WHY ANSWER ONLY TO HANG UP?!
PSST
PSST
YOU'RE THE ONE WHO'S WEIRD.
YOU ADDED YOUR NUMBER TO MY PHONE.
IT'S NOT APPROPRIATE ...
USE MY PDA FROM NOW ON.
YOU'RE SO PETTY! IT'S NO BIG DEAL!!
IT ISN'T? IT'S AN INVASION OF PRIVACY!
...
ALL RIGHT, PLEASE TAKE THE STAGE!
CREAK
...

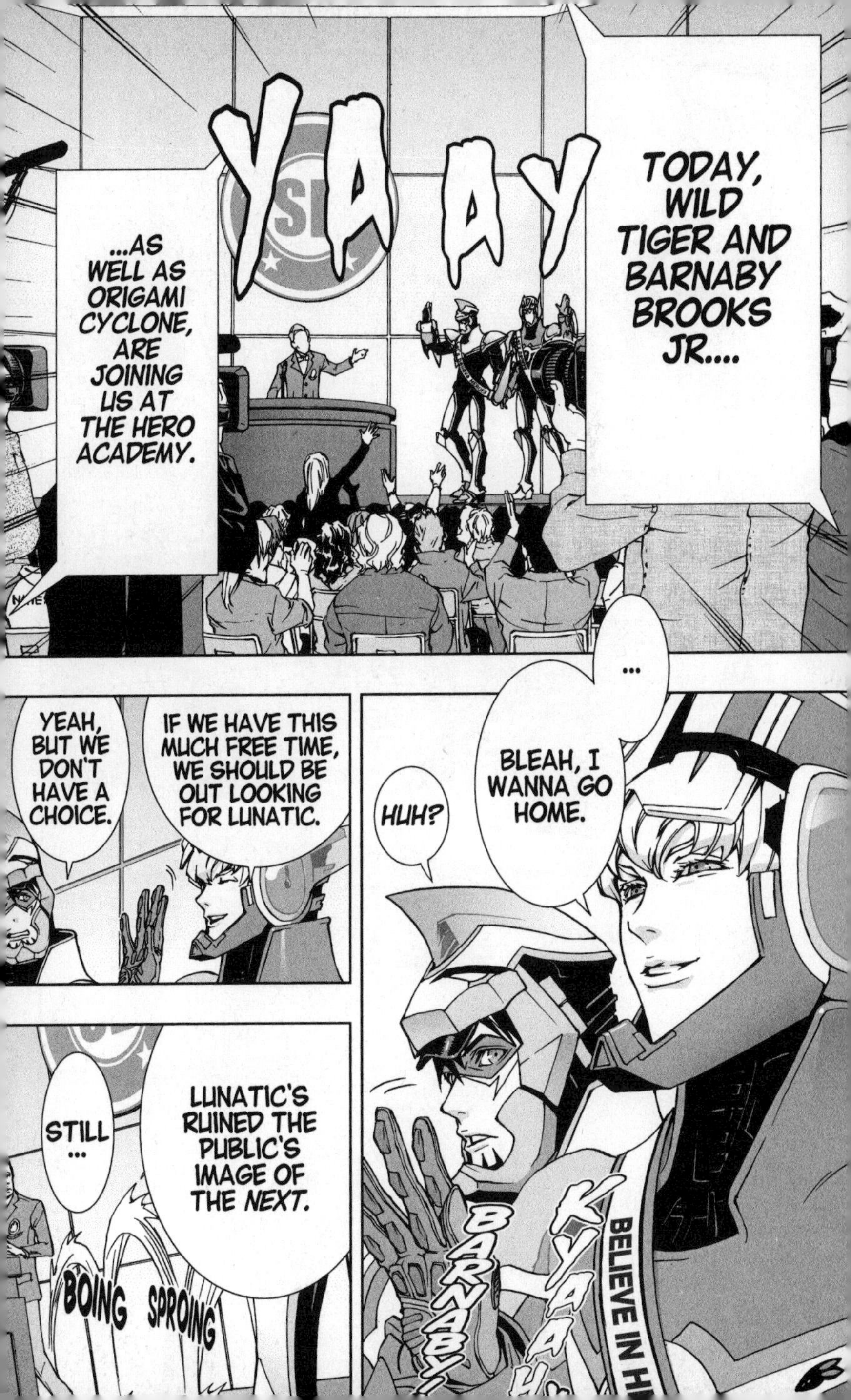
TODAY, WILD TIGER AND BARNABY BROOKS JR....
YAAY
...AS WELL AS ORIGAMI CYCLONE, ARE JOINING US AT THE HERO ACADEMY.
...
BLEAH, I WANNA GO HOME.
HUH?
BARNABY
IF WE HAVE THIS MUCH FREE TIME, WE SHOULD BE OUT LOOKING FOR LUNATIC.
YEAH, BUT WE DON'T HAVE A CHOICE.
LUNATIC'S RUINED THE PUBLIC'S IMAGE OF THE NEXT.
STILL ...
BOING SPRONG

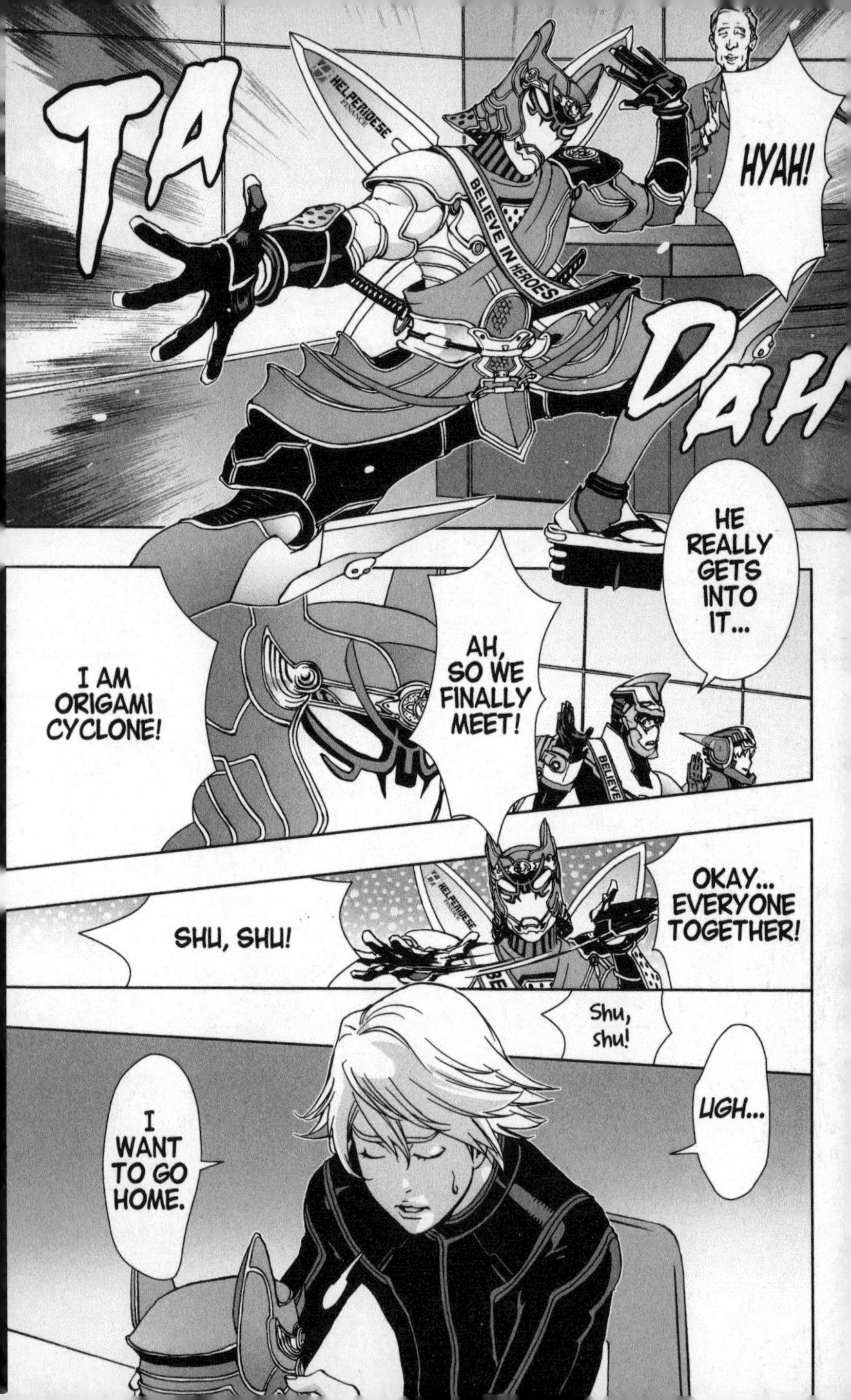
HYAH!
TA
HELPERIDESE FINANCE
BELIEVE IN HEROES
DAH
HE REALLY GETS INTO IT...
AH, SO WE FINALLY MEET!
I AM ORIGAMI CYCLONE!
BELIEVE
OKAY... EVERYONE TOGETHER!
SHU, SHU!
HELPERIDESE FINANCE
Shu, shu!
UGH...
I WANT TO GO HOME.

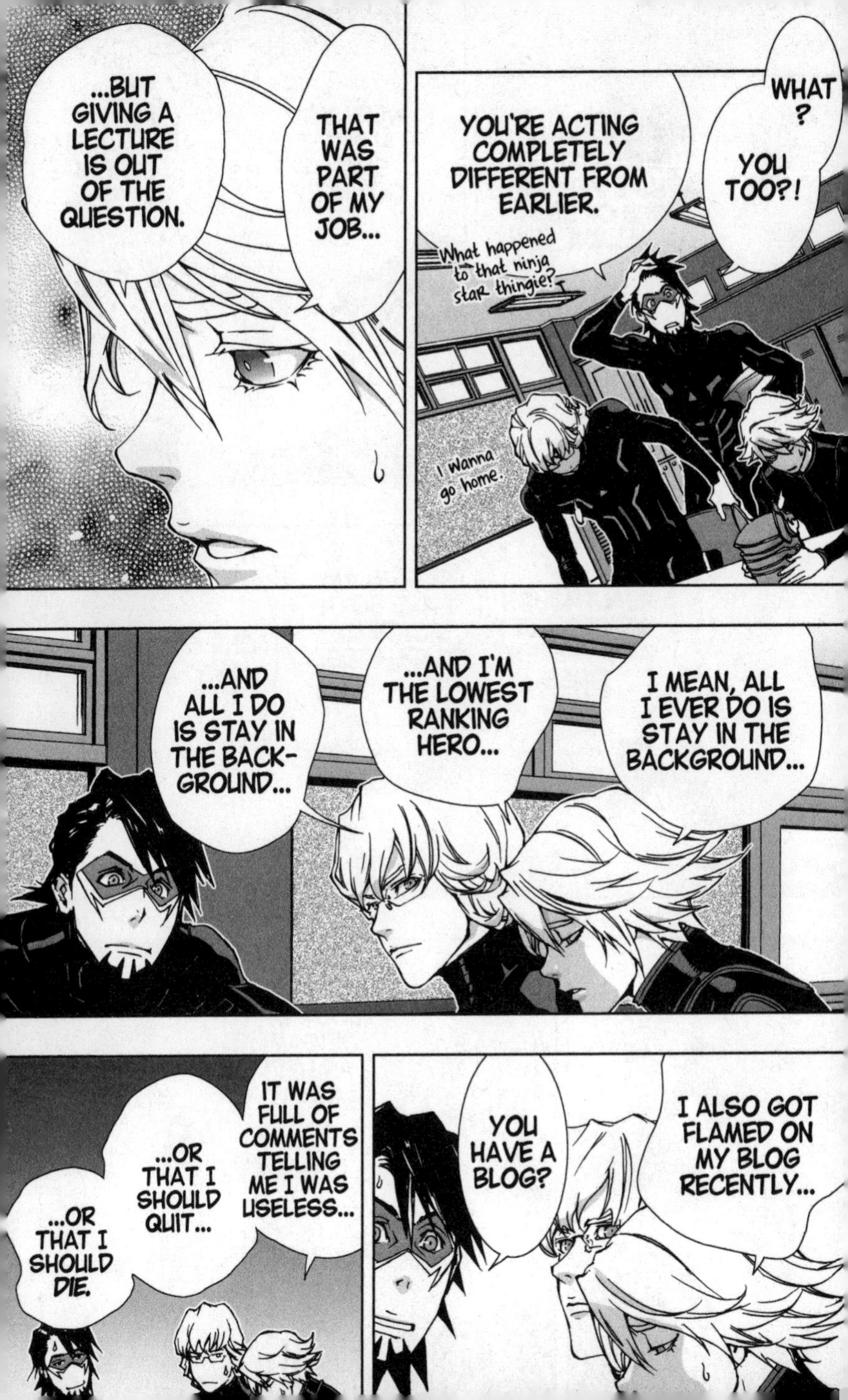
WHAT? YOU TOO?!
YOU'RE ACTING COMPLETELY DIFFERENT FROM EARLIER.
What happened to that ninja star thingie?
I wanna go home.
THAT WAS PART OF MY JOB...
...BUT GIVING A LECTURE IS OUT OF THE QUESTION.
I MEAN, ALL I EVER DO IS STAY IN THE BACKGROUND...
...AND I'M THE LOWEST RANKING HERO...
...AND ALL I DO IS STAY IN THE BACK-GROUND...
I ALSO GOT FLAMED ON MY BLOG RECENTLY...
YOU HAVE A BLOG?
IT WAS FULL OF COMMENTS TELLING ME I WAS USELESS...
...OR THAT I SHOULD QUIT...
...OR THAT I SHOULD DIE.

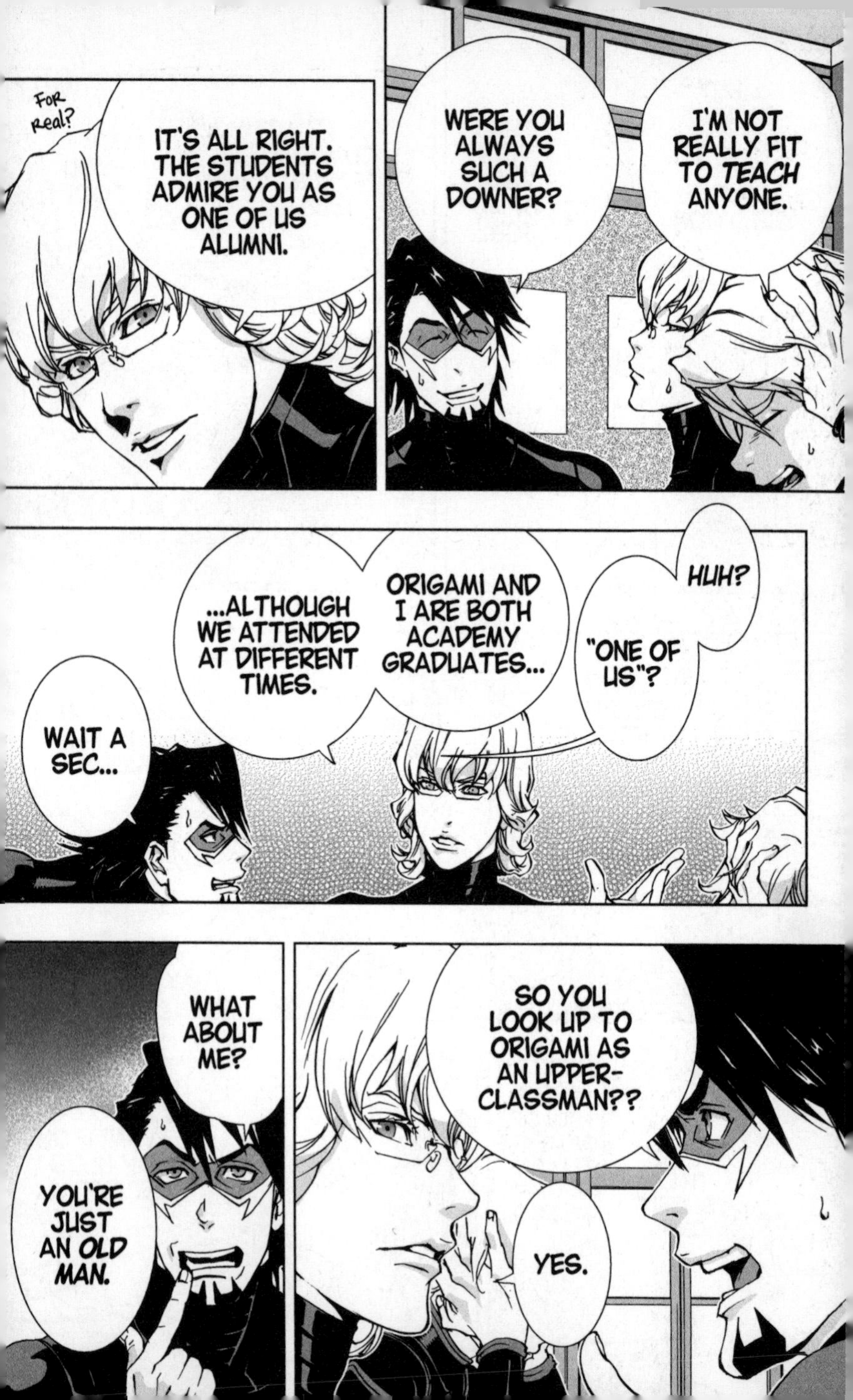
I'M NOT REALLY FIT TO *TEACH* ANYONE.
WERE YOU ALWAYS SUCH A DOWNER?
IT'S ALL RIGHT. THE STUDENTS ADMIRE YOU AS ONE OF US ALUMNI.
For real?
HUH?
"ONE OF US"?
ORIGAMI AND I ARE BOTH ACADEMY GRADUATES...
...ALTHOUGH WE ATTENDED AT DIFFERENT TIMES.
WAIT A SEC...
SO YOU LOOK UP TO ORIGAMI AS AN UPPER-CLASSMAN??
YES.
WHAT ABOUT ME?
YOU'RE JUST AN OLD MAN.

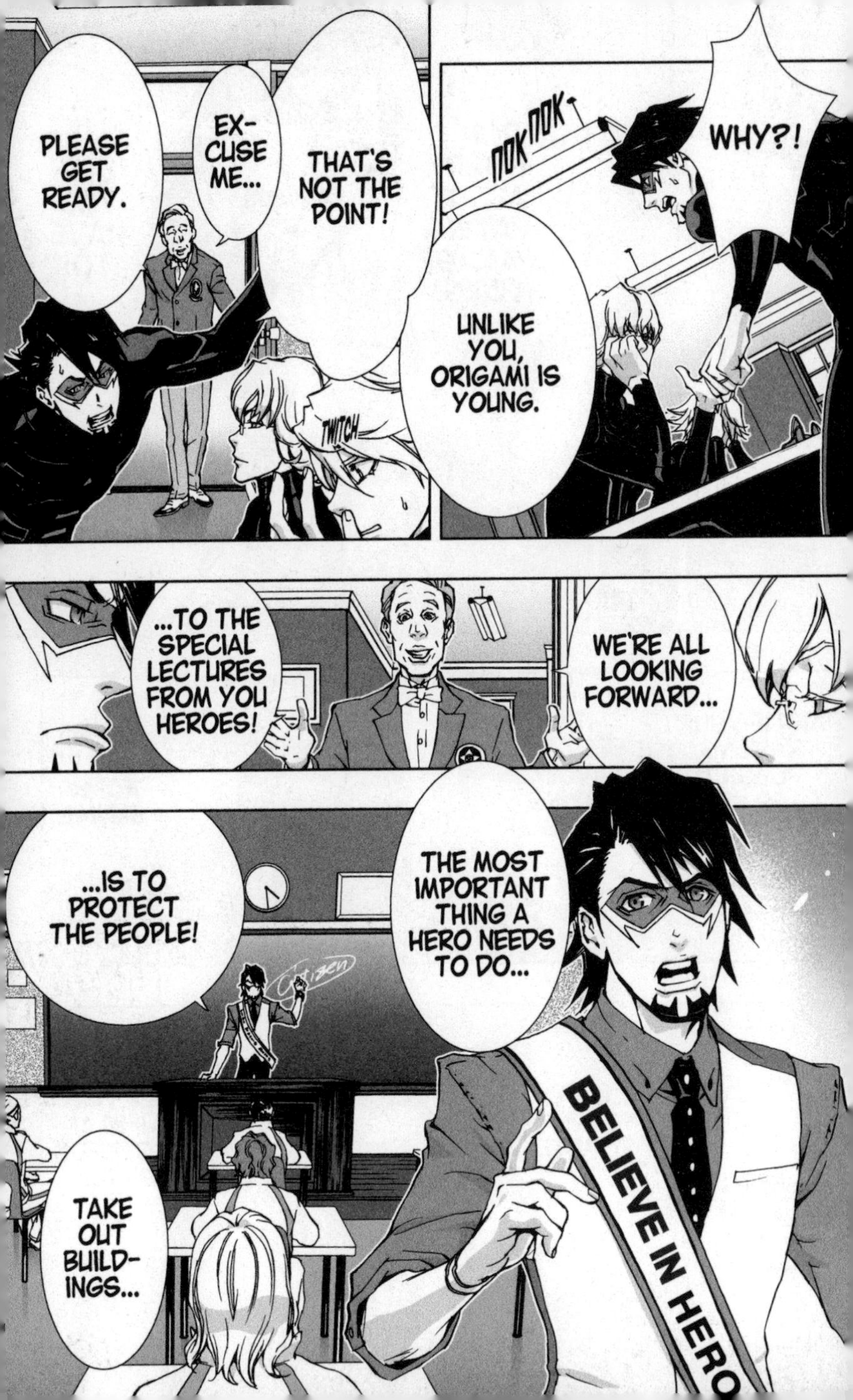
WHY?!
NOK NOK
UNLIKE YOU, ORIGAMI IS YOUNG.
THAT'S NOT THE POINT!
EX-CUSE ME...
PLEASE GET READY.
TWITCH
WE'RE ALL LOOKING FORWARD...
...TO THE SPECIAL LECTURES FROM YOU HEROES!
THE MOST IMPORTANT THING A HERO NEEDS TO DO...
...IS TO PROTECT THE PEOPLE!
TAKE OUT BUILD-INGS...
BELIEVE IN HERO

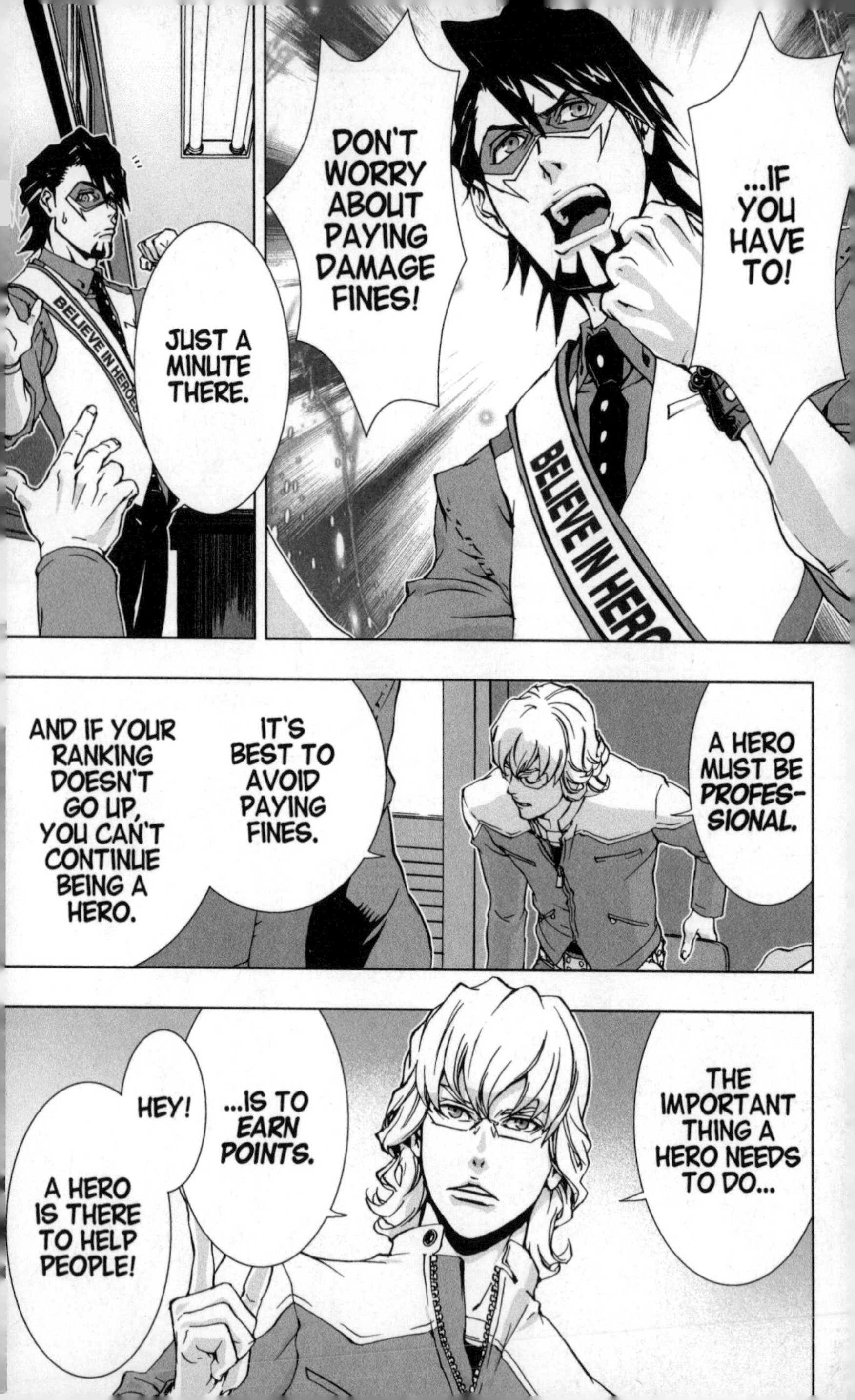

...IF YOU HAVE TO!
DON'T WORRY ABOUT PAYING DAMAGE FINES!
JUST A MINUTE THERE.
A HERO MUST BE PROFES-SIONAL.
IT'S BEST TO AVOID PAYING FINES.
AND IF YOUR RANKING DOESN'T GO UP, YOU CAN'T CONTINUE BEING A HERO.
THE IMPORTANT THING A HERO NEEDS TO DO...
...IS TO EARN POINTS.
HEY!
A HERO IS THERE TO HELP PEOPLE!

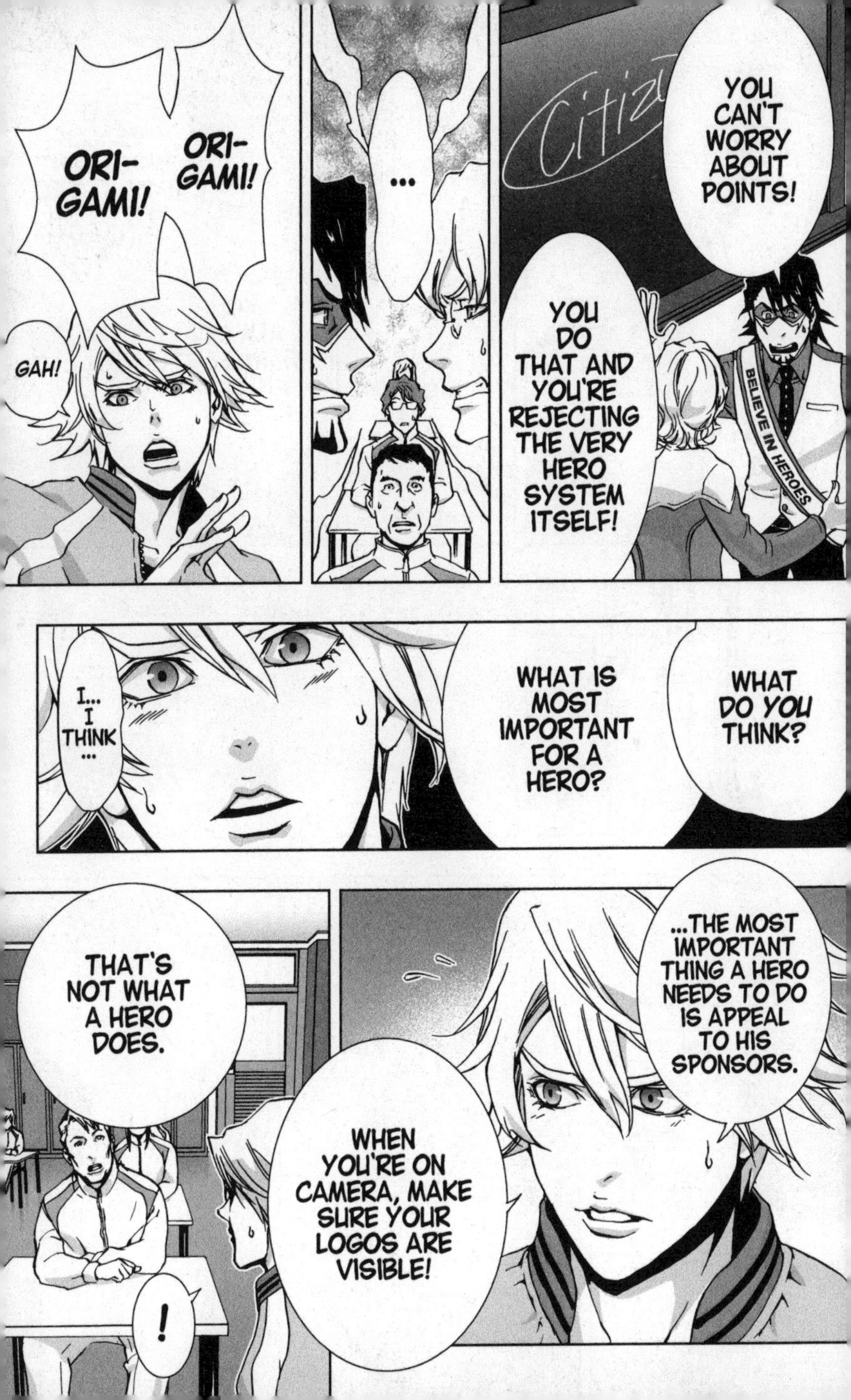
YOU CAN'T WORRY ABOUT POINTS!
BELIEVE IN HEROES
YOU DO THAT AND YOU'RE REJECTING THE VERY HERO SYSTEM ITSELF!
...
ORI-GAMI!
ORI-GAMI!
GAH!
WHAT DO YOU THINK?
WHAT IS MOST IMPORTANT FOR A HERO?
I... I THINK...
...THE MOST IMPORTANT THING A HERO NEEDS TO DO IS APPEAL TO HIS SPONSORS.
WHEN YOU'RE ON CAMERA, MAKE SURE YOUR LOGOS ARE VISIBLE!
THAT'S NOT WHAT A HERO DOES.
!

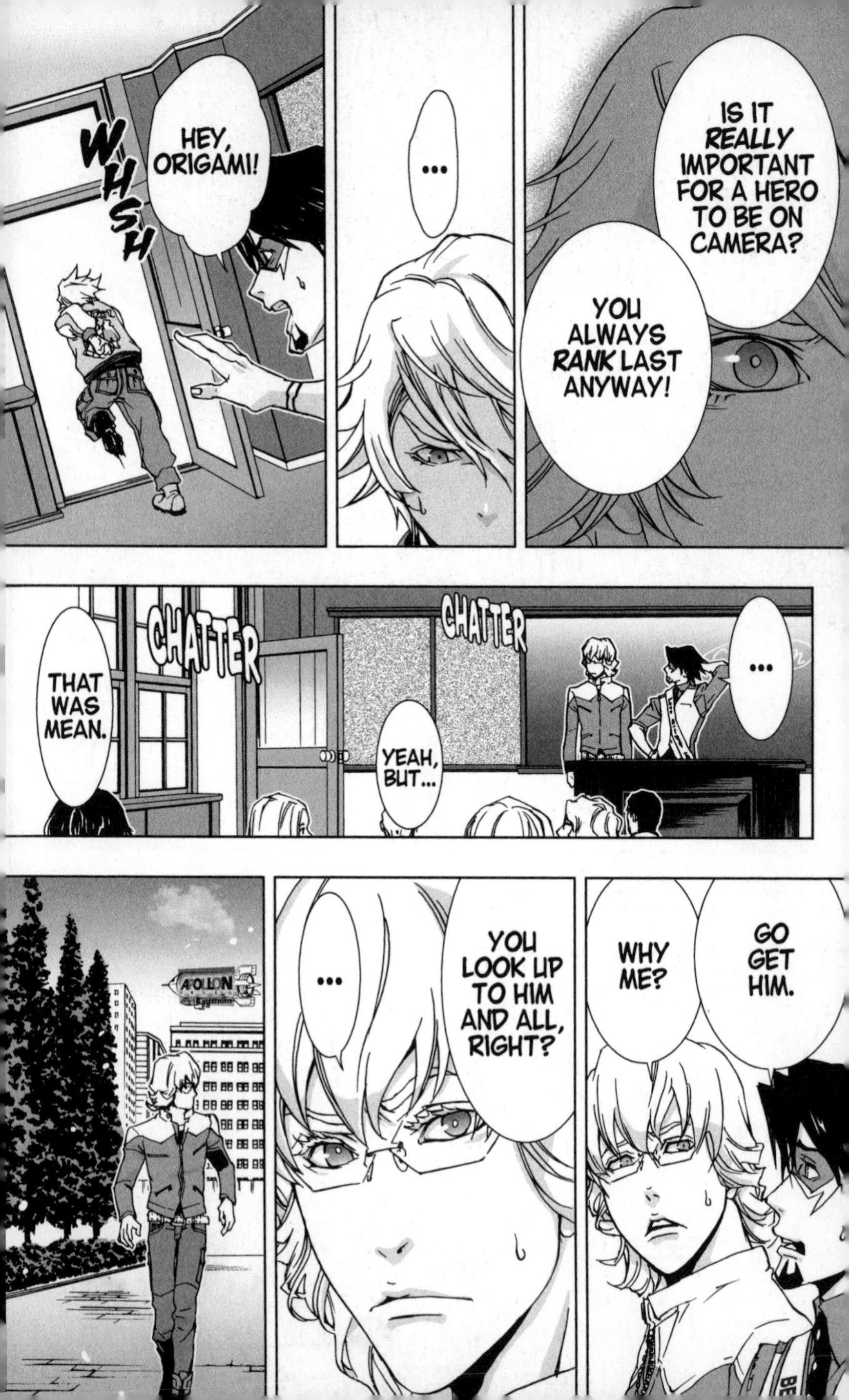
IS IT REALLY IMPORTANT FOR A HERO TO BE ON CAMERA?
YOU ALWAYS RANK LAST ANYWAY!
...
HEY, ORIGAMI!
WHSH
...
CHATTER
YEAH, BUT...
CHATTER
THAT WAS MEAN.
GO GET HIM.
WHY ME?
YOU LOOK UP TO HIM AND ALL, RIGHT?
...
APOLLON

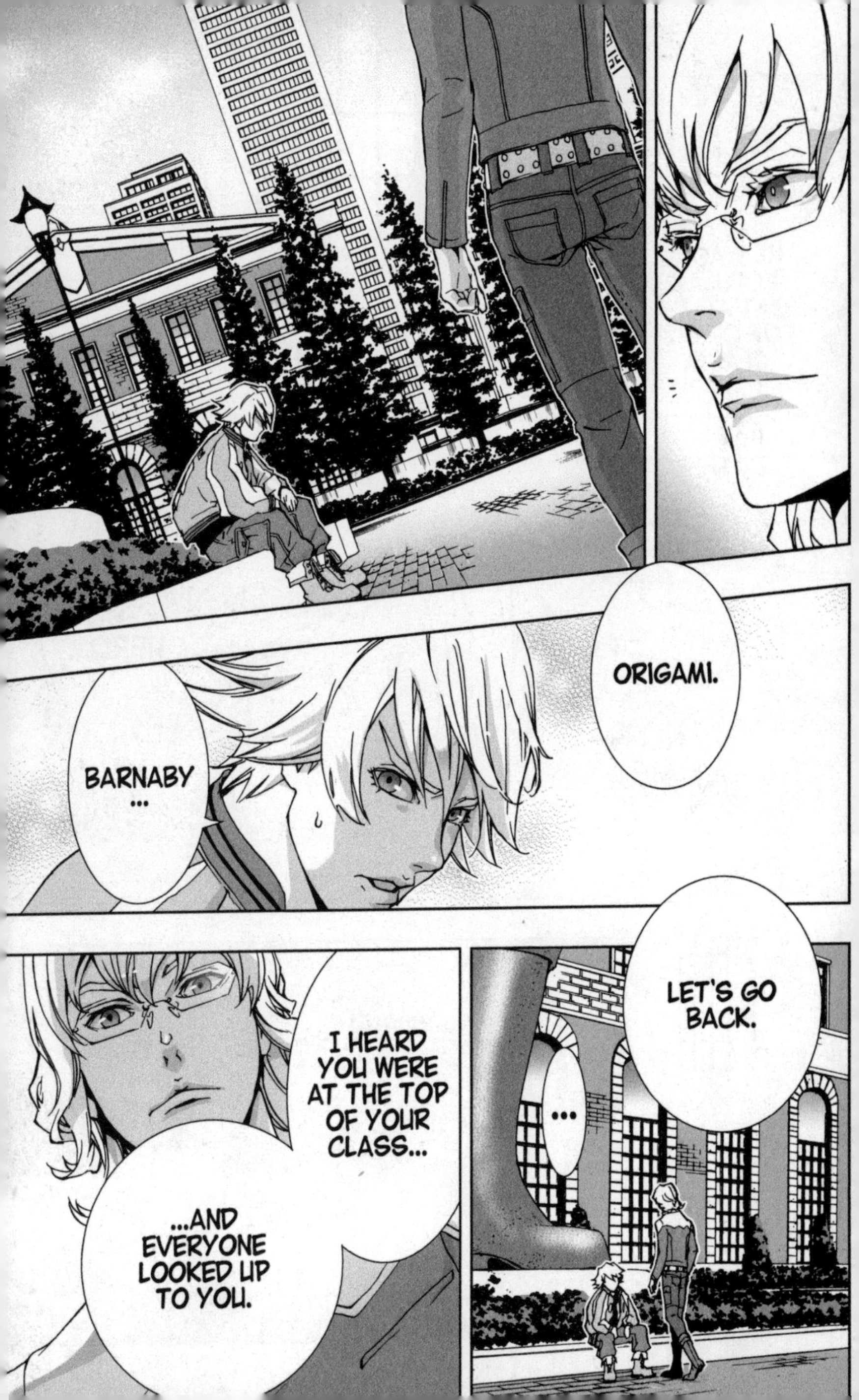
ORIGAMI.
BARNABY ...
LET'S GO BACK.
...
I HEARD YOU WERE AT THE TOP OF YOUR CLASS...
...AND EVERYONE LOOKED UP TO YOU.

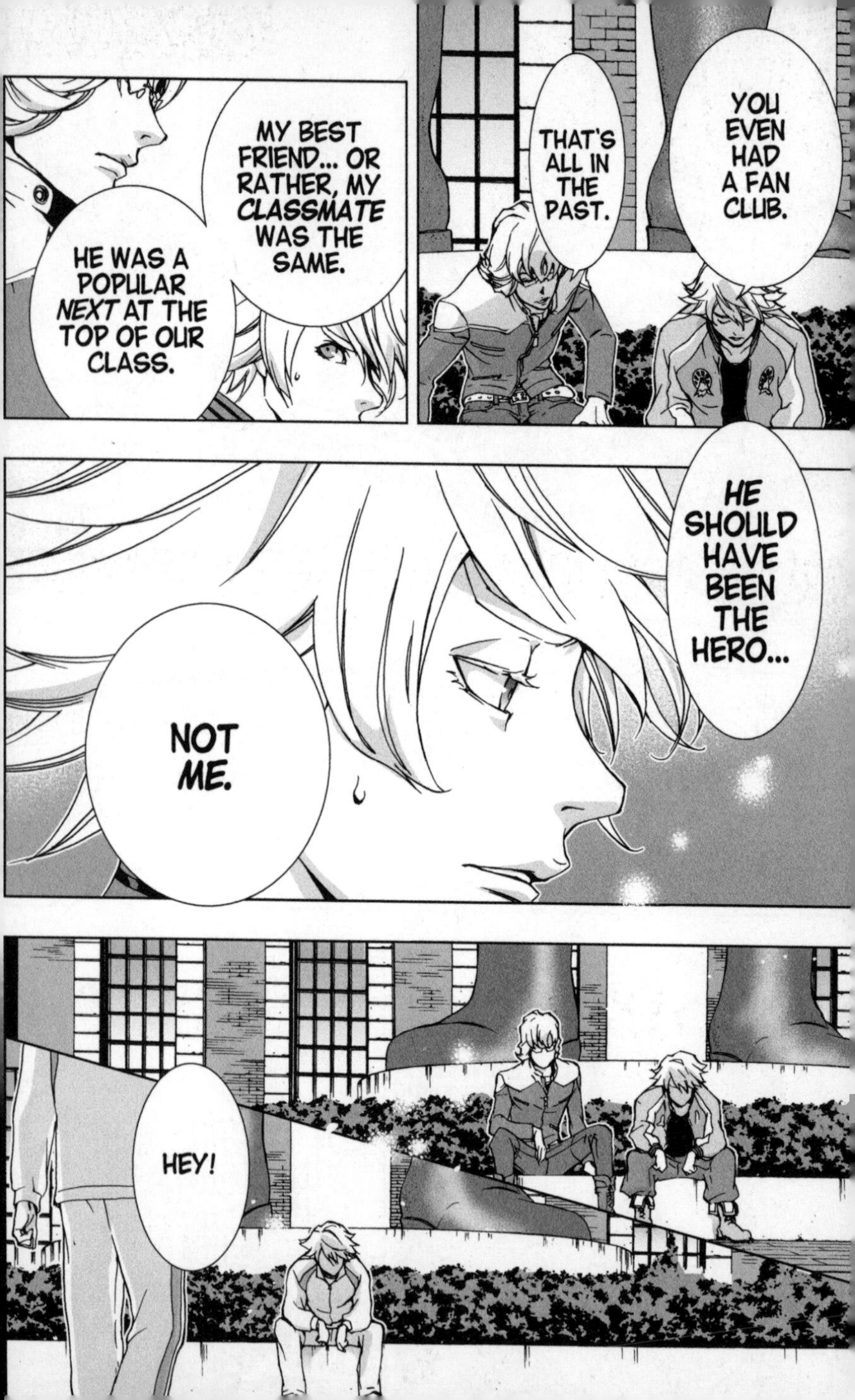
YOU EVEN HAD A FAN CLUB.
THAT'S ALL IN THE PAST.
MY BEST FRIEND... OR RATHER, MY *CLASSMATE* WAS THE SAME.
HE WAS A POPULAR *NEXT* AT THE TOP OF OUR CLASS.
HE SHOULD HAVE BEEN THE HERO...
NOT *ME*.
HEY!

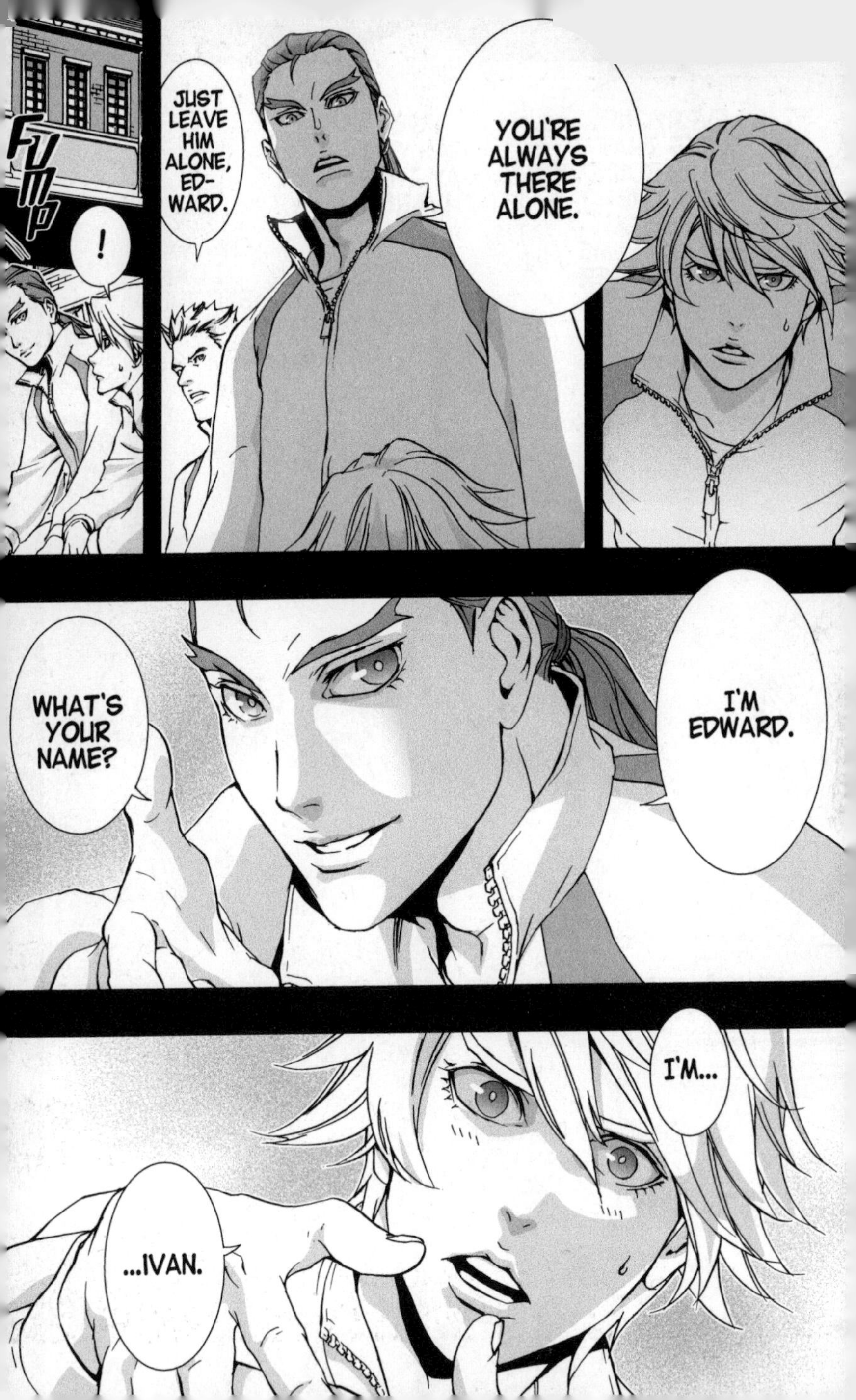

YOU'RE ALWAYS THERE ALONE.
JUST LEAVE HIM ALONE, ED-WARD.
FUMP
!
I'M EDWARD.
WHAT'S YOUR NAME?
I'M...
...IVAN.

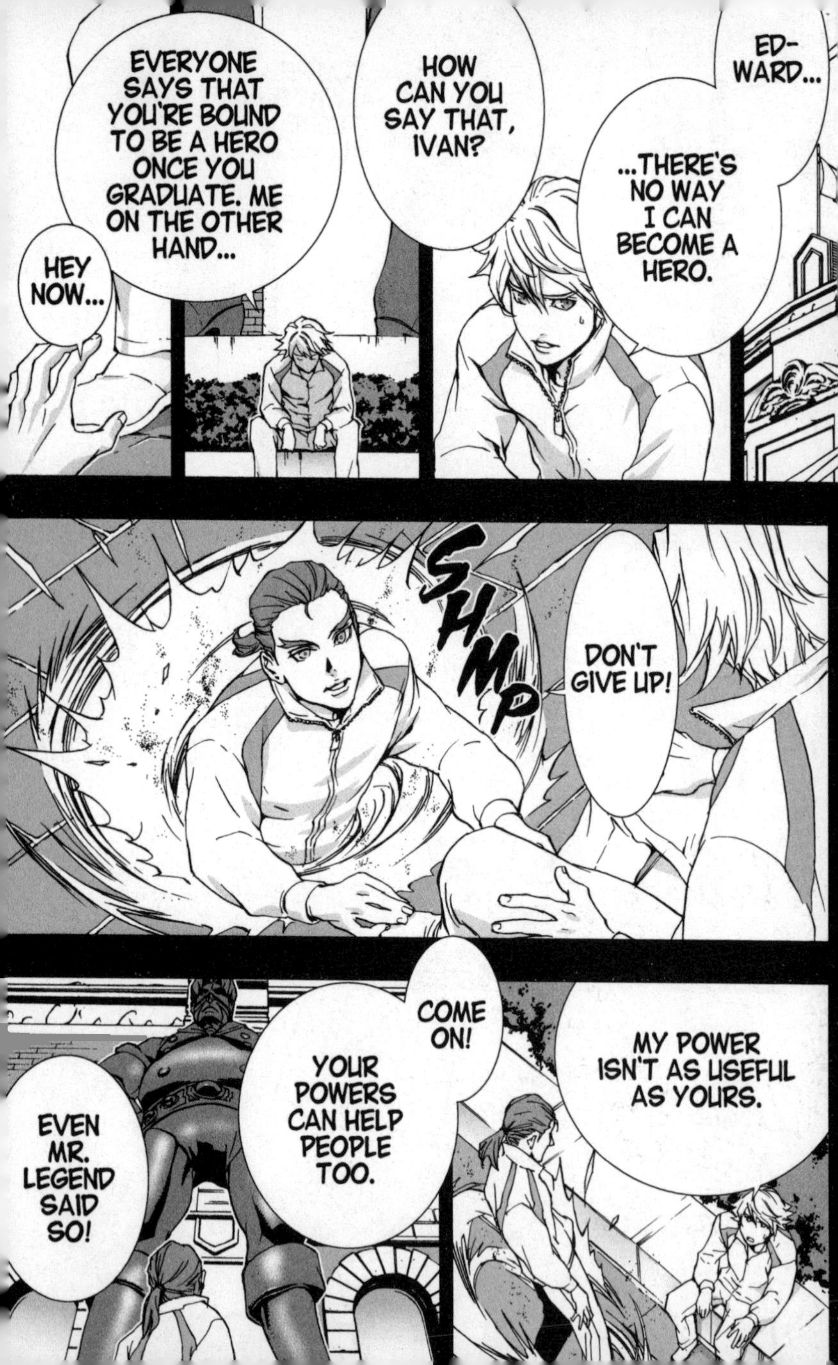
ED-WARD...
...THERE'S NO WAY I CAN BECOME A HERO.
HOW CAN YOU SAY THAT, IVAN?
EVERYONE SAYS THAT YOU'RE BOUND TO BE A HERO ONCE YOU GRADUATE. ME ON THE OTHER HAND...
HEY NOW...
SHMP
DON'T GIVE UP!
MY POWER ISN'T AS USEFUL AS YOURS.
COME ON!
YOUR POWERS CAN HELP PEOPLE TOO.
EVEN MR. LEGEND SAID SO!

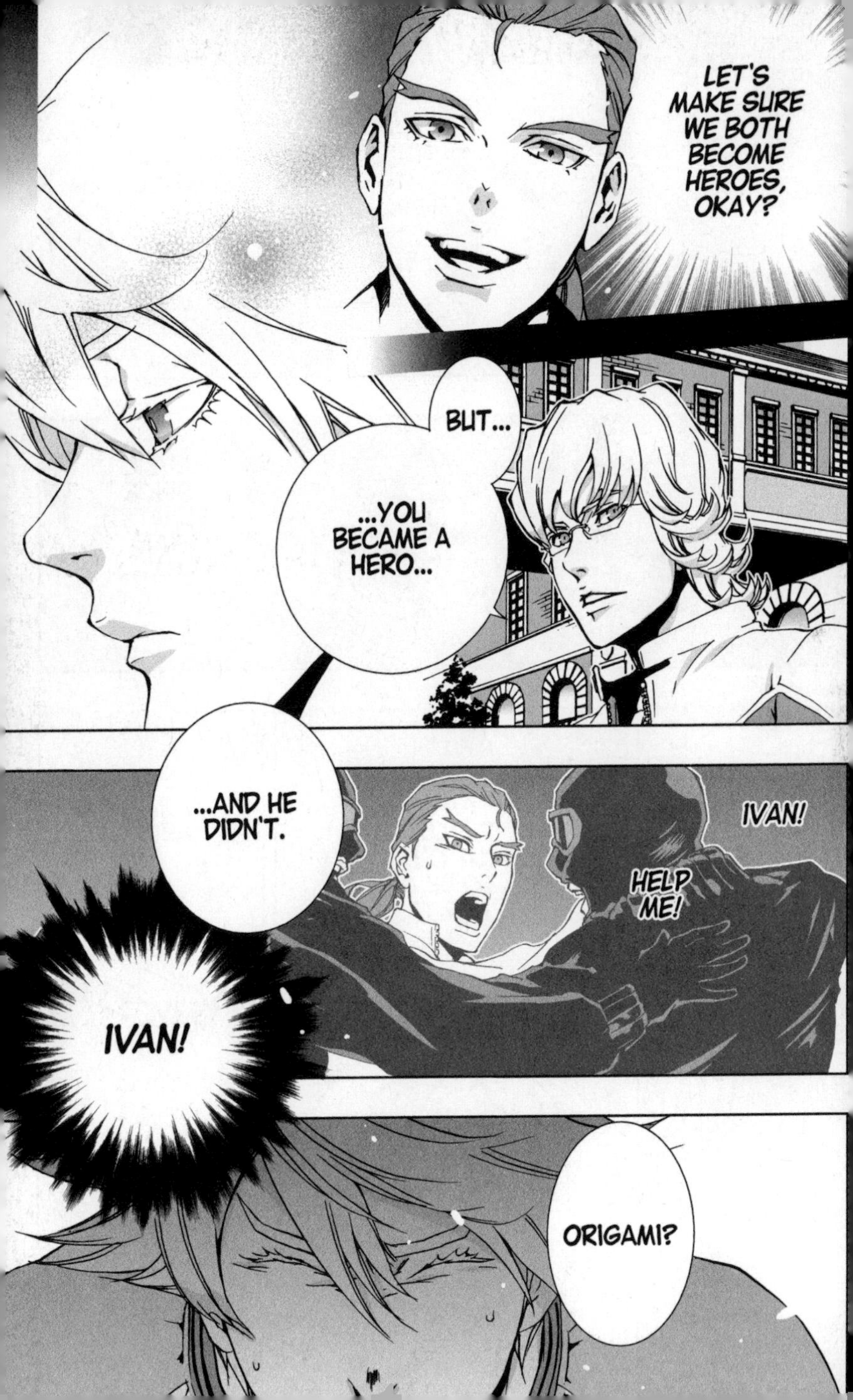
LET'S MAKE SURE WE BOTH BECOME HEROES, OKAY?
BUT...
...YOU BECAME A HERO...
...AND HE DIDN'T.
IVAN!
HELP ME!
IVAN!
ORIGAMI?

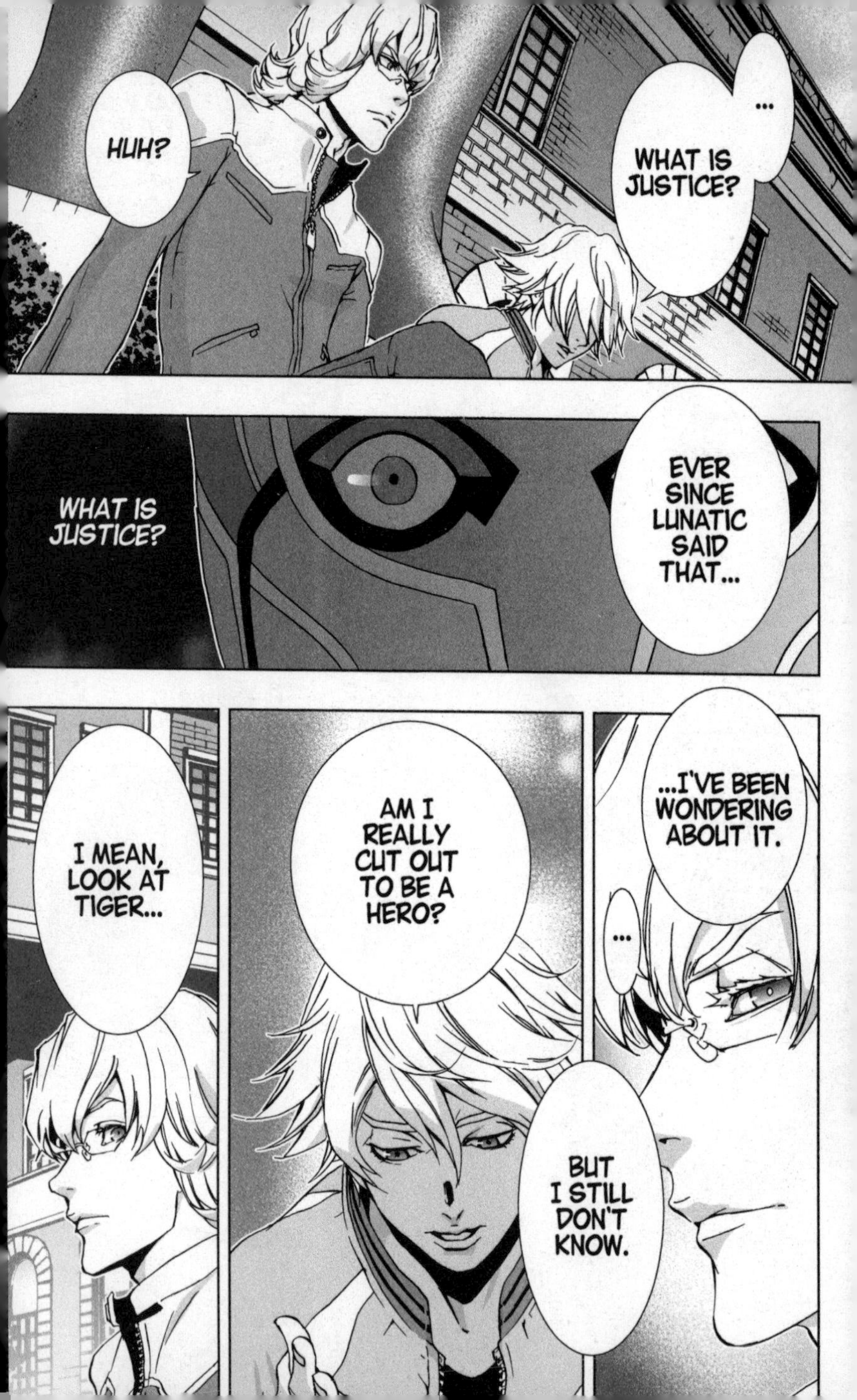
...
WHAT IS JUSTICE?
HUH?
EVER SINCE LUNATIC SAID THAT...
WHAT IS JUSTICE?
...I'VE BEEN WONDERING ABOUT IT.
...
BUT I STILL DON'T KNOW.
AM I REALLY CUT OUT TO BE A HERO?
I MEAN, LOOK AT TIGER...

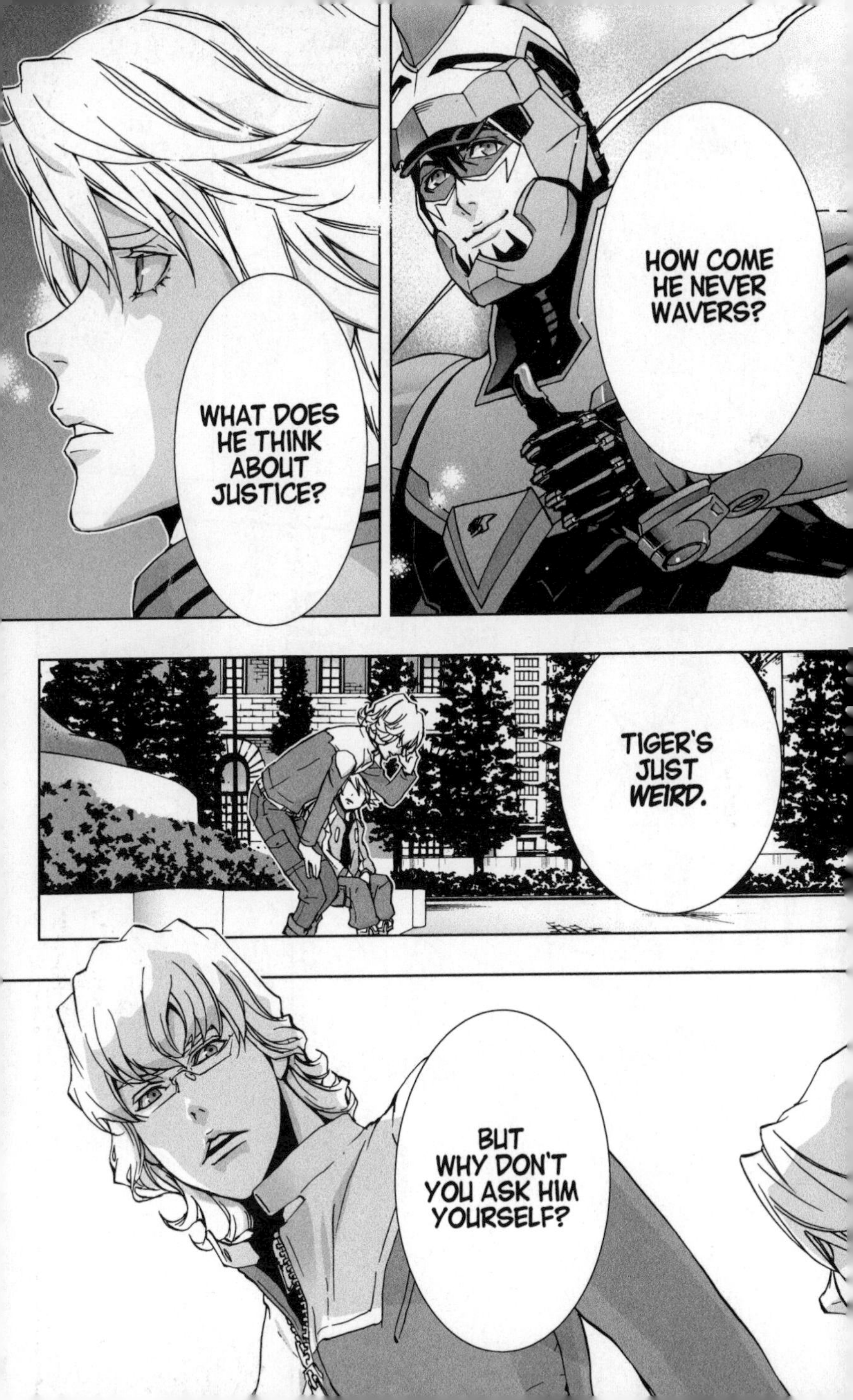
HOW COME HE NEVER WAVERS?
WHAT DOES HE THINK ABOUT JUSTICE?
TIGER'S JUST WEIRD.
BUT WHY DON'T YOU ASK HIM YOURSELF?

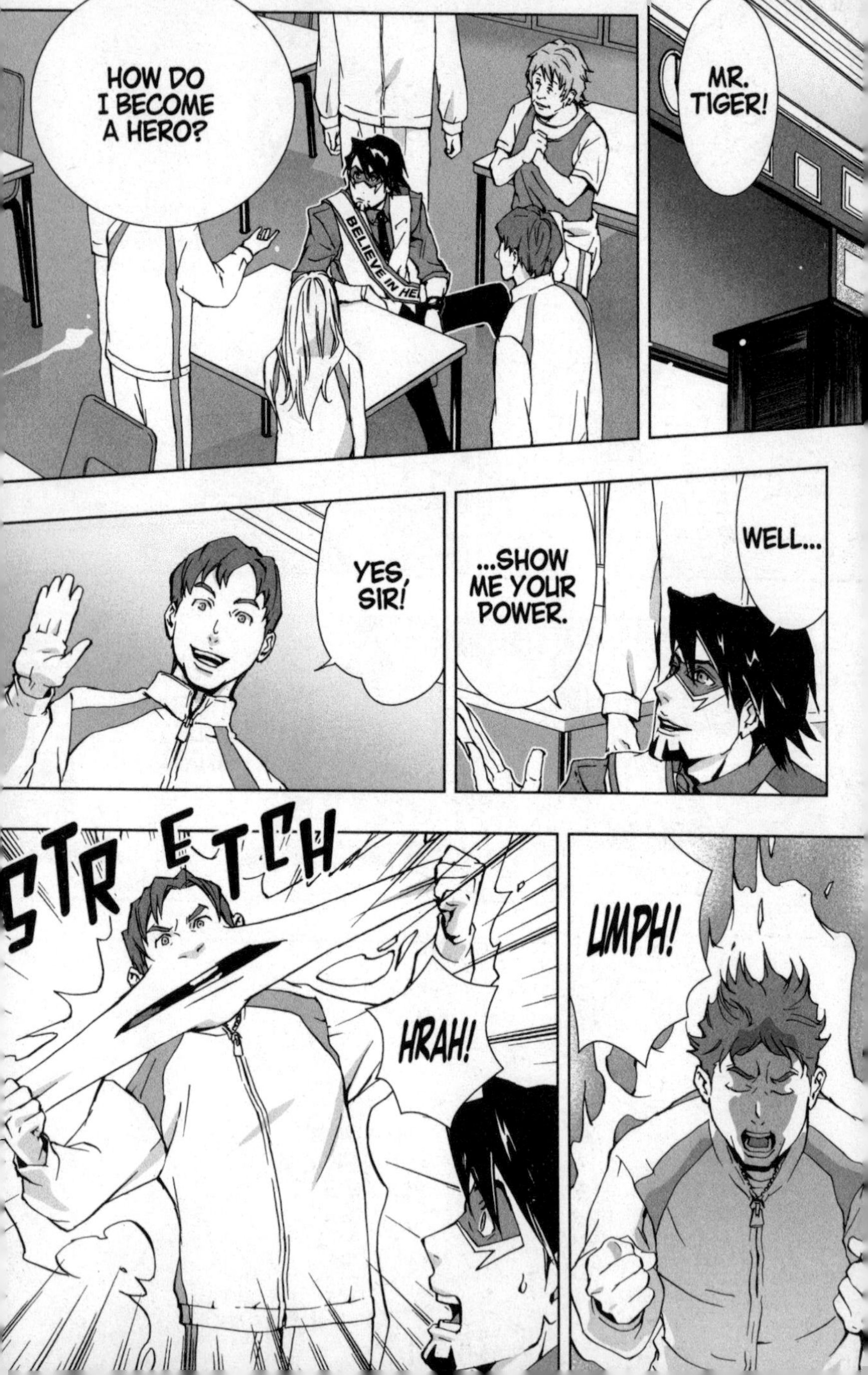
MR. TIGER!
HOW DO I BECOME A HERO?
WELL...
...SHOW ME YOUR POWER.
YES, SIR!
UMPH!
STRETCH
HRAH!

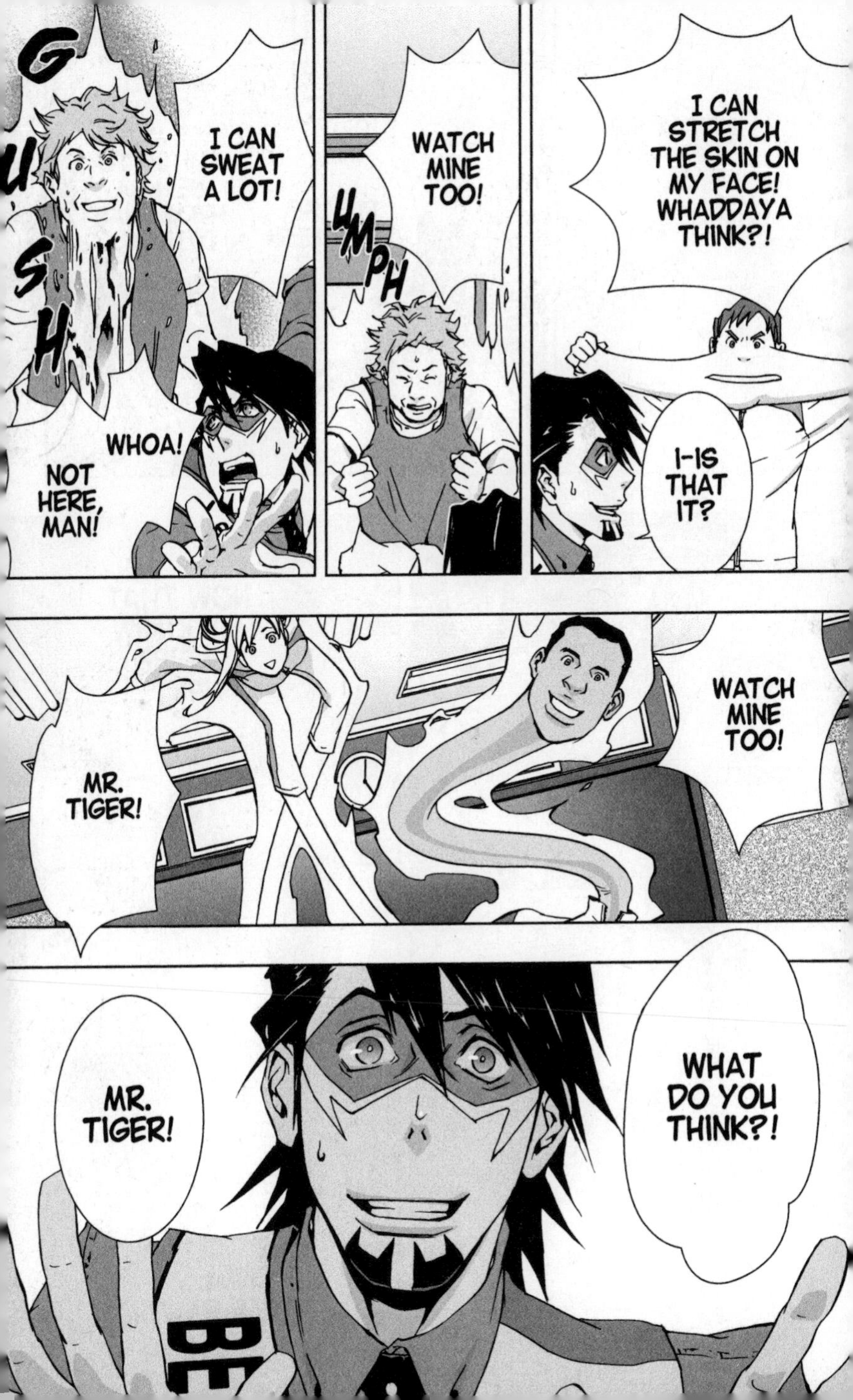
I CAN STRETCH THE SKIN ON MY FACE! WHADDAYA THINK?!
I-IS THAT IT?
WATCH MINE TOO!
UMPH
I CAN SWEAT A LOT!
GUSH
WHOA!
NOT HERE, MAN!
WATCH MINE TOO!
MR. TIGER!
WHAT DO YOU THINK?!
MR. TIGER!

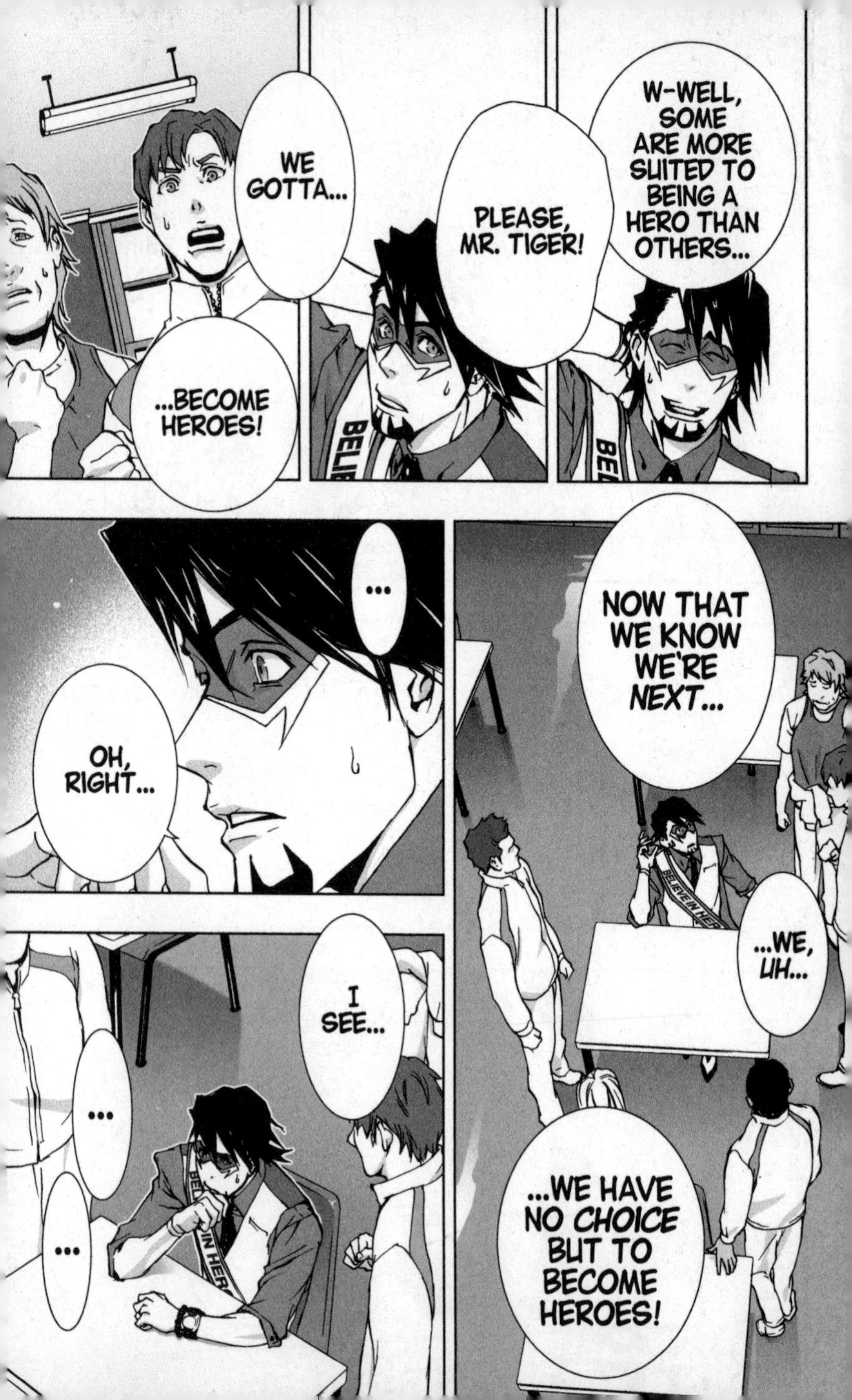
W-WELL, SOME ARE MORE SUITED TO BEING A HERO THAN OTHERS...
PLEASE, MR. TIGER!
WE GOTTA...
...BECOME HEROES!
NOW THAT WE KNOW WE'RE NEXT...
...WE, UH...
...WE HAVE NO CHOICE BUT TO BECOME HEROES!
...
OH, RIGHT...
I SEE...
...
...

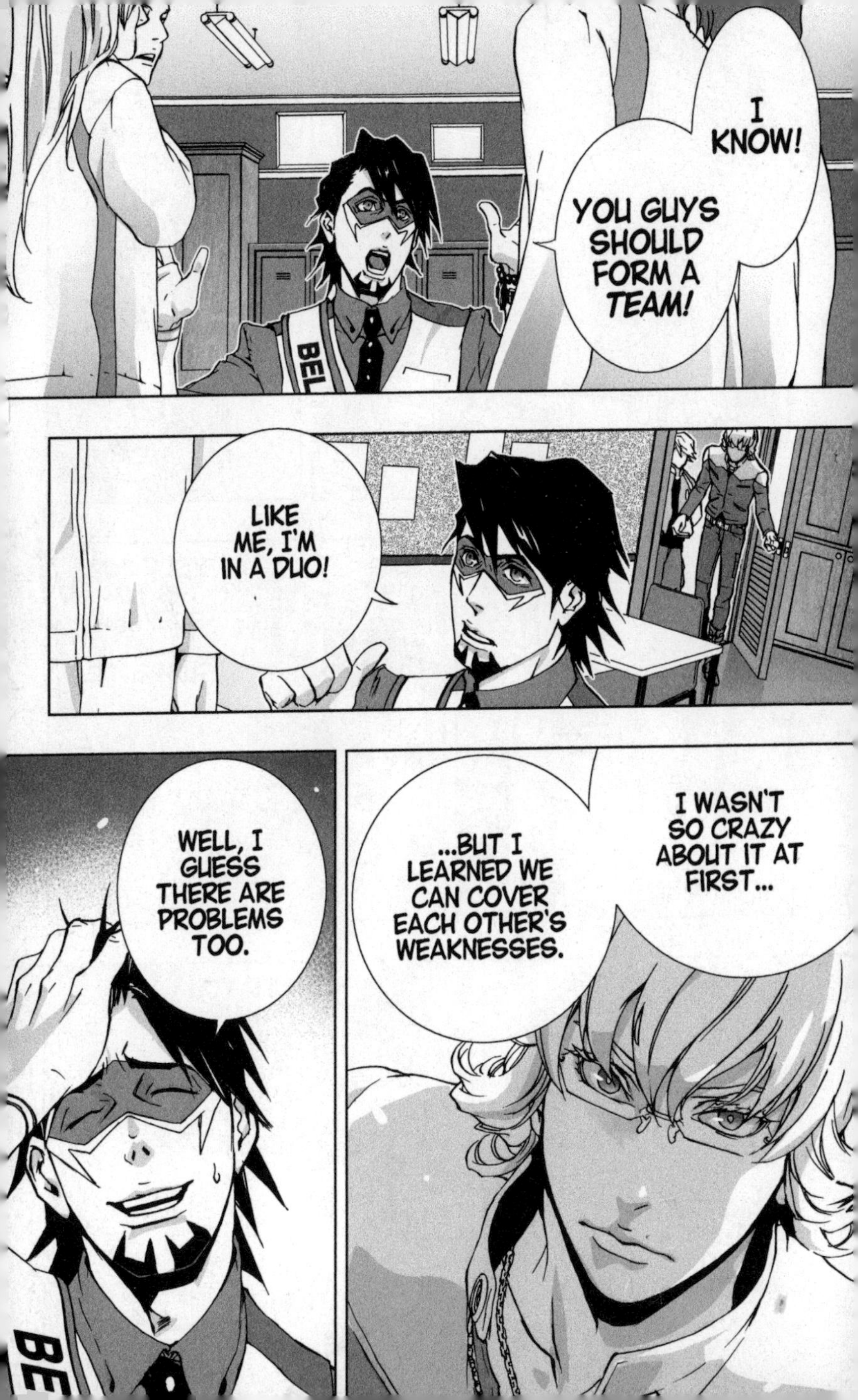
I KNOW!
YOU GUYS SHOULD FORM A TEAM!
LIKE ME, I'M IN A DUO!
I WASN'T SO CRAZY ABOUT IT AT FIRST...
...BUT I LEARNED WE CAN COVER EACH OTHER'S WEAKNESSES.
WELL, I GUESS THERE ARE PROBLEMS TOO.

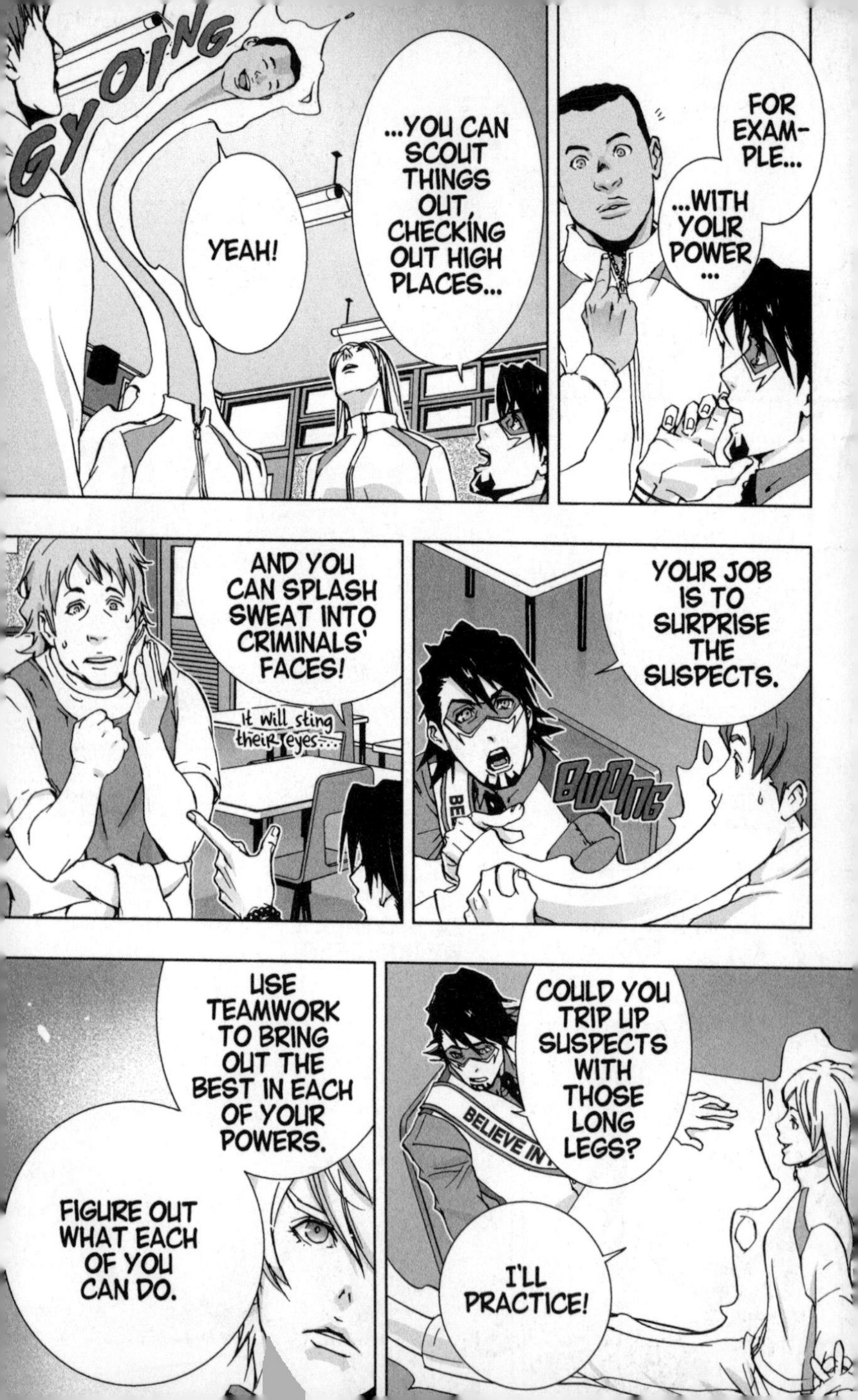
FOR EXAMPLE...
...WITH YOUR POWER...
...YOU CAN SCOUT THINGS OUT, CHECKING OUT HIGH PLACES...
GY-OING
YEAH!
YOUR JOB IS TO SURPRISE THE SUSPECTS.
BUOING
AND YOU CAN SPLASH SWEAT INTO CRIMINALS' FACES!
It will sting their eyes...
COULD YOU TRIP UP SUSPECTS WITH THOSE LONG LEGS?
I'LL PRACTICE!
USE TEAMWORK TO BRING OUT THE BEST IN EACH OF YOUR POWERS.
FIGURE OUT WHAT EACH OF YOU CAN DO.

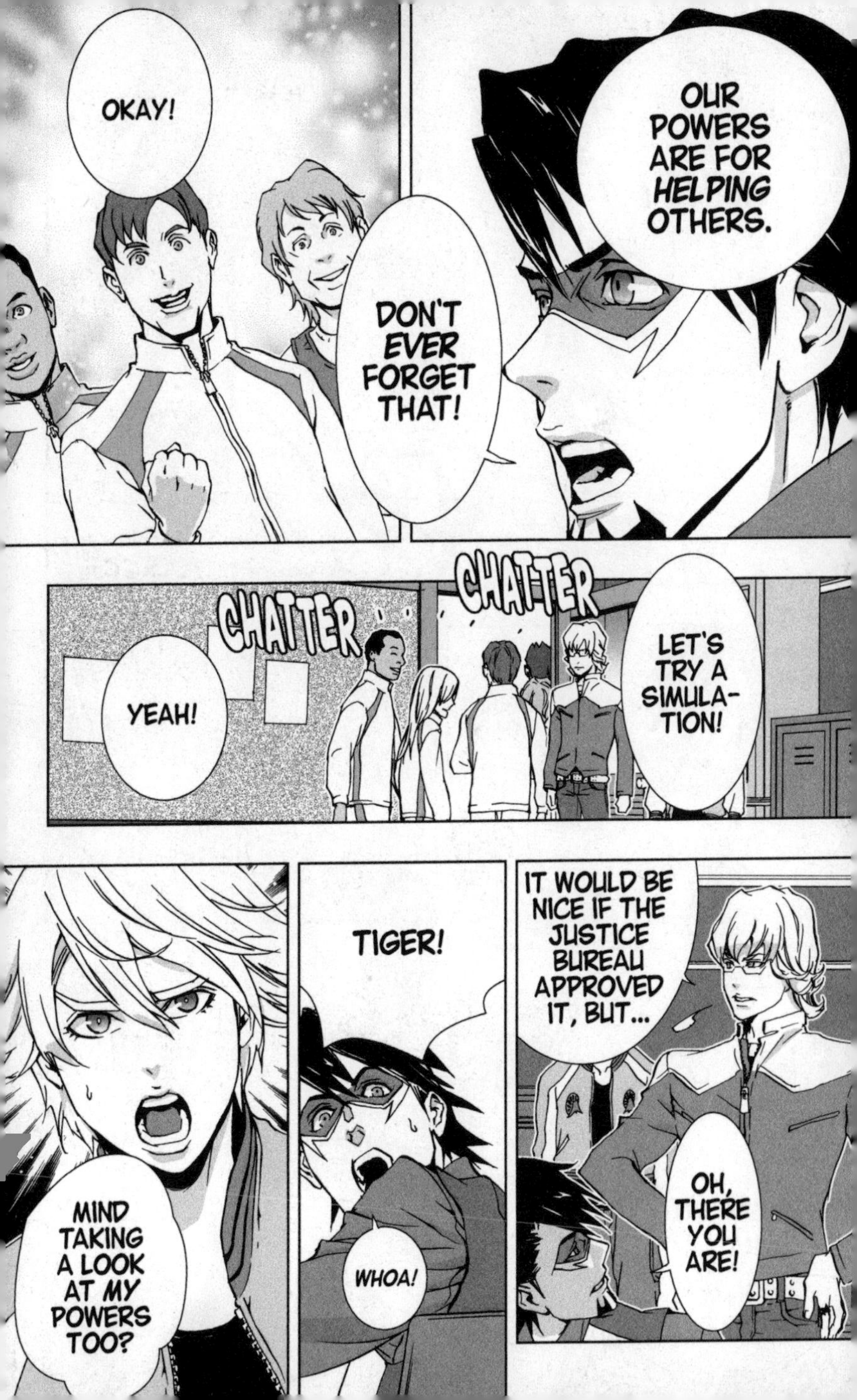
OUR POWERS ARE FOR HELPING OTHERS.
DON'T EVER FORGET THAT!
OKAY!
LET'S TRY A SIMULA-TION!
CHATTER
CHATTER
YEAH!
IT WOULD BE NICE IF THE JUSTICE BUREAU APPROVED IT, BUT...
OH, THERE YOU ARE!
TIGER!
WHOA!
MIND TAKING A LOOK AT MY POWERS TOO?

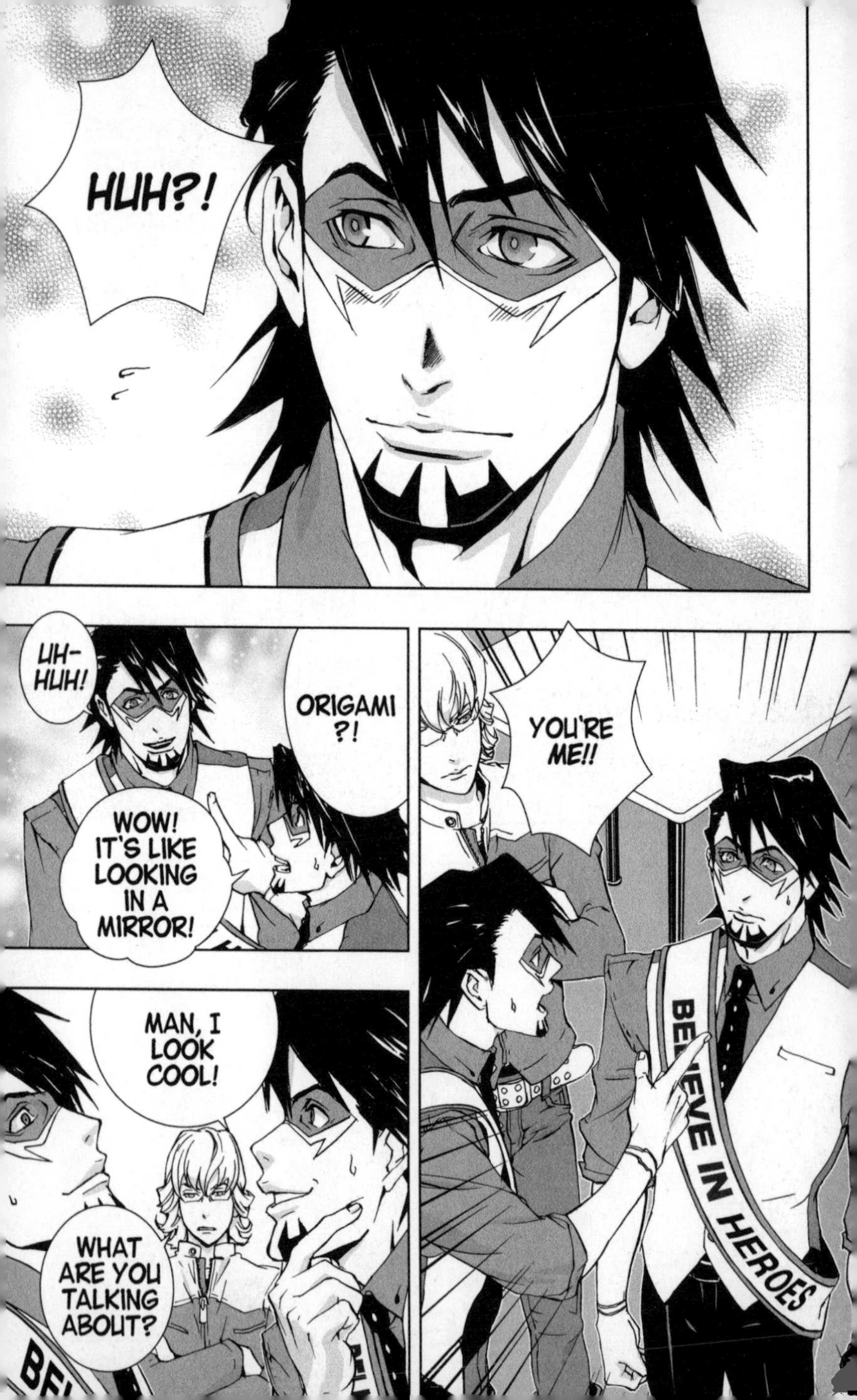
HUH?!
YOU'RE ME!!
ORIGAMI?!
UH-HUH!
WOW! IT'S LIKE LOOKING IN A MIRROR!
MAN, I LOOK COOL!
WHAT ARE YOU TALKING ABOUT?

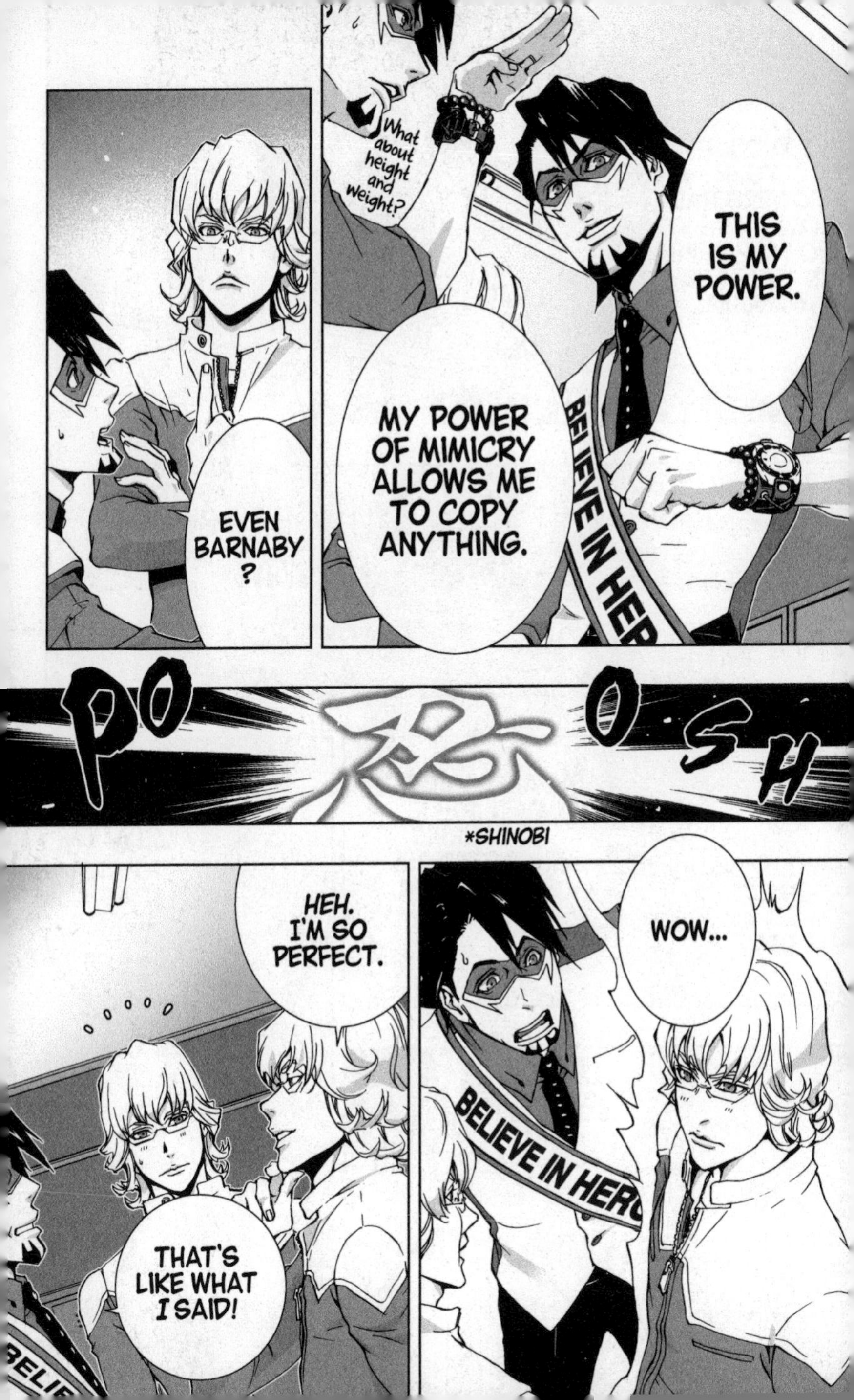
THIS IS MY POWER.
MY POWER OF MIMICRY ALLOWS ME TO COPY ANYTHING.
What about height and weight?
EVEN BARNABY ?
POOSH
*SHINOBI
WOW...
HEH. I'M SO PERFECT.
THAT'S LIKE WHAT I SAID!

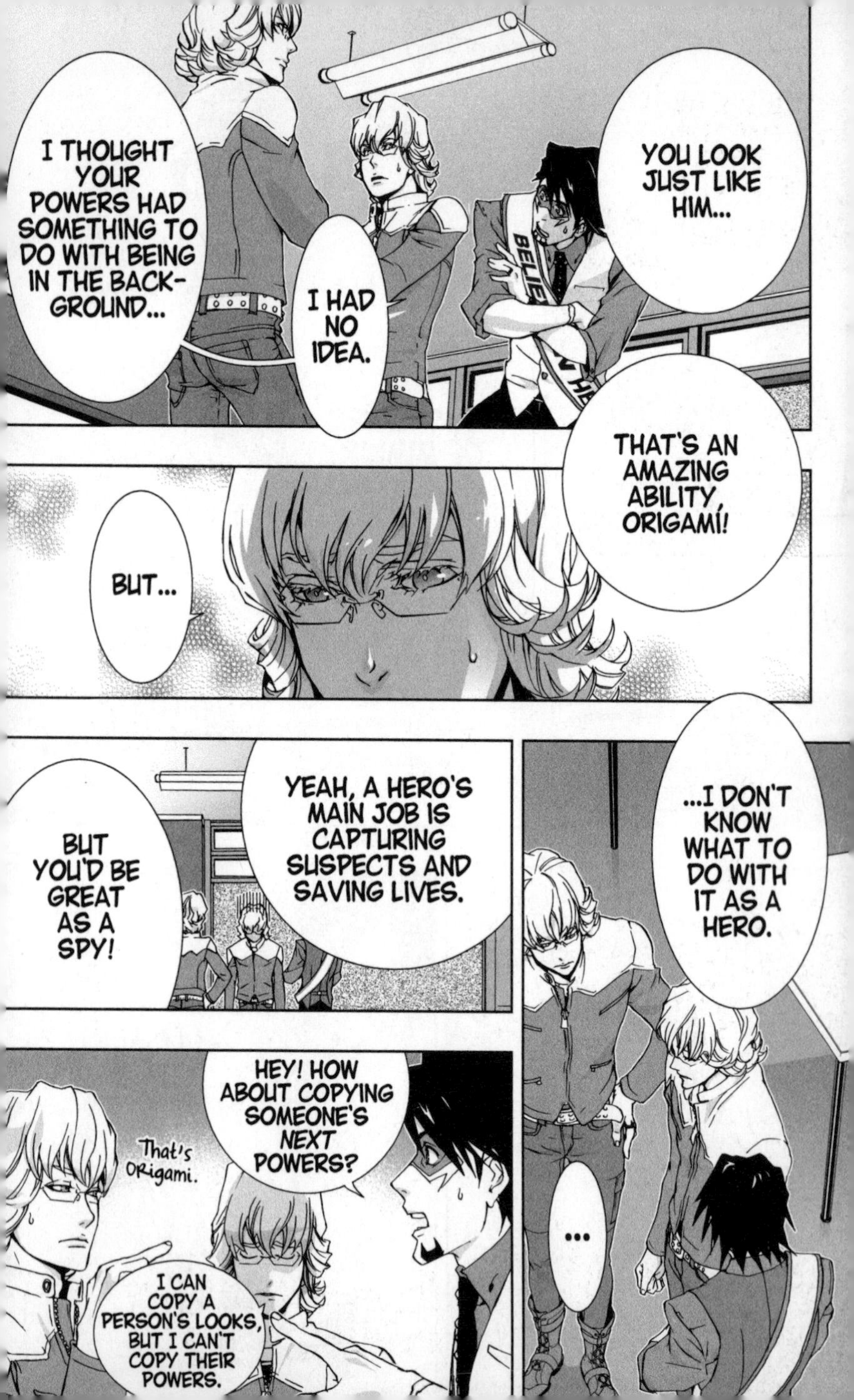
YOU LOOK JUST LIKE HIM...
I HAD NO IDEA.
I THOUGHT YOUR POWERS HAD SOMETHING TO DO WITH BEING IN THE BACK-GROUND...
THAT'S AN AMAZING ABILITY, ORIGAMI!
BUT...
...I DON'T KNOW WHAT TO DO WITH IT AS A HERO.
...
YEAH, A HERO'S MAIN JOB IS CAPTURING SUSPECTS AND SAVING LIVES.
BUT YOU'D BE GREAT AS A SPY!
HEY! HOW ABOUT COPYING SOMEONE'S NEXT POWERS?
That's Origami.
I CAN COPY A PERSON'S LOOKS, BUT I CAN'T COPY THEIR POWERS.

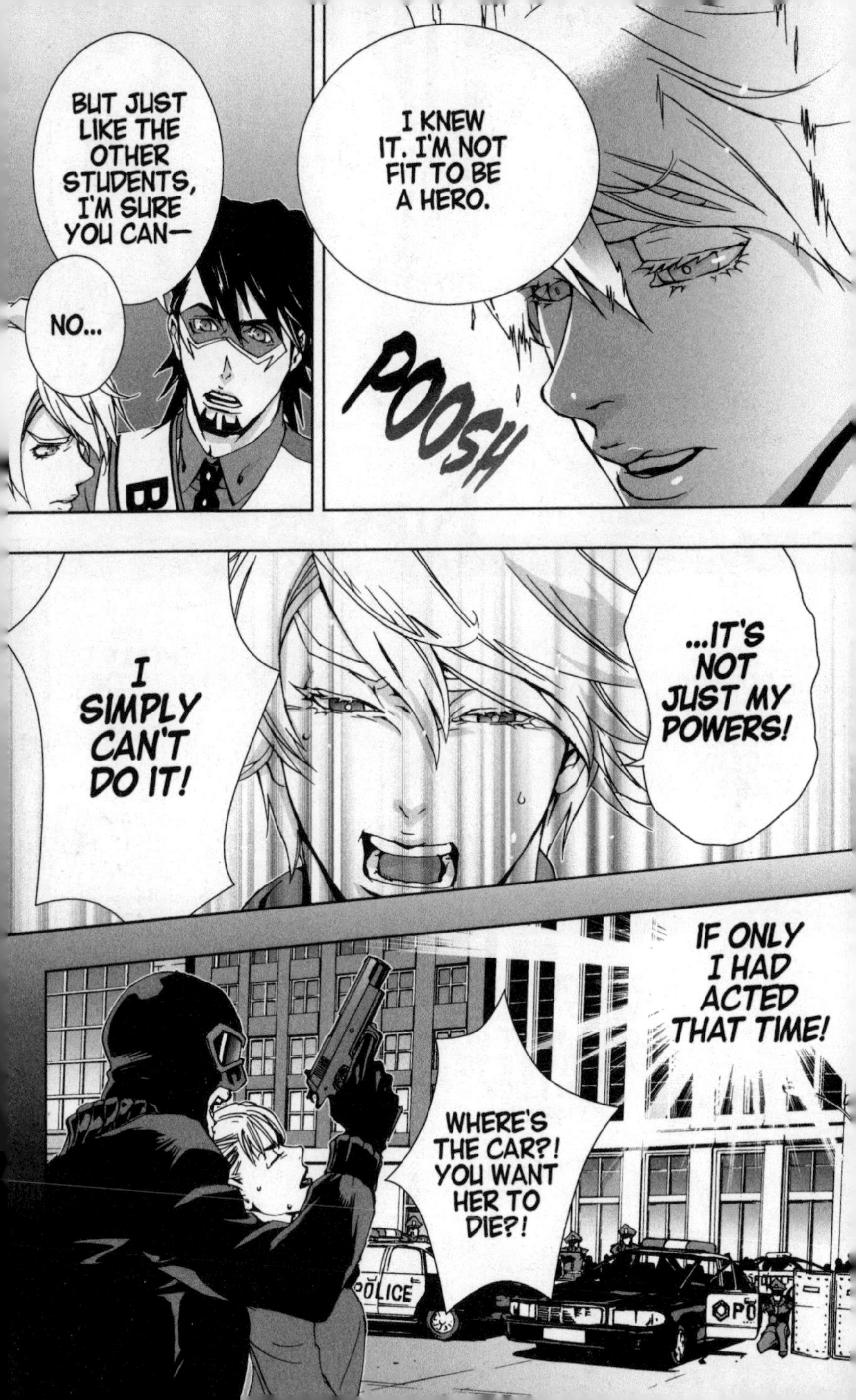
I KNEW IT. I'M NOT FIT TO BE A HERO.
POOSH
BUT JUST LIKE THE OTHER STUDENTS, I'M SURE YOU CAN—
NO...
...IT'S NOT JUST MY POWERS!
I SIMPLY CAN'T DO IT!
IF ONLY I HAD ACTED THAT TIME!
WHERE'S THE CAR?! YOU WANT HER TO DIE?!
POLICE

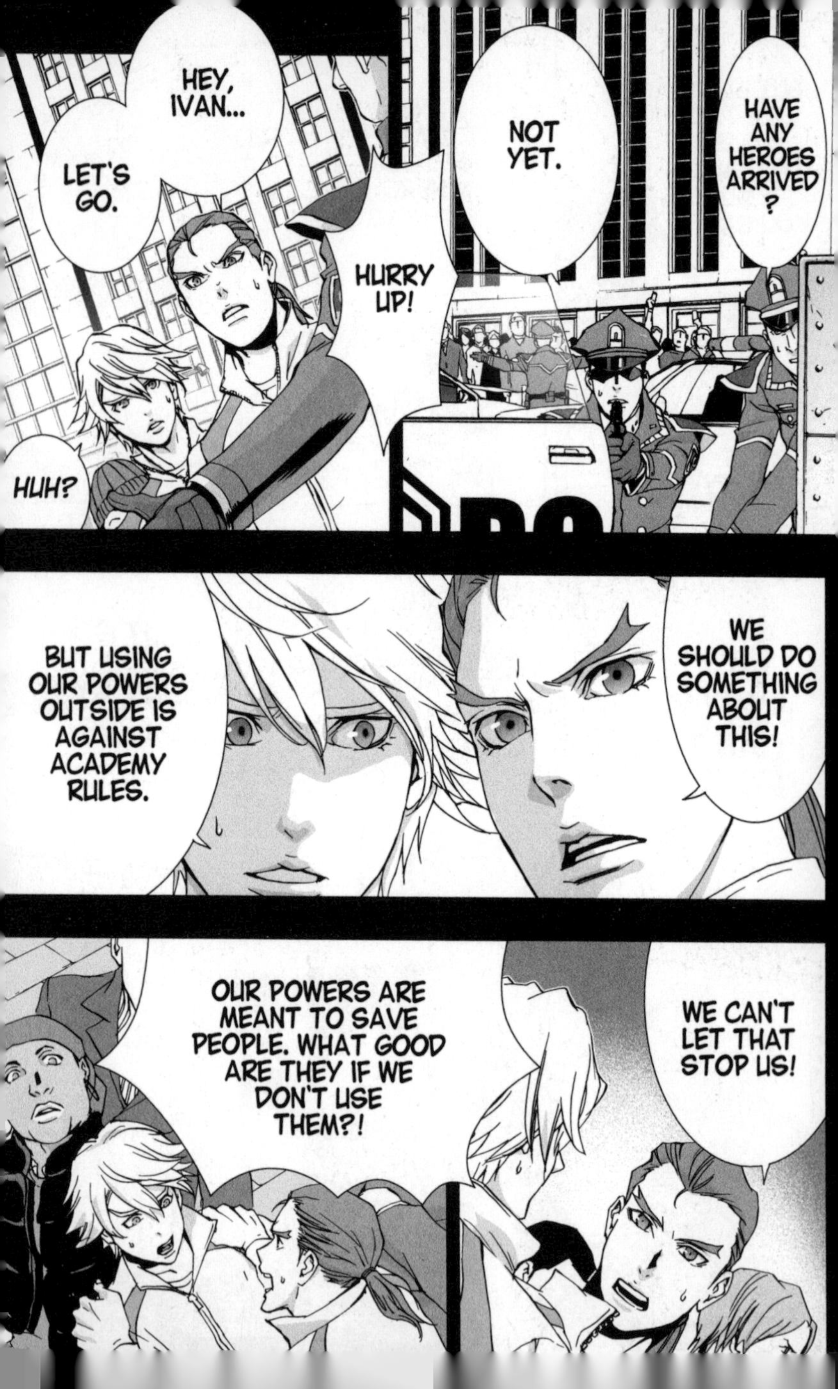
HAVE ANY HEROES ARRIVED?
NOT YET.
HEY, IVAN...
LET'S GO.
HURRY UP!
HUH?
WE SHOULD DO SOMETHING ABOUT THIS!
BUT USING OUR POWERS OUTSIDE IS AGAINST ACADEMY RULES.
WE CAN'T LET THAT STOP US!
OUR POWERS ARE MEANT TO SAVE PEOPLE. WHAT GOOD ARE THEY IF WE DON'T USE THEM?!

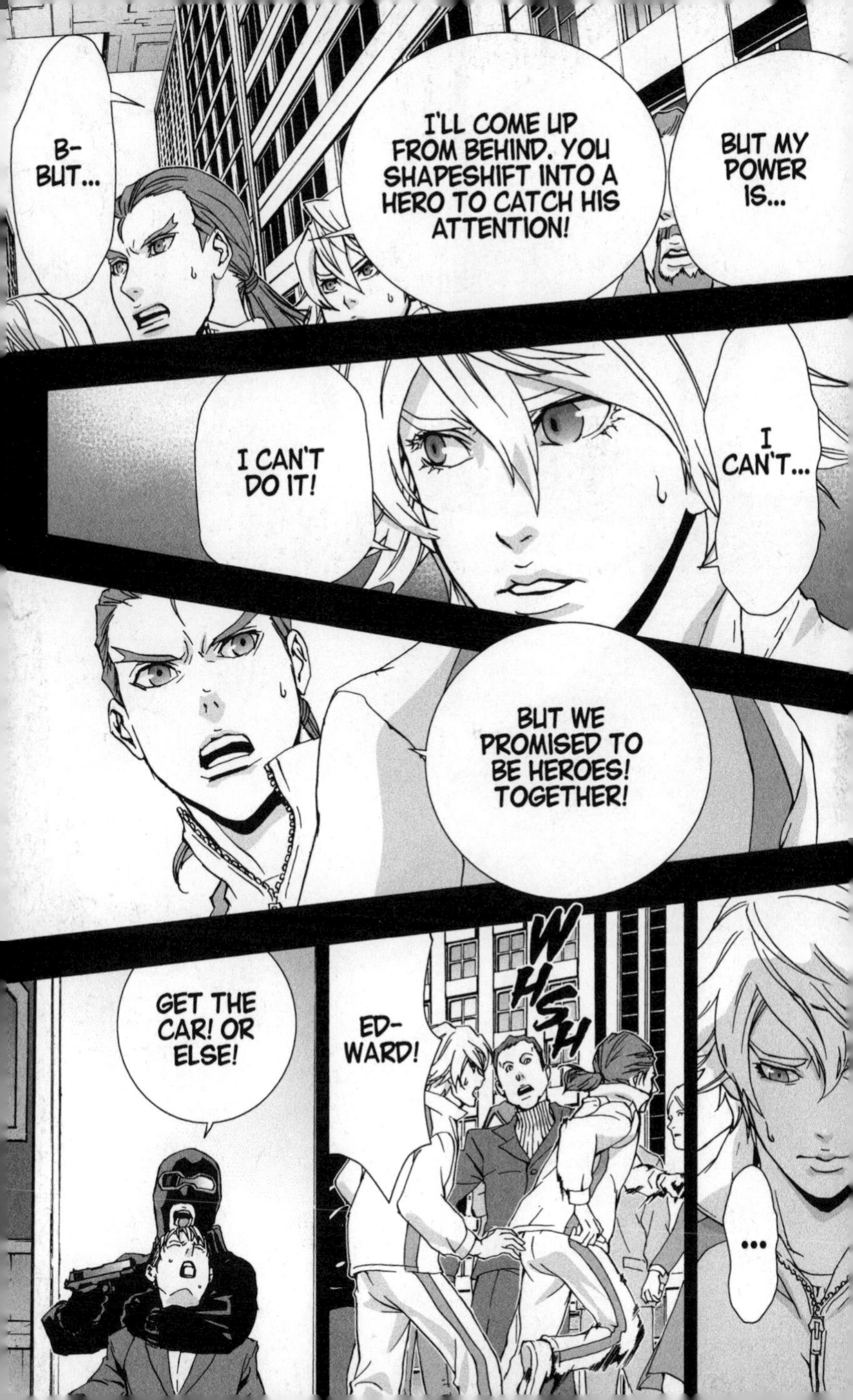
BUT MY POWER IS...
I'LL COME UP FROM BEHIND. YOU SHAPESHIFT INTO A HERO TO CATCH HIS ATTENTION!
B-BUT...
I CAN'T...
I CAN'T DO IT!
BUT WE PROMISED TO BE HEROES! TOGETHER!
...
WHSH
ED-WARD!
GET THE CAR! OR ELSE!

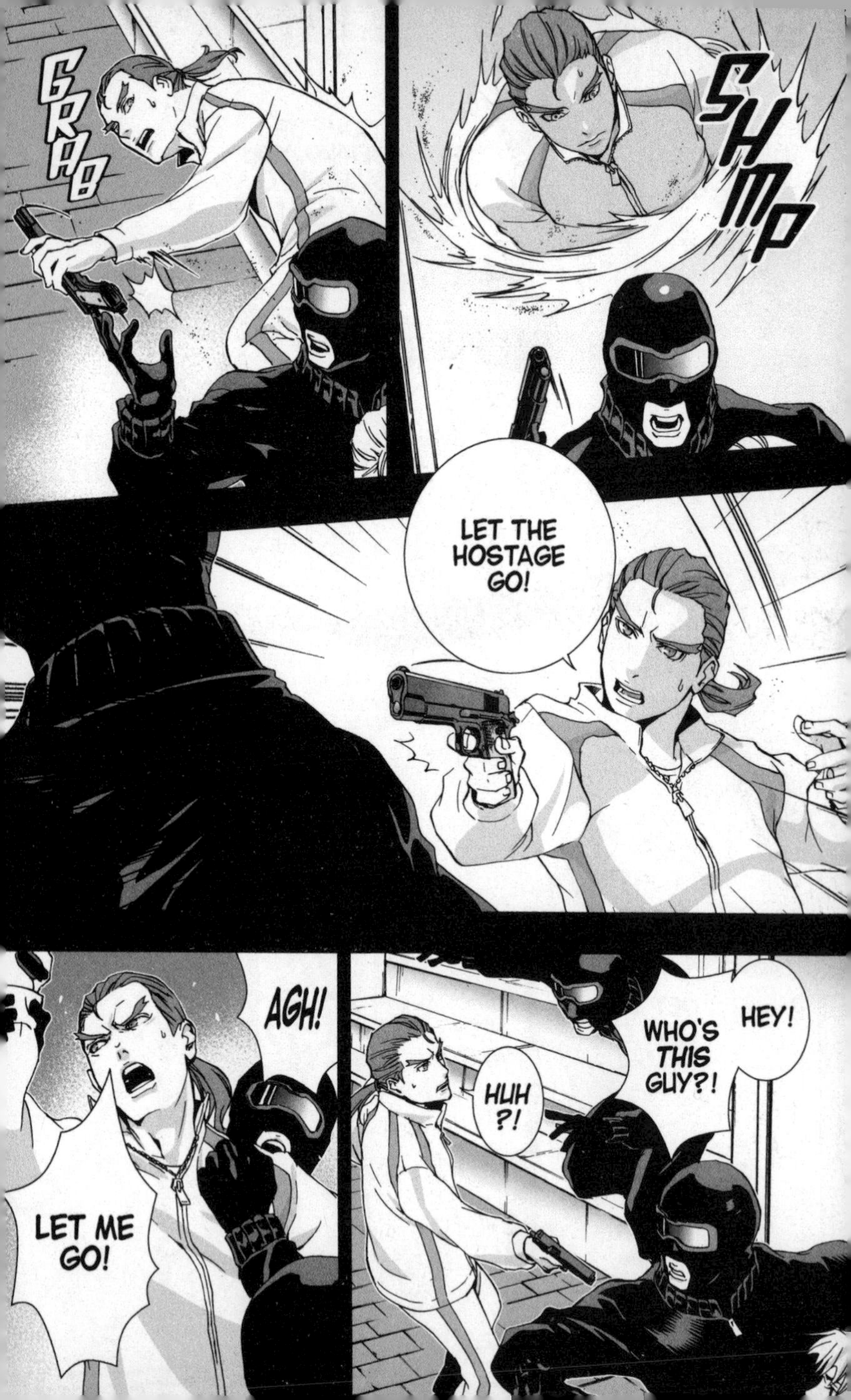
SHMP
GRAB
LET THE HOSTAGE GO!
HEY!
WHO'S THIS GUY?!
HUH?!
AGH!
LET ME GO!

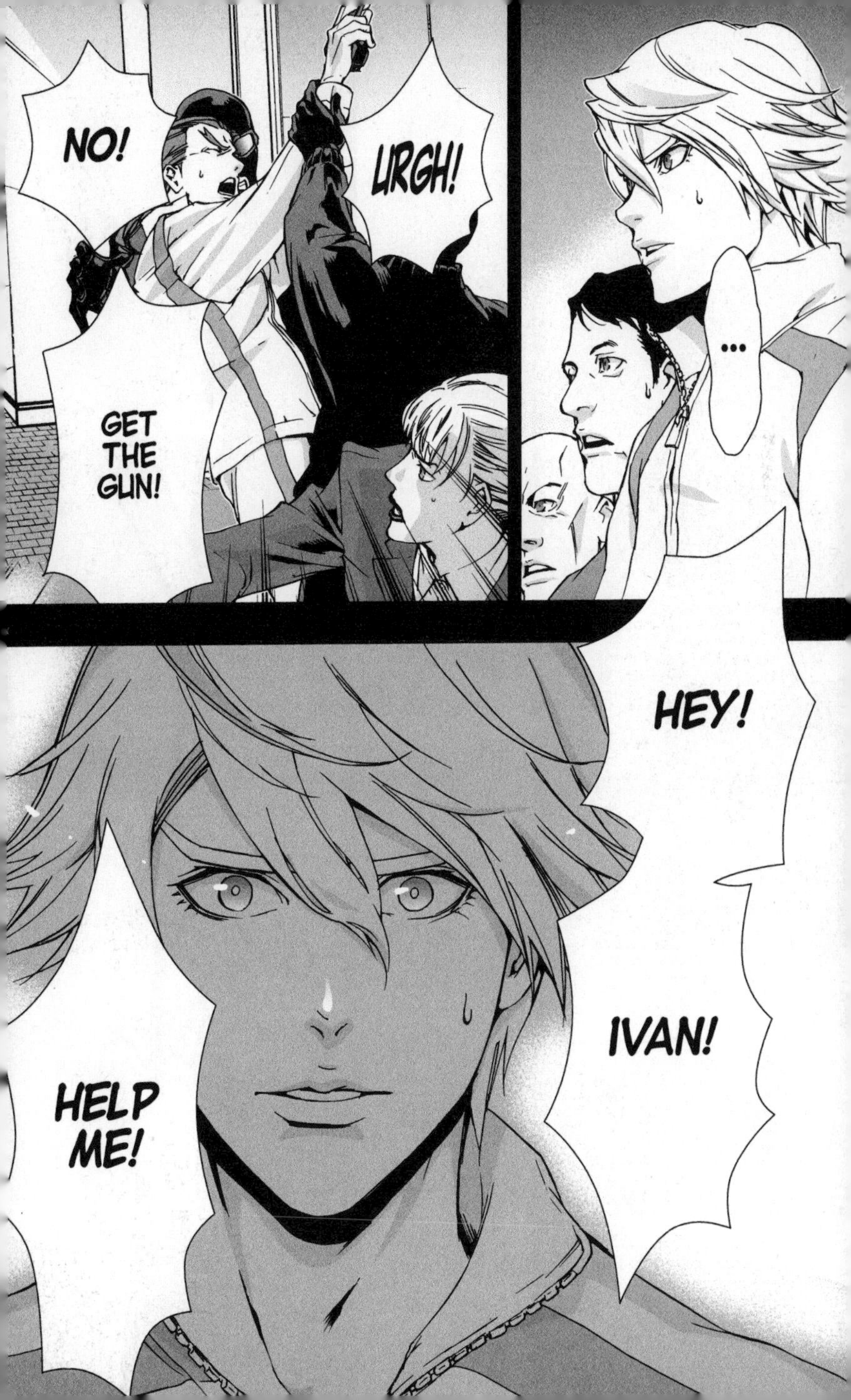
...
URGH!
NO!
GET THE GUN!
HEY!
IVAN!
HELP ME!

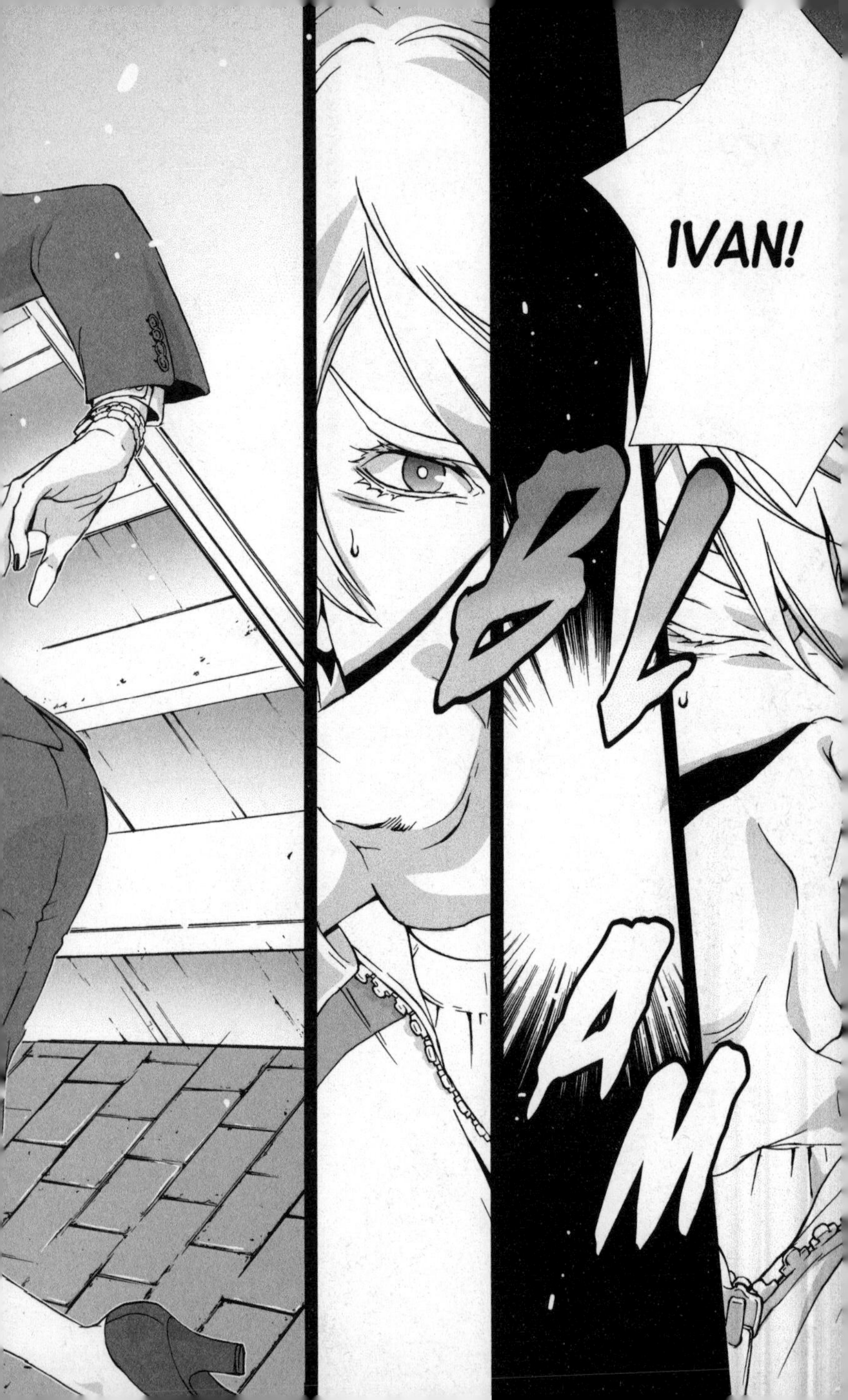
IVAN!
BLAM

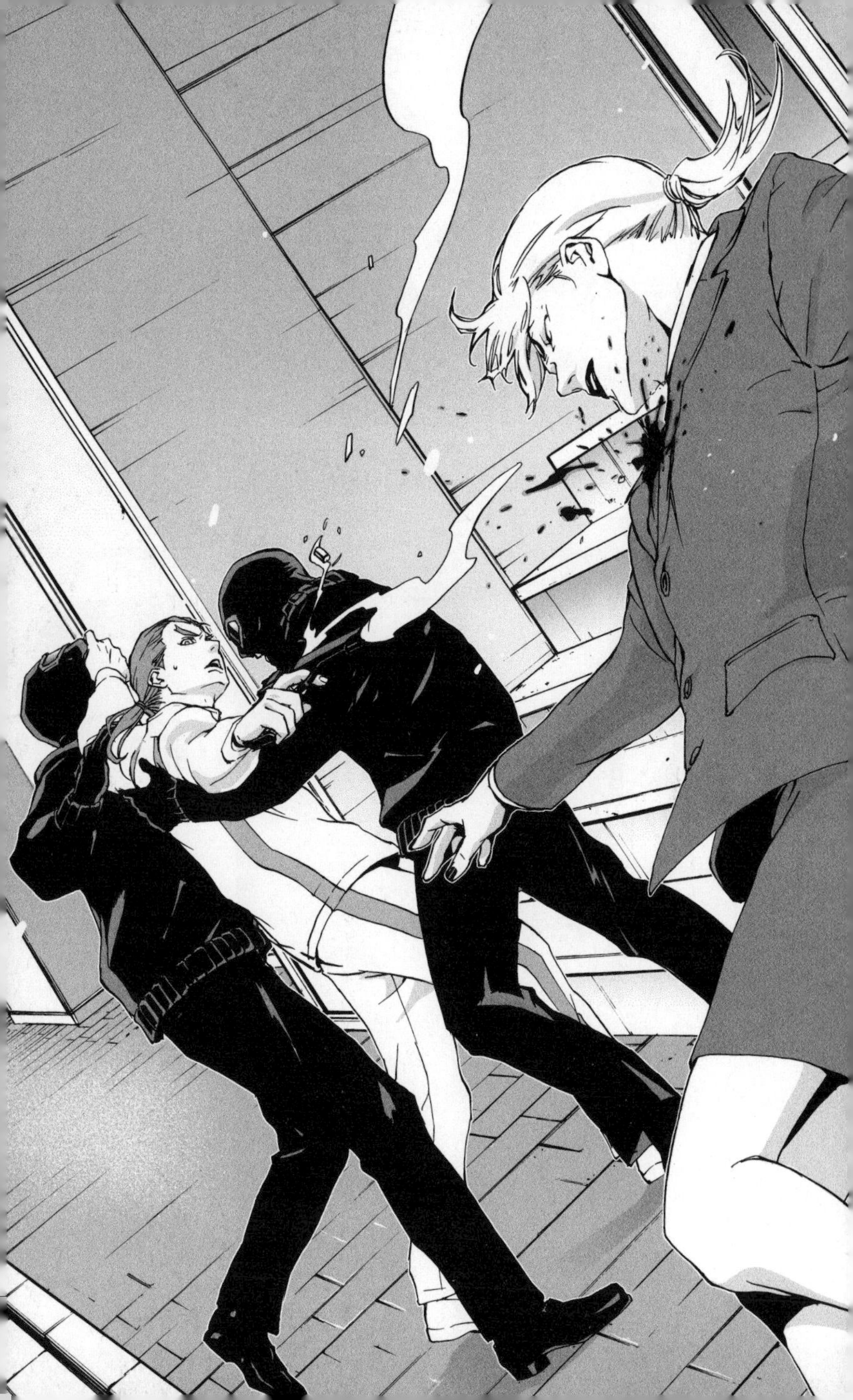

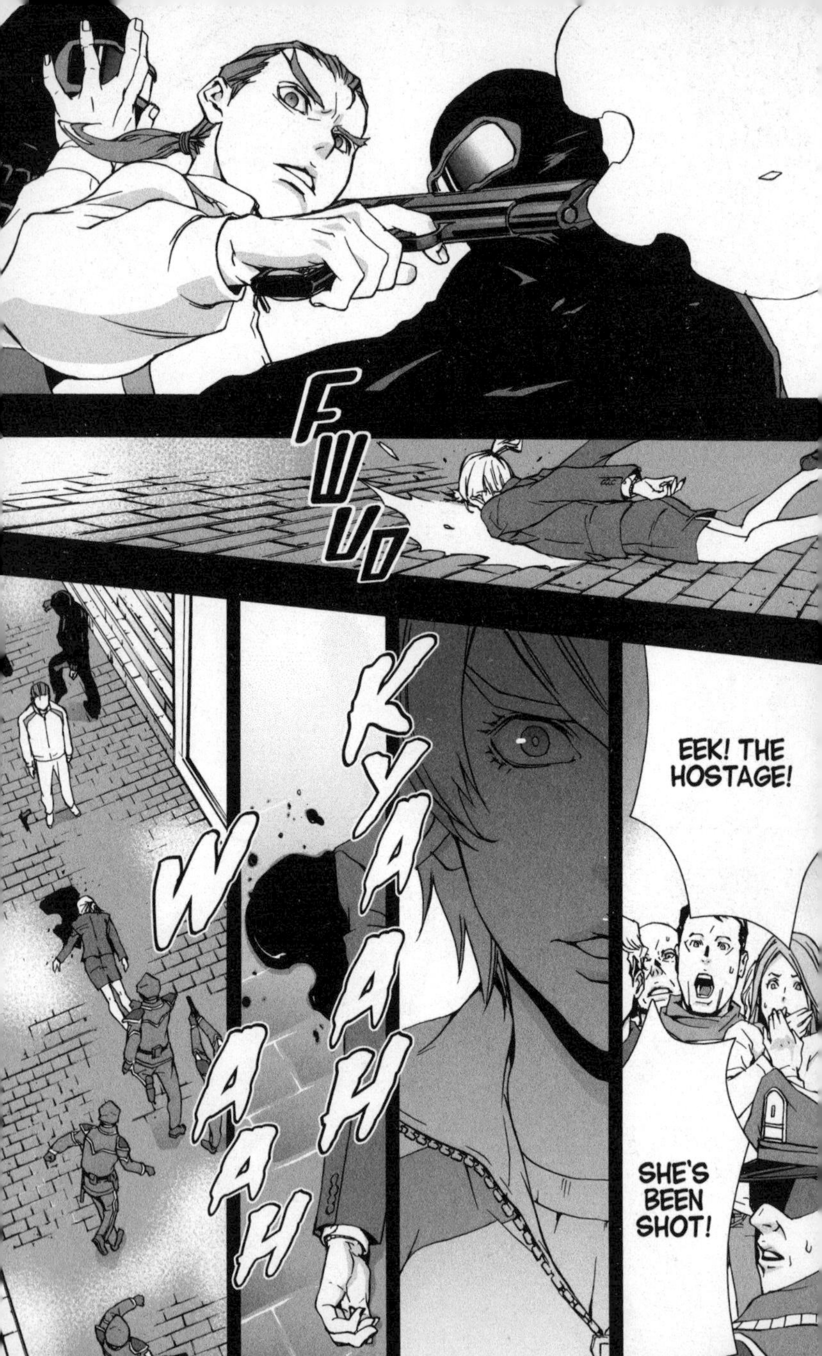
FWUD
EEK! THE HOSTAGE!
SHE'S BEEN SHOT!
KYAAAH
WAAH

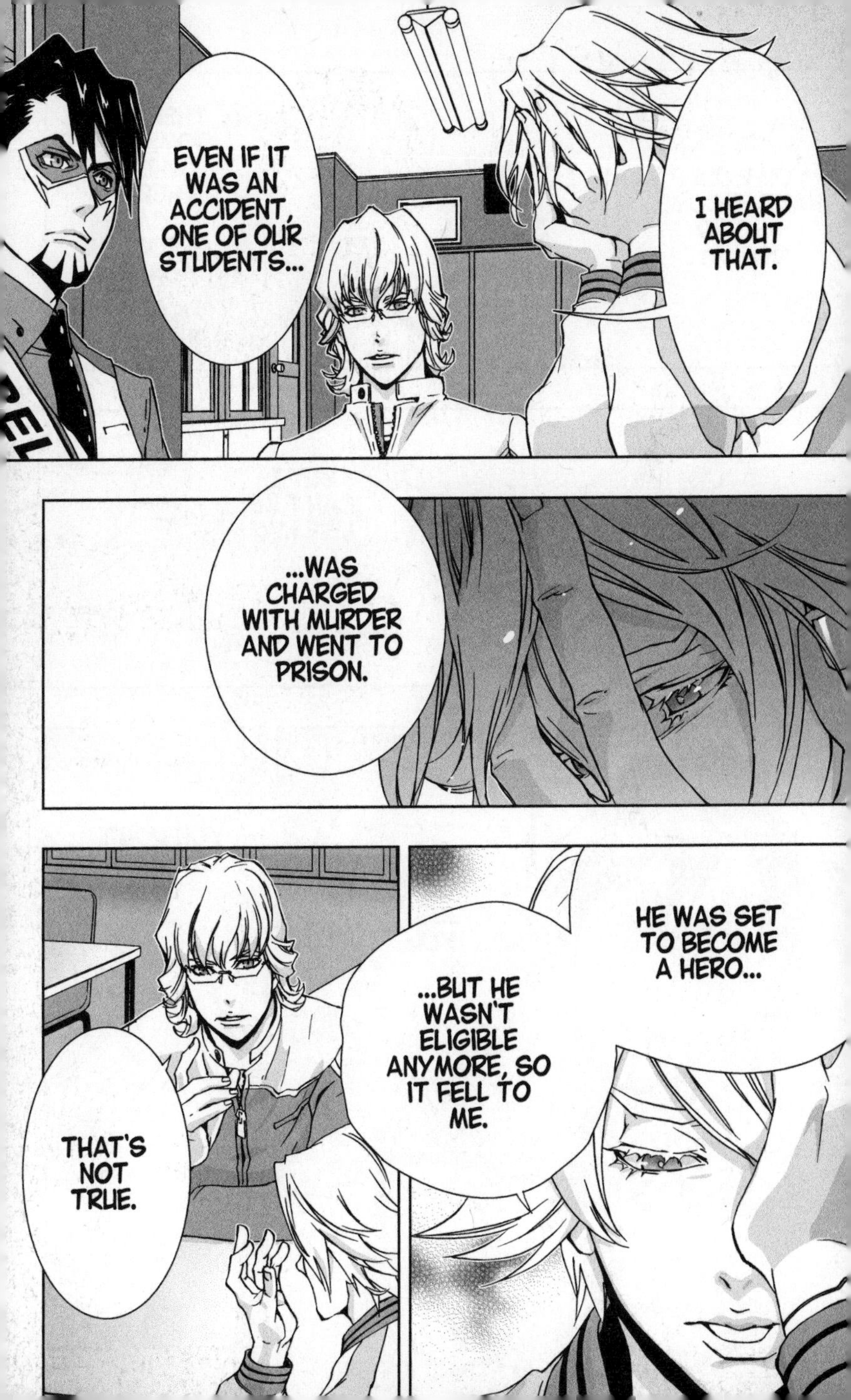
I HEARD ABOUT THAT.
EVEN IF IT WAS AN ACCIDENT, ONE OF OUR STUDENTS...
...WAS CHARGED WITH MURDER AND WENT TO PRISON.
HE WAS SET TO BECOME A HERO...
...BUT HE WASN'T ELIGIBLE ANYMORE, SO IT FELL TO ME.
THAT'S NOT TRUE.

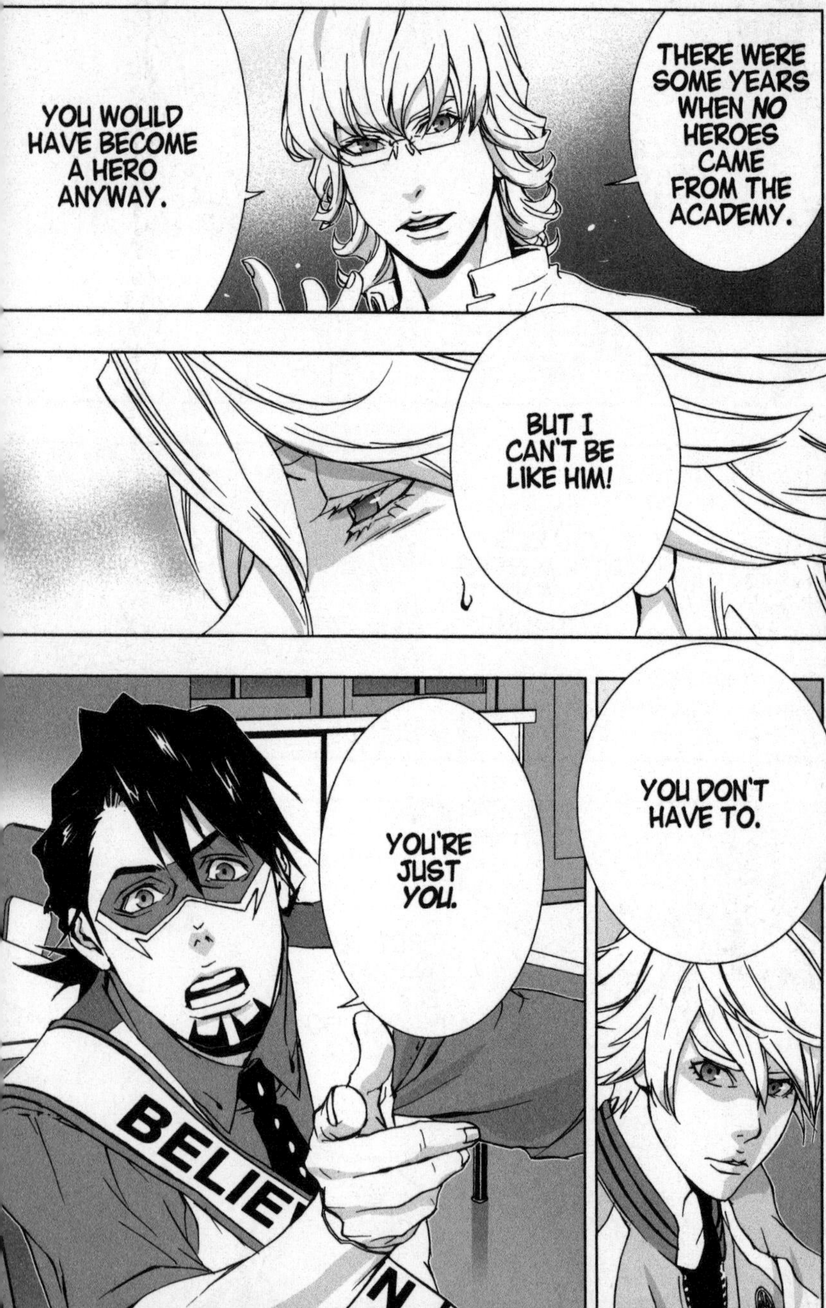
THERE WERE SOME YEARS WHEN NO HEROES CAME FROM THE ACADEMY.
YOU WOULD HAVE BECOME A HERO ANYWAY.
BUT I CAN'T BE LIKE HIM!
YOU DON'T HAVE TO.
YOU'RE JUST YOU.

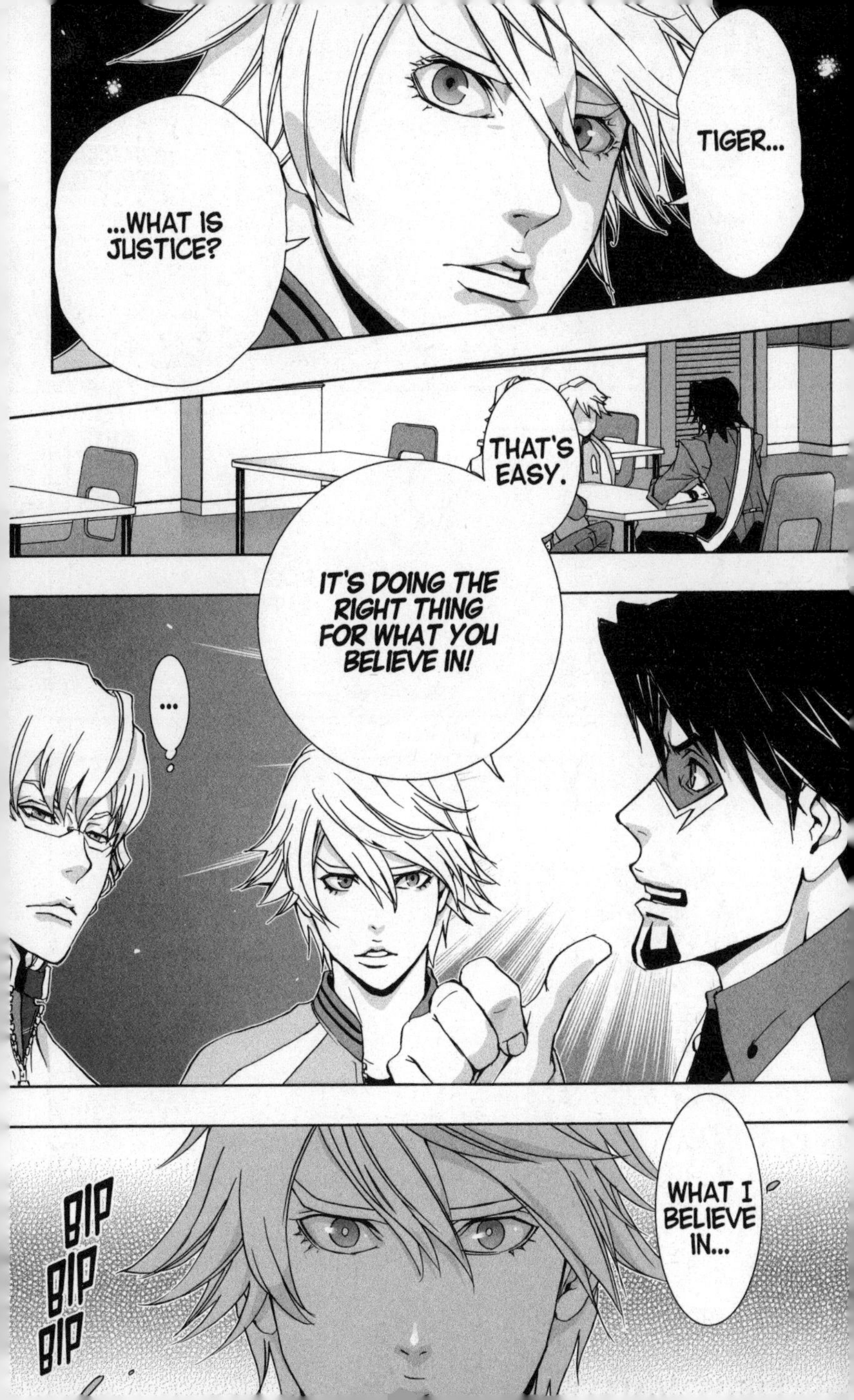
TIGER...
...WHAT IS JUSTICE?
THAT'S EASY.
IT'S DOING THE RIGHT THING FOR WHAT YOU BELIEVE IN!
...
WHAT I BELIEVE IN...
BIP BIP BIP

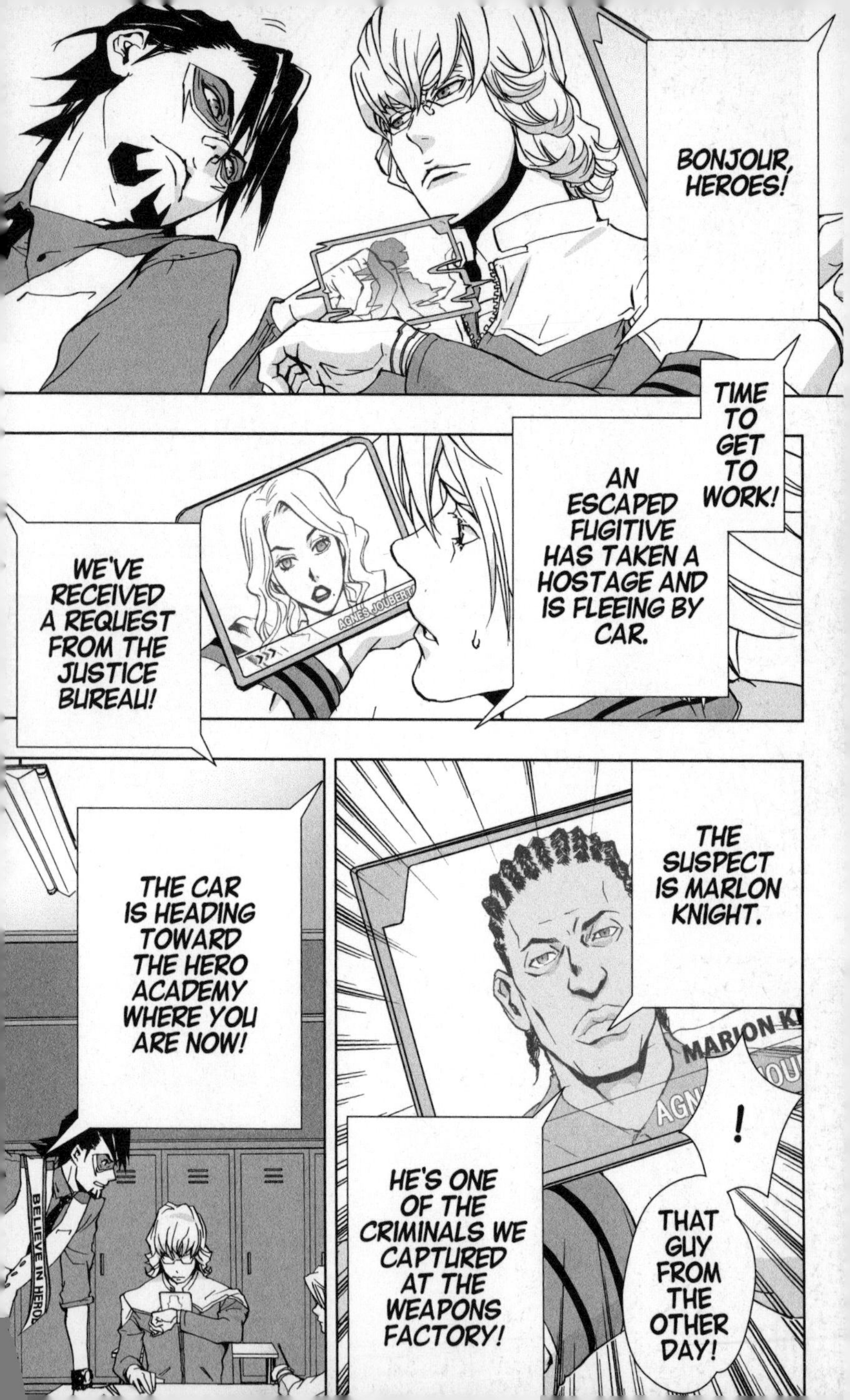
BONJOUR, HEROES!
TIME TO GET TO WORK!
AN ESCAPED FUGITIVE HAS TAKEN A HOSTAGE AND IS FLEEING BY CAR.
WE'VE RECEIVED A REQUEST FROM THE JUSTICE BUREAU!
THE SUSPECT IS MARLON KNIGHT.
HE'S ONE OF THE CRIMINALS WE CAPTURED AT THE WEAPONS FACTORY!
!
THAT GUY FROM THE OTHER DAY!
THE CAR IS HEADING TOWARD THE HERO ACADEMY WHERE YOU ARE NOW!

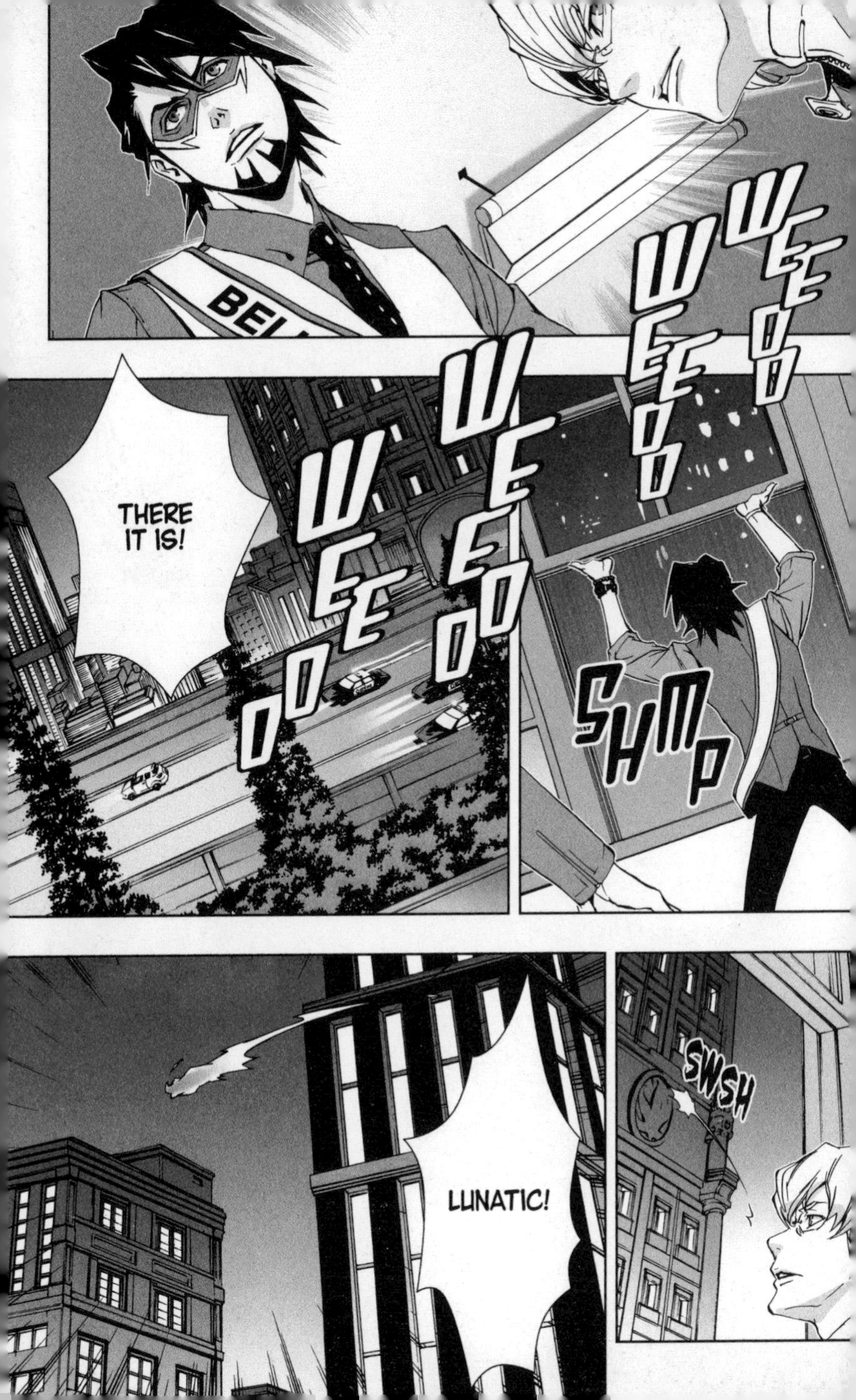
WEEOO
WEEOO
SHMP
WEEOO
WEEOO
THERE IT IS!
SWSH
LUNATIC!

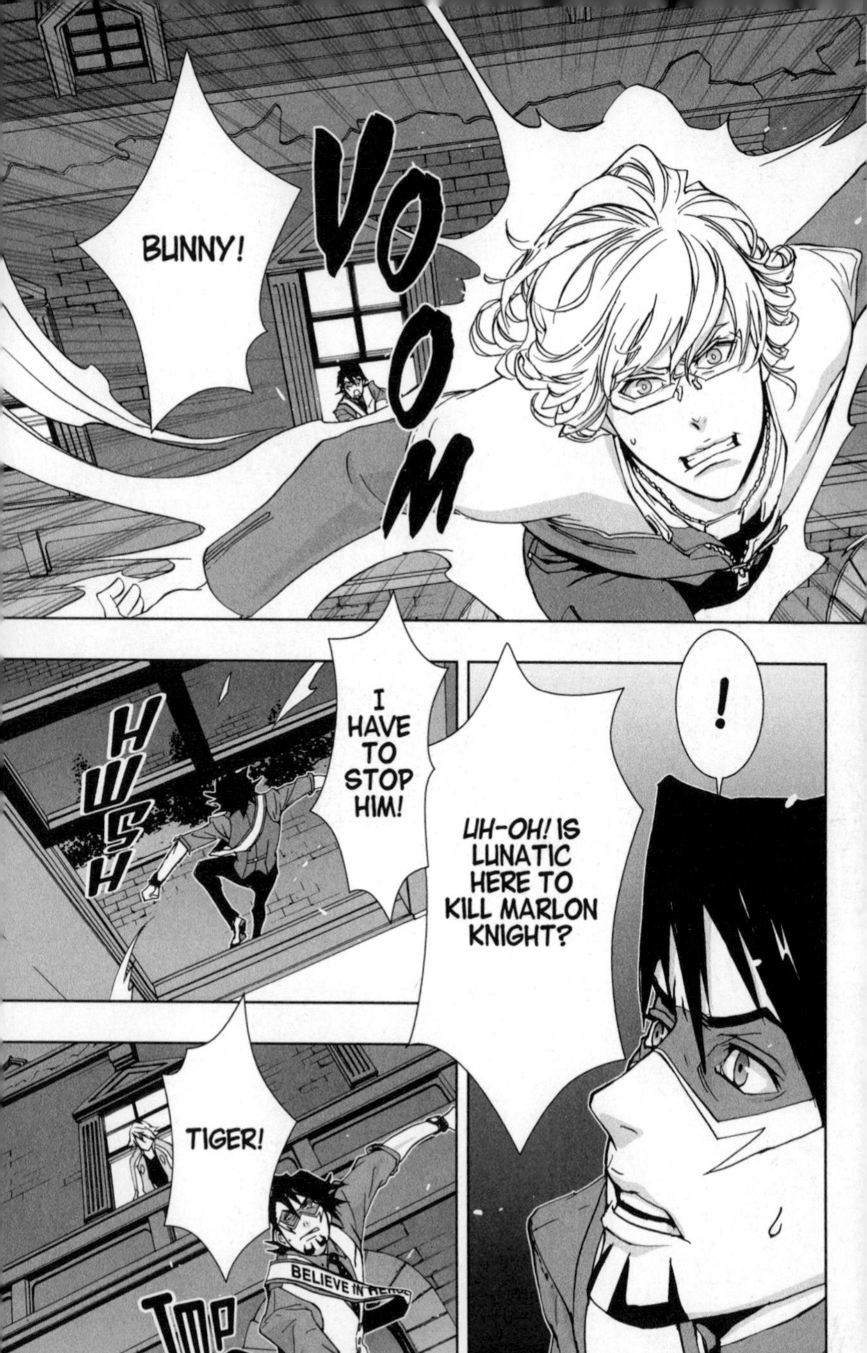
VOOM
BUNNY!
!
UH-OH! IS LUNATIC HERE TO KILL MARLON KNIGHT?
I HAVE TO STOP HIM!
HWSH
TIGER!
BELIEVE IN
TMP

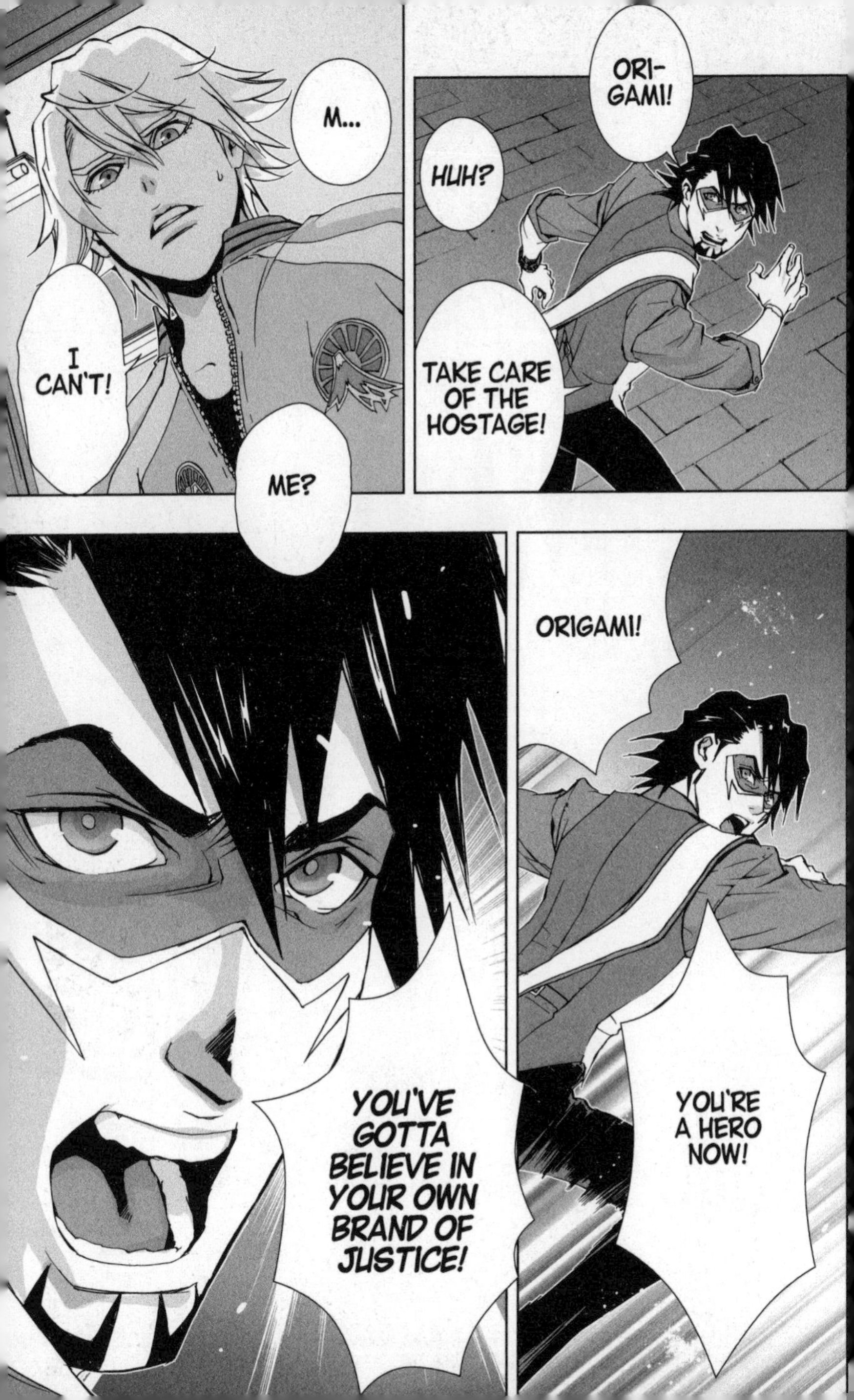
ORI-GAMI!
HUH?
TAKE CARE OF THE HOSTAGE!
ME?
M...
I CAN'T!
ORIGAMI!
YOU'RE A HERO NOW!
YOU'VE GOTTA BELIEVE IN YOUR OWN BRAND OF JUSTICE!

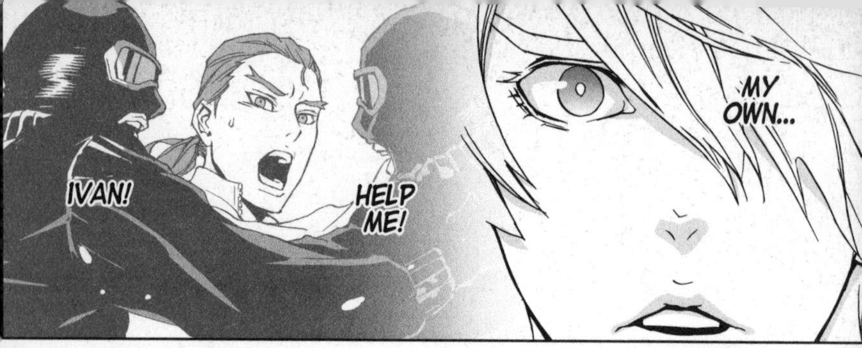
MY OWN...
HELP ME!
IVAN!

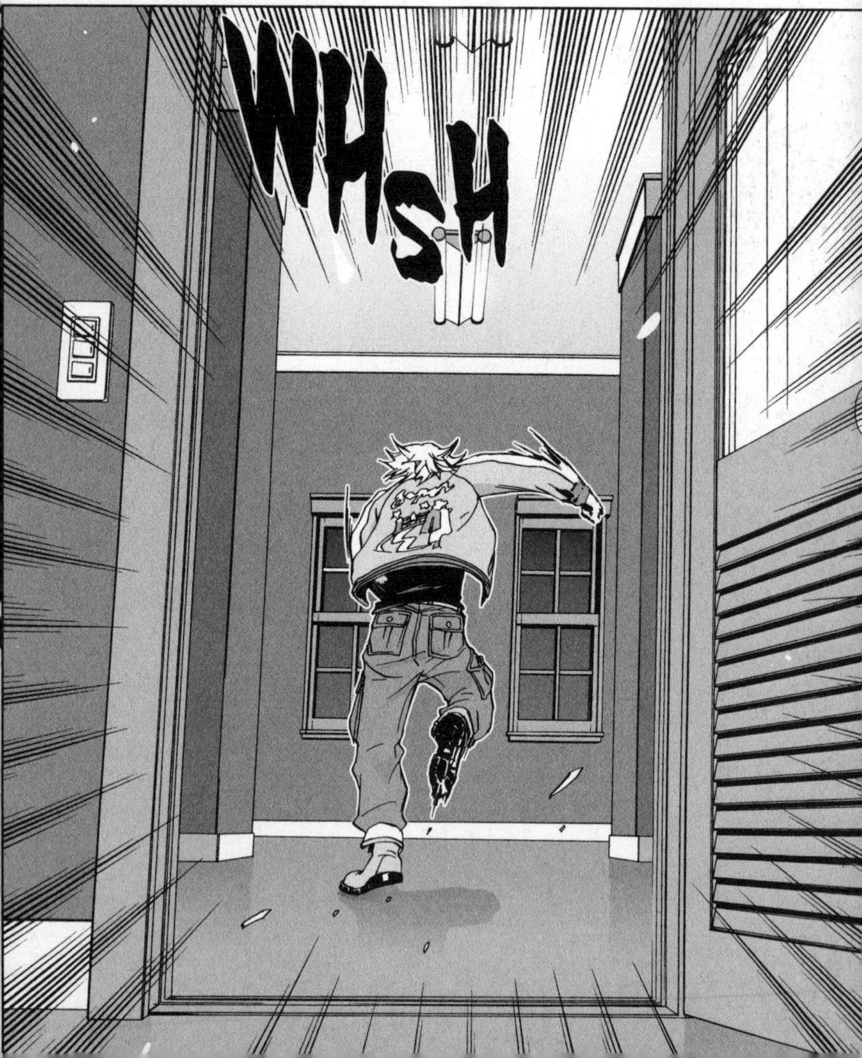
WHSH

TIGER & BUNNY

TIGER&BUNNY

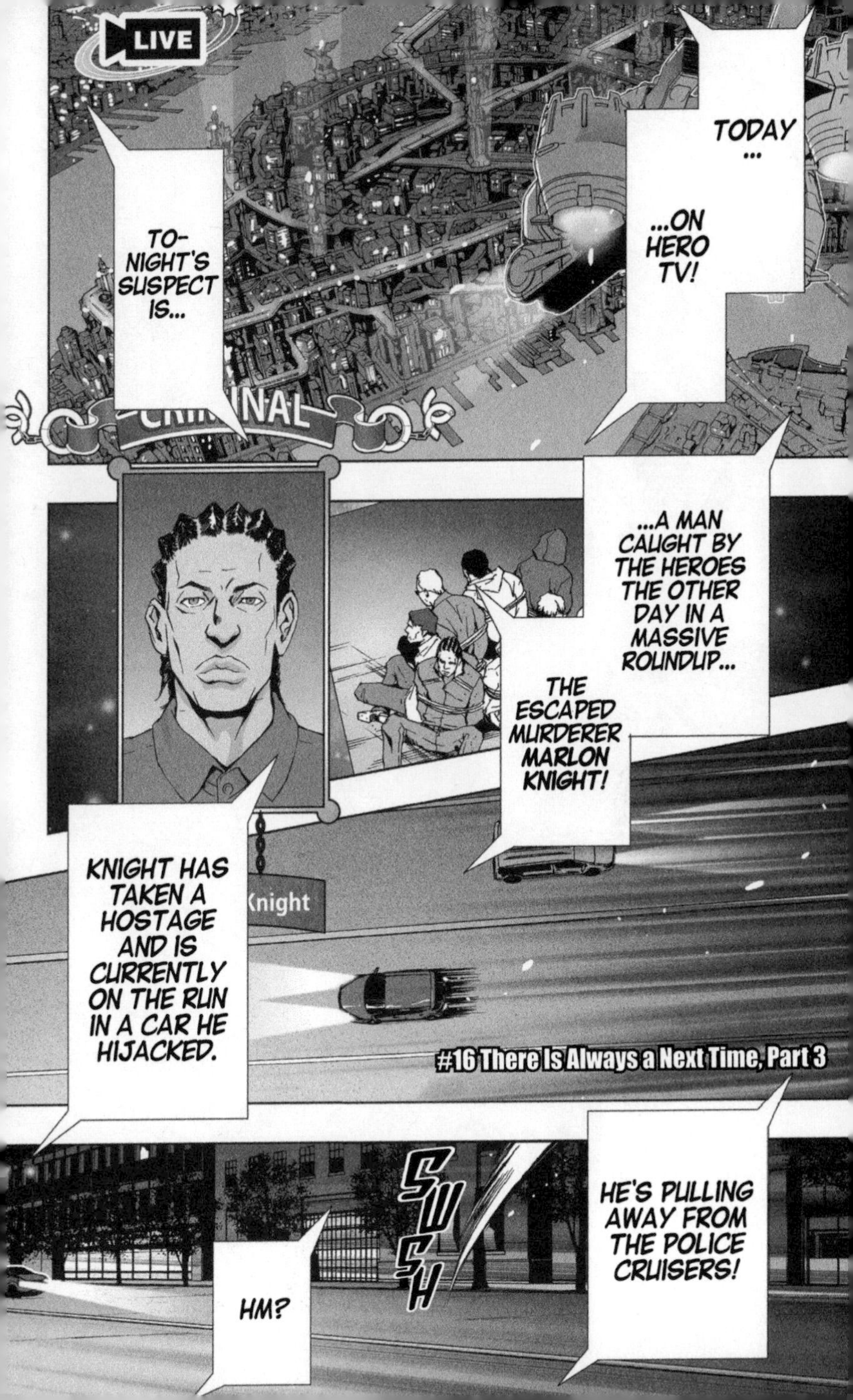
LIVE
TODAY...
...ON HERO TV!
TO-NIGHT'S SUSPECT IS...
...A MAN CAUGHT BY THE HEROES THE OTHER DAY IN A MASSIVE ROUNDUP...
THE ESCAPED MURDERER MARLON KNIGHT!
Knight
KNIGHT HAS TAKEN A HOSTAGE AND IS CURRENTLY ON THE RUN IN A CAR HE HIJACKED.
#16 There Is Always a Next Time, Part 3
HE'S PULLING AWAY FROM THE POLICE CRUISERS!
SWISH
HM?

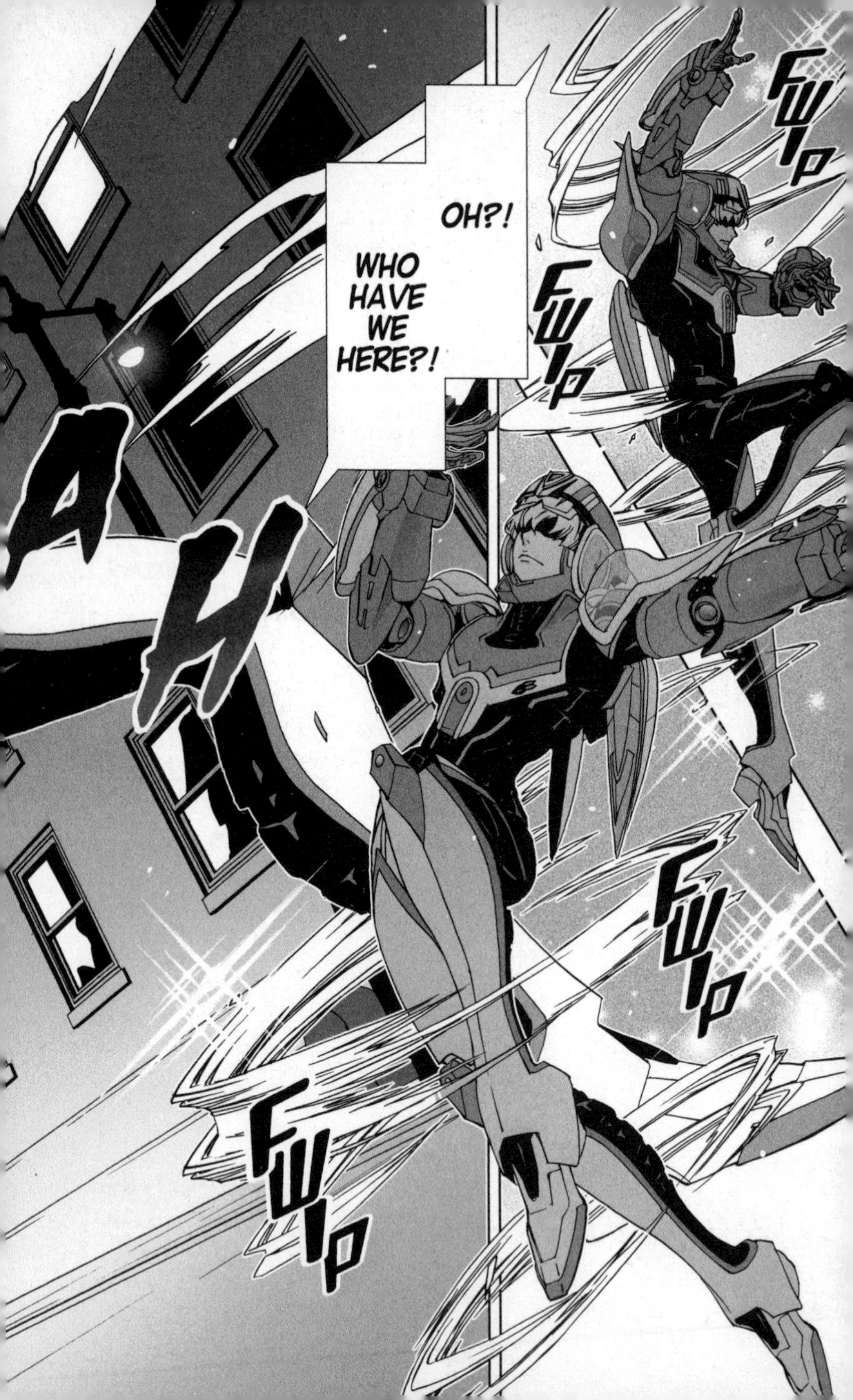
FWIP
OH?!
WHO HAVE WE HERE?!
FWIP
FWIP
FWIP

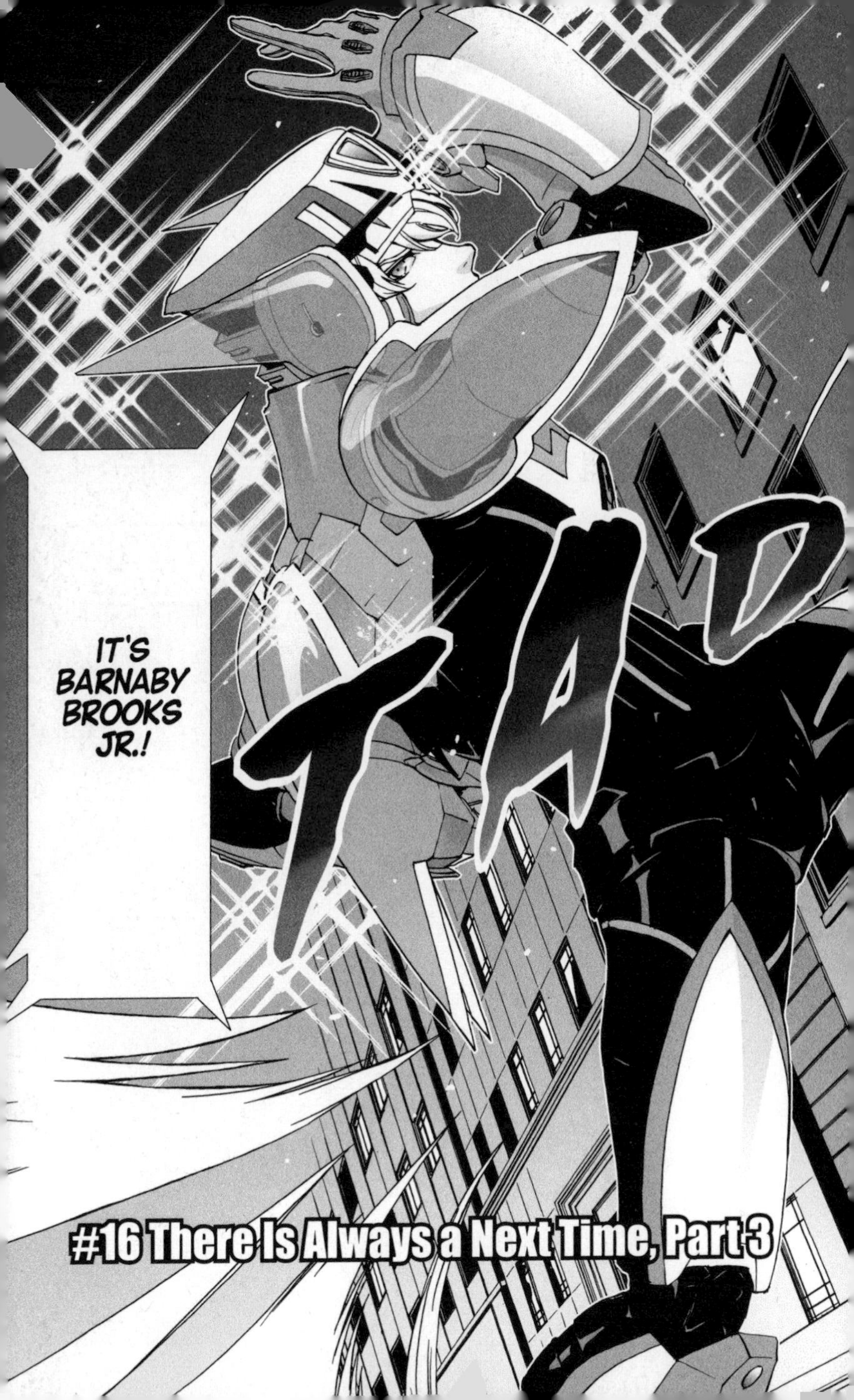
IT'S BARNABY BROOKS JR.!
#16 There Is Always a Next Time, Part 3

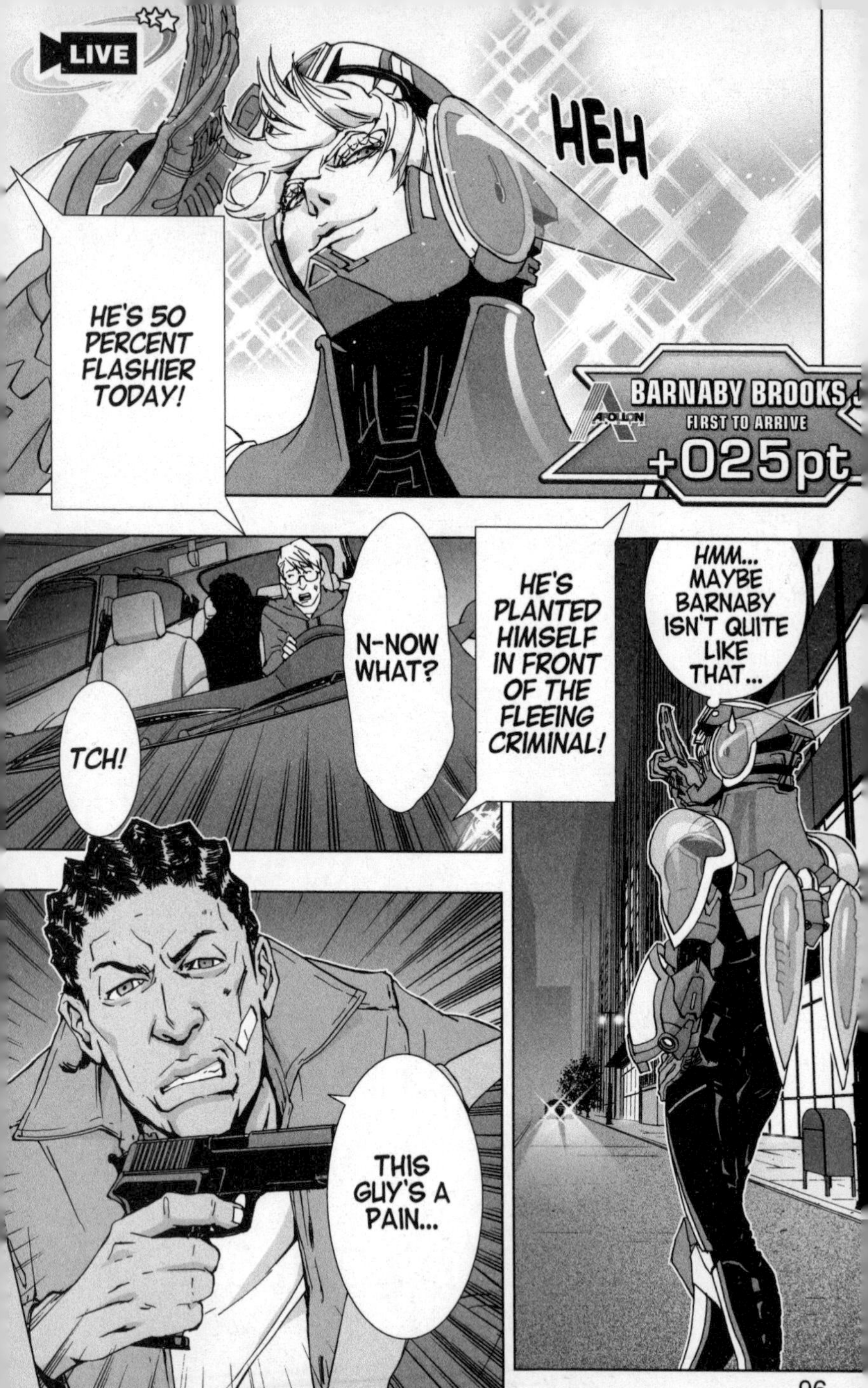
LIVE
HEH
BARNABY BROOKS
FIRST TO ARRIVE
+025pt
HE'S 50 PERCENT FLASHIER TODAY!
HMM... MAYBE BARNABY ISN'T QUITE LIKE THAT...
HE'S PLANTED HIMSELF IN FRONT OF THE FLEEING CRIMINAL!
N-NOW WHAT?
TCH!
THIS GUY'S A PAIN...

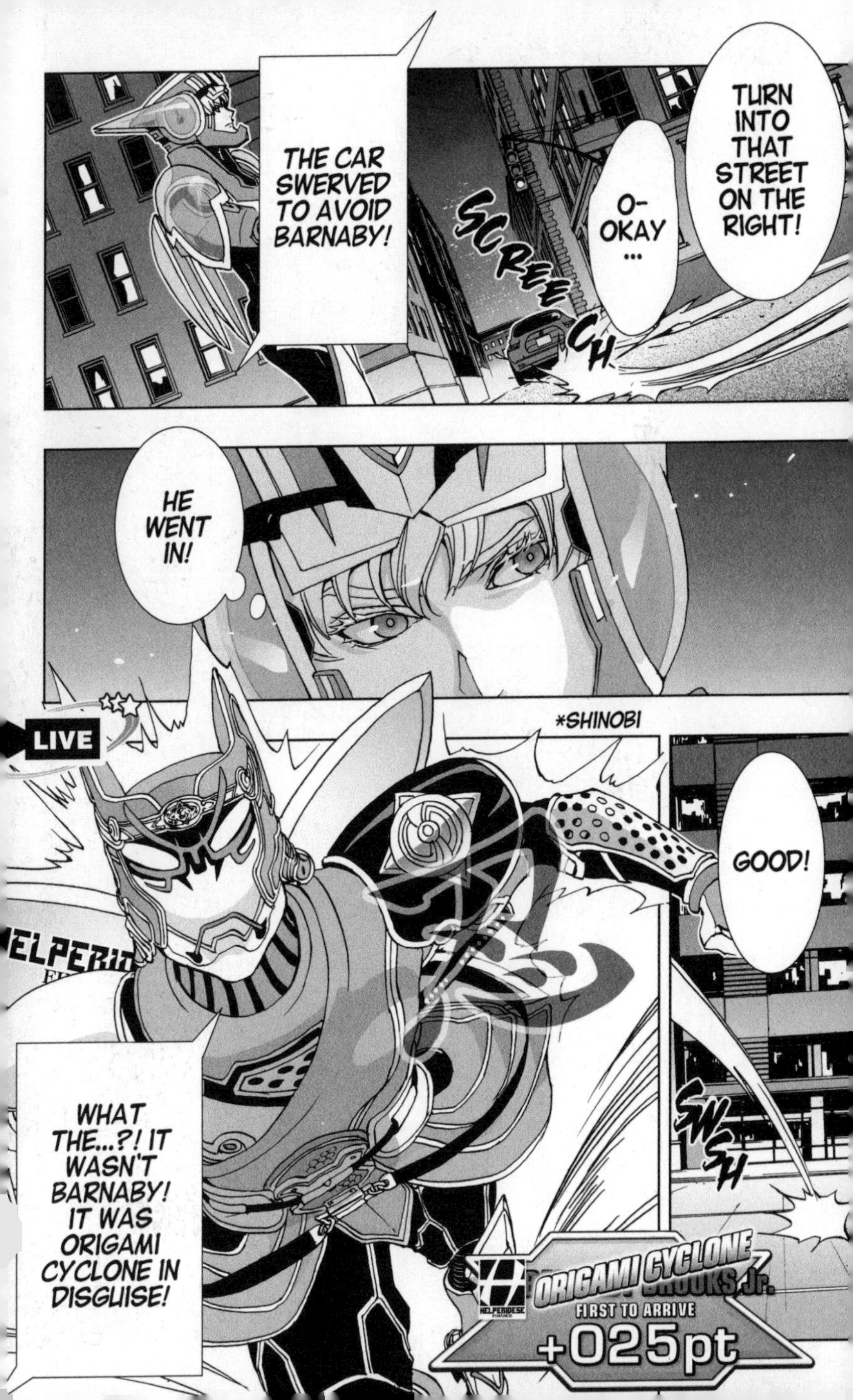
TURN INTO THAT STREET ON THE RIGHT!
O-OKAY...
SCREEECH
THE CAR SWERVED TO AVOID BARNABY!
HE WENT IN!
*SHINOBI
GOOD!
SWSH
LIVE
WHAT THE...?! IT WASN'T BARNABY! IT WAS ORIGAMI CYCLONE IN DISGUISE!
ORIGAMI CYCLONE
BROOKS Jr.
FIRST TO ARRIVE
+025pt

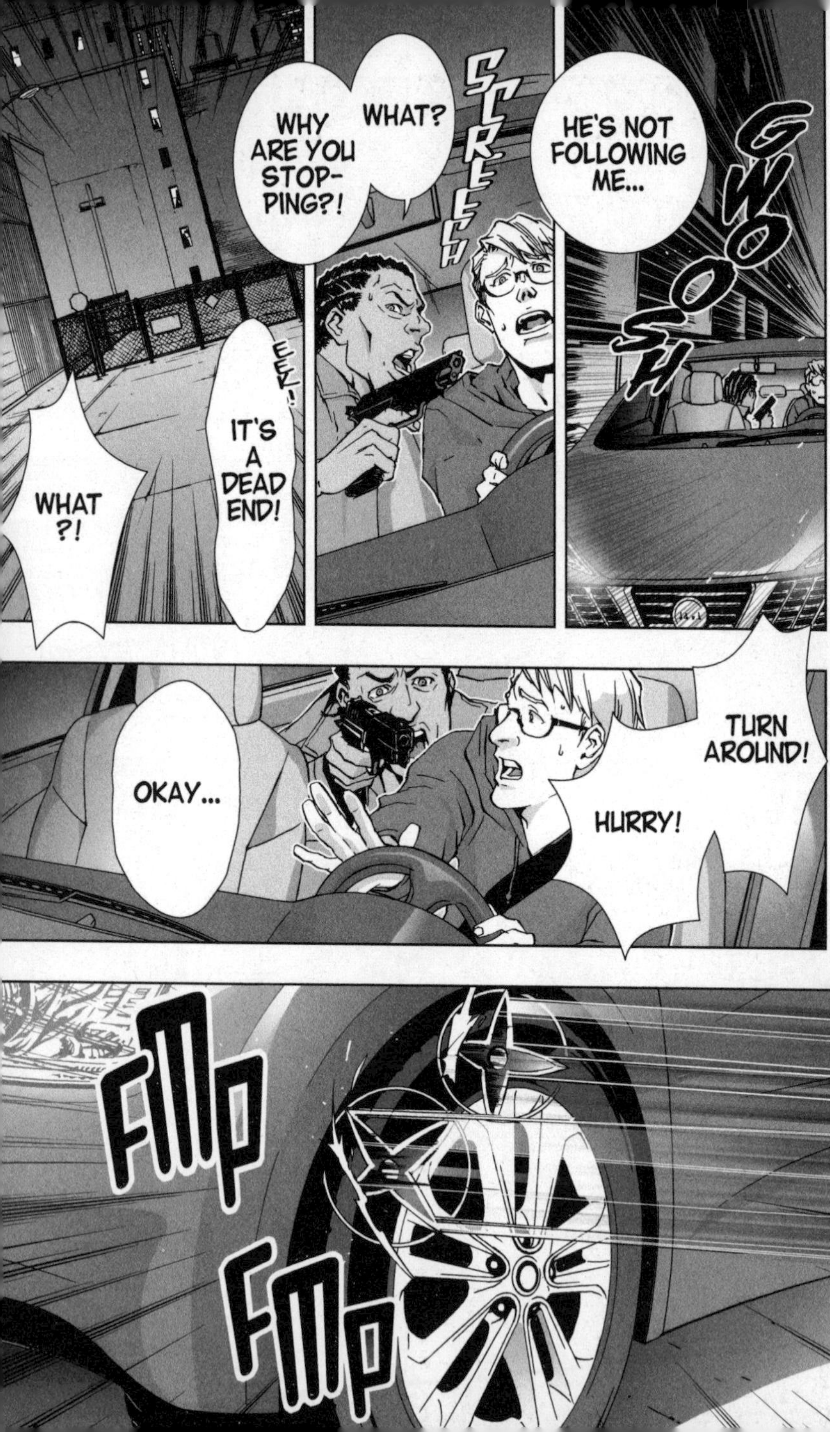
HE'S NOT FOLLOWING ME...
GWOOOSH
SCREEECH
WHAT?
WHY ARE YOU STOP-PING?!
EEK!
IT'S A DEAD END!
WHAT?!
TURN AROUND!
HURRY!
OKAY...
FMP
FMP

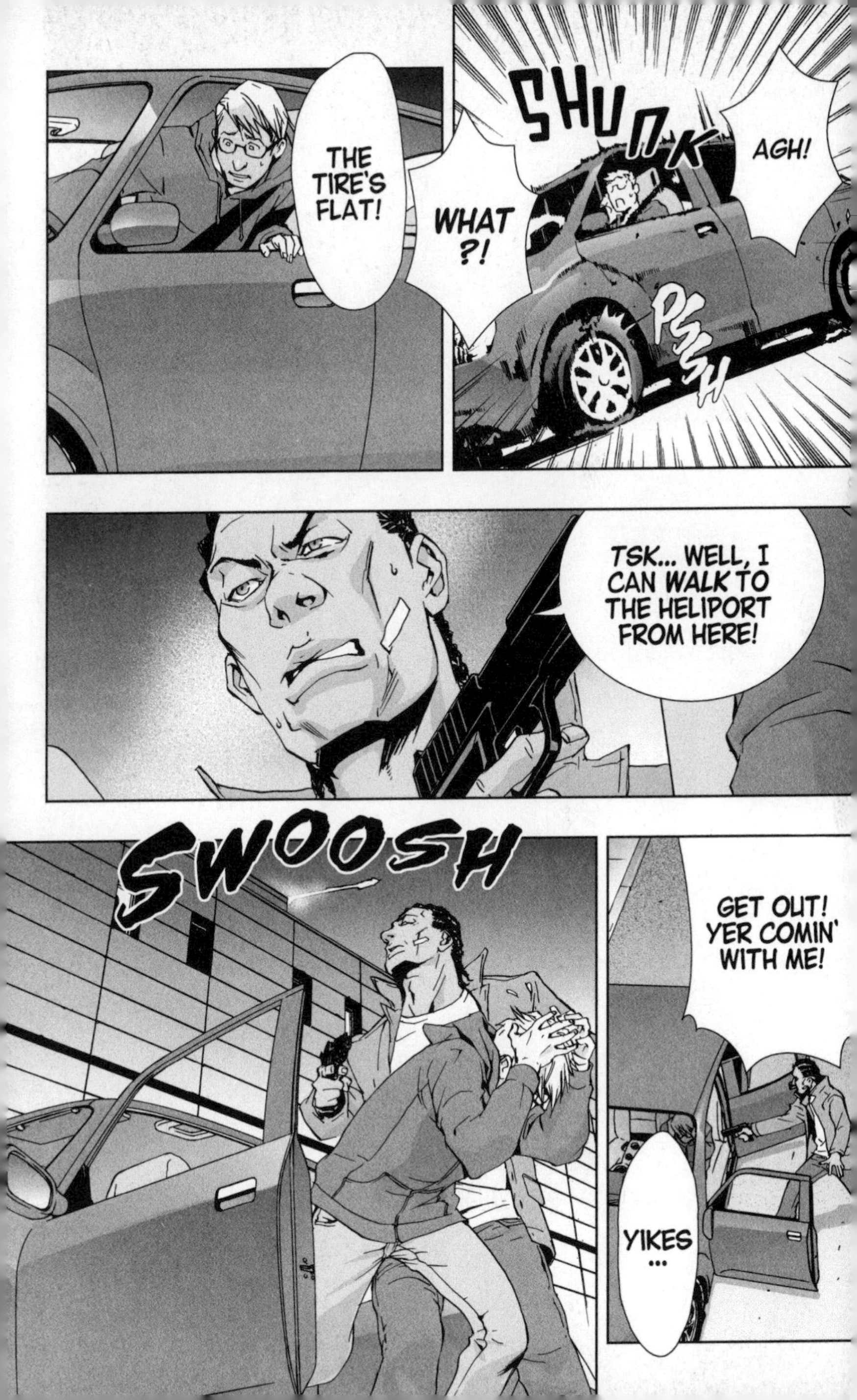
AGH!
SHUNK
WHAT?!
PSSH
THE TIRE'S FLAT!
TSK... WELL, I CAN *WALK* TO THE HELIPORT FROM HERE!
GET OUT! YER COMIN' WITH ME!
YIKES...
SWOOSH

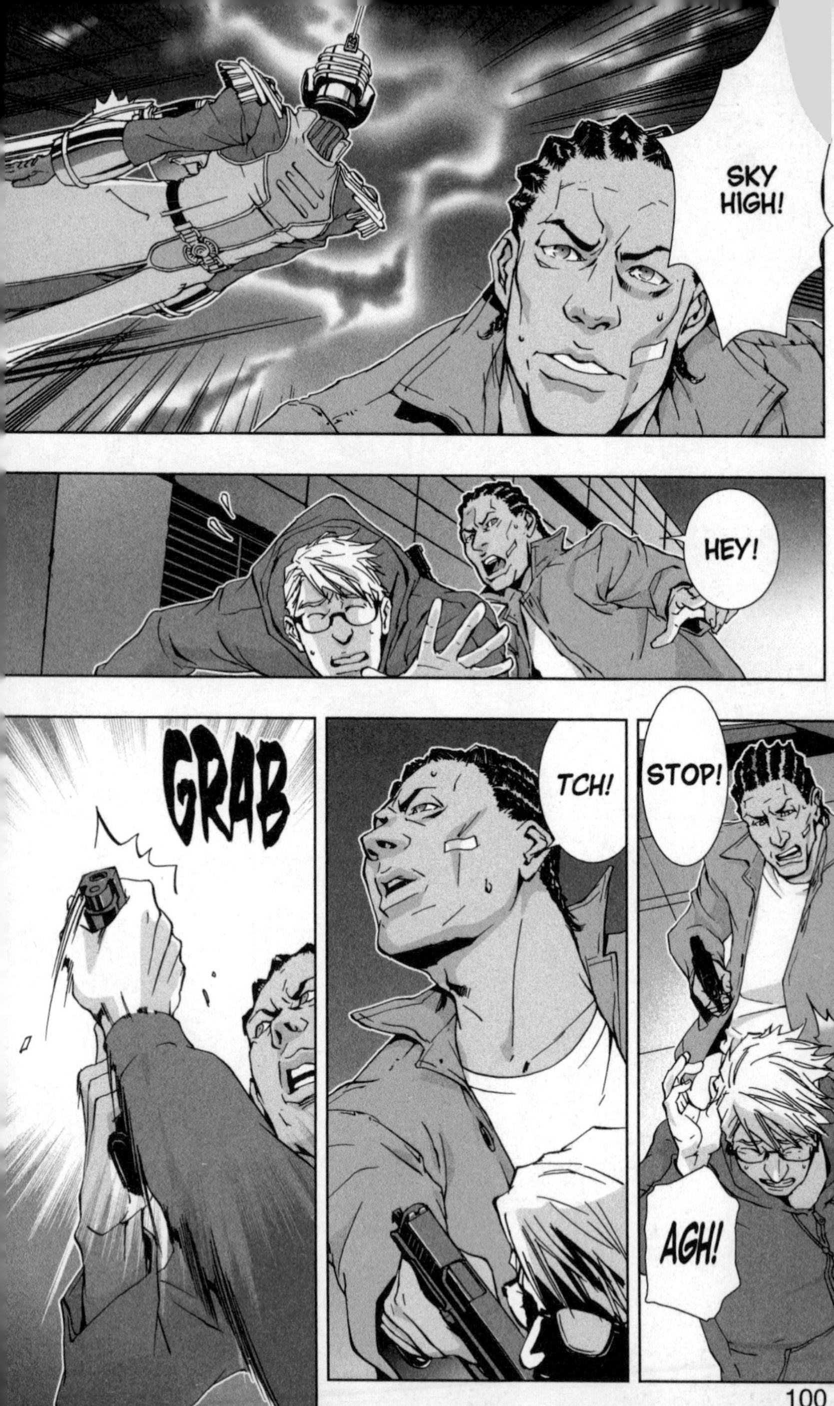
SKY HIGH!
HEY!
STOP!
AGH!
TCH!
GRAB

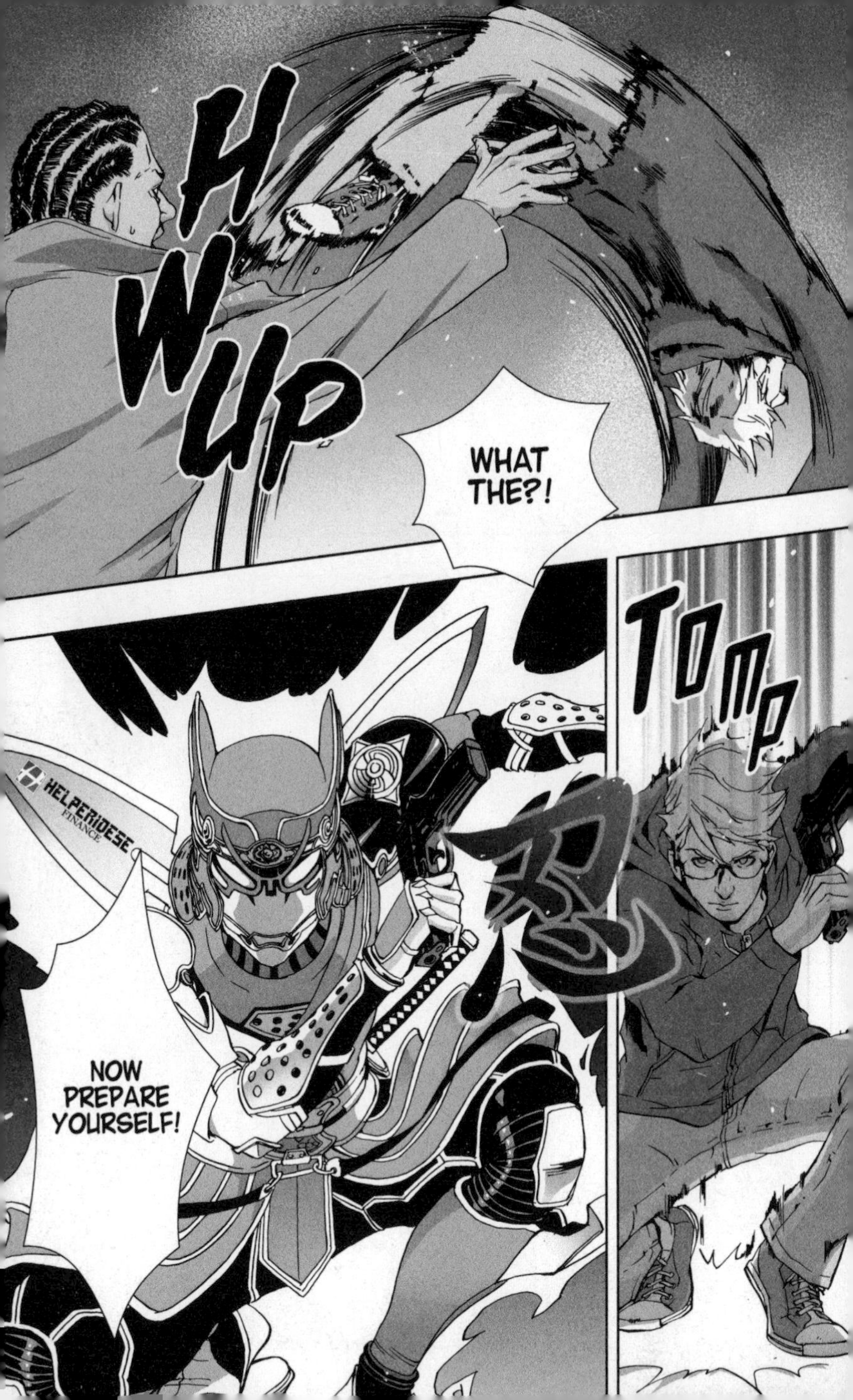
HWUP
WHAT THE?!
TOMP
HELPERIDESE FINANCE
NOW PREPARE YOURSELF!

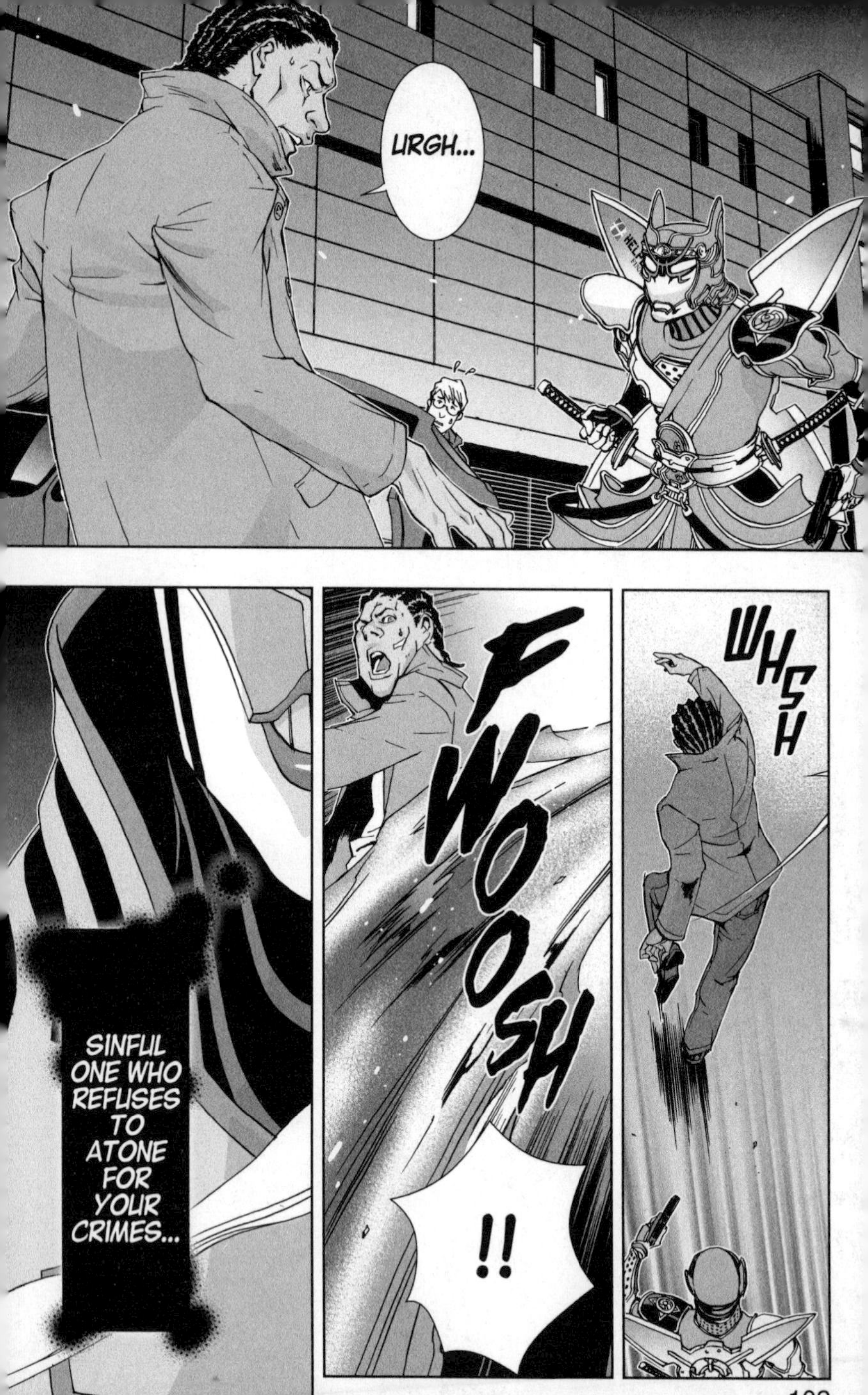
URGH...
WHSH
FWOOSH
!!
SINFUL ONE WHO REFUSES TO ATONE FOR YOUR CRIMES...

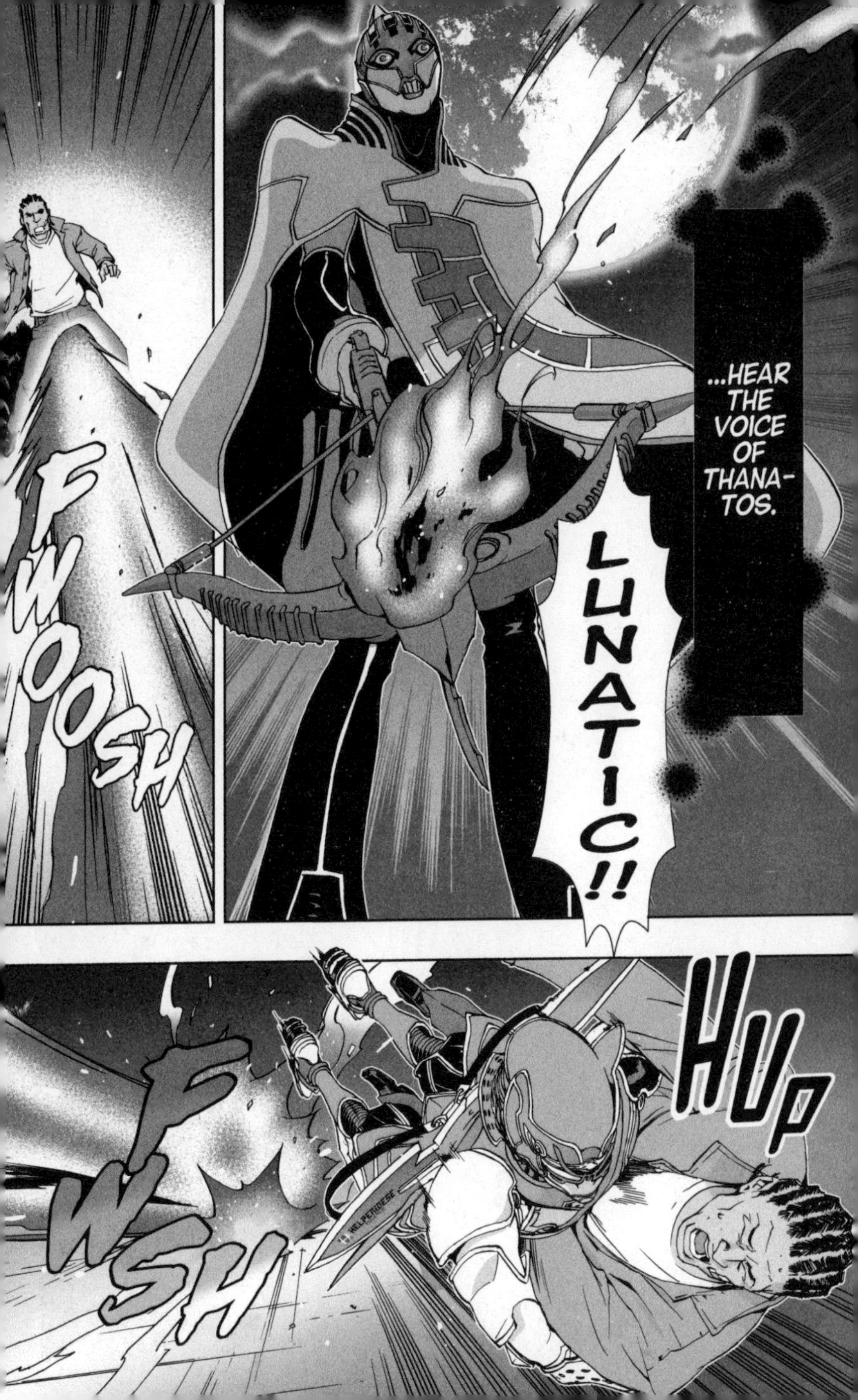
...HEAR THE VOICE OF THANA-TOS.
LUNATIC!!
FWOOSH
HUP
FWSH

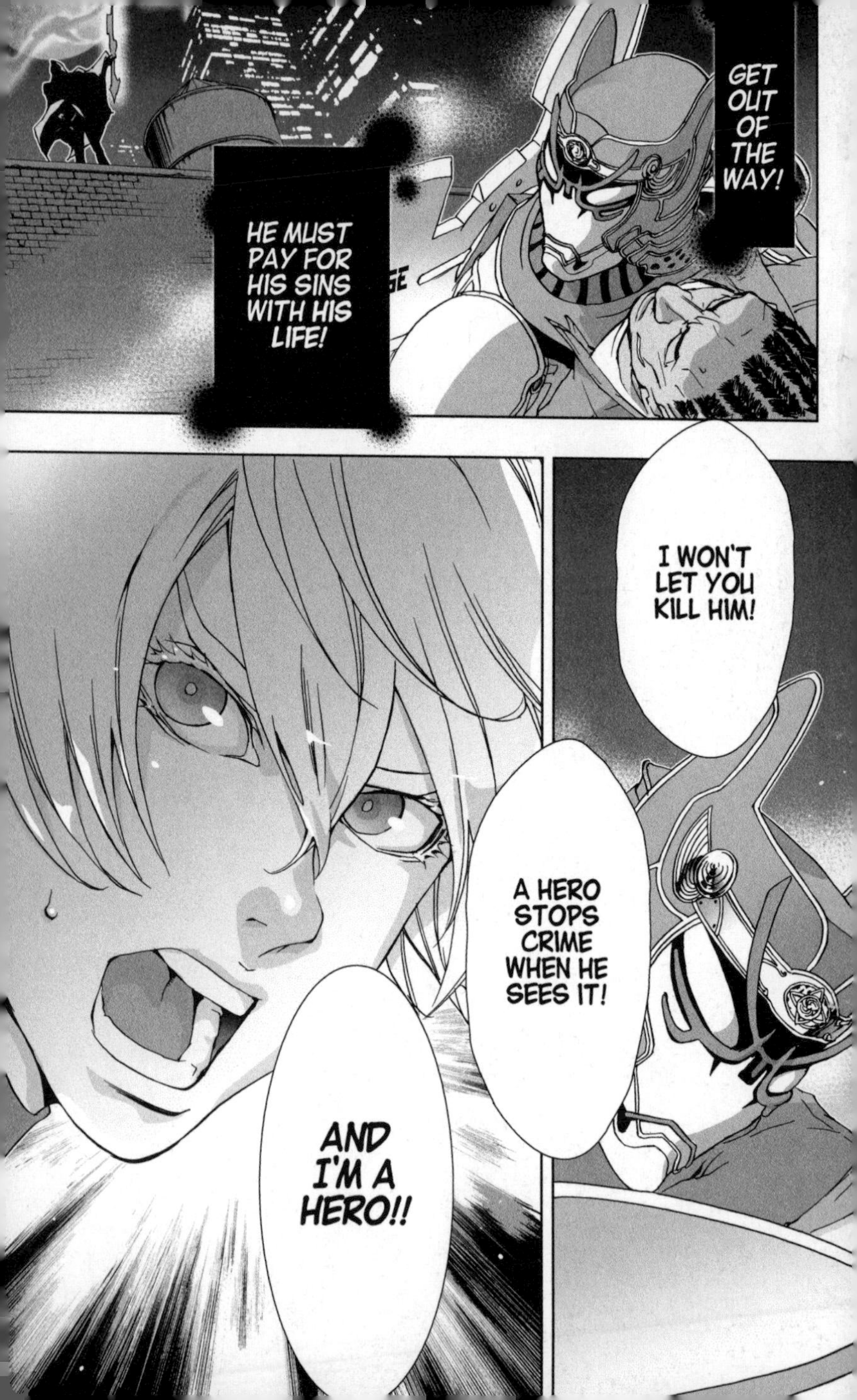
GET OUT OF THE WAY!
HE MUST PAY FOR HIS SINS WITH HIS LIFE!
I WON'T LET YOU KILL HIM!
A HERO STOPS CRIME WHEN HE SEES IT!
AND I'M A HERO!!

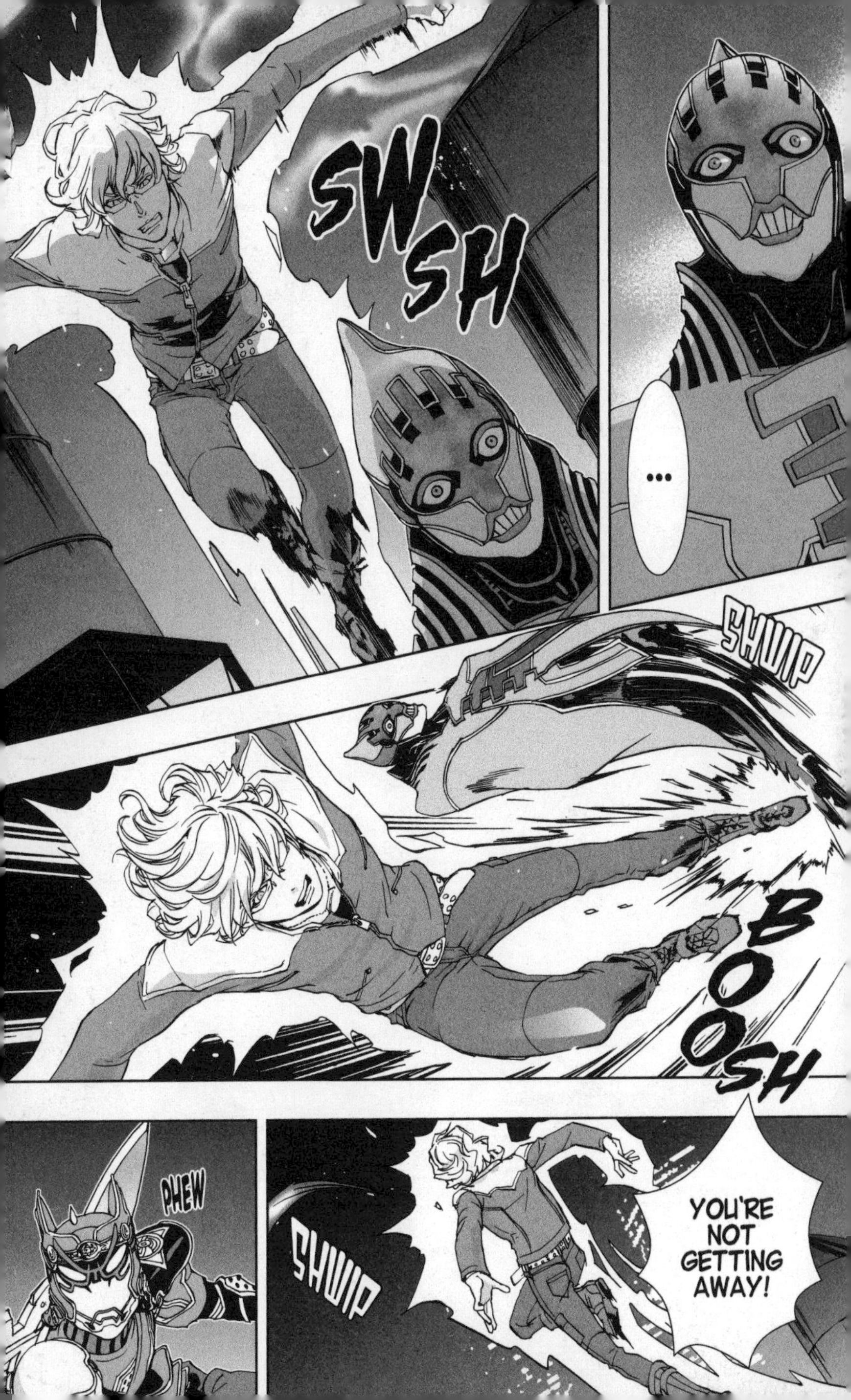
...
SWSH
SHWIP
BOOOSH
YOU'RE NOT GETTING AWAY!
SHWIP
PHEW

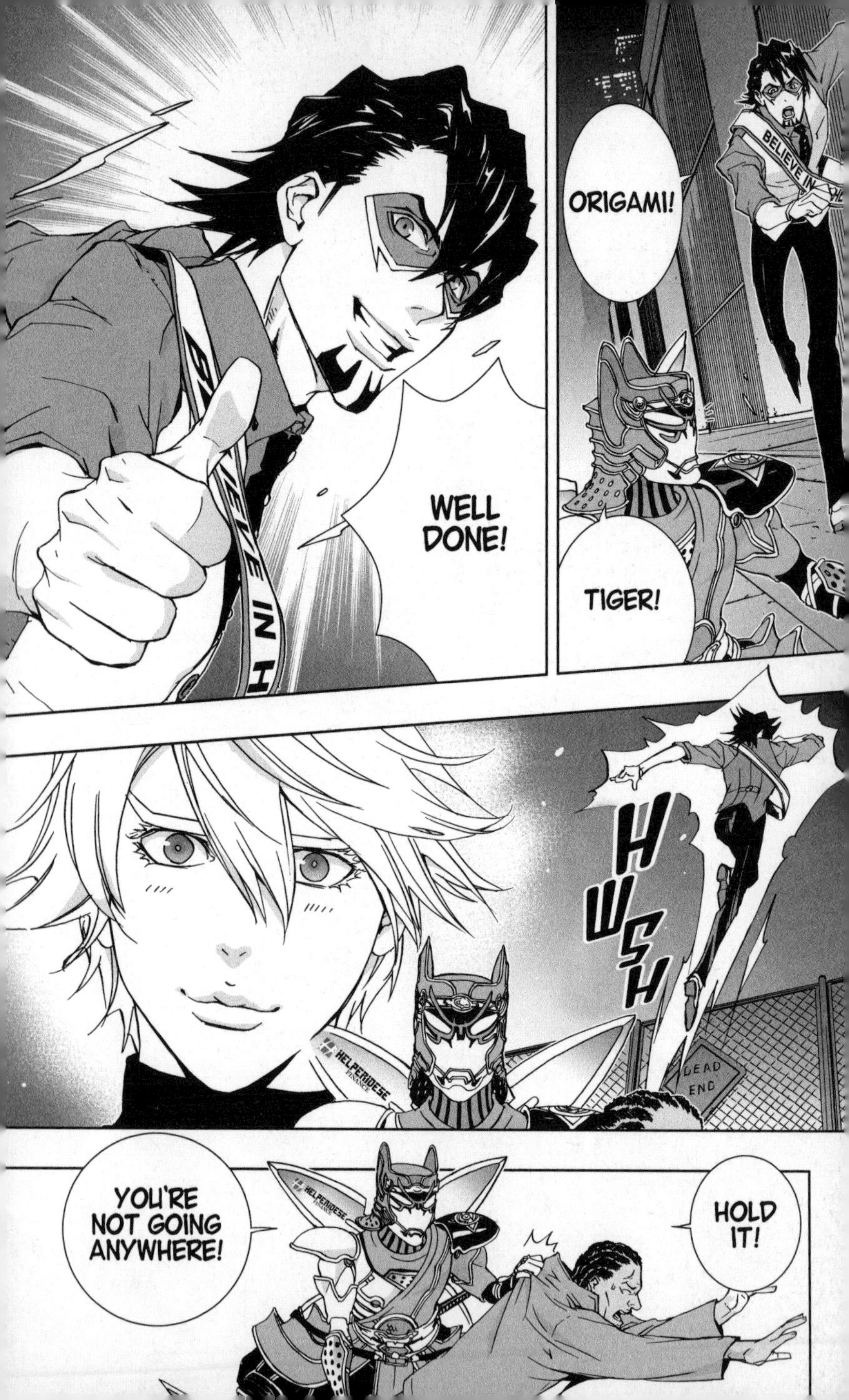

ORIGAMI!
BELIEVE IN
TIGER!
WELL DONE!
HWSH
HELPERIDESE FINANCE
DEAD END
HOLD IT!
YOU'RE NOT GOING ANYWHERE!
HELPERIDESE FINANCE

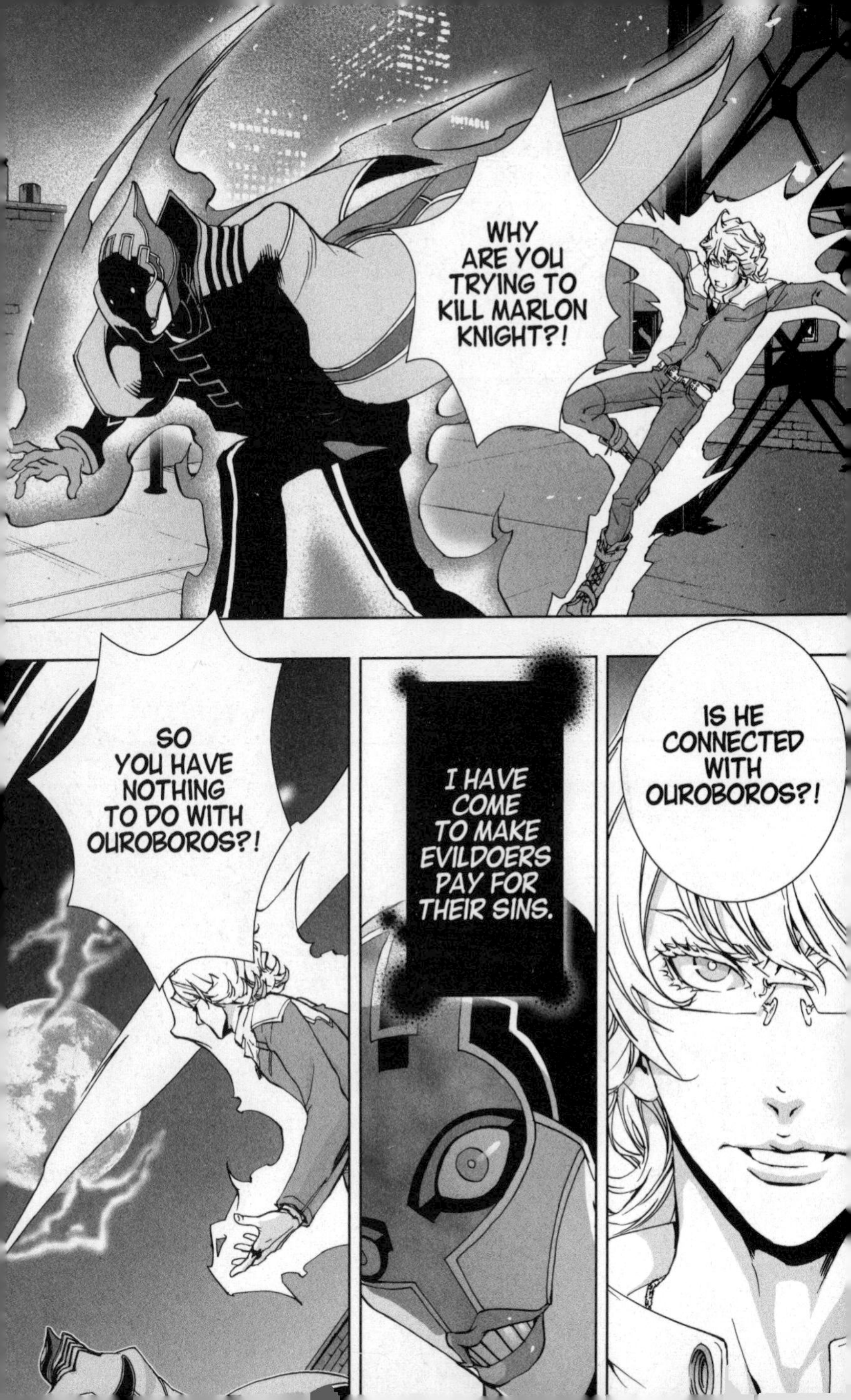
WHY ARE YOU TRYING TO KILL MARLON KNIGHT?!
IS HE CONNECTED WITH OUROBOROS?!
I HAVE COME TO MAKE EVILDOERS PAY FOR THEIR SINS.
SO YOU HAVE NOTHING TO DO WITH OUROBOROS?!

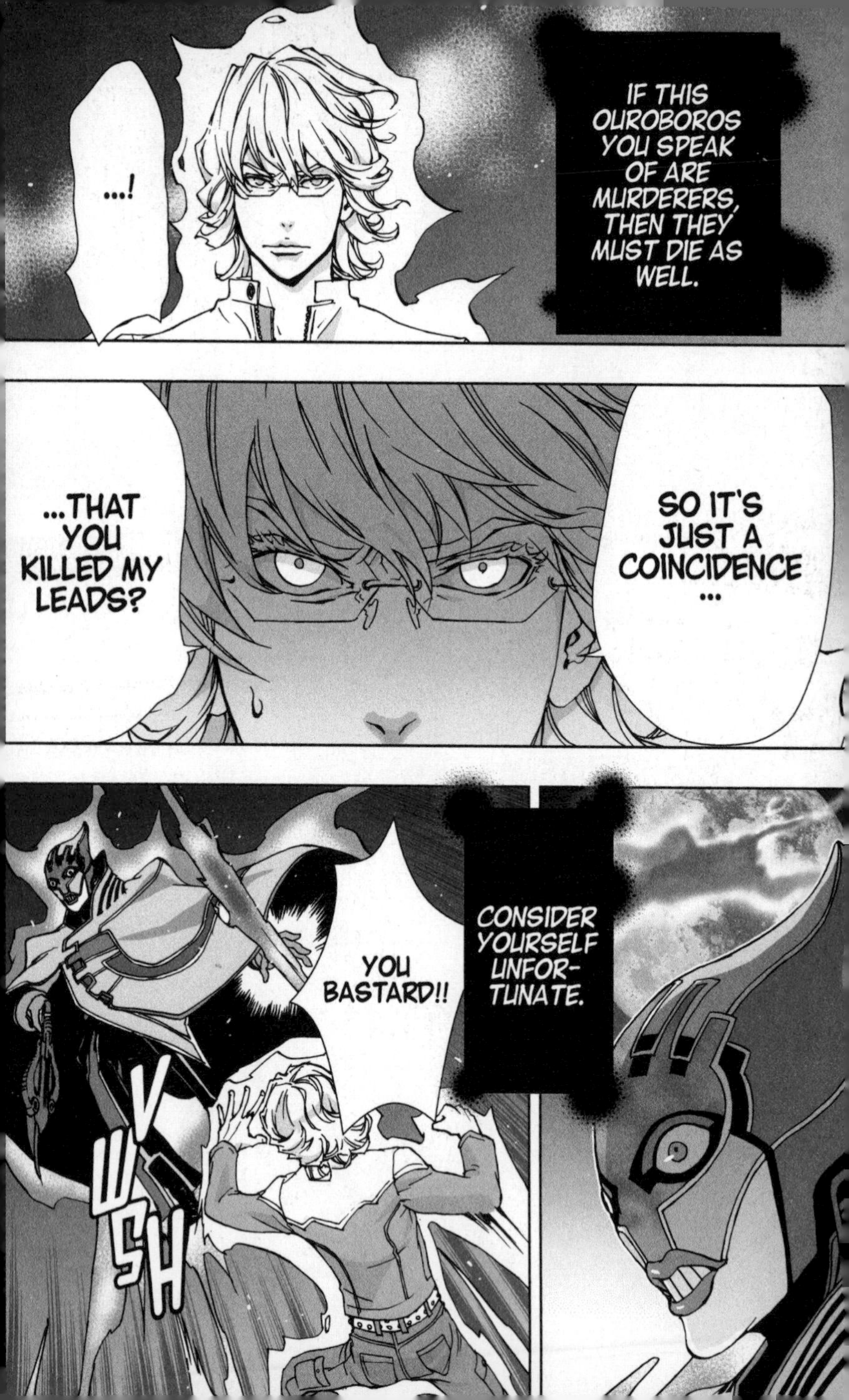
IF THIS OUROBOROS YOU SPEAK OF ARE MURDERERS, THEN THEY MUST DIE AS WELL.
...!
SO IT'S JUST A COINCIDENCE...
...THAT YOU KILLED MY LEADS?
CONSIDER YOURSELF UNFORTUNATE.
YOU BASTARD!!
VWSH

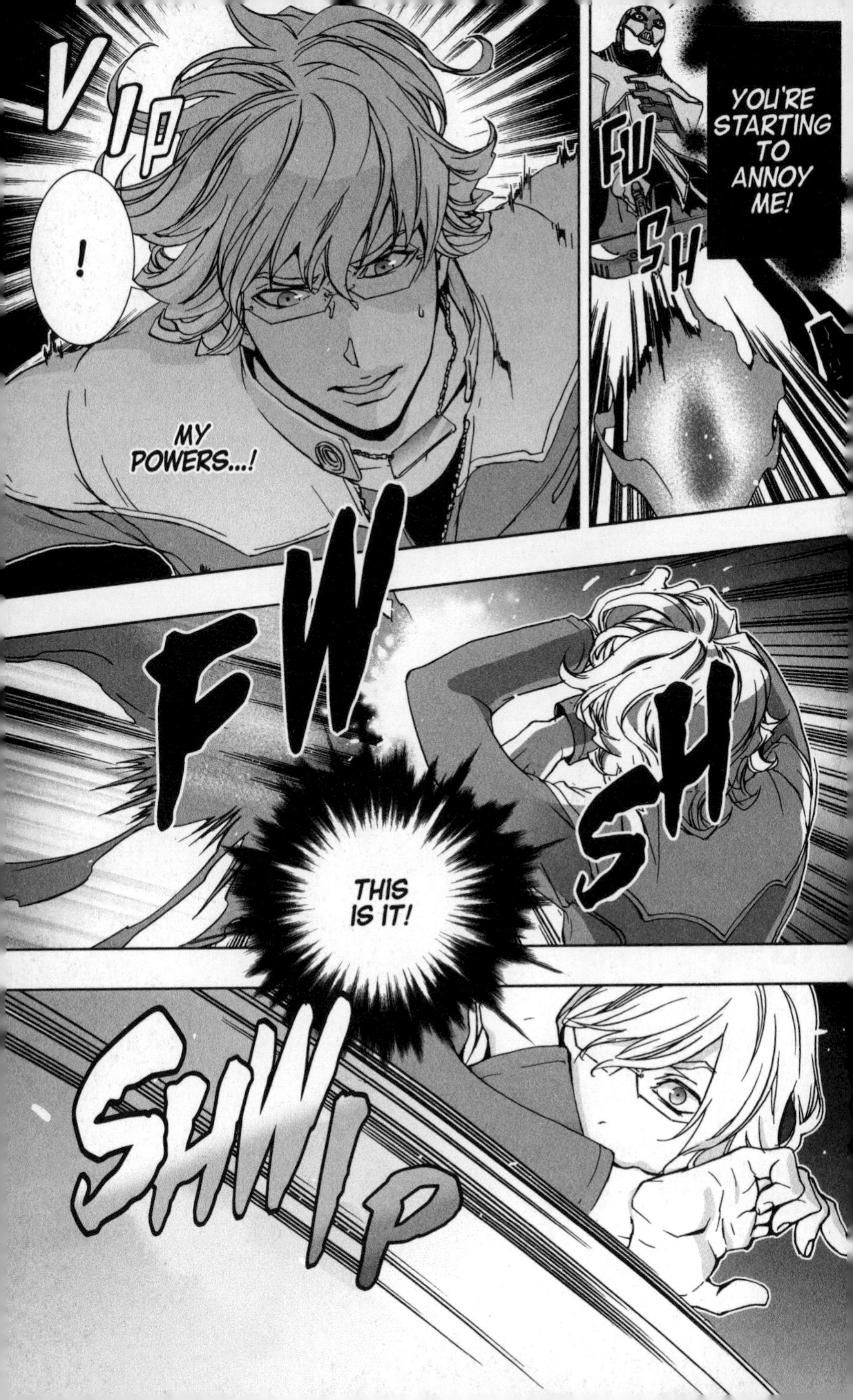
YOU'RE STARTING TO ANNOY ME!
FUSH
VIP
!
MY POWERS...!
FWSH
THIS IS IT!
SHWIP

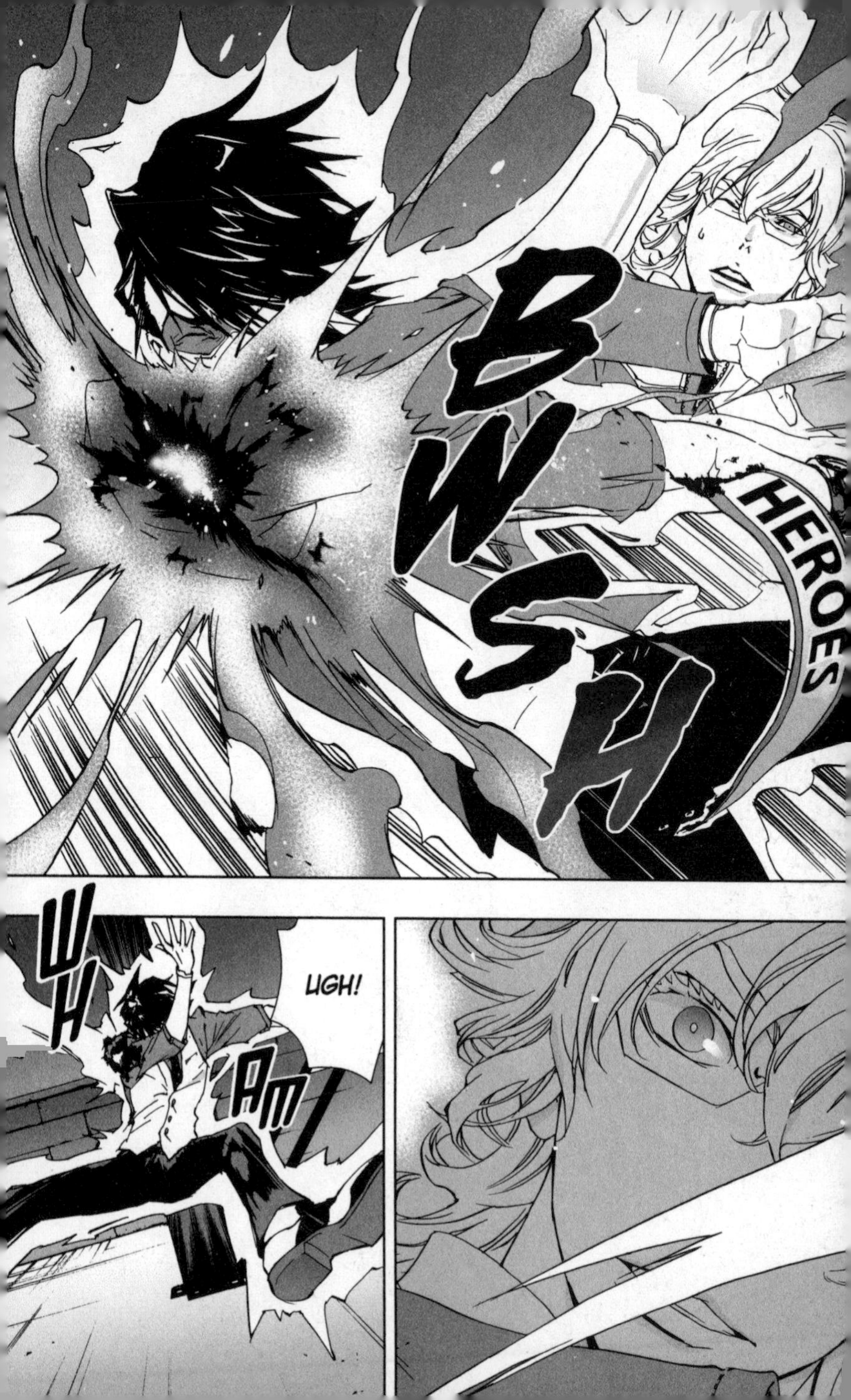
BWSH
HEROES
UGH!
WH
AM

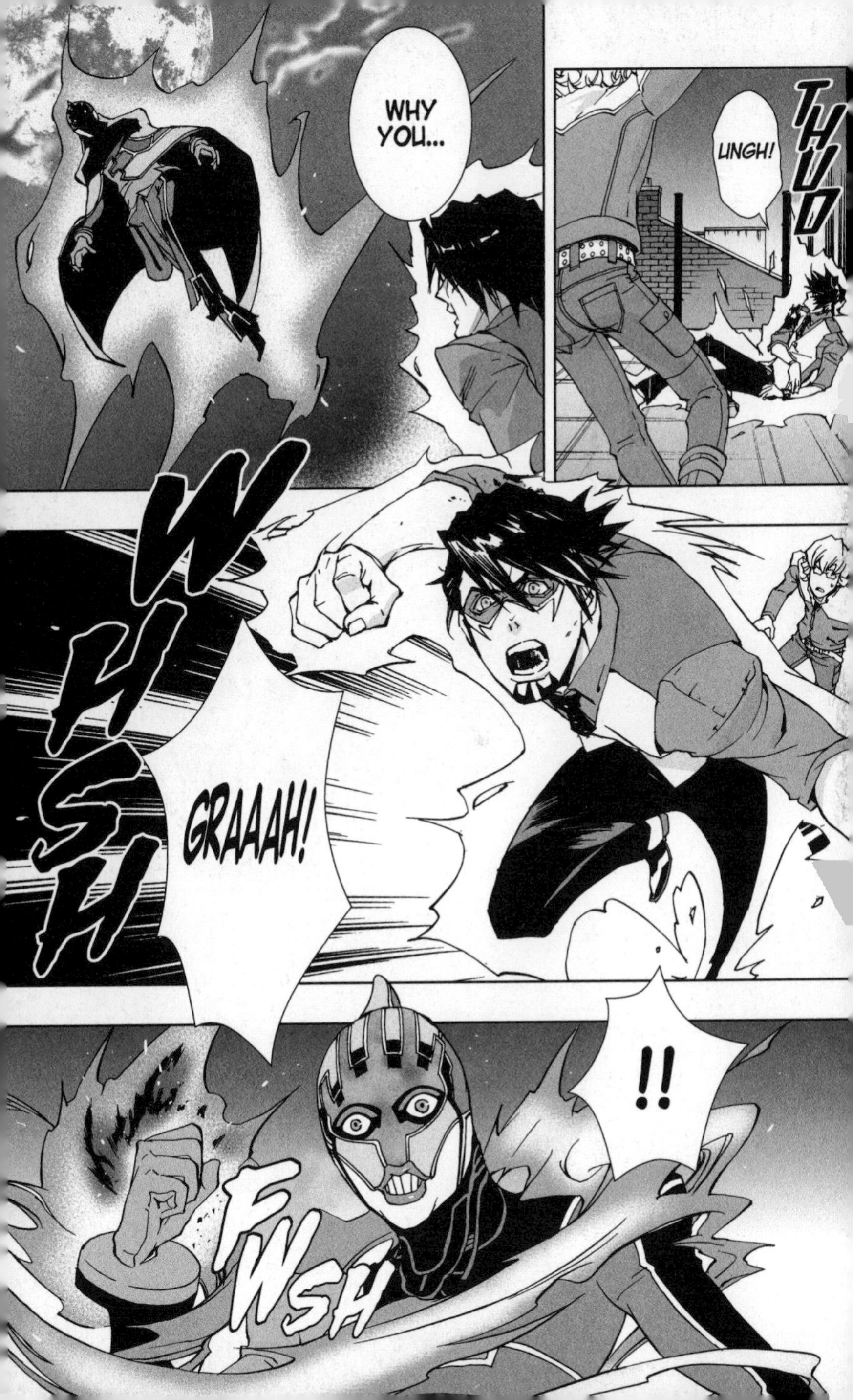

THUD
UNGH!
WHY YOU...
GRAAAH!
WHUSH
!!
FWSH

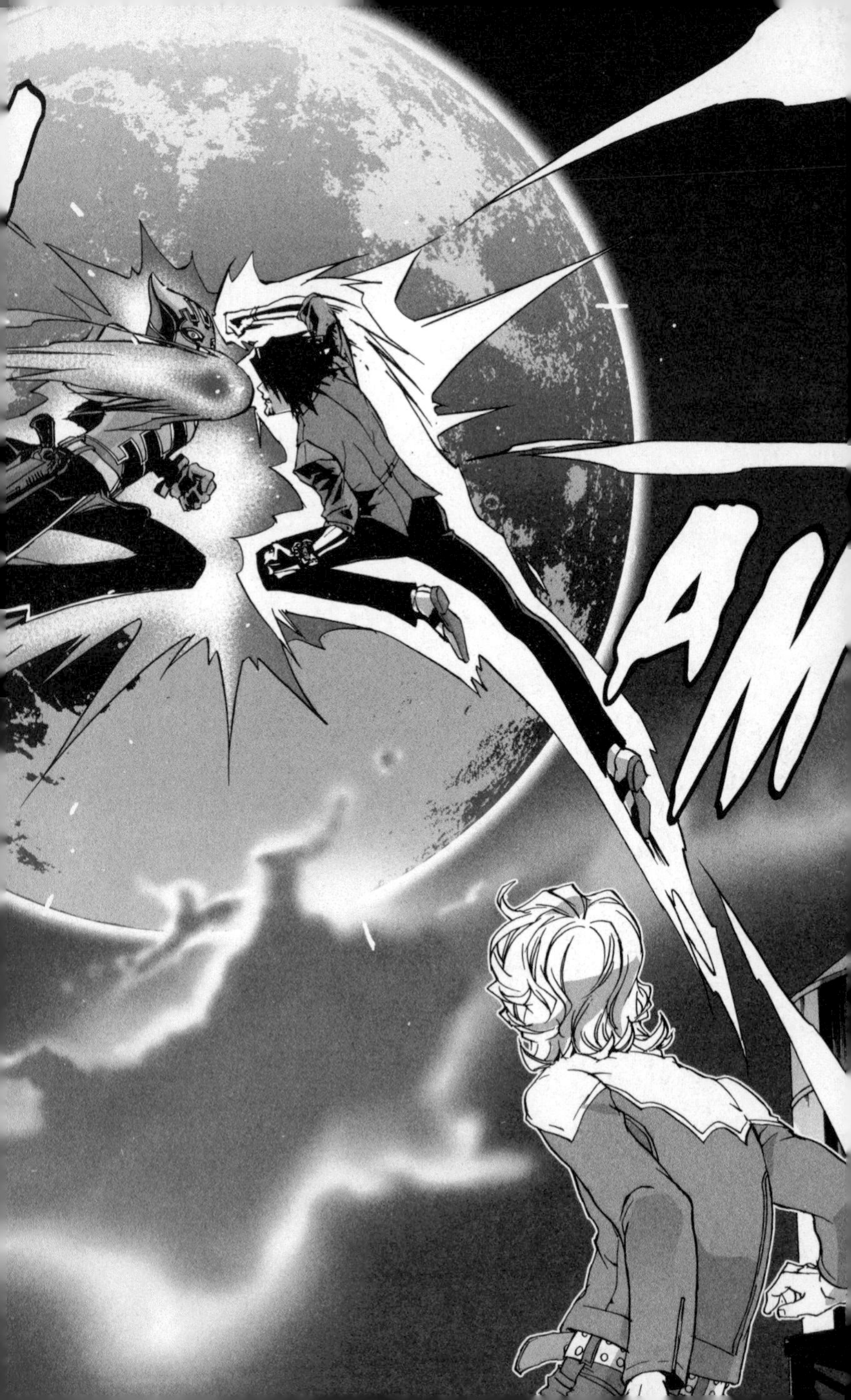
AM

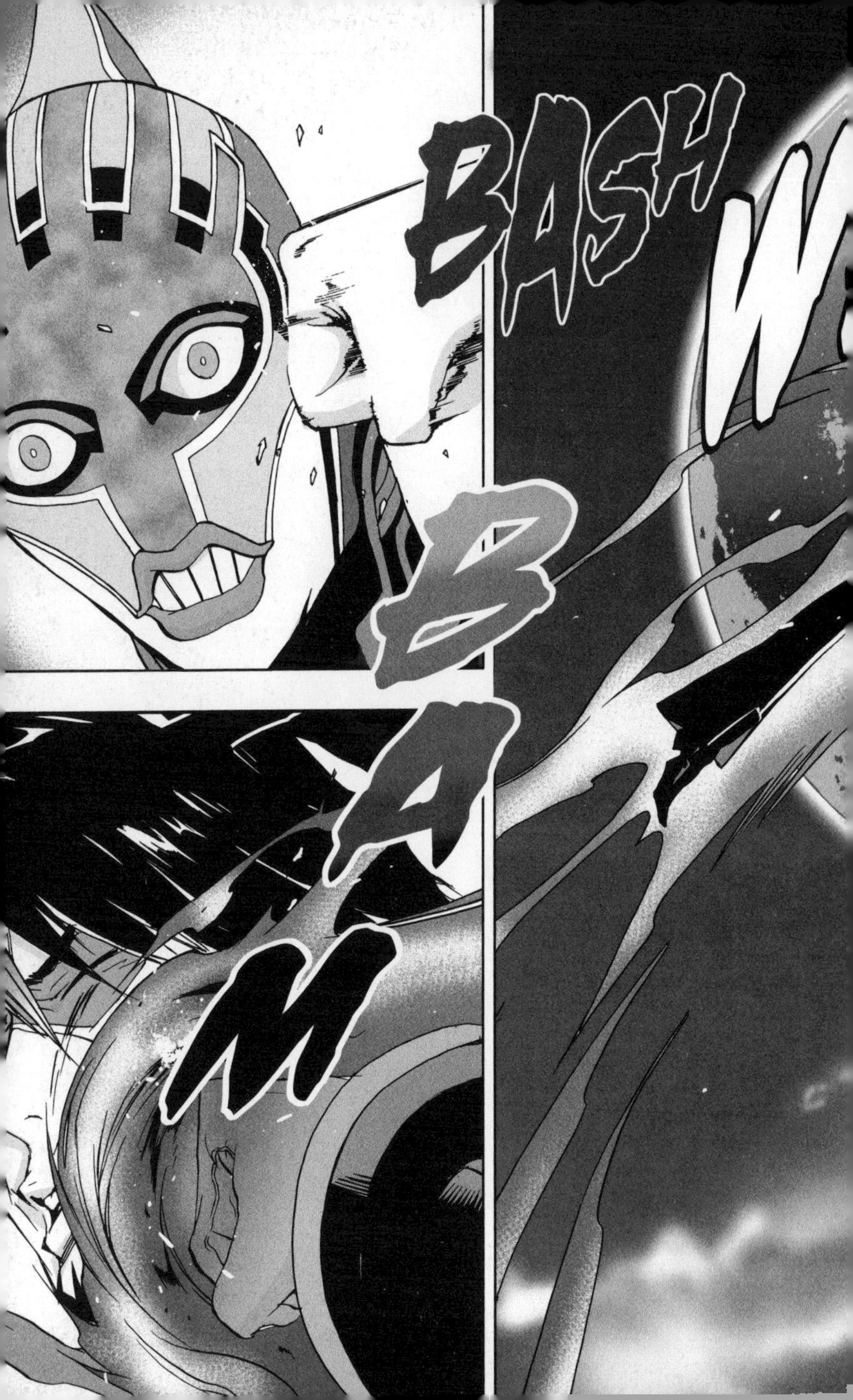
BASH
BAM

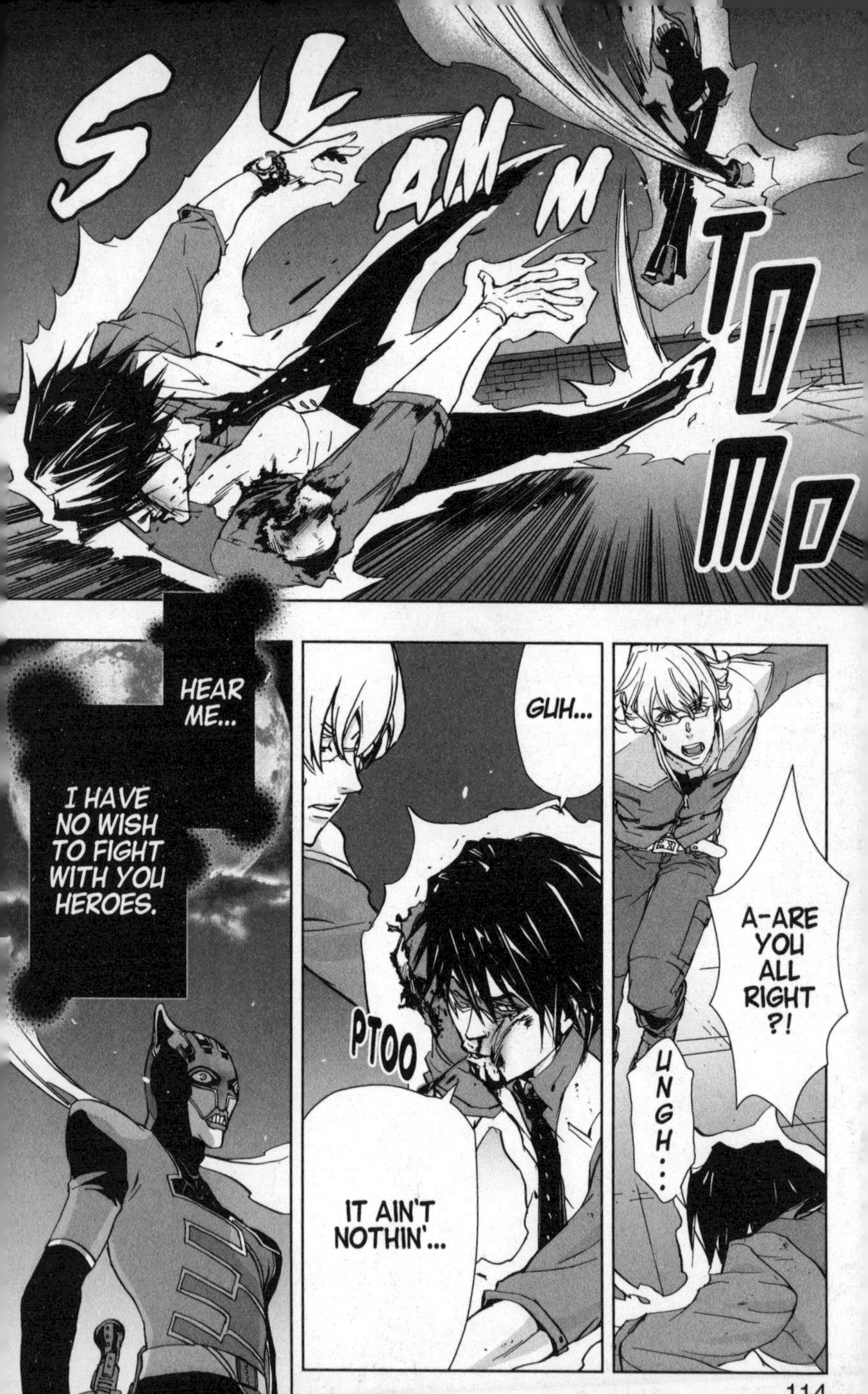
SLAMM
TOMP
A-ARE YOU ALL RIGHT?!
UNGH...
GUH...
PTOO
IT AIN'T NOTHIN'...
HEAR ME...
I HAVE NO WISH TO FIGHT WITH YOU HEROES.

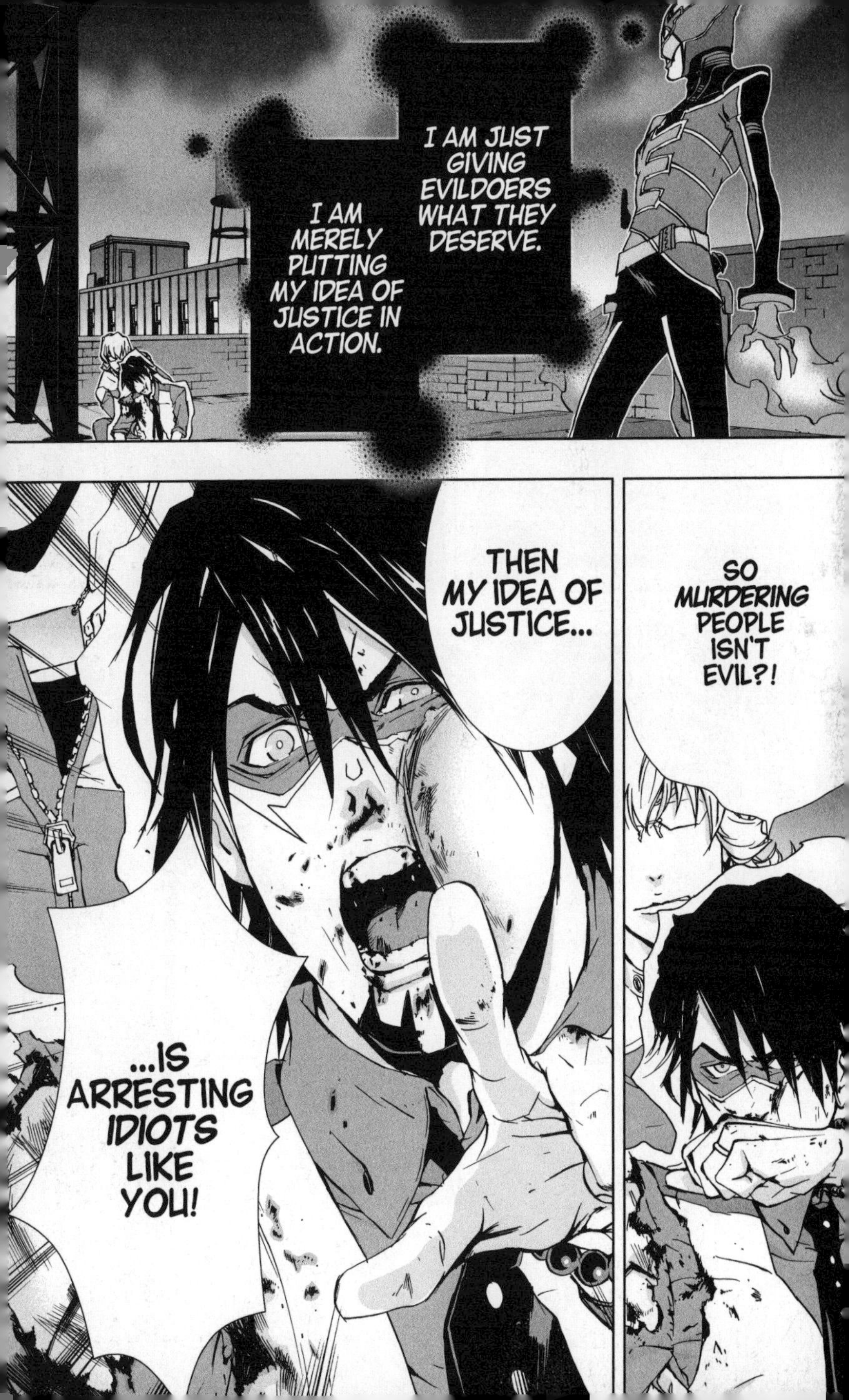
I AM JUST GIVING EVILDOERS WHAT THEY DESERVE.
I AM MERELY PUTTING MY IDEA OF JUSTICE IN ACTION.
SO MURDERING PEOPLE ISN'T EVIL?!
THEN MY IDEA OF JUSTICE...
...IS ARRESTING IDIOTS LIKE YOU!

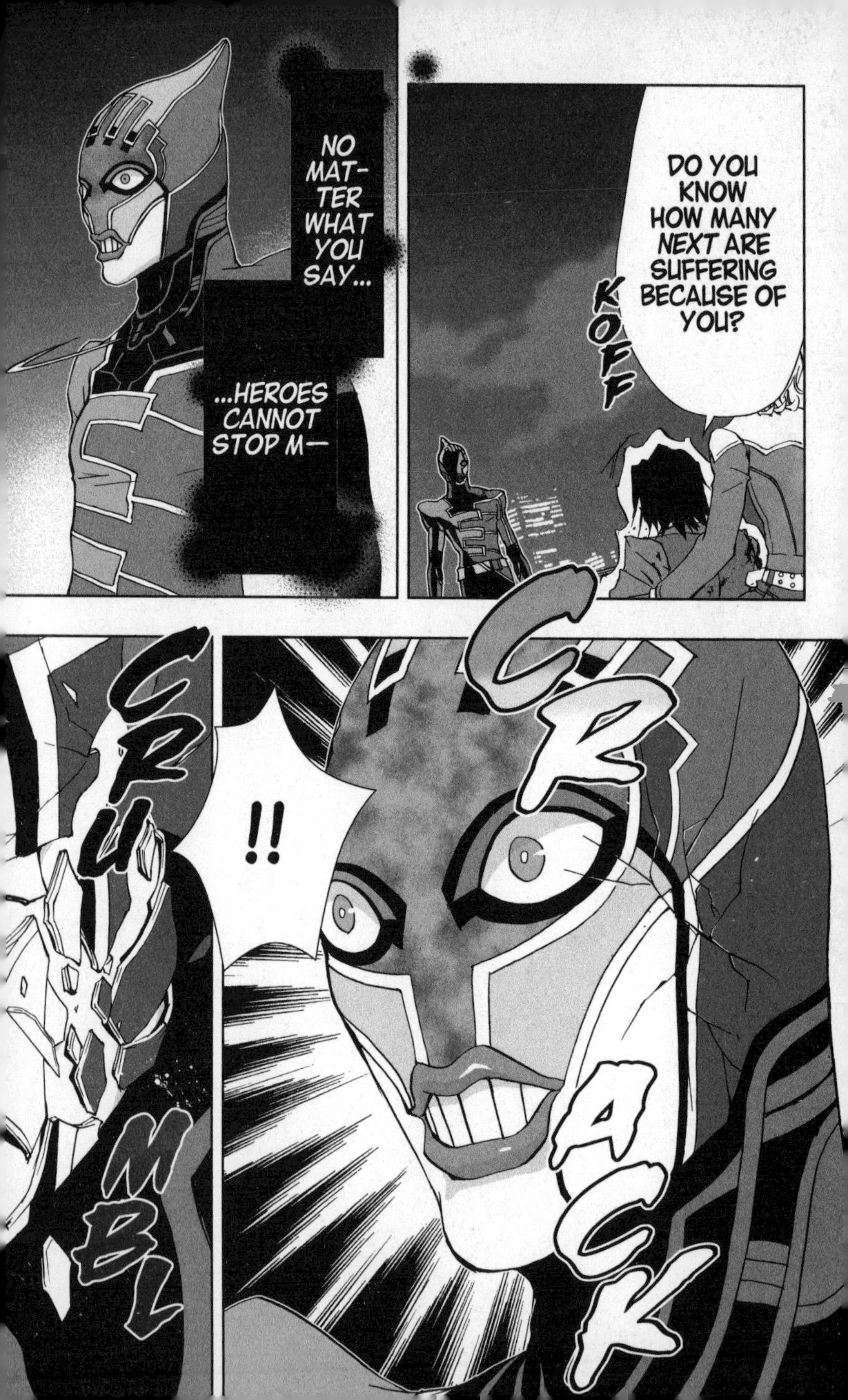
DO YOU KNOW HOW MANY NEXT ARE SUFFERING BECAUSE OF YOU?
KOFF
NO MAT-TER WHAT YOU SAY...
...HEROES CANNOT STOP M—
CRACK
!!
CRUMBL

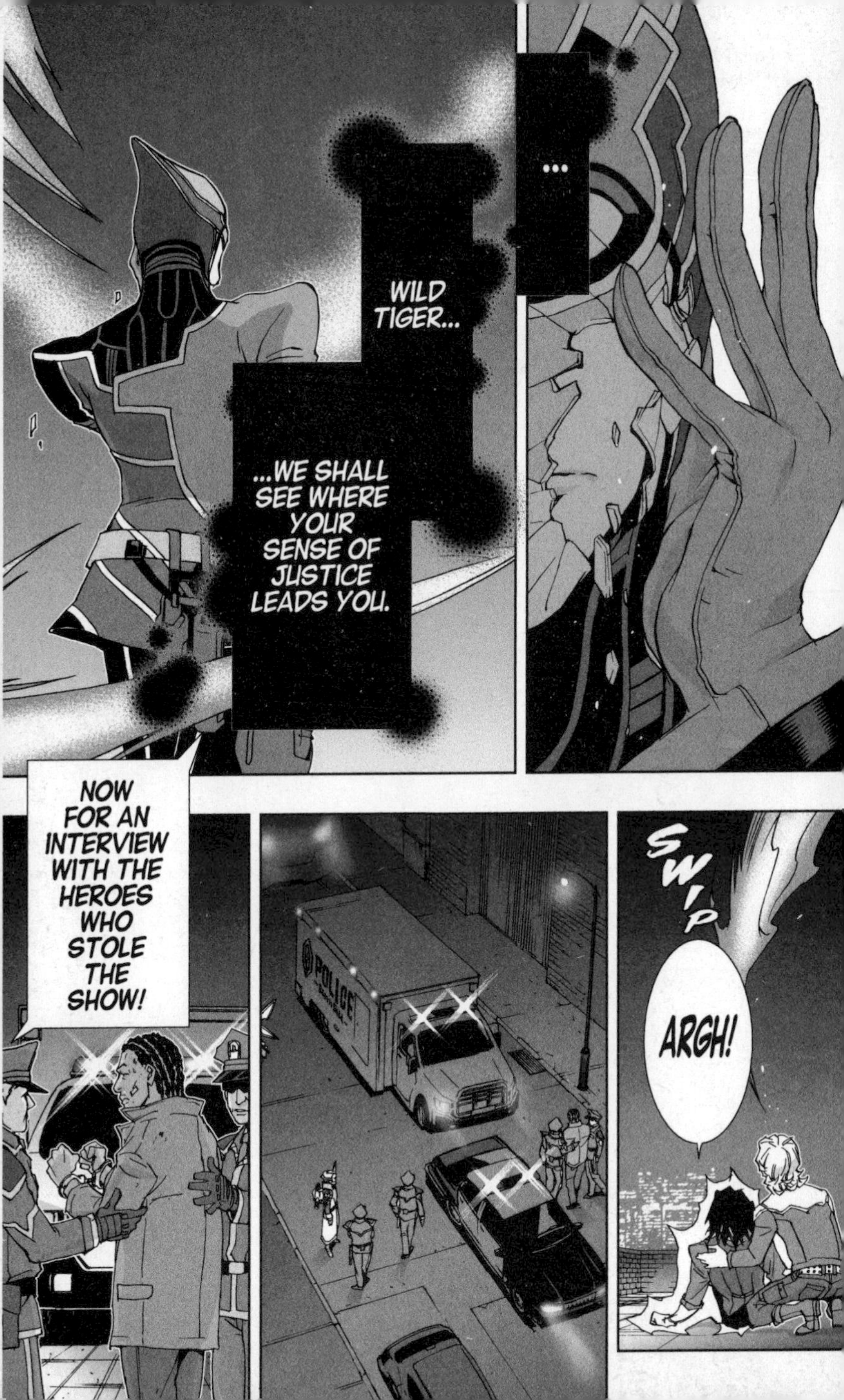
...
WILD TIGER...
...WE SHALL SEE WHERE YOUR SENSE OF JUSTICE LEADS YOU.
SWIP
ARGH!
NOW FOR AN INTERVIEW WITH THE HEROES WHO STOLE THE SHOW!

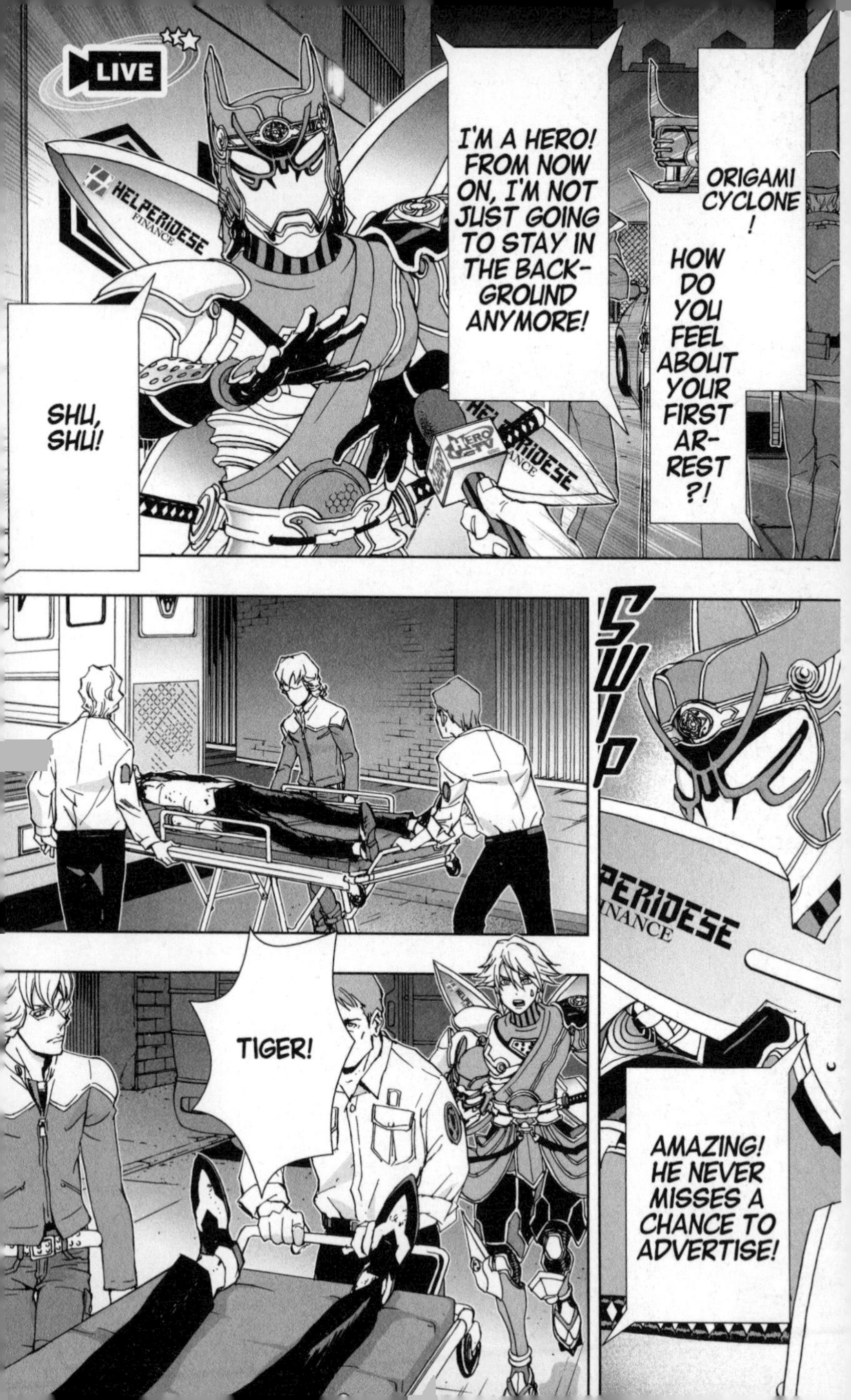
LIVE
ORIGAMI CYCLONE! HOW DO YOU FEEL ABOUT YOUR FIRST AR-REST?!
I'M A HERO! FROM NOW ON, I'M NOT JUST GOING TO STAY IN THE BACK-GROUND ANYMORE!
SHU, SHU!
HELPERIDESE FINANCE
HERO TV
SWIP
AMAZING! HE NEVER MISSES A CHANCE TO ADVERTISE!
TIGER!

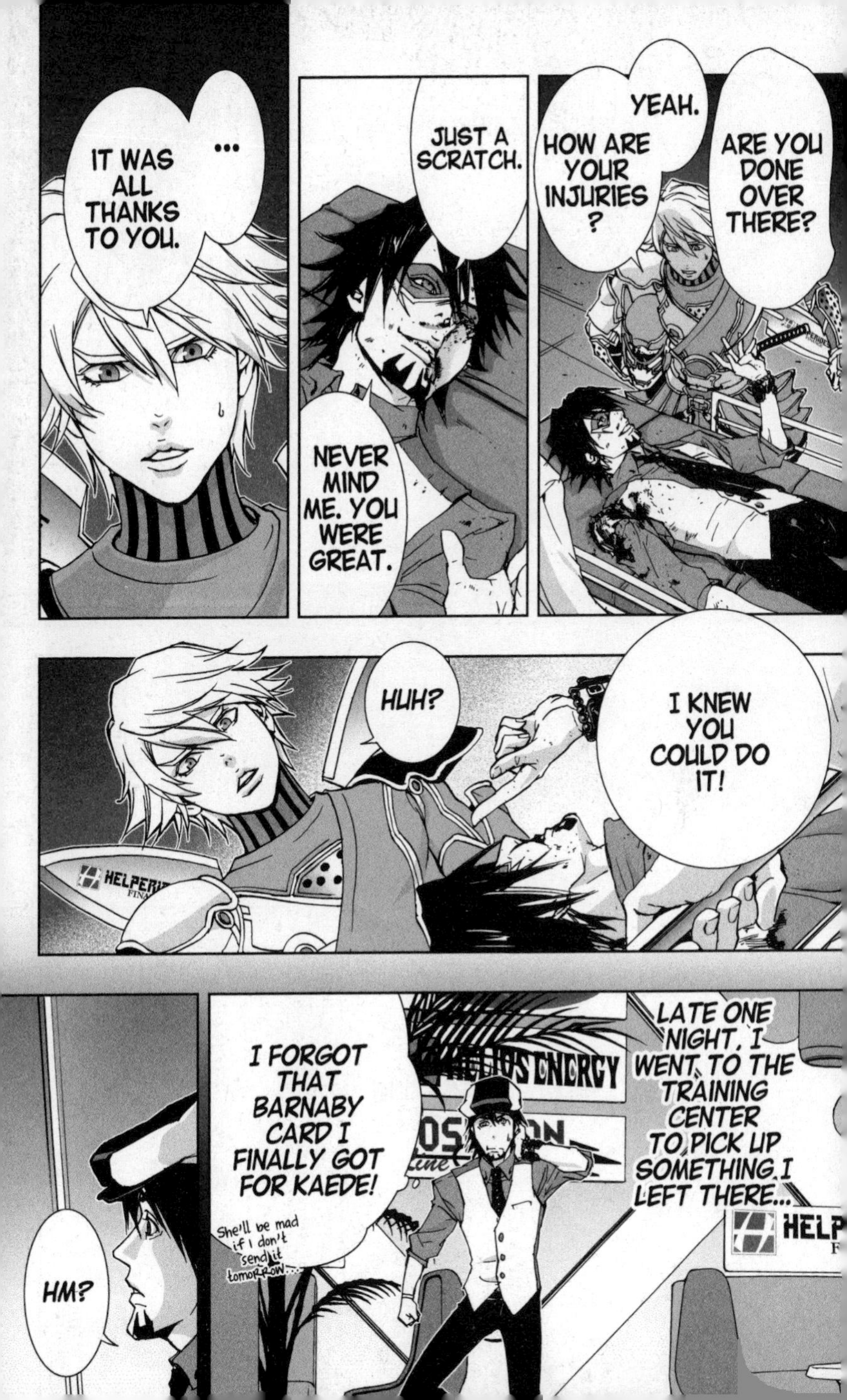
ARE YOU DONE OVER THERE?
YEAH.
HOW ARE YOUR INJURIES ?
JUST A SCRATCH.
NEVER MIND ME. YOU WERE GREAT.
...
IT WAS ALL THANKS TO YOU.
I KNEW YOU COULD DO IT!
HUH?
LATE ONE NIGHT, I WENT TO THE TRAINING CENTER TO PICK UP SOMETHING I LEFT THERE...
HELIOS ENERGY
I FORGOT THAT BARNABY CARD I FINALLY GOT FOR KAEDE!
She'll be mad if I don't send it tomorrow...
HM?

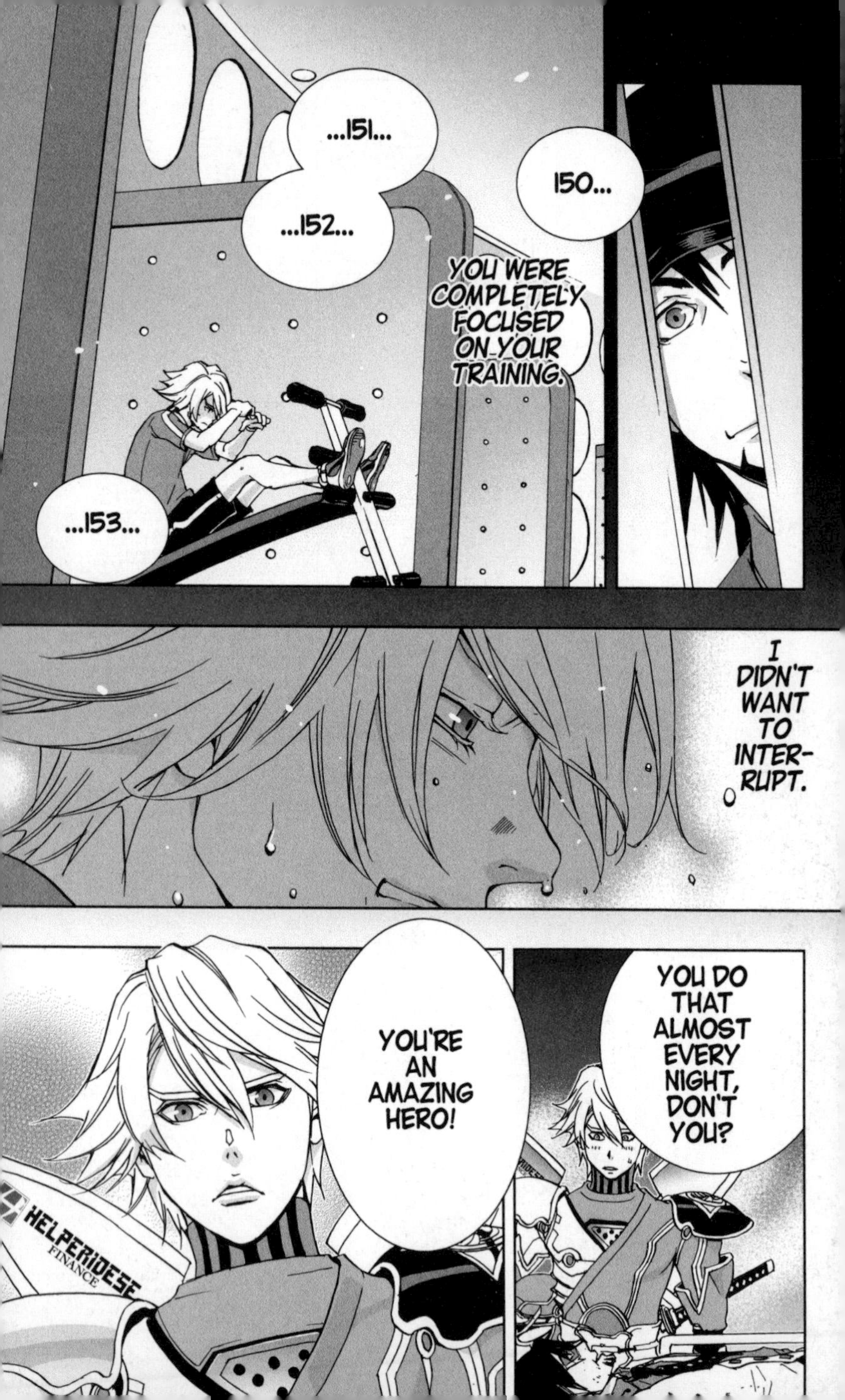
150...
...151...
...152...
YOU WERE COMPLETELY FOCUSED ON YOUR TRAINING.
...153...
I DIDN'T WANT TO INTER-RUPT.
YOU DO THAT ALMOST EVERY NIGHT, DON'T YOU?
YOU'RE AN AMAZING HERO!
HELPERIDESE FINANCE

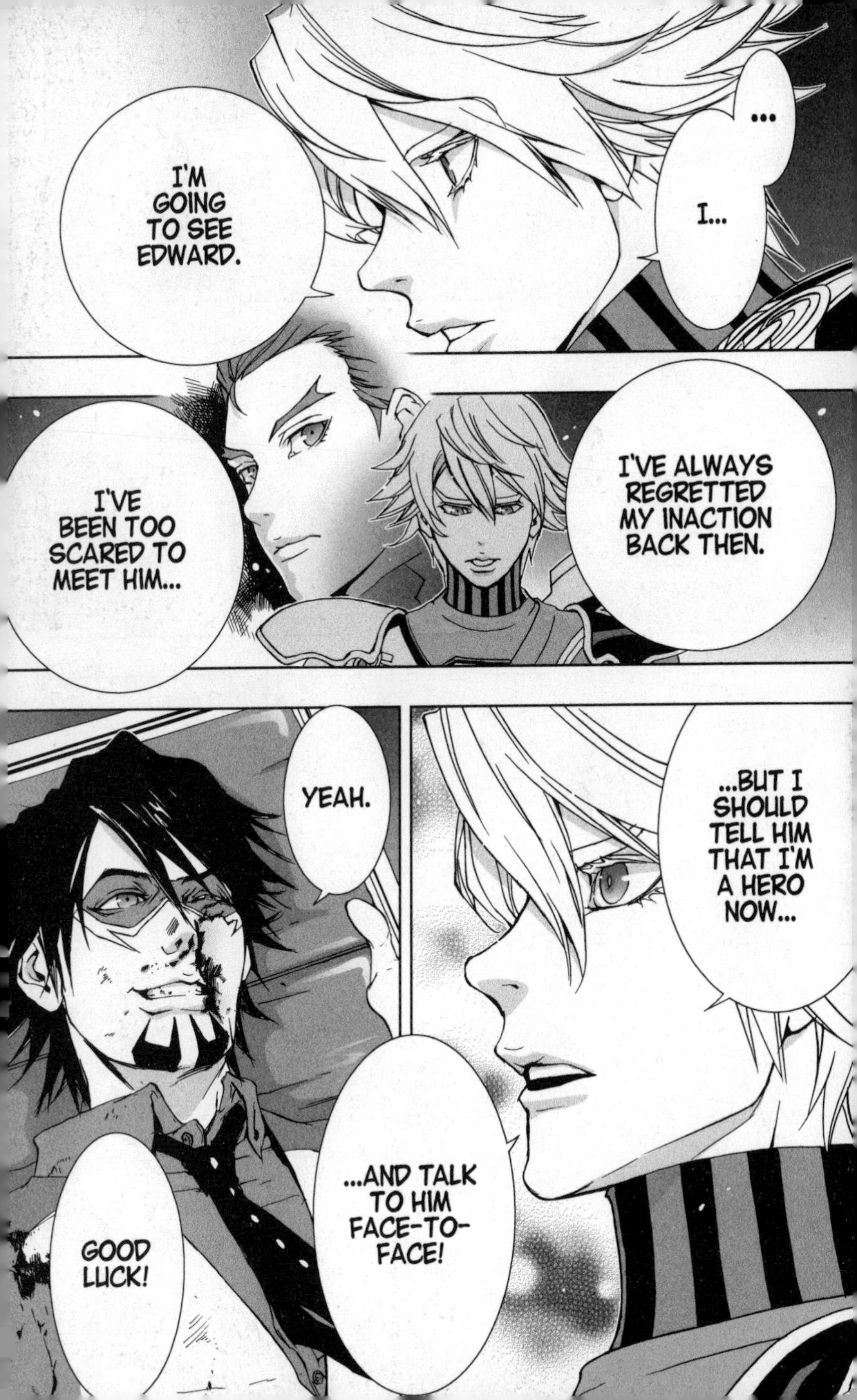
...
I...
I'M GOING TO SEE EDWARD.
I'VE ALWAYS REGRETTED MY INACTION BACK THEN.
I'VE BEEN TOO SCARED TO MEET HIM...
...BUT I SHOULD TELL HIM THAT I'M A HERO NOW...
...AND TALK TO HIM FACE-TO-FACE!
YEAH.
GOOD LUCK!

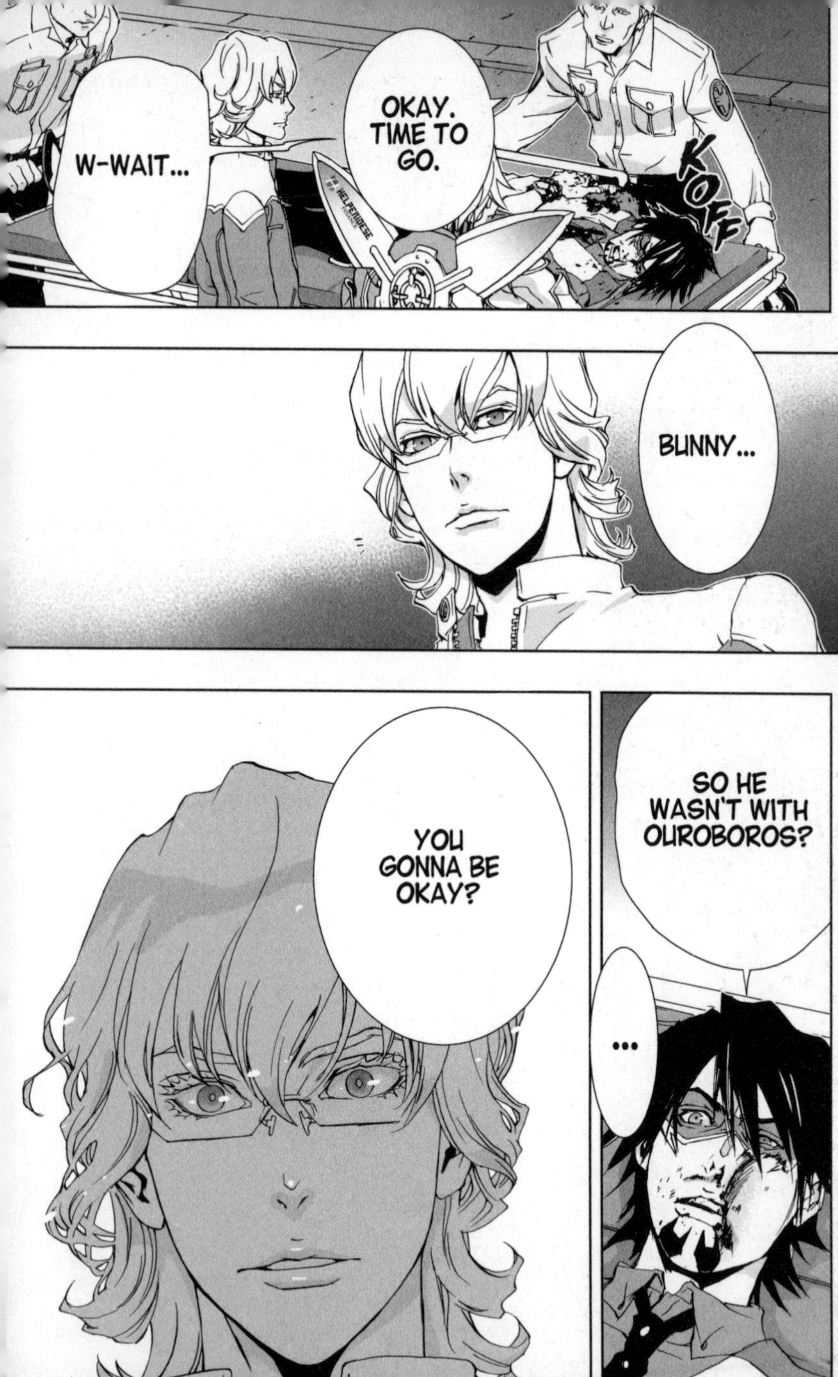
KOFF
OKAY. TIME TO GO.
W-WAIT...
BUNNY...
SO HE WASN'T WITH OUROBOROS?
...
YOU GONNA BE OKAY?

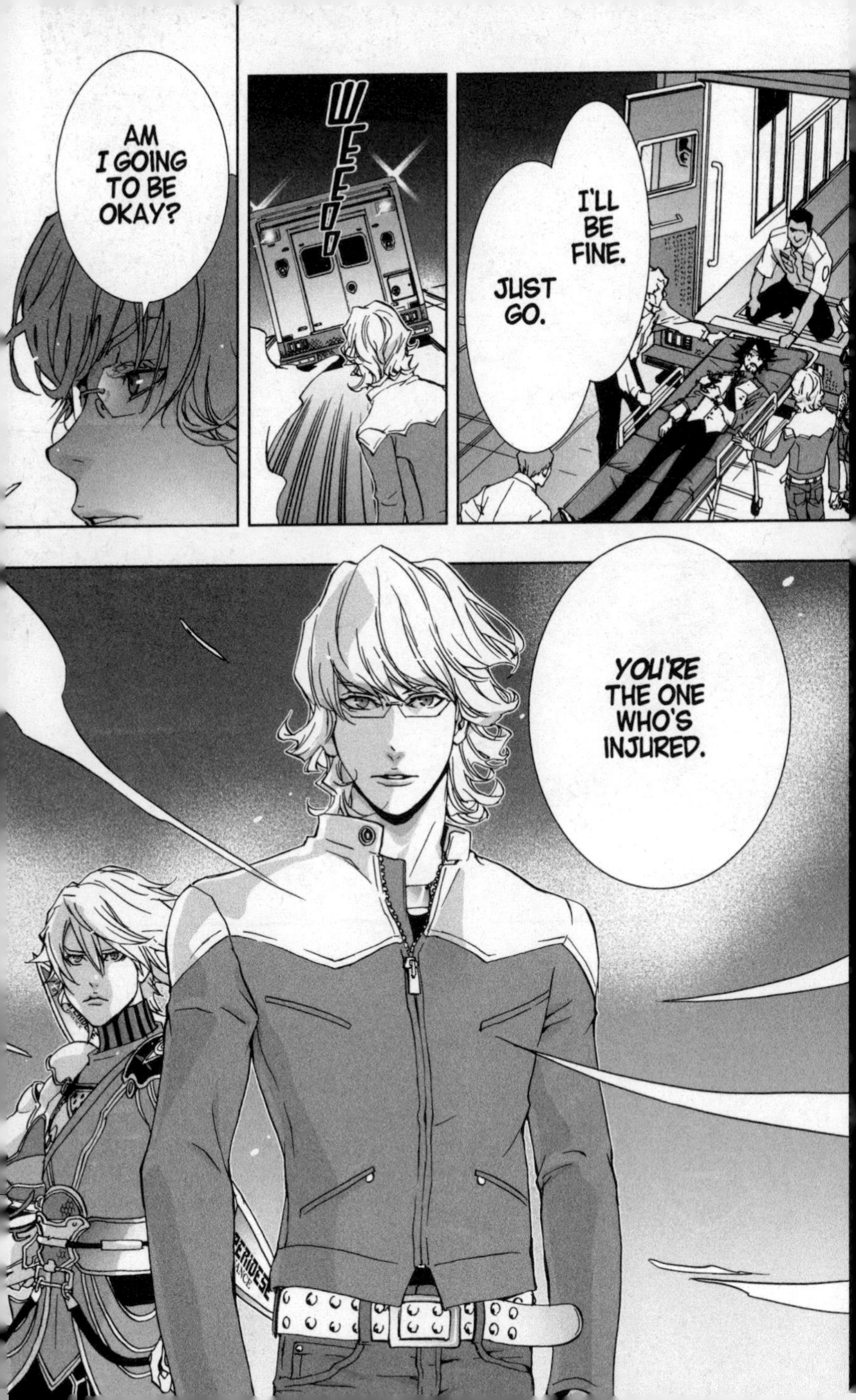
I'LL BE FINE.
JUST GO.
WEEOO
AM I GOING TO BE OKAY?
YOU'RE THE ONE WHO'S INJURED.

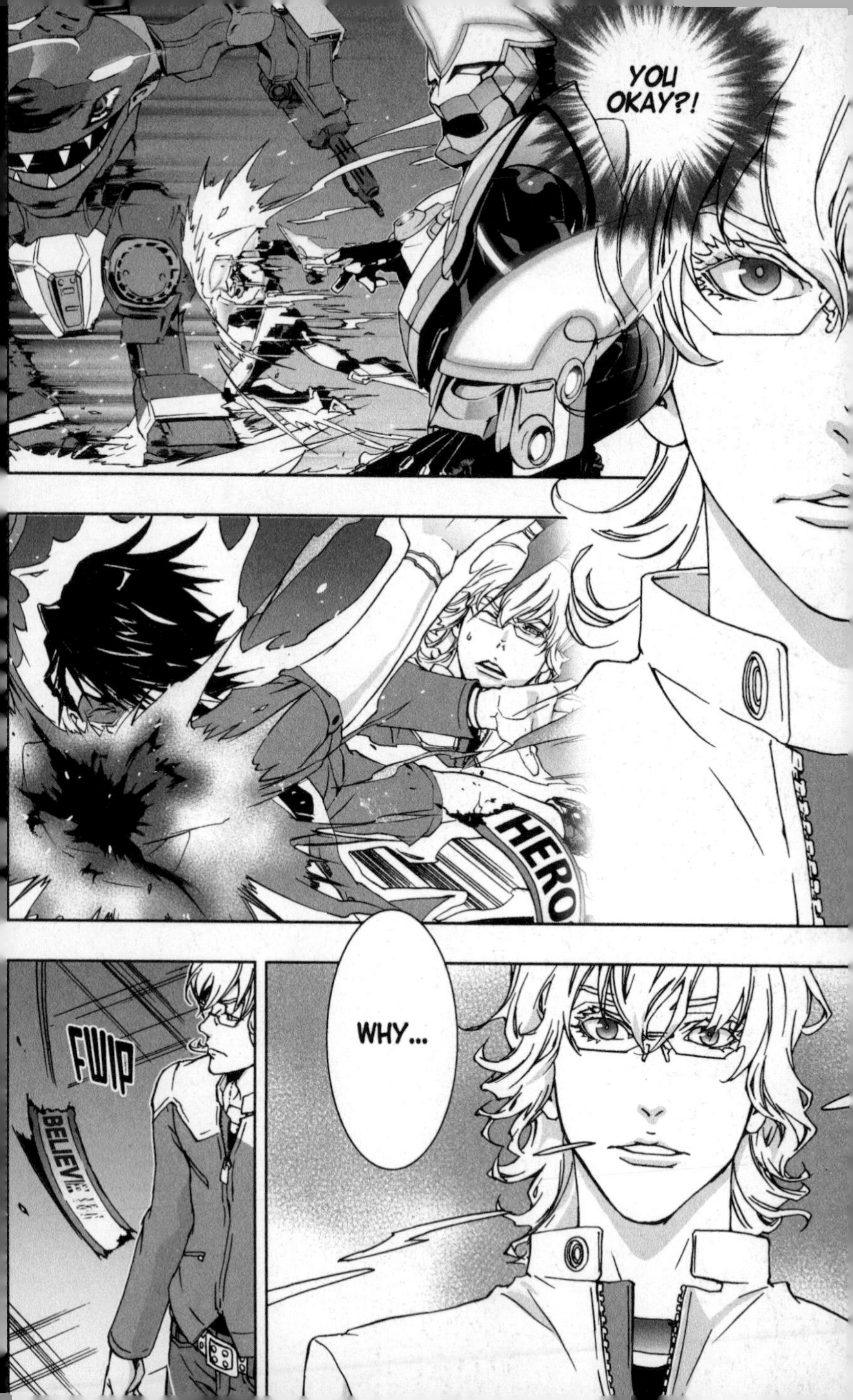
YOU OKAY?!
HERO
WHY...
FWIP
BELIEV

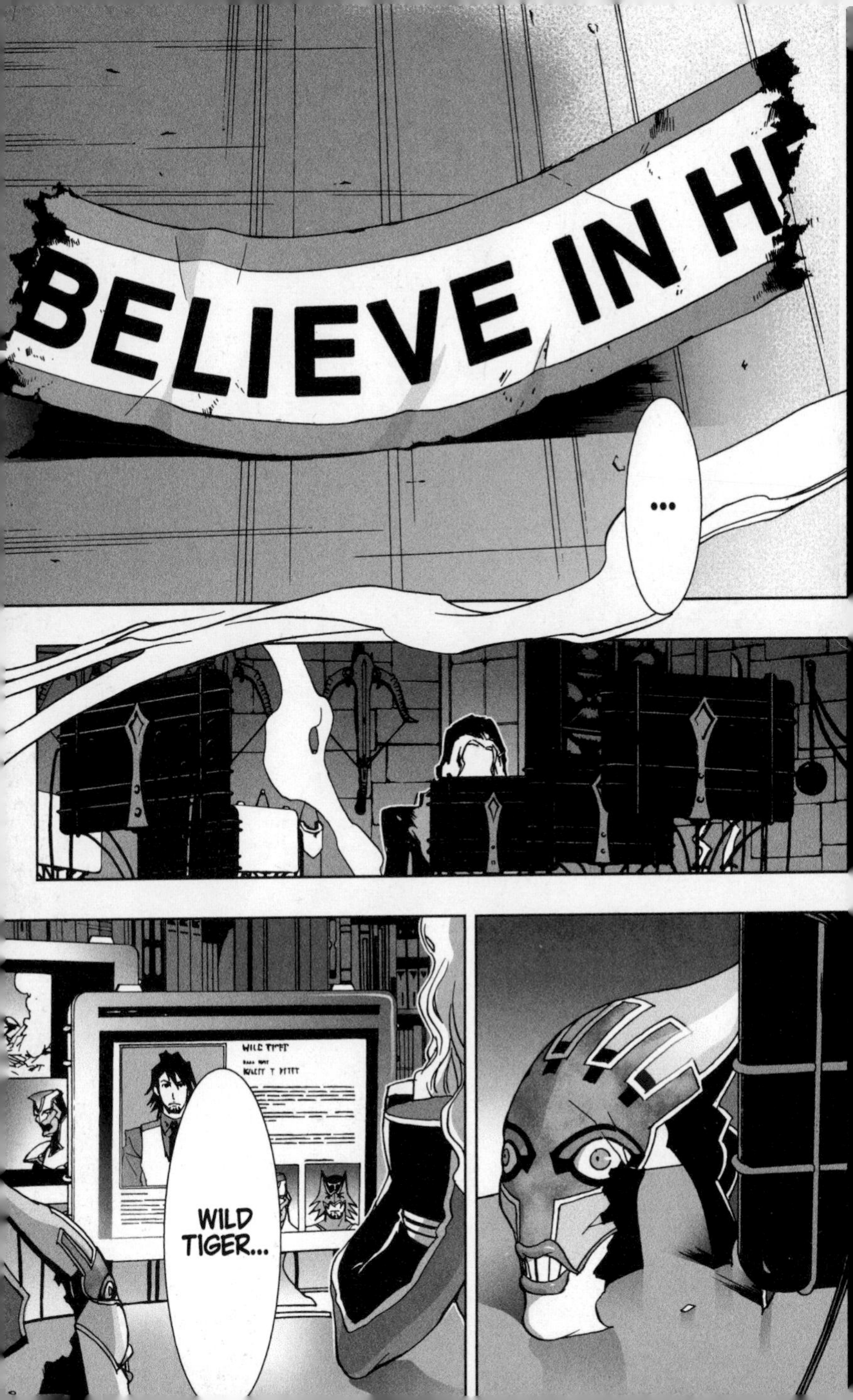
BELIEVE IN H
...
WILD TIGER...

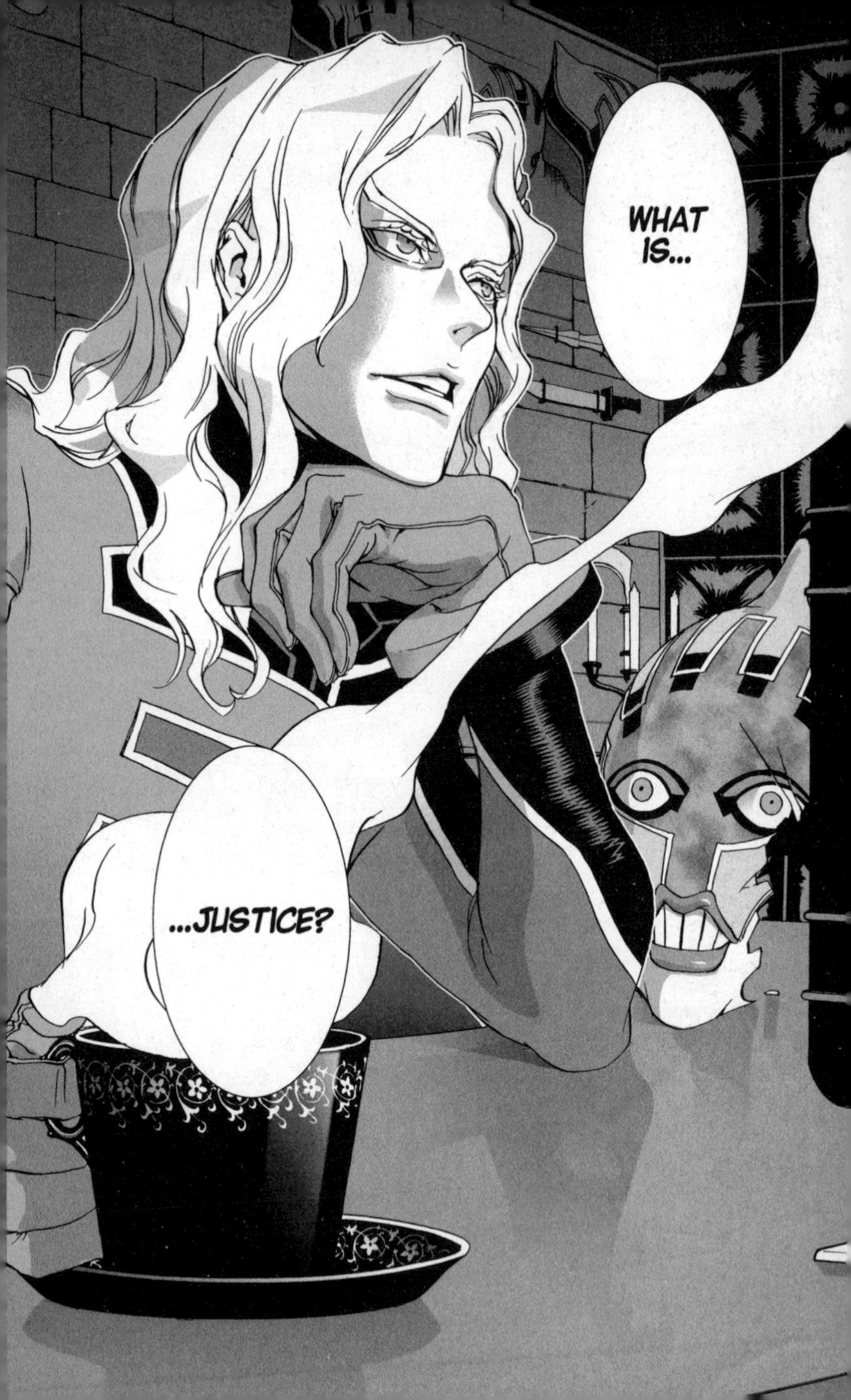
WHAT IS...
...JUSTICE?

TIGER&BUNNY

TIGER&BUNNY

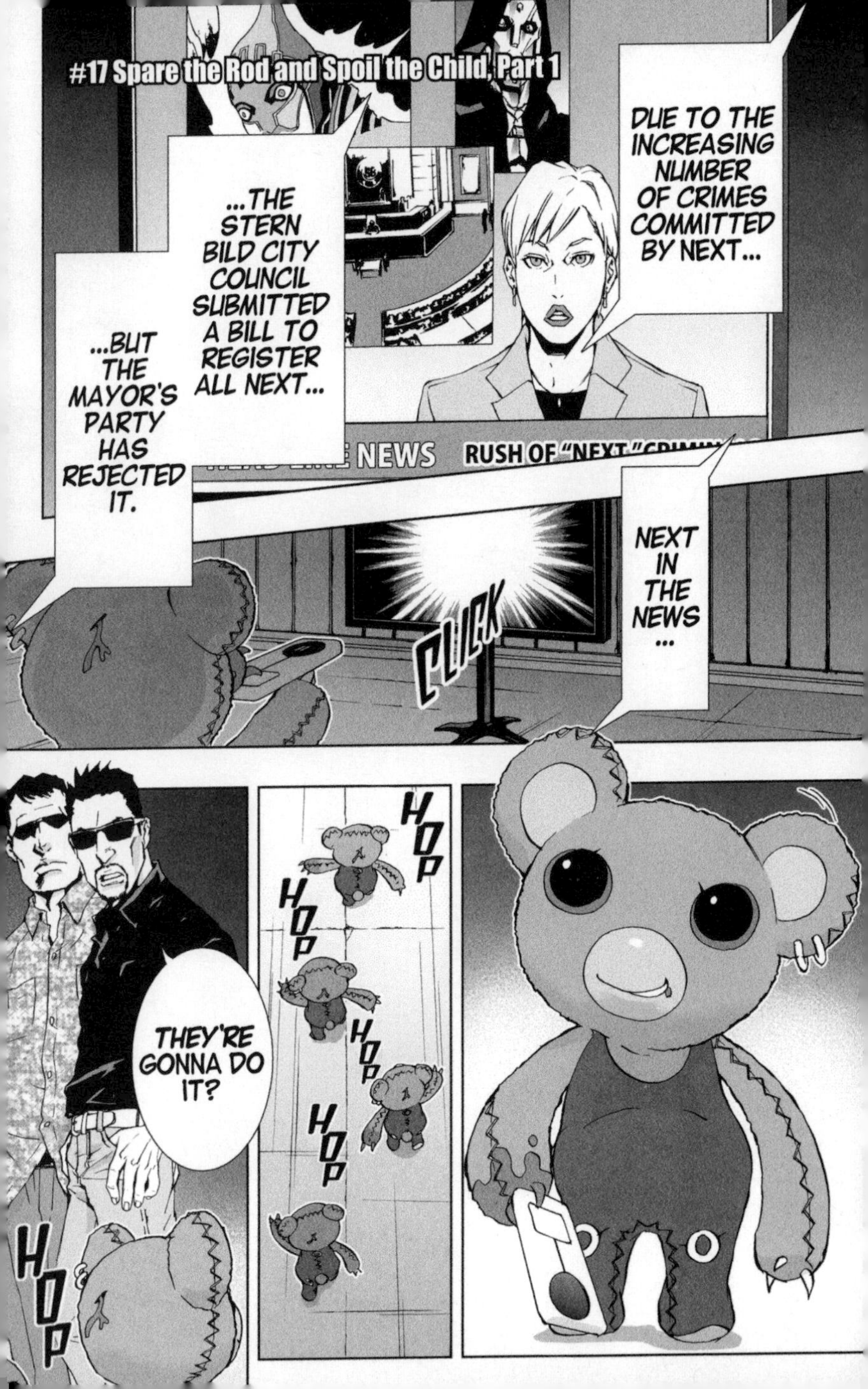
#17 Spare the Rod and Spoil the Child, Part 1
DUE TO THE INCREASING NUMBER OF CRIMES COMMITTED BY NEXT...
...THE STERN BILD CITY COUNCIL SUBMITTED A BILL TO REGISTER ALL NEXT...
...BUT THE MAYOR'S PARTY HAS REJECTED IT.
NEWS
RUSH OF
NEXT IN THE NEWS ...
CLICK
HOP
HOP
HOP
HOP
THEY'RE GONNA DO IT?
HOP

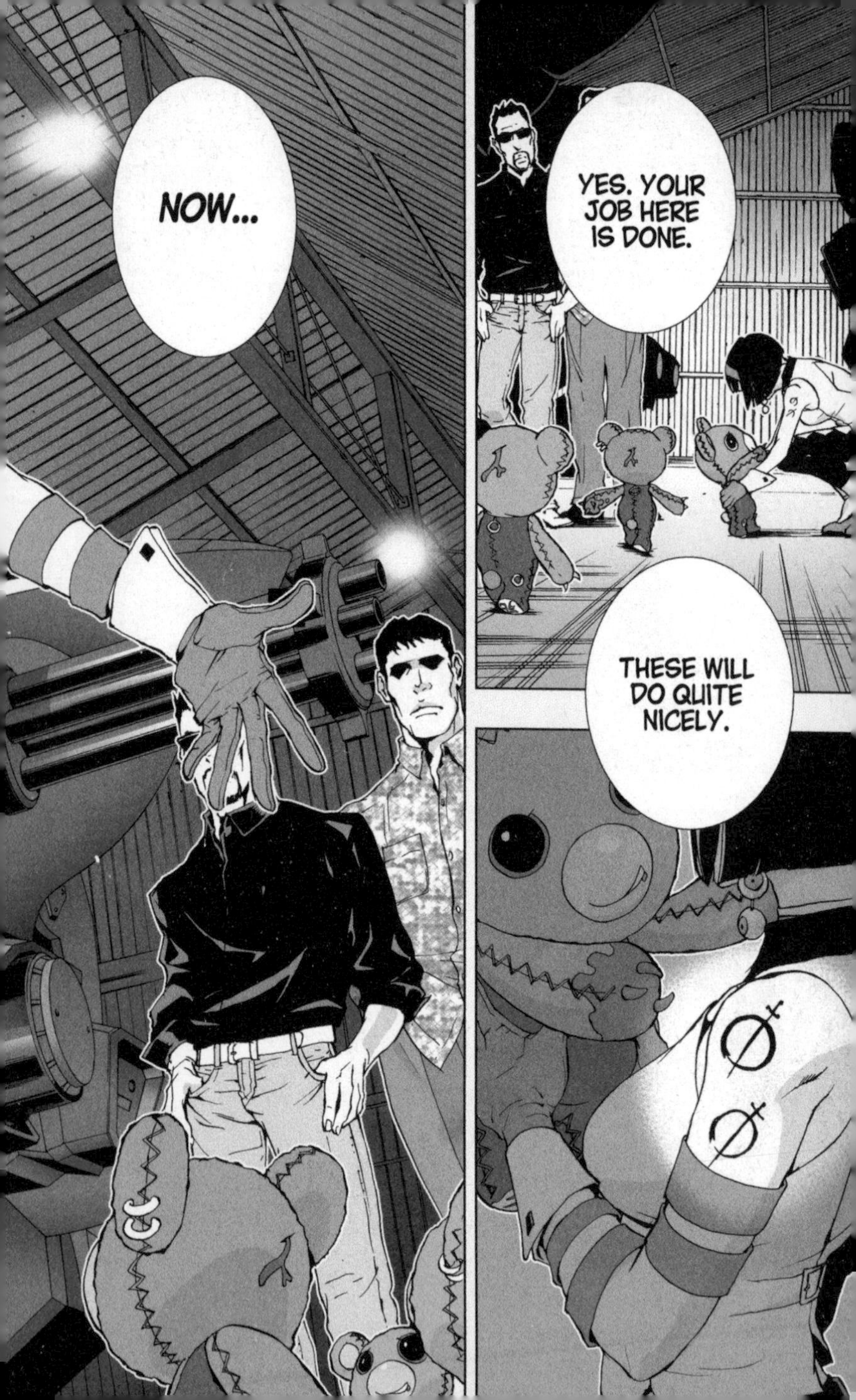
YES. YOUR JOB HERE IS DONE.
THESE WILL DO QUITE NICELY.
NOW...

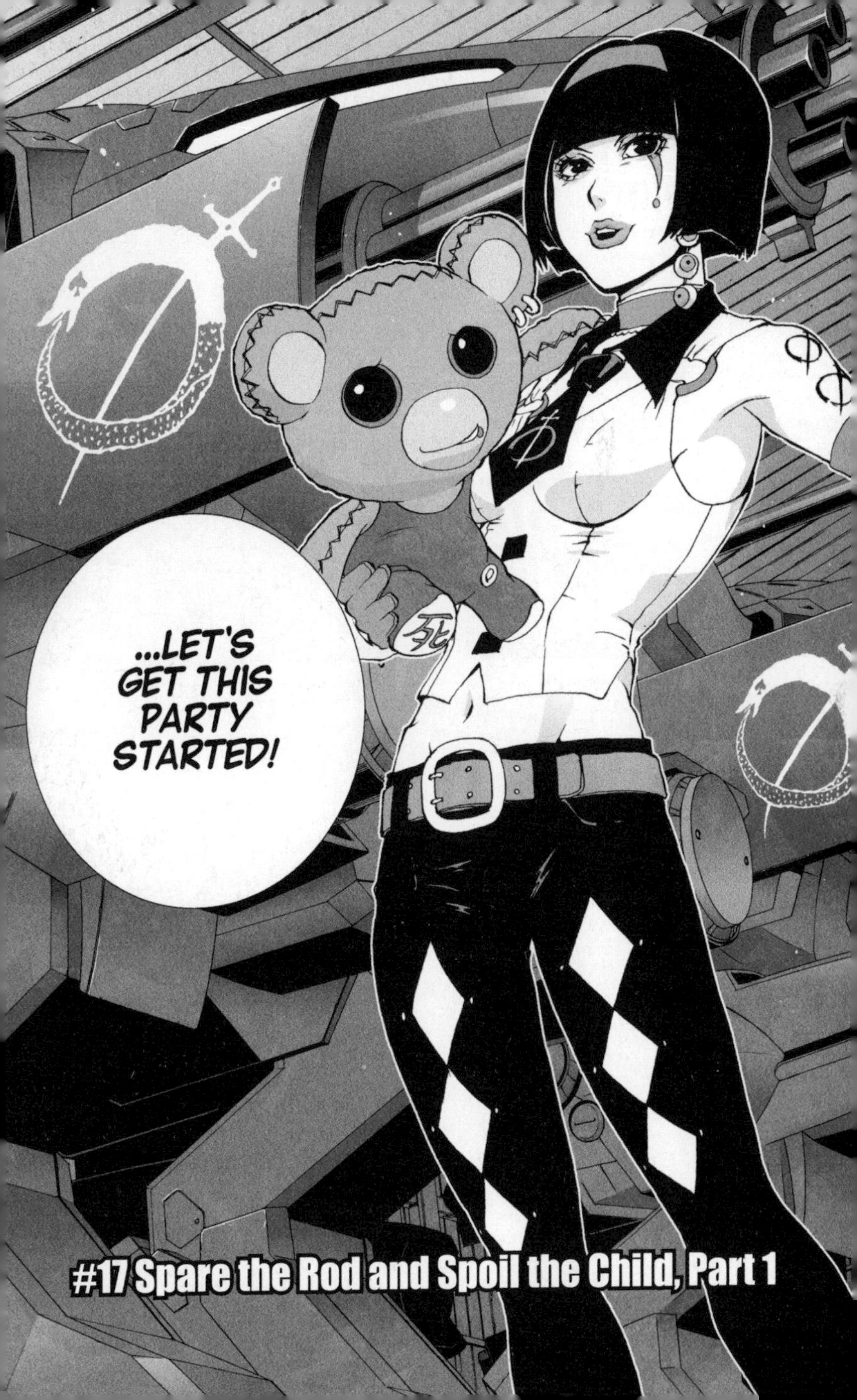
...LET'S GET THIS PARTY STARTED!

#17 Spare the Rod and Spoil the Child, Part 1

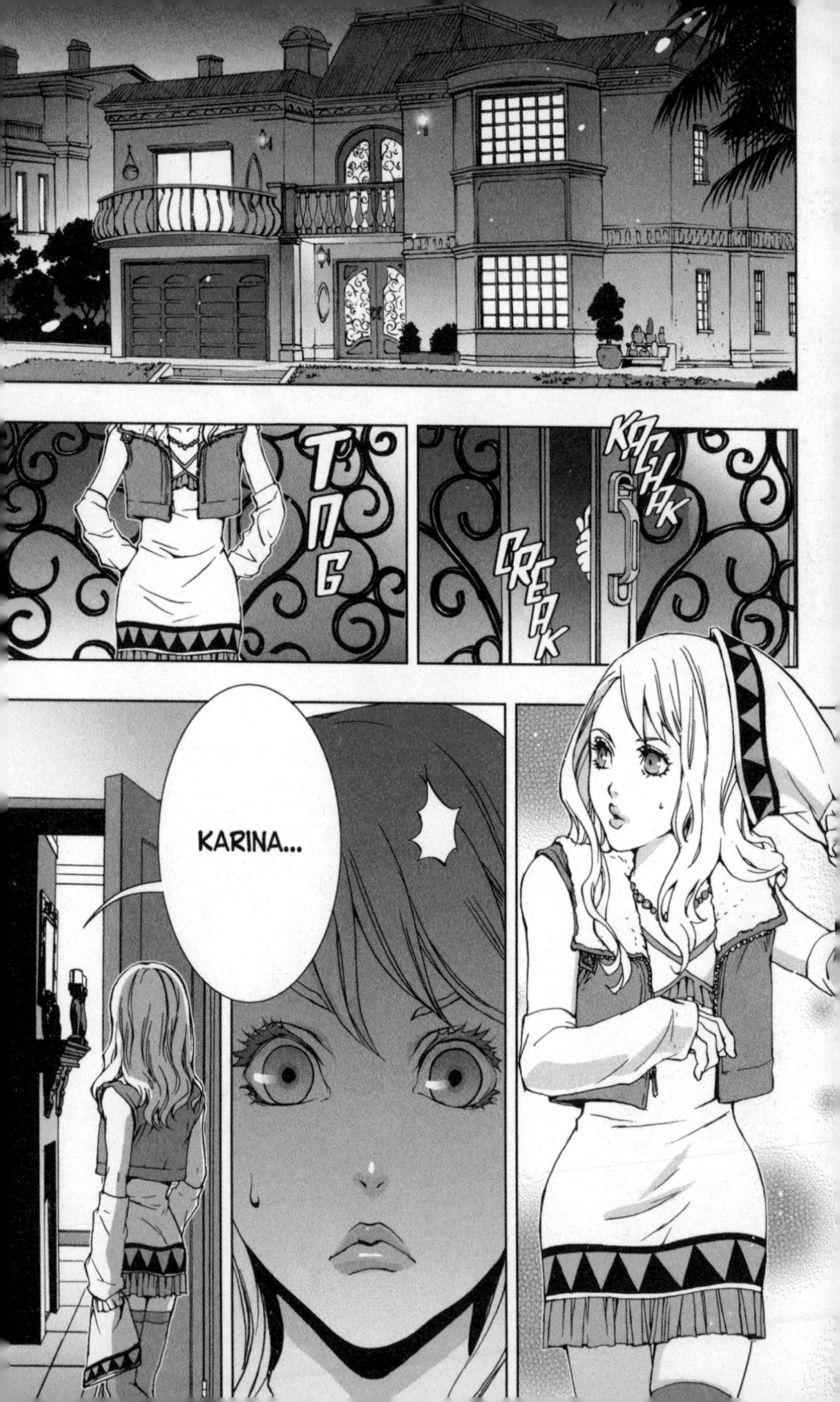
KACHAK
CREAK
TING
KARINA...

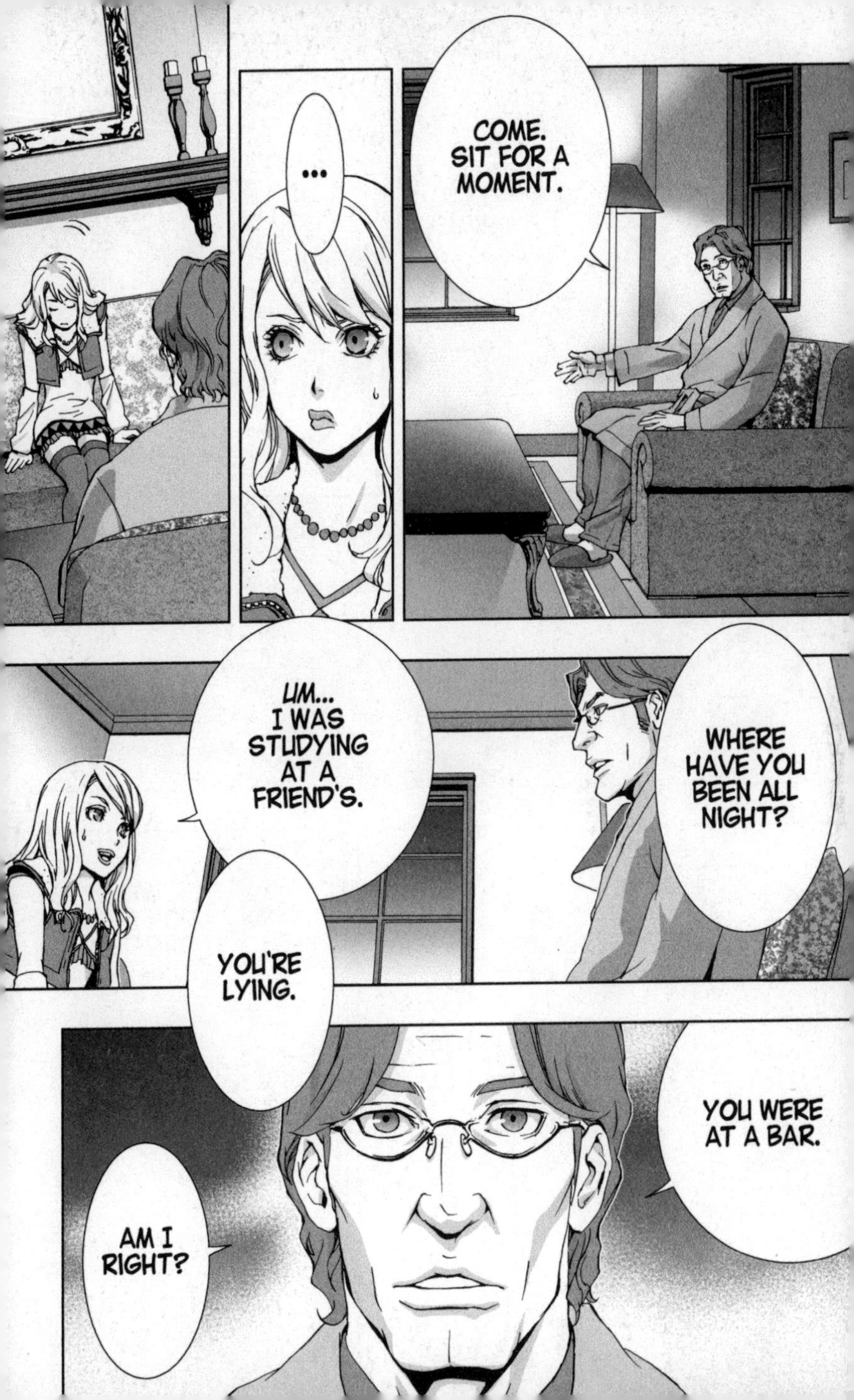
COME. SIT FOR A MOMENT.
...
WHERE HAVE YOU BEEN ALL NIGHT?
UM... I WAS STUDYING AT A FRIEND'S.
YOU'RE LYING.
YOU WERE AT A BAR.
AM I RIGHT?

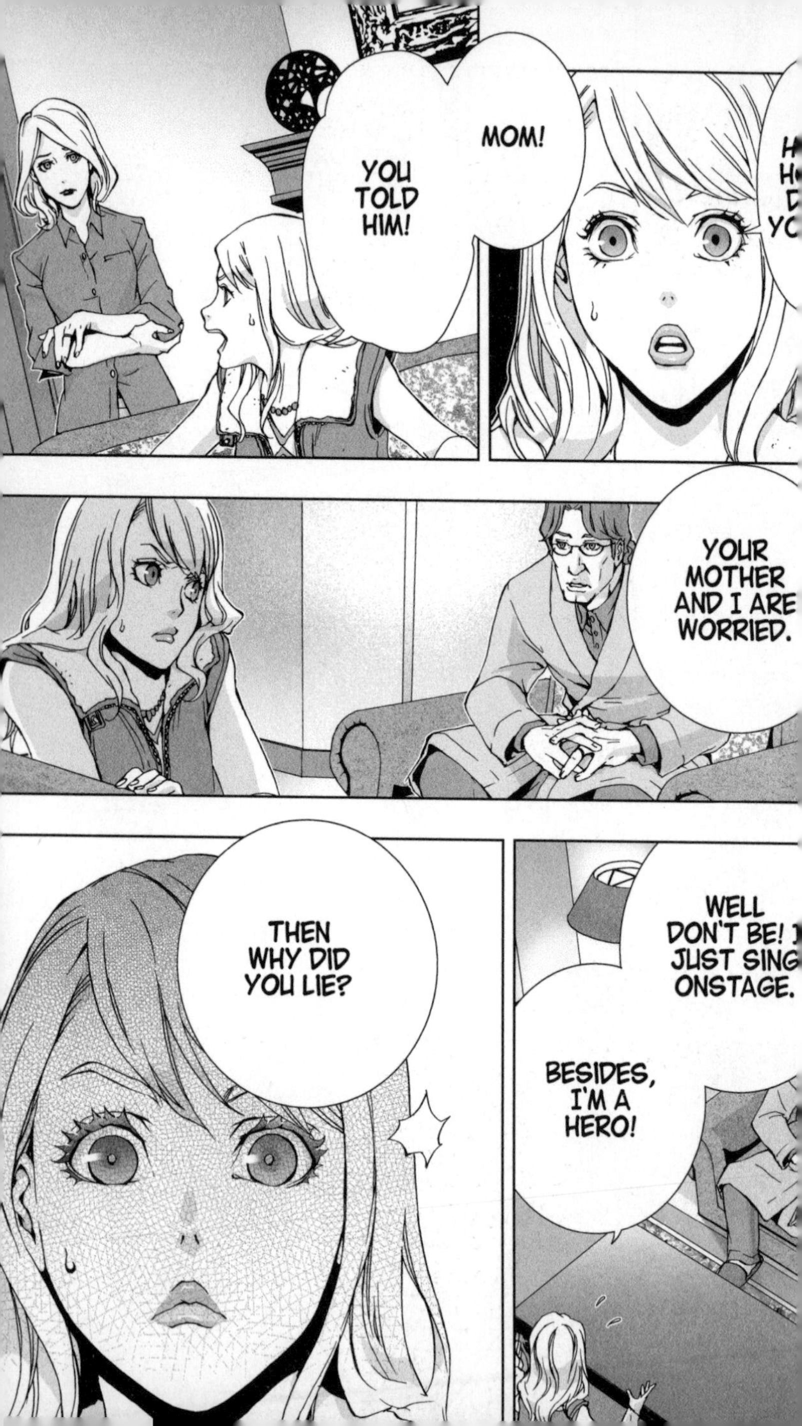
MOM!
YOU TOLD HIM!
YOUR MOTHER AND I ARE WORRIED.
WELL DON'T BE! I JUST SING ONSTAGE.
BESIDES, I'M A HERO!
THEN WHY DID YOU LIE?

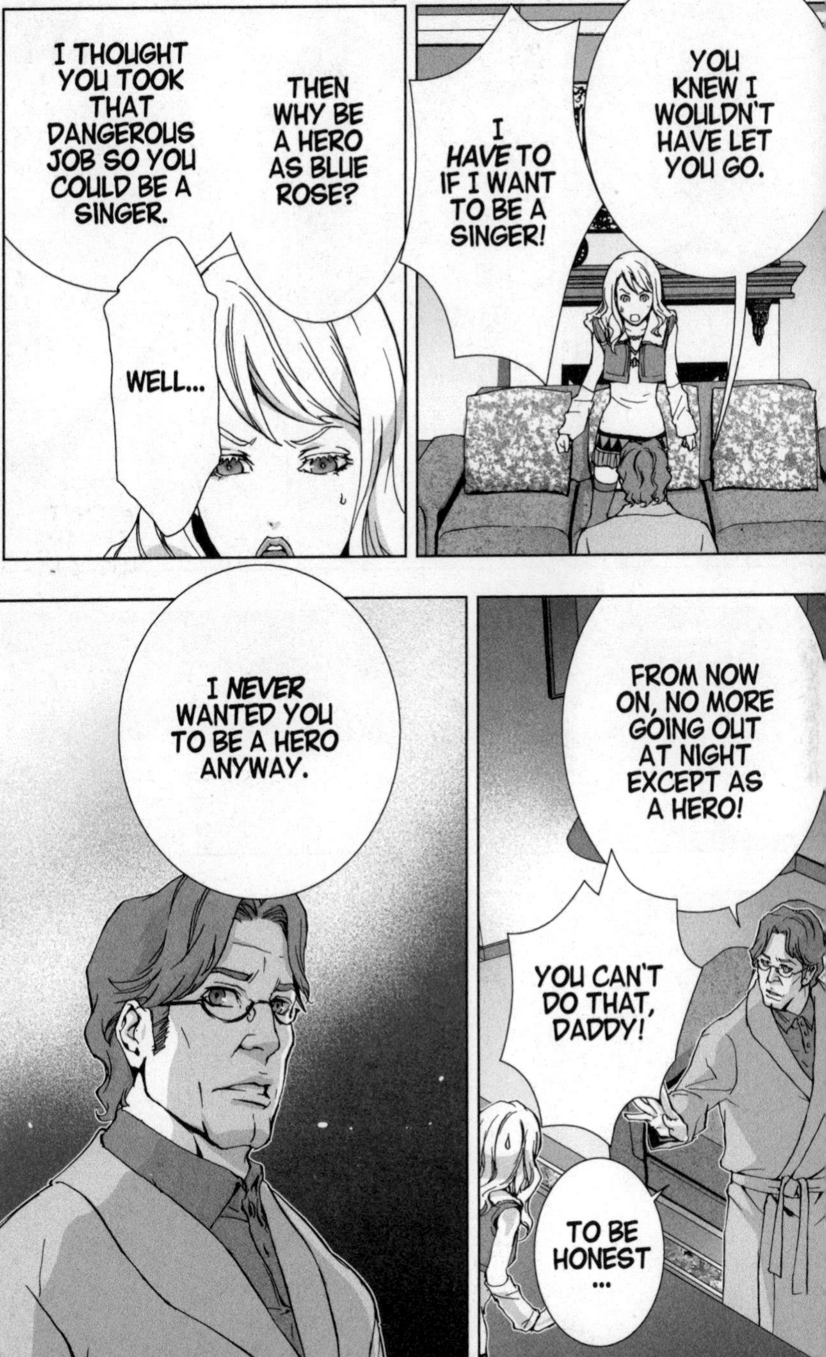
YOU KNEW I WOULDN'T HAVE LET YOU GO.
I *HAVE* TO IF I WANT TO BE A SINGER!
THEN WHY BE A HERO AS BLUE ROSE?
I THOUGHT YOU TOOK THAT DANGEROUS JOB SO YOU COULD BE A SINGER.
WELL...
FROM NOW ON, NO MORE GOING OUT AT NIGHT EXCEPT AS A HERO!
YOU CAN'T DO THAT, DADDY!
TO BE HONEST...
I *NEVER* WANTED YOU TO BE A HERO ANYWAY.

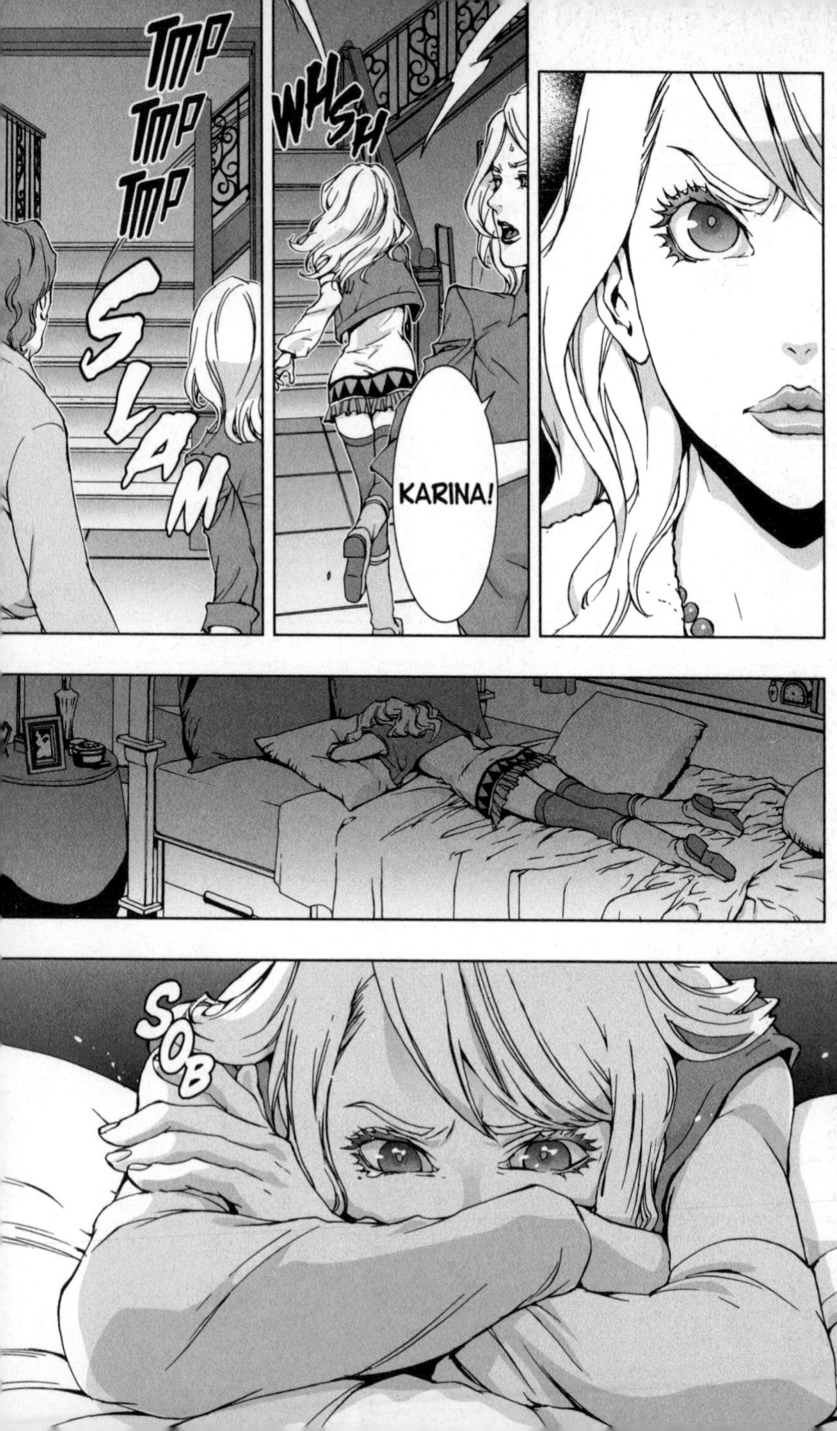
WHSH
KARINA!
TMP
TMP
TMP
SLAM
SOB

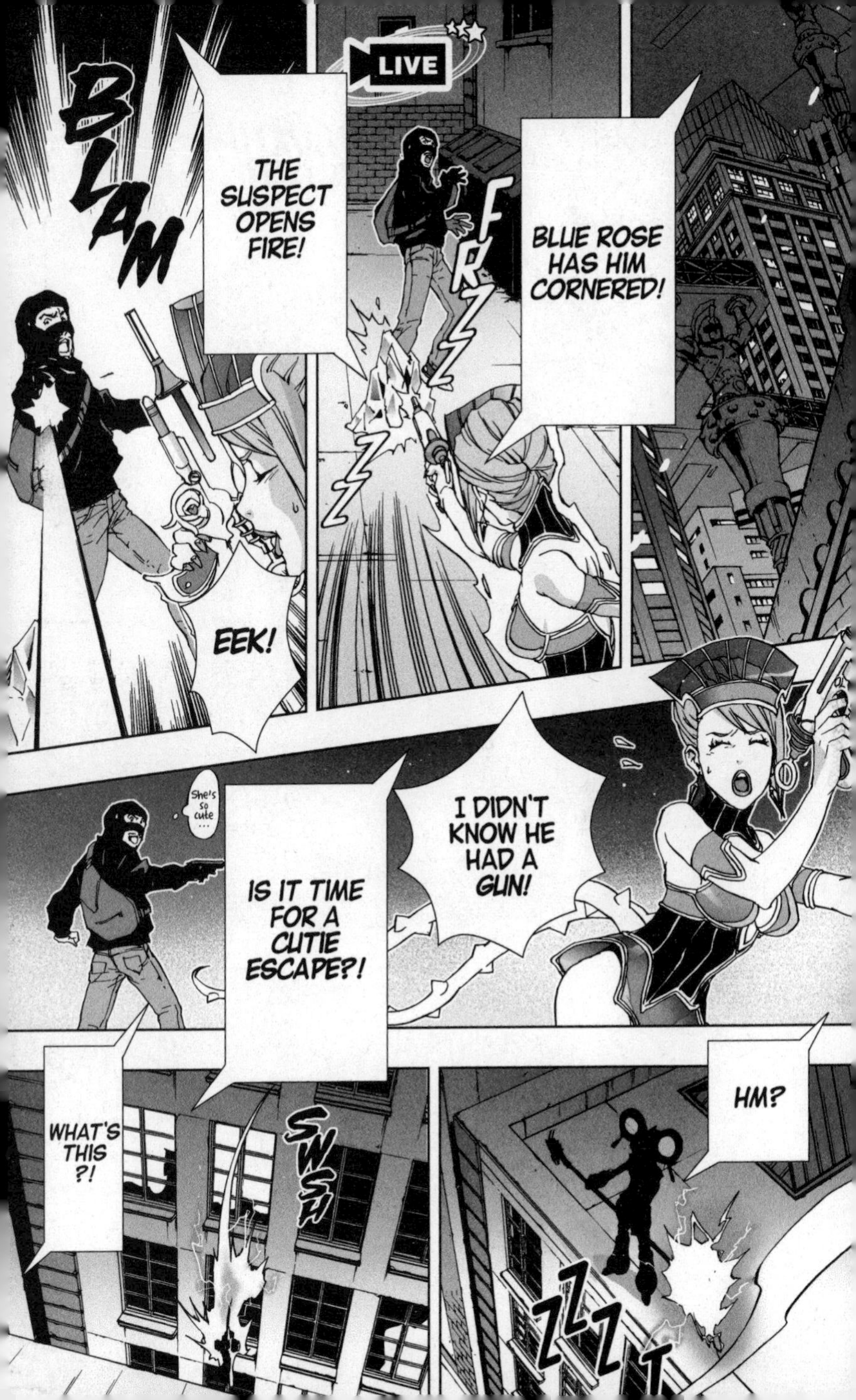
LIVE
BLUE ROSE HAS HIM CORNERED!
FRZZZ
THE SUSPECT OPENS FIRE!
BLAM
EEK!
I DIDN'T KNOW HE HAD A GUN!
IS IT TIME FOR A CUTIE ESCAPE?!
She's so cute...
HM?
ZZZT
SWSH
WHAT'S THIS?!

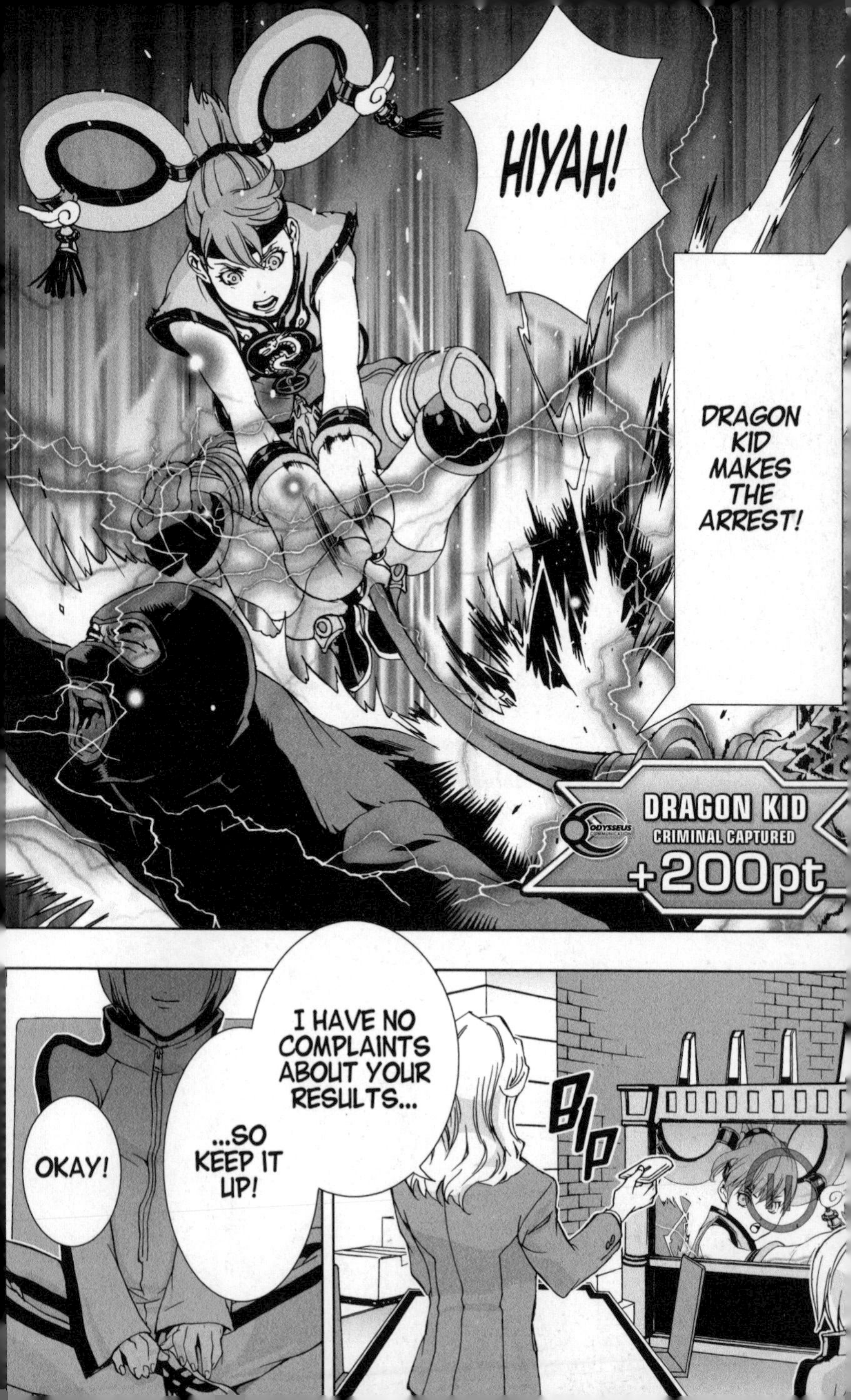
HIYAH!
DRAGON KID MAKES THE ARREST!
DRAGON KID
CRIMINAL CAPTURED
+200pt
I HAVE NO COMPLAINTS ABOUT YOUR RESULTS...
...SO KEEP IT UP!
BIP
OKAY!

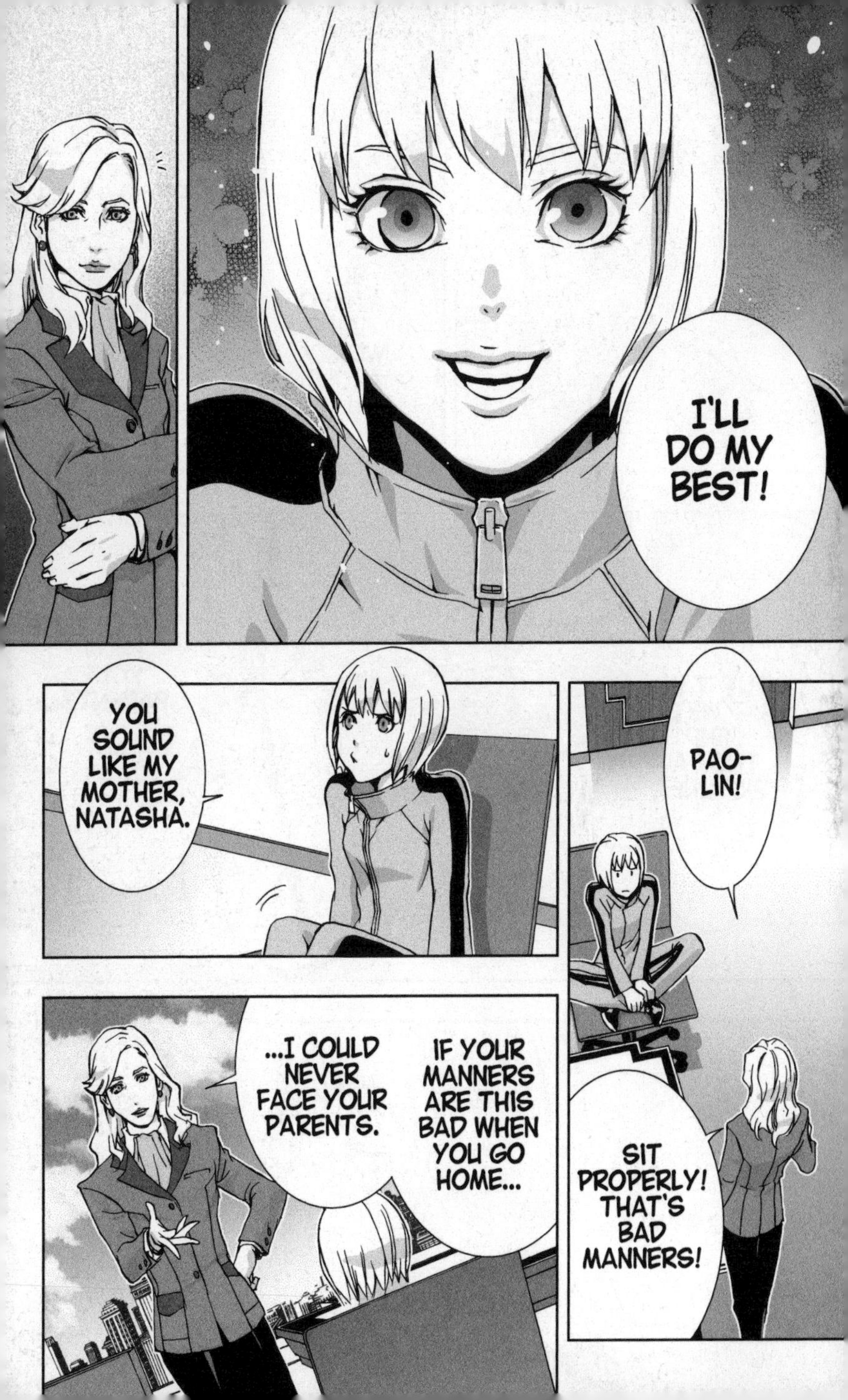
I'LL DO MY BEST!
PAO-LIN!
SIT PROPERLY! THAT'S BAD MANNERS!
YOU SOUND LIKE MY MOTHER, NATASHA.
IF YOUR MANNERS ARE THIS BAD WHEN YOU GO HOME...
...I COULD NEVER FACE YOUR PARENTS.

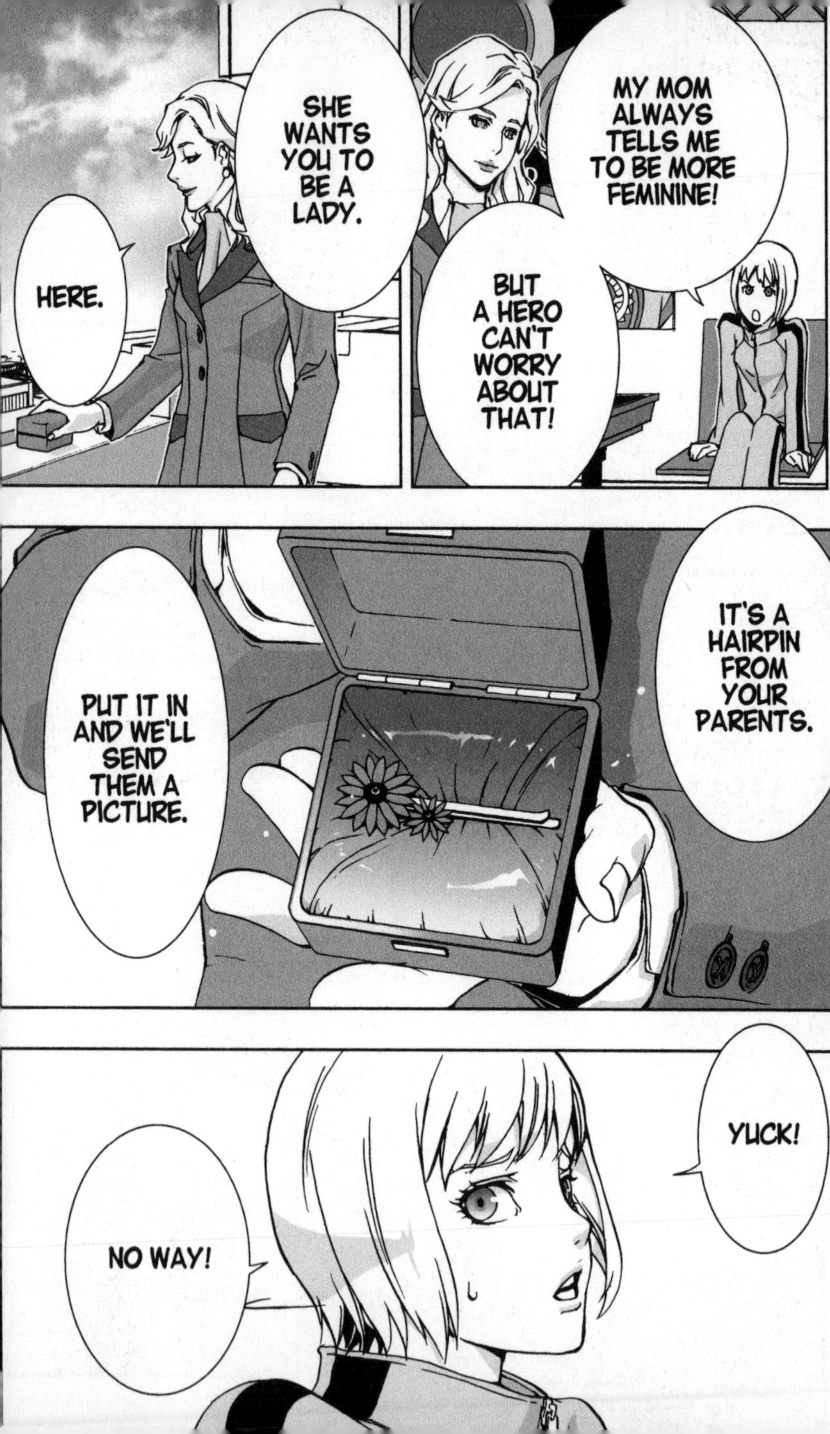
MY MOM ALWAYS TELLS ME TO BE MORE FEMININE!
BUT A HERO CAN'T WORRY ABOUT THAT!
SHE WANTS YOU TO BE A LADY.
HERE.
IT'S A HAIRPIN FROM YOUR PARENTS.
PUT IT IN AND WE'LL SEND THEM A PICTURE.
YUCK!
NO WAY!

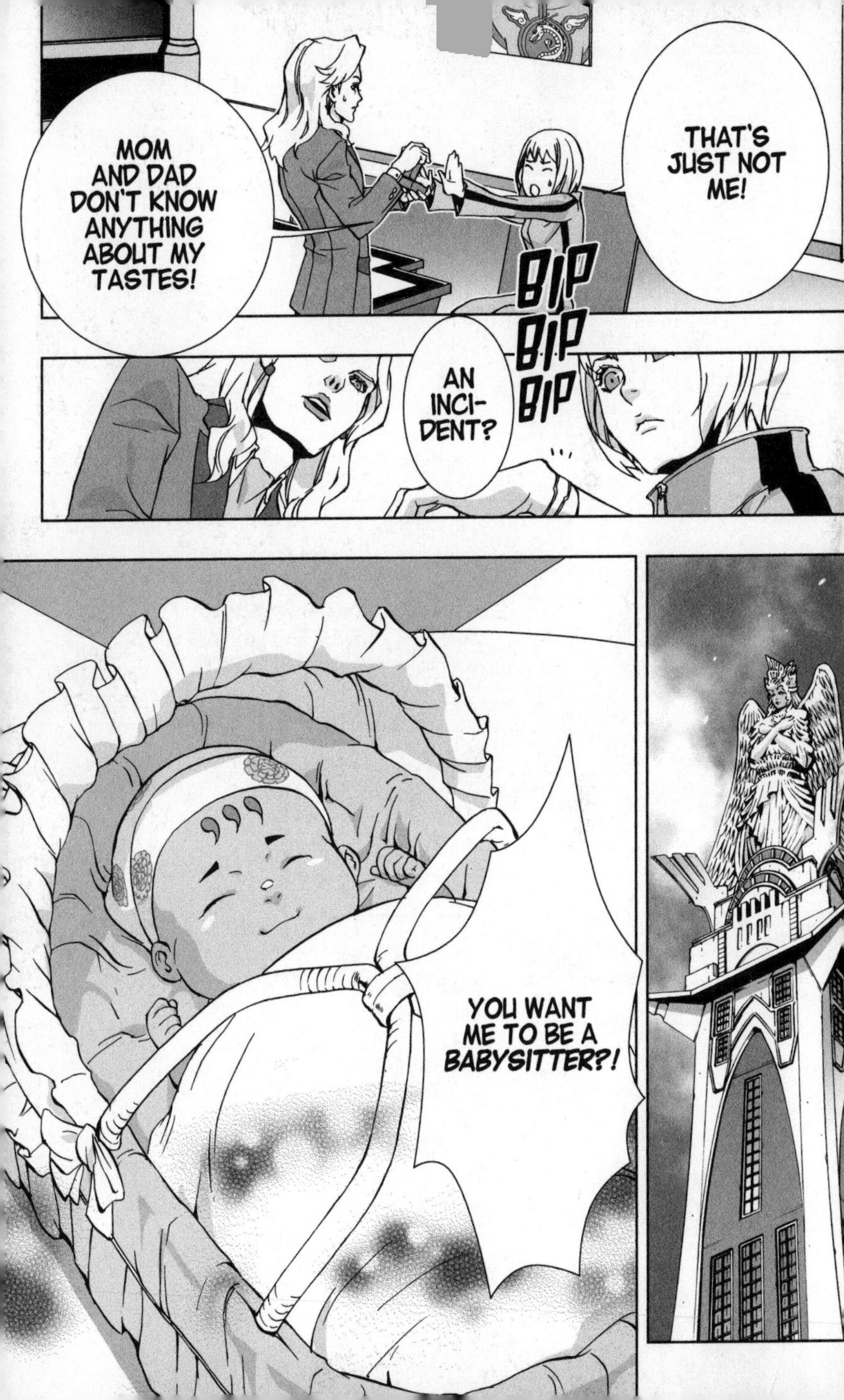
THAT'S JUST NOT ME!
MOM AND DAD DON'T KNOW ANYTHING ABOUT MY TASTES!
BIP BIP BIP
AN INCI-DENT?
...
YOU WANT ME TO BE A BABYSITTER?!

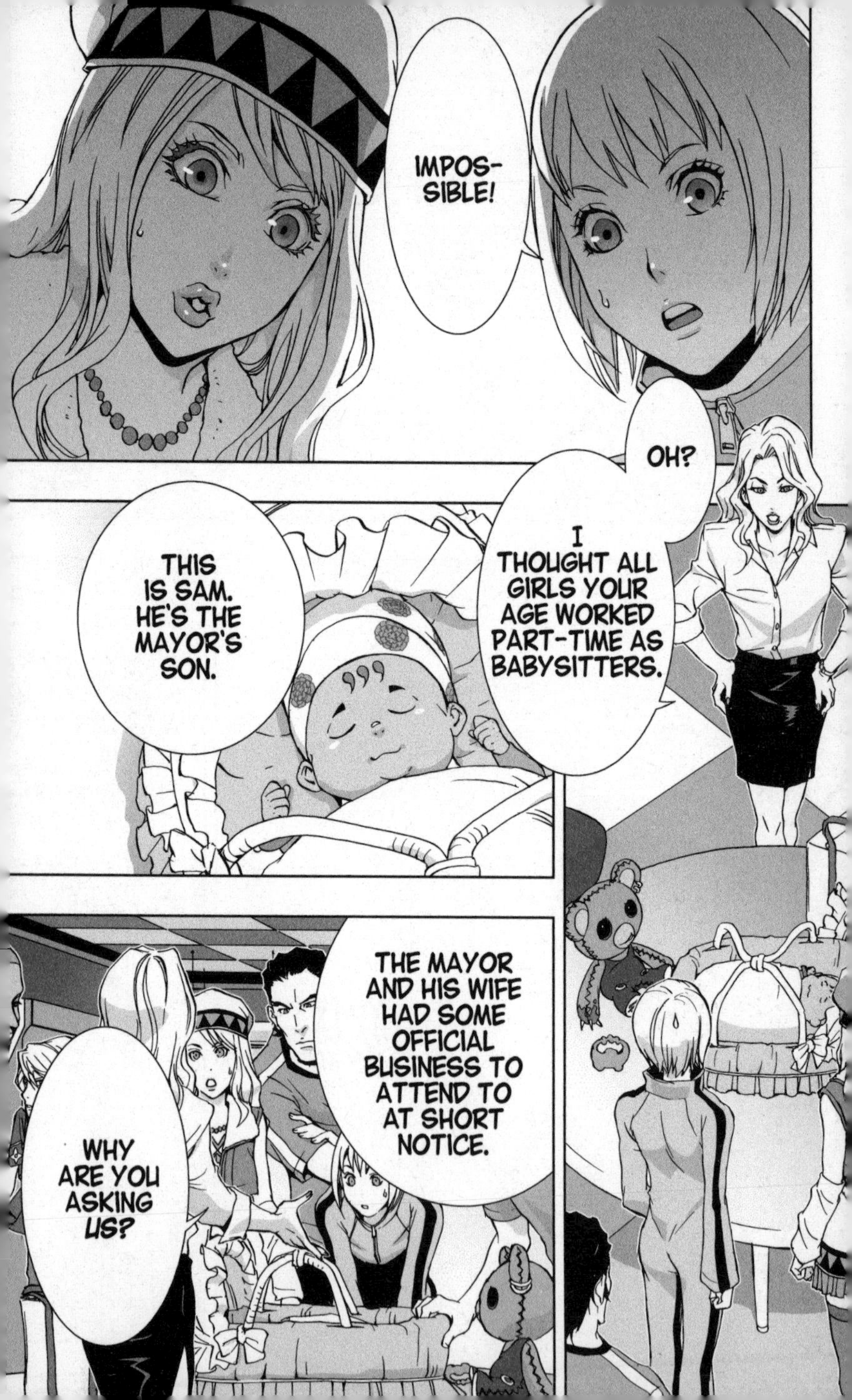
IMPOS-SIBLE!
OH?
I THOUGHT ALL GIRLS YOUR AGE WORKED PART-TIME AS BABYSITTERS.
THIS IS SAM. HE'S THE MAYOR'S SON.
THE MAYOR AND HIS WIFE HAD SOME OFFICIAL BUSINESS TO ATTEND TO AT SHORT NOTICE.
WHY ARE YOU ASKING US?

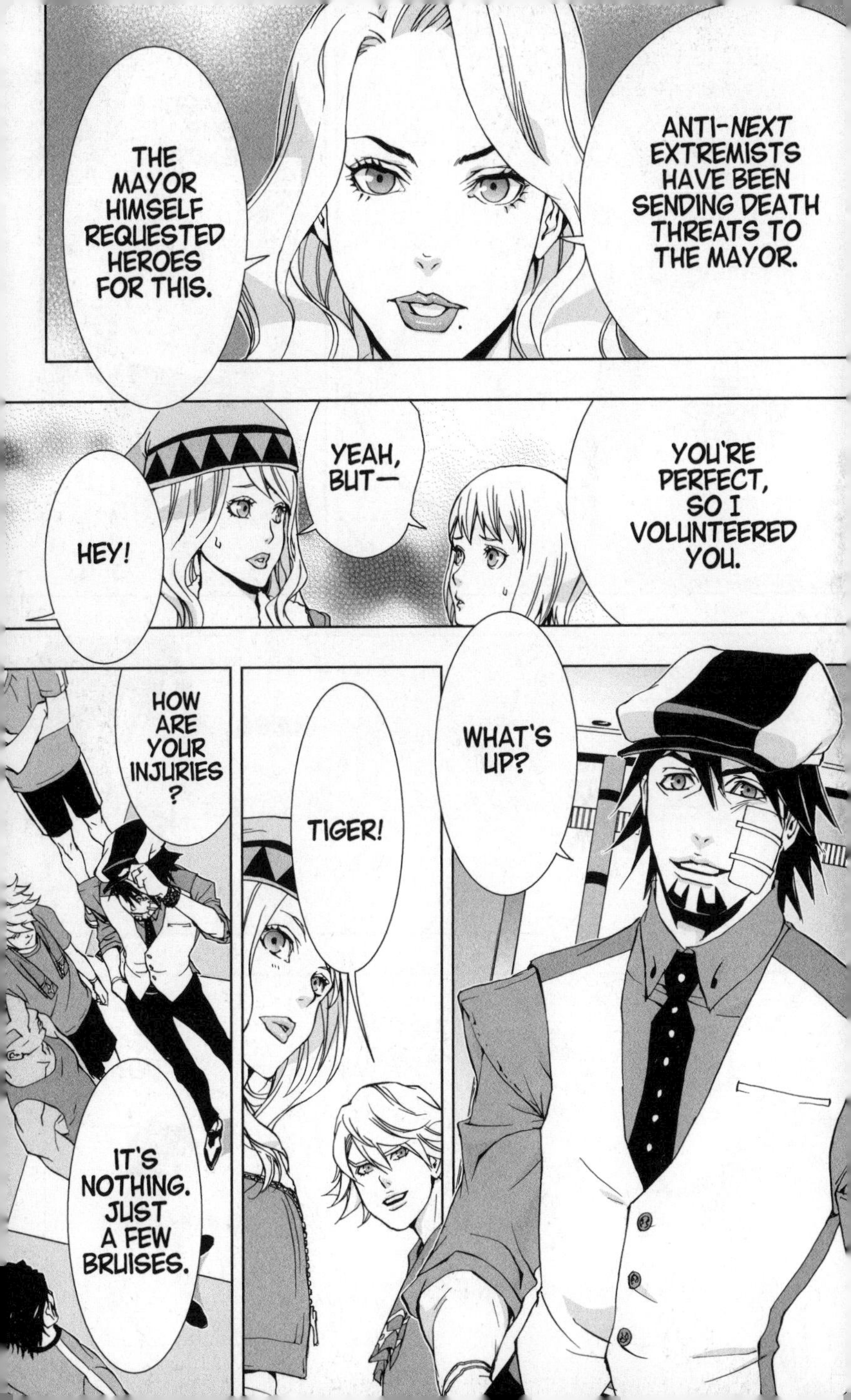
ANTI-NEXT EXTREMISTS HAVE BEEN SENDING DEATH THREATS TO THE MAYOR.
THE MAYOR HIMSELF REQUESTED HEROES FOR THIS.
YOU'RE PERFECT, SO I VOLUNTEERED YOU.
YEAH, BUT—
HEY!
WHAT'S UP?
TIGER!
HOW ARE YOUR INJURIES?
IT'S NOTHING. JUST A FEW BRUISES.

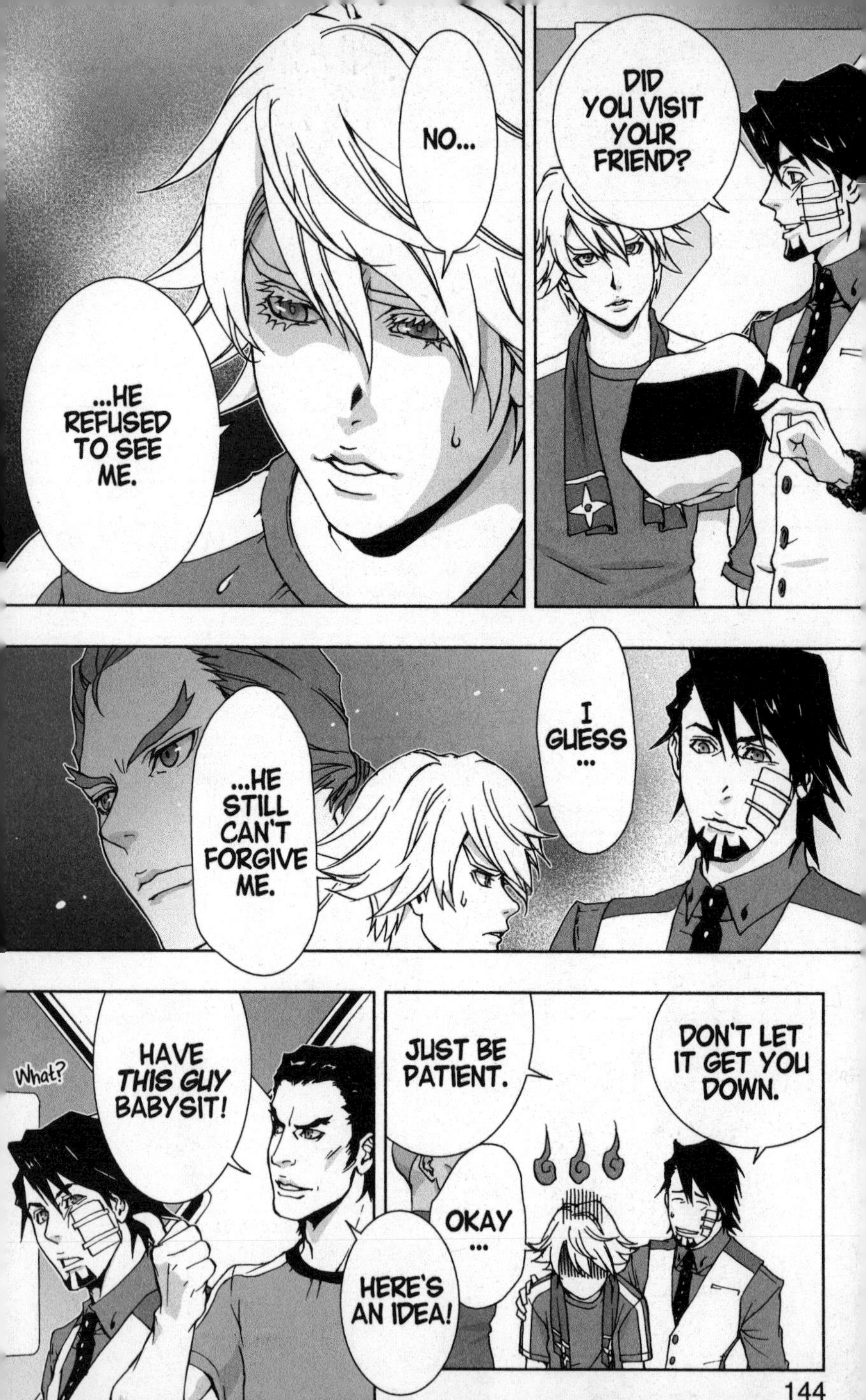
DID YOU VISIT YOUR FRIEND?
NO...
...HE REFUSED TO SEE ME.
I GUESS...
...HE STILL CAN'T FORGIVE ME.
DON'T LET IT GET YOU DOWN.
JUST BE PATIENT.
OKAY...
HERE'S AN IDEA!
HAVE *THIS GUY* BABYSIT!
What?

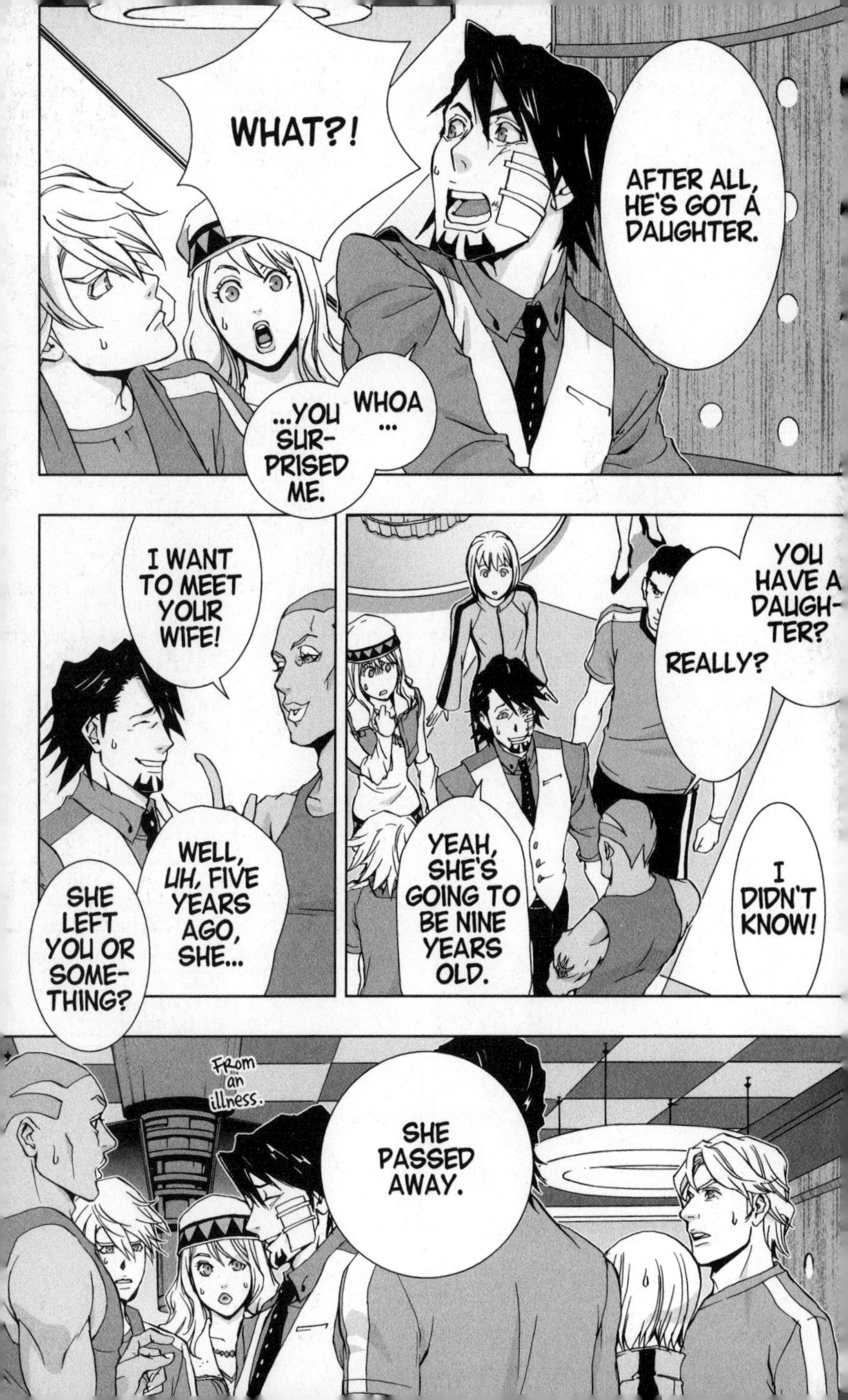
AFTER ALL, HE'S GOT A DAUGHTER.
WHAT?!
WHOA ...
...YOU SUR-PRISED ME.
YOU HAVE A DAUGH-TER?
REALLY?
I DIDN'T KNOW!
YEAH, SHE'S GOING TO BE NINE YEARS OLD.
I WANT TO MEET YOUR WIFE!
WELL, UH, FIVE YEARS AGO, SHE...
SHE LEFT YOU OR SOME-THING?
SHE PASSED AWAY.
From an illness.

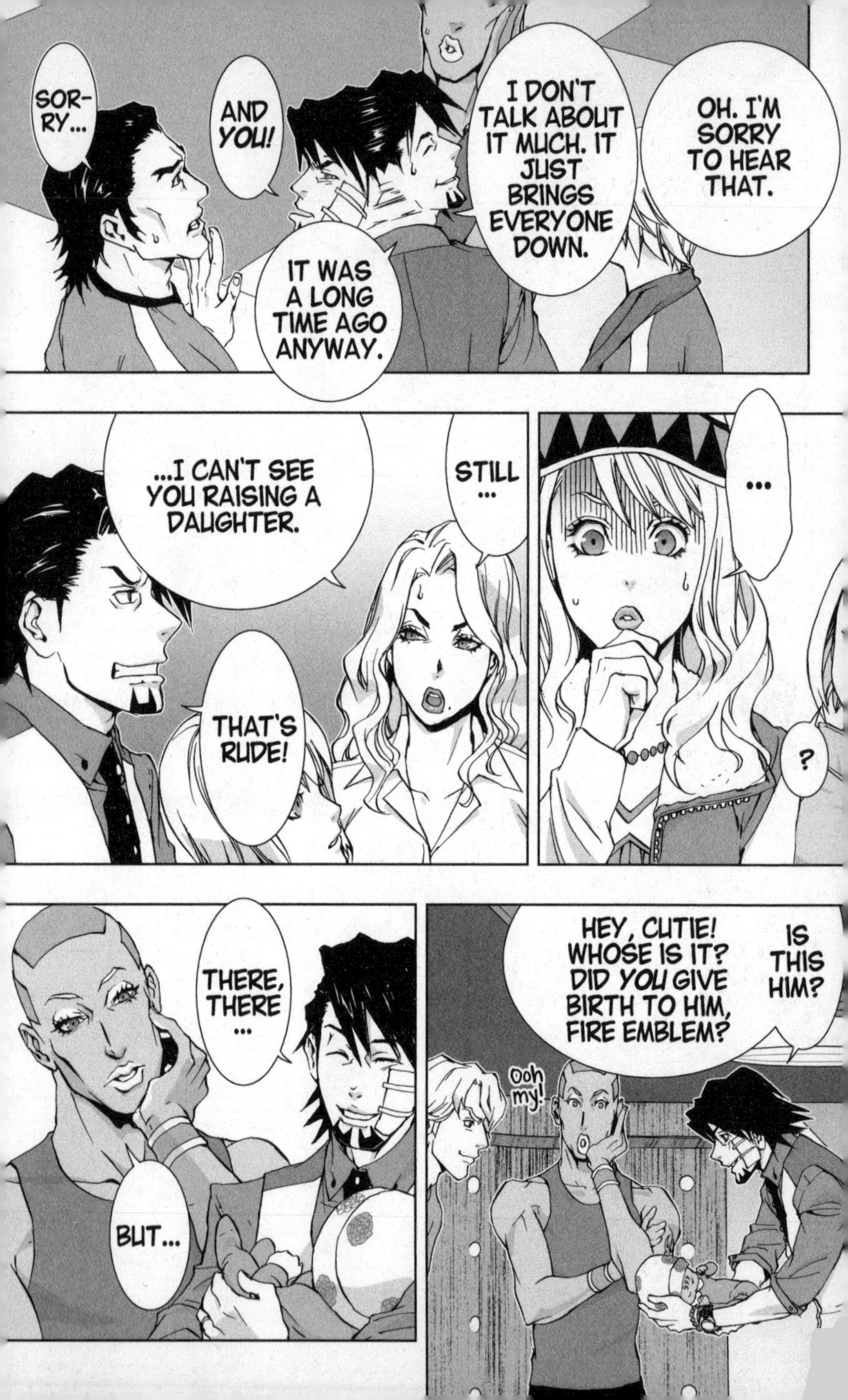
OH. I'M SORRY TO HEAR THAT.
I DON'T TALK ABOUT IT MUCH. IT JUST BRINGS EVERYONE DOWN.
IT WAS A LONG TIME AGO ANYWAY.
AND YOU!
SOR-RY...
...
?
STILL ...
...I CAN'T SEE YOU RAISING A DAUGHTER.
THAT'S RUDE!
IS THIS HIM?
HEY, CUTIE! WHOSE IS IT? DID YOU GIVE BIRTH TO HIM, FIRE EMBLEM?
Ooh my!
THERE, THERE ...
BUT...

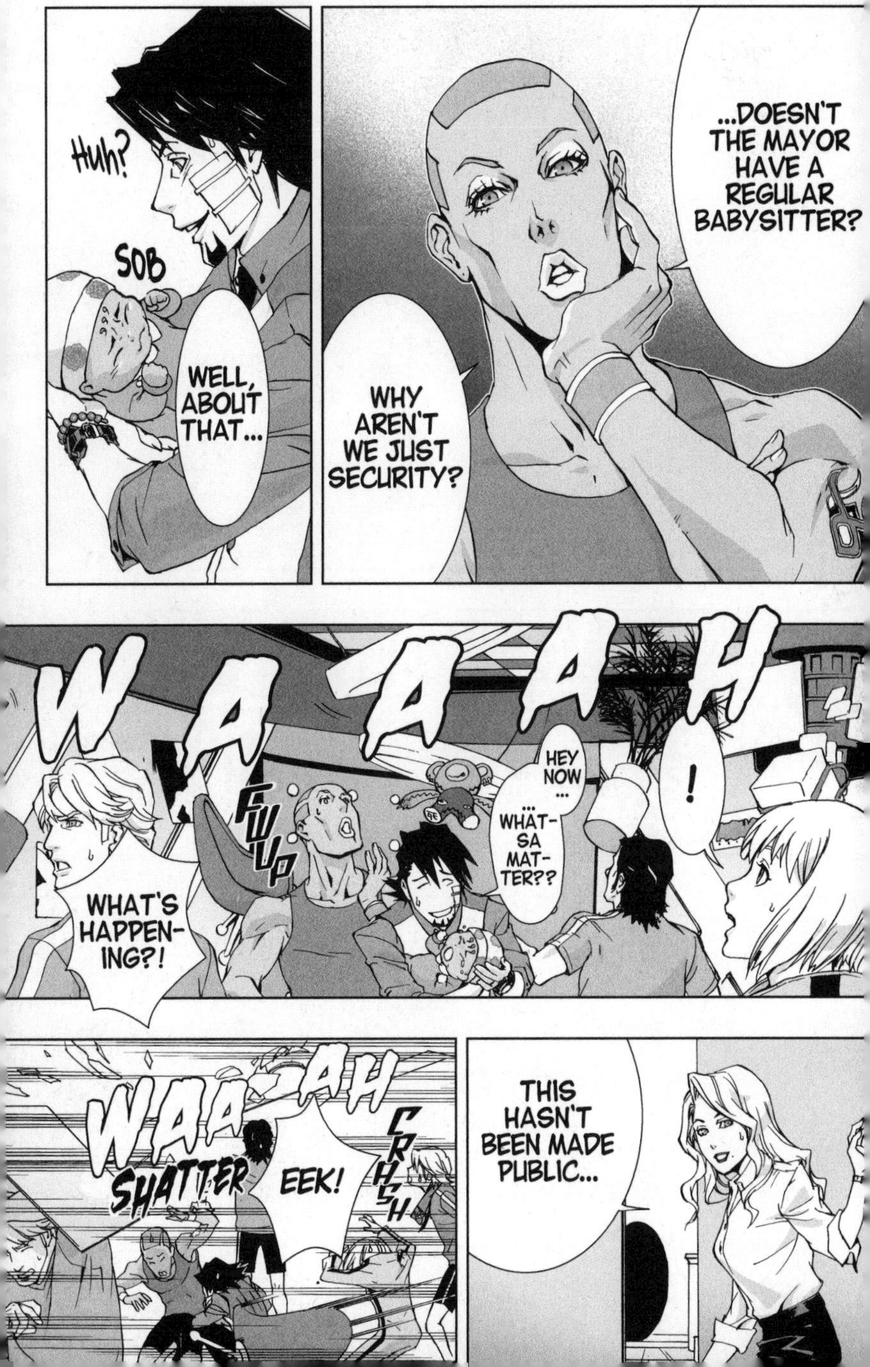
...DOESN'T THE MAYOR HAVE A REGULAR BABYSITTER?
WHY AREN'T WE JUST SECURITY?
Huh?
SOB
WELL, ABOUT THAT...
WAAAH
!
HEY NOW... ...WHAT-SA MAT-TER??
FWUP
WHAT'S HAPPEN-ING?!
THIS HASN'T BEEN MADE PUBLIC...
WAA-AH
CRASH
EEK!
SHATTER

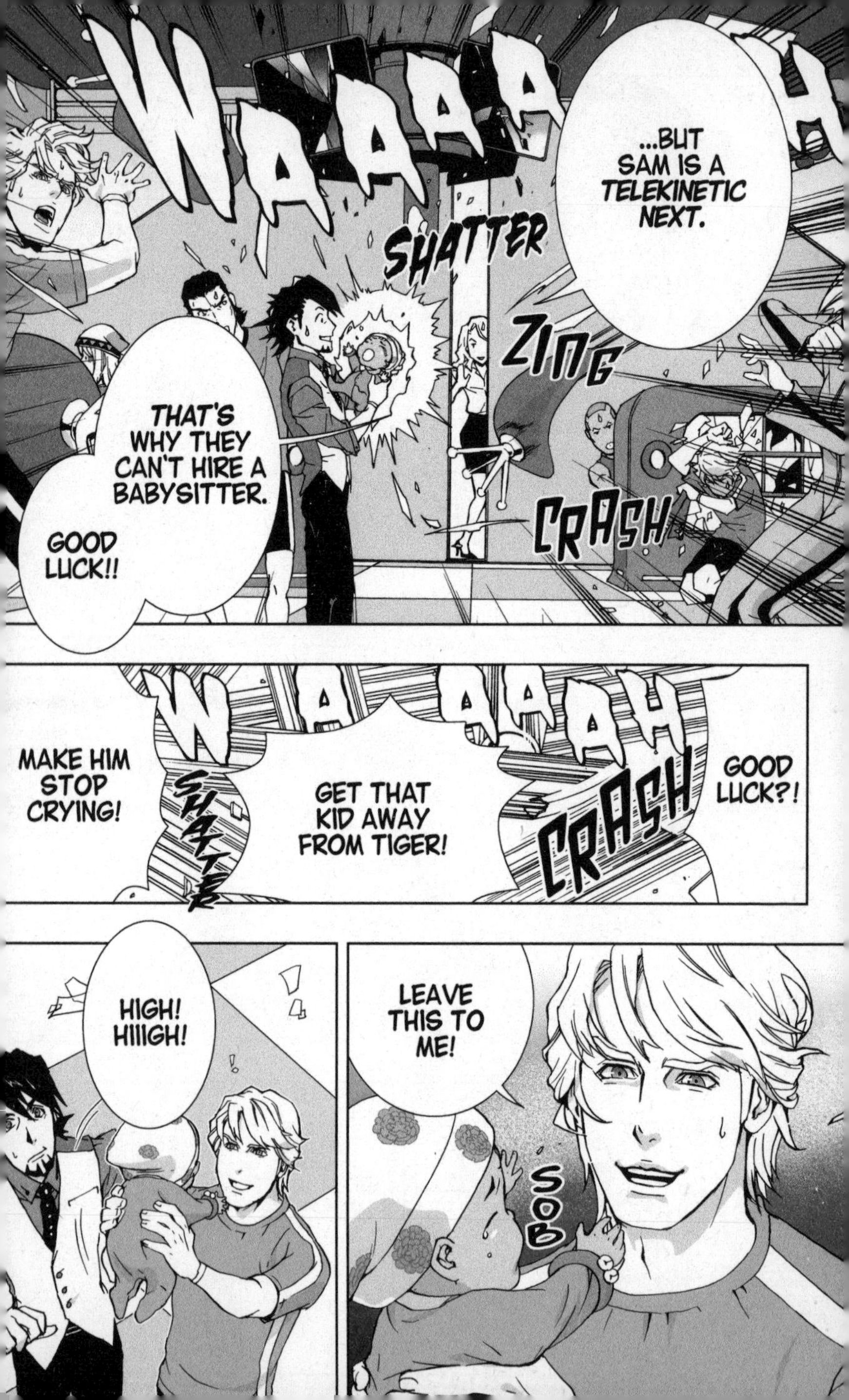
WAAAAH
...BUT SAM IS A TELEKINETIC NEXT.
SHATTER
ZING
CRASH
THAT'S WHY THEY CAN'T HIRE A BABYSITTER.
GOOD LUCK!!
GOOD LUCK?!
CRASH
WAAAAH
GET THAT KID AWAY FROM TIGER!
SHATTER
MAKE HIM STOP CRYING!
LEAVE THIS TO ME!
SOB
HIGH! HIIIGH!

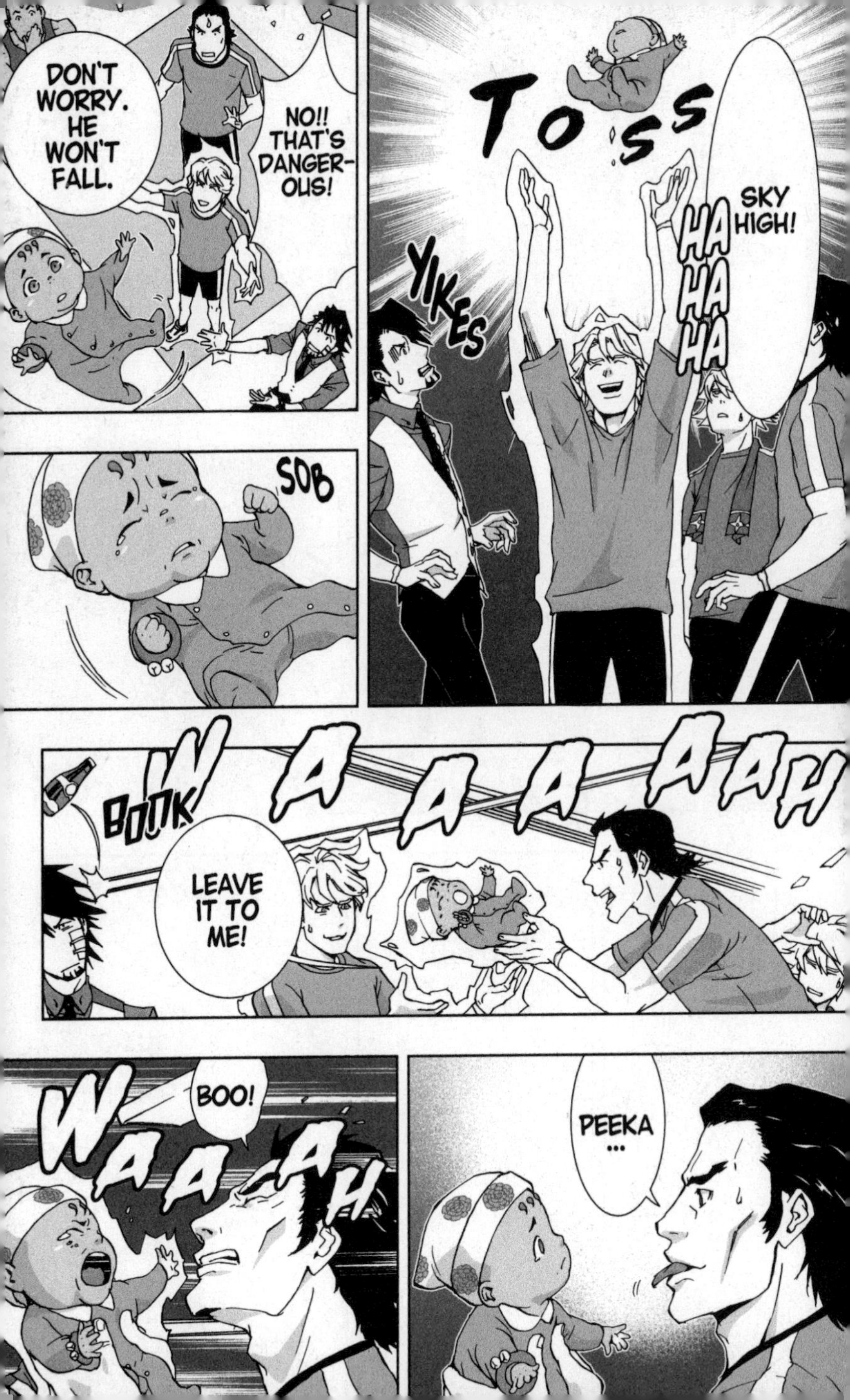
TOSS
SKY HIGH!
HA HA HA HA
YIKES
NO!! THAT'S DANGER-OUS!
DON'T WORRY. HE WON'T FALL.
SOB
WAAAAAH
LEAVE IT TO ME!
BOOK
PEEKA ...
BOO!
WAAAH

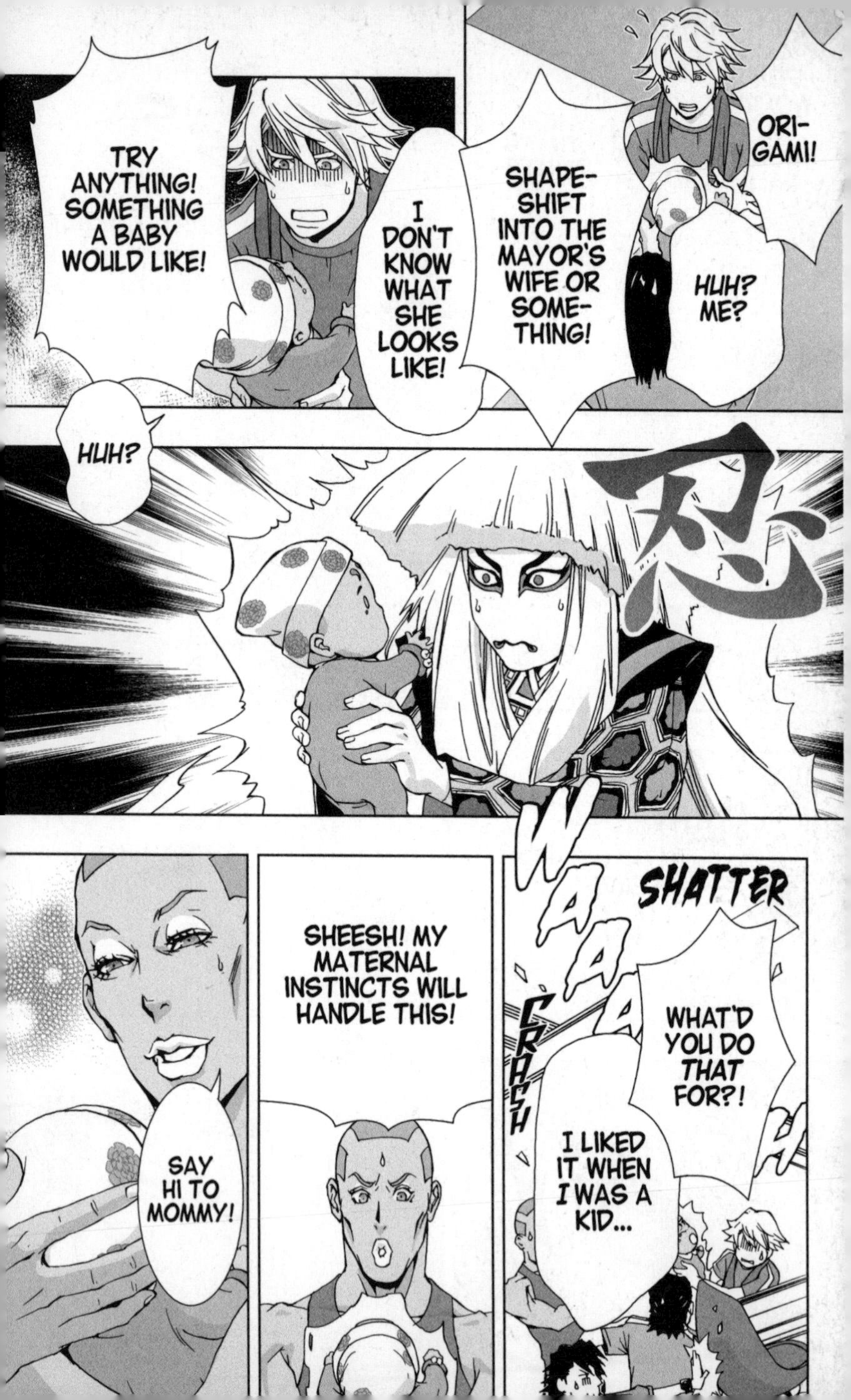
ORI-GAMI!
HUH? ME?
SHAPE-SHIFT INTO THE MAYOR'S WIFE OR SOME-THING!
I DON'T KNOW WHAT SHE LOOKS LIKE!
TRY ANYTHING! SOMETHING A BABY WOULD LIKE!
忍
HUH?
WAAAA
SHATTER
CRASH
WHAT'D YOU DO THAT FOR?!
I LIKED IT WHEN I WAS A KID...
SHEESH! MY MATERNAL INSTINCTS WILL HANDLE THIS!
SAY HI TO MOMMY!

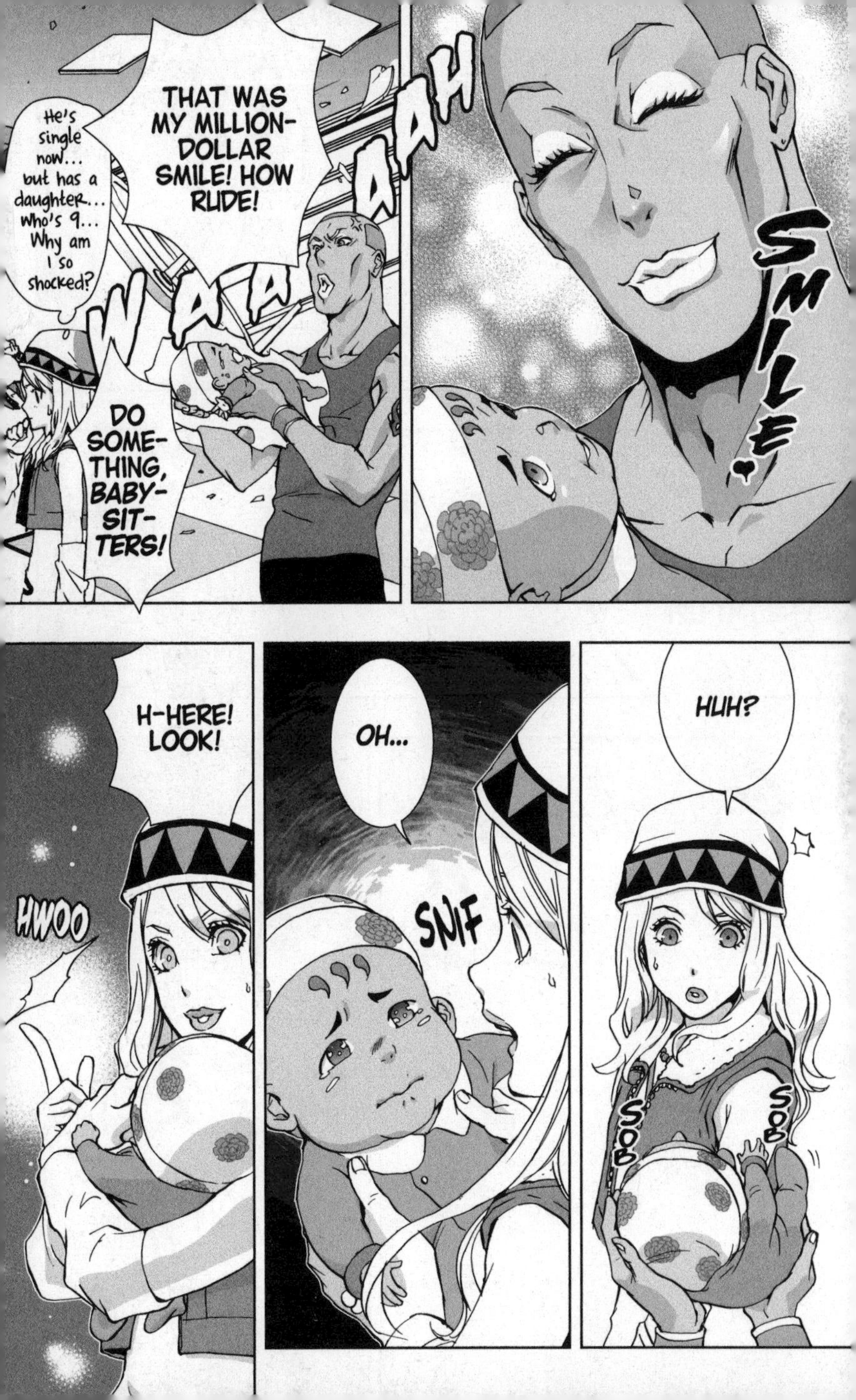
SMILE
WAAAAH
THAT WAS MY MILLION-DOLLAR SMILE! HOW RUDE!
He's single now... but has a daughter... who's 9... Why am I so shocked?
DO SOMETHING, BABYSITTERS!
HUH?
SOB SOB
OH...
SNIF
H-HERE! LOOK!
HWOO

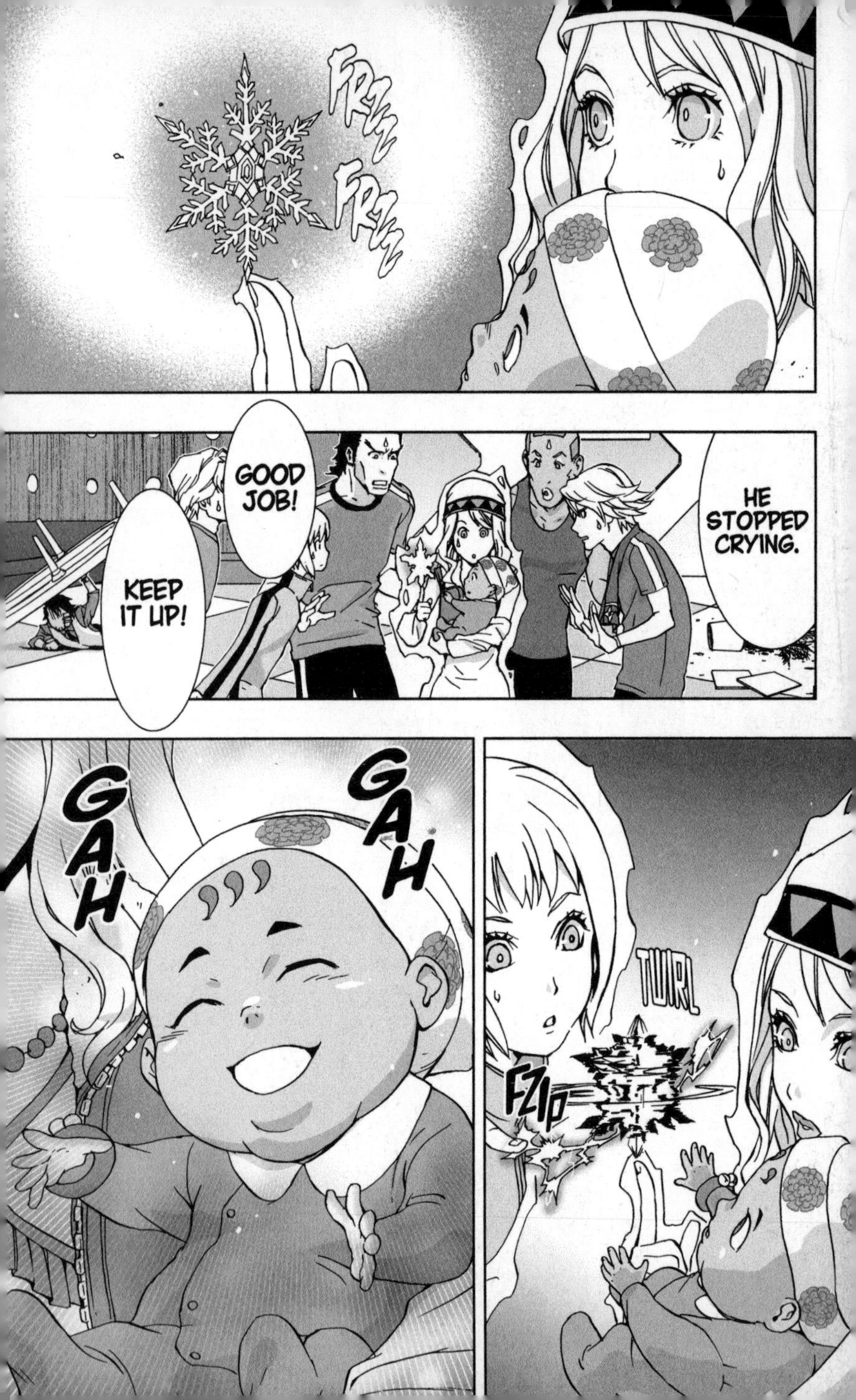
FRZN
FRZN
HE STOPPED CRYING.
GOOD JOB!
KEEP IT UP!
TWIRL
FZIP
GAH
GAH

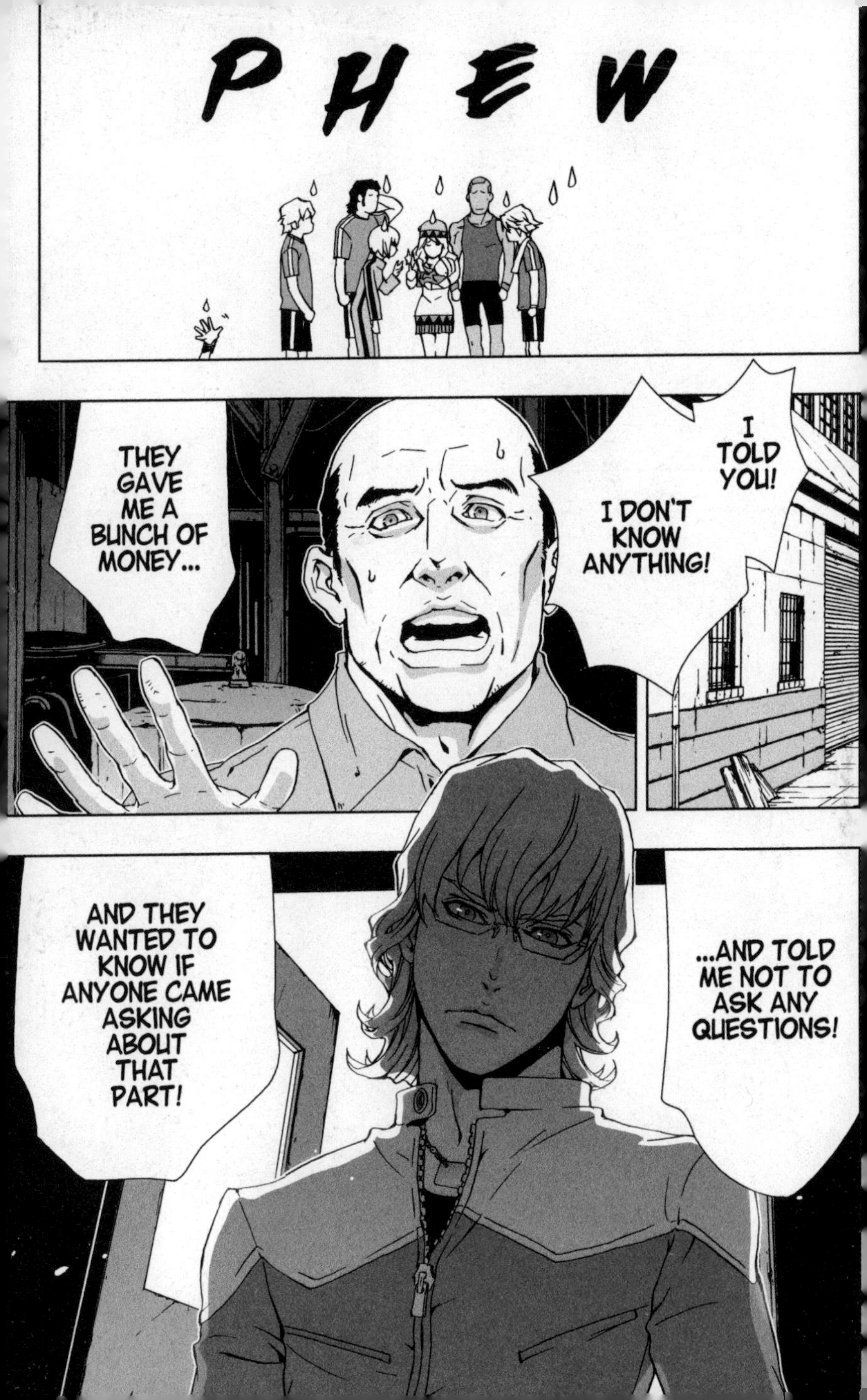
PHEW
I TOLD YOU!
I DON'T KNOW ANYTHING!
THEY GAVE ME A BUNCH OF MONEY...
...AND TOLD ME NOT TO ASK ANY QUESTIONS!
AND THEY WANTED TO KNOW IF ANYONE CAME ASKING ABOUT THAT PART!

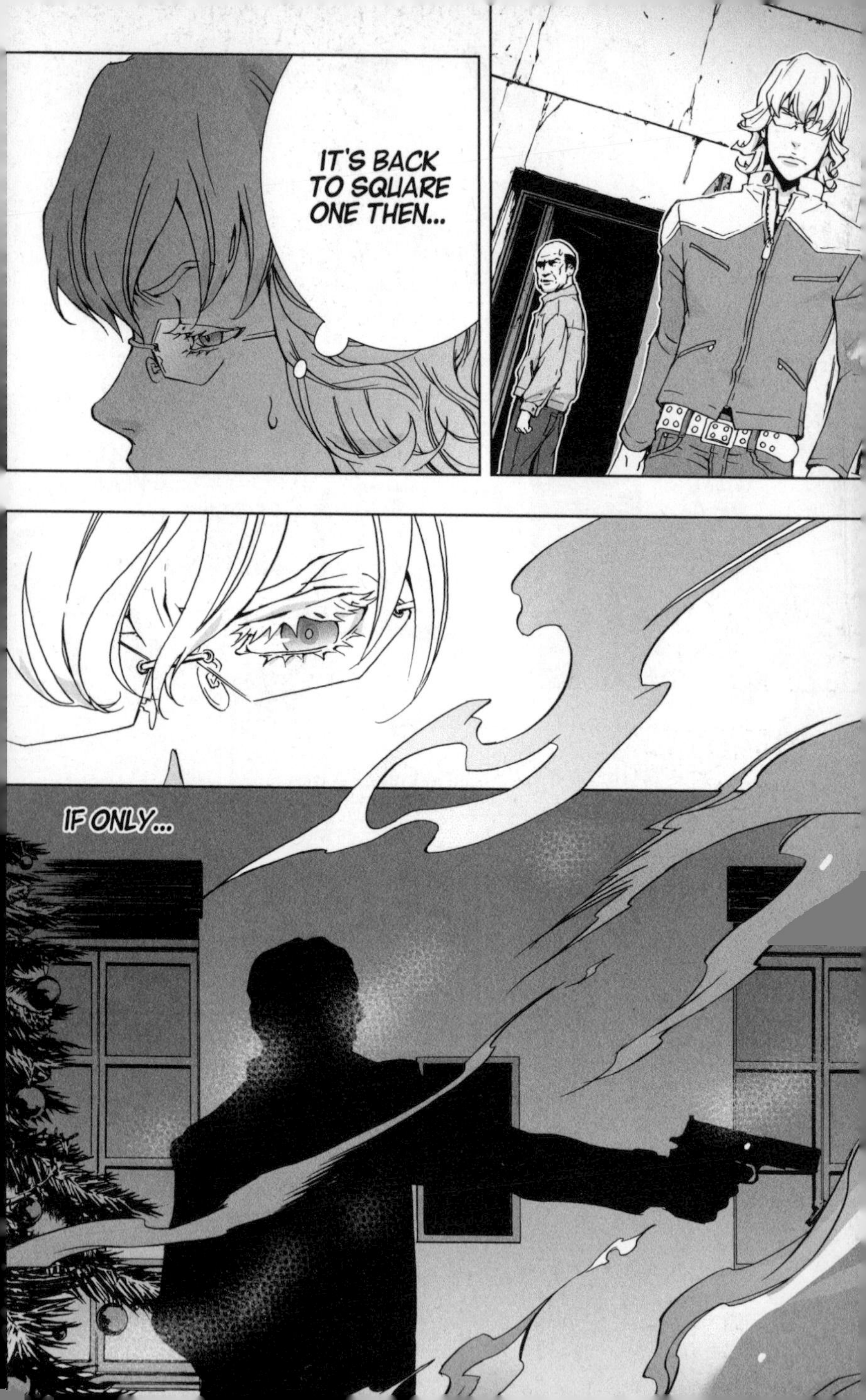
IT'S BACK TO SQUARE ONE THEN...
IF ONLY...

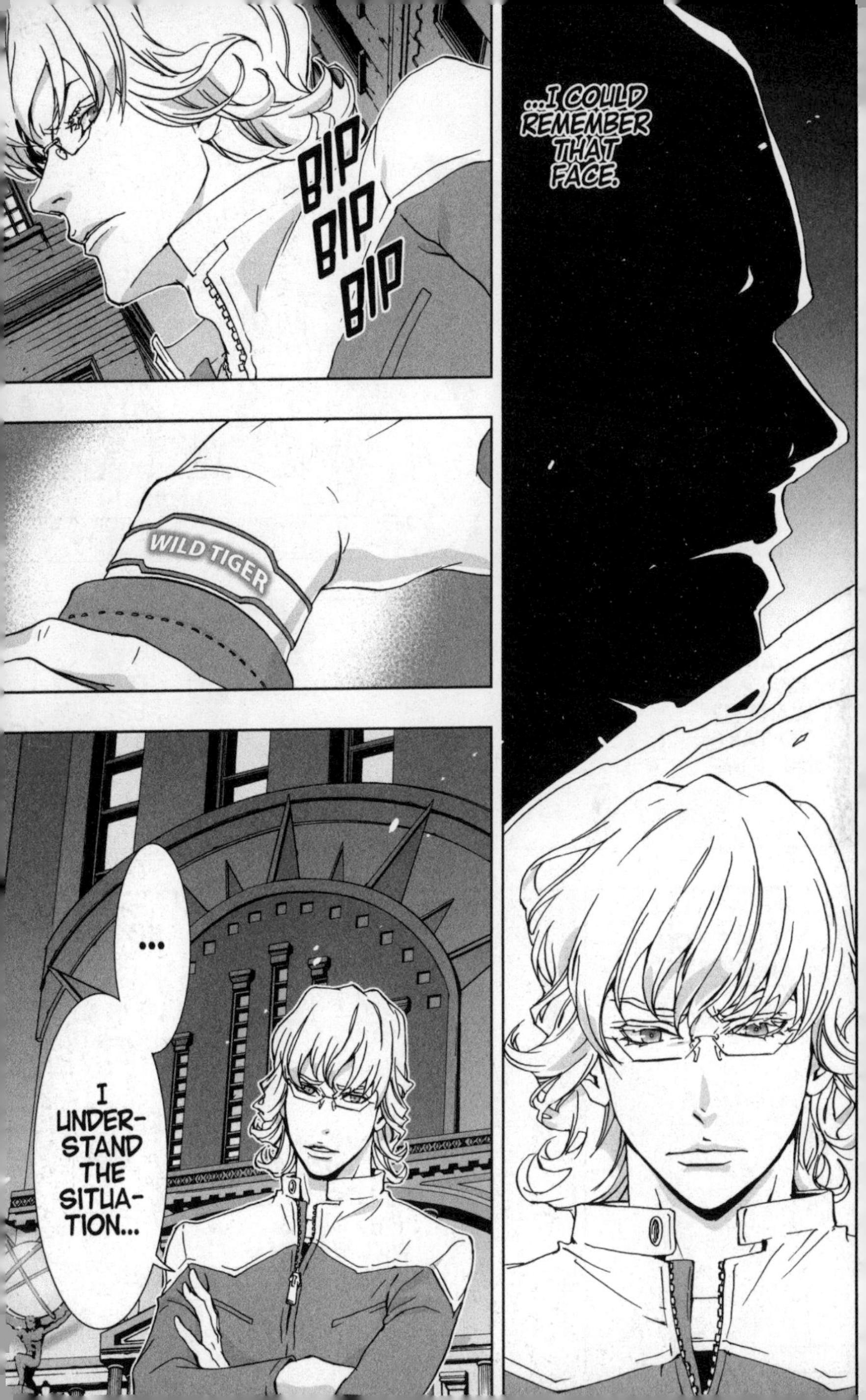
...I COULD REMEMBER THAT FACE.
BIP BIP BIP
WILD TIGER
...
I UNDER-STAND THE SITUA-TION...

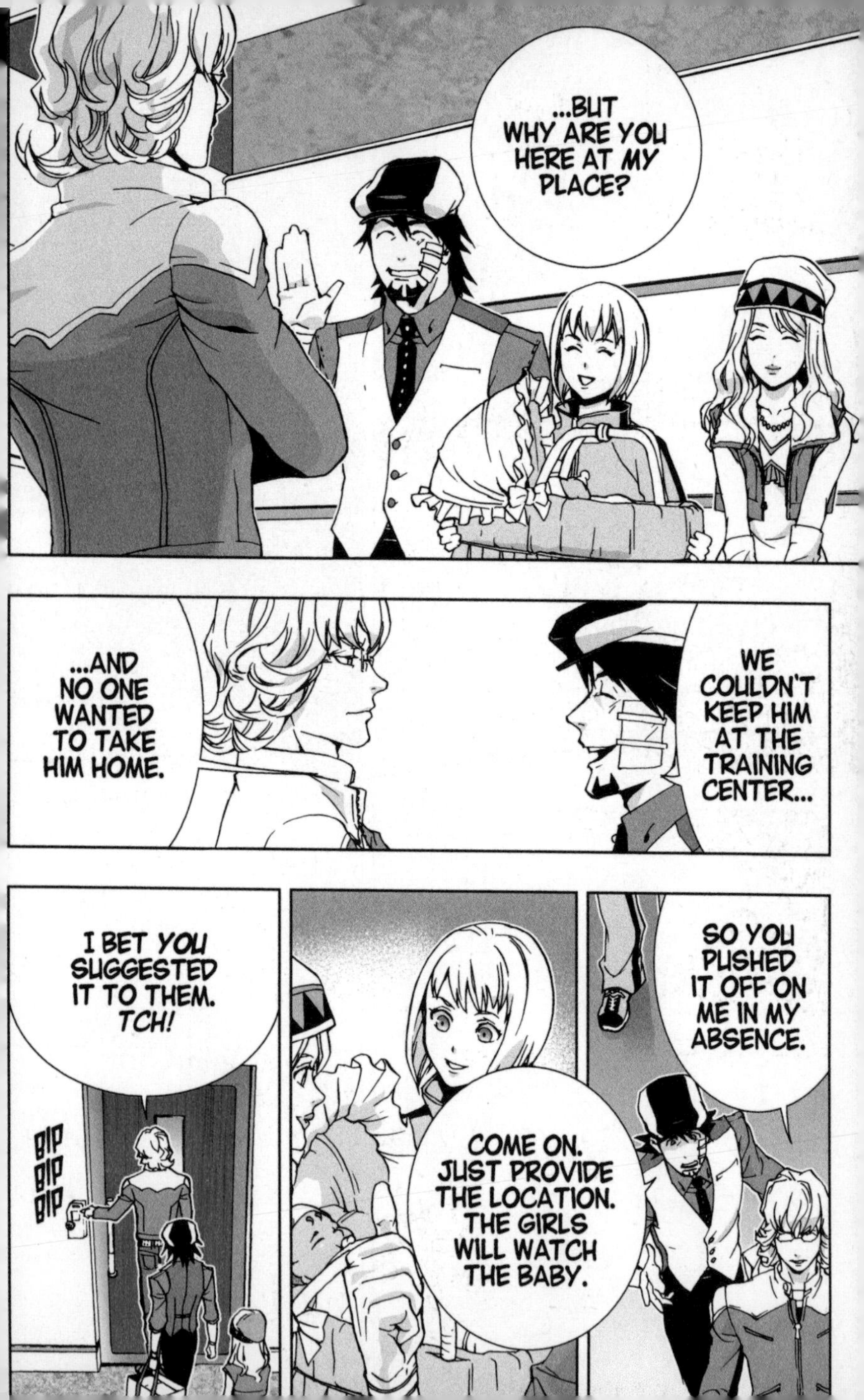
...BUT WHY ARE YOU HERE AT MY PLACE?
WE COULDN'T KEEP HIM AT THE TRAINING CENTER...
...AND NO ONE WANTED TO TAKE HIM HOME.
SO YOU PUSHED IT OFF ON ME IN MY ABSENCE.
COME ON. JUST PROVIDE THE LOCATION. THE GIRLS WILL WATCH THE BABY.
I BET *YOU* SUGGESTED IT TO THEM. *TCH!*
BIP BIP BIP

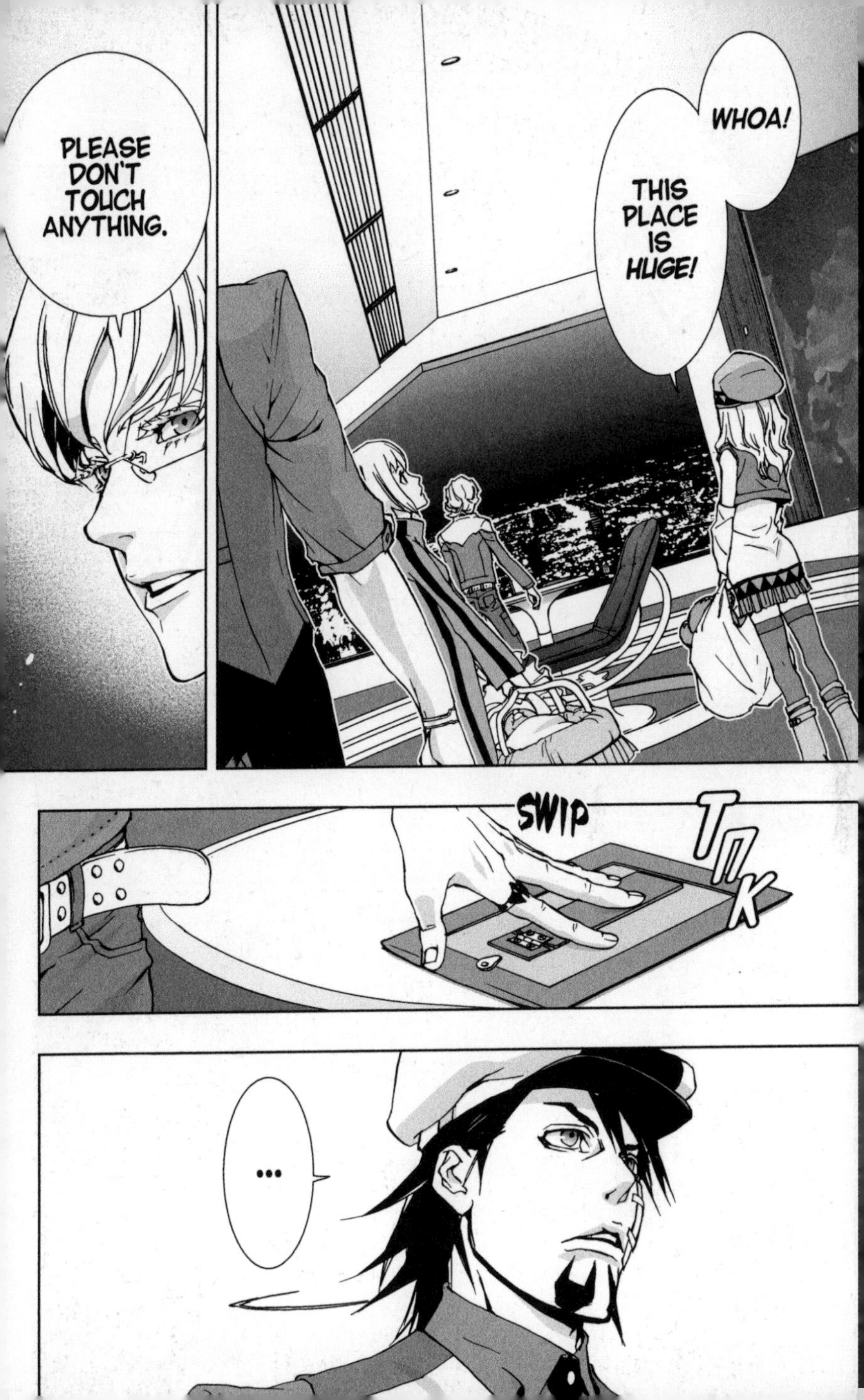
WHOA!
THIS PLACE IS HUGE!
PLEASE DON'T TOUCH ANYTHING.
TOK
SWIP
...

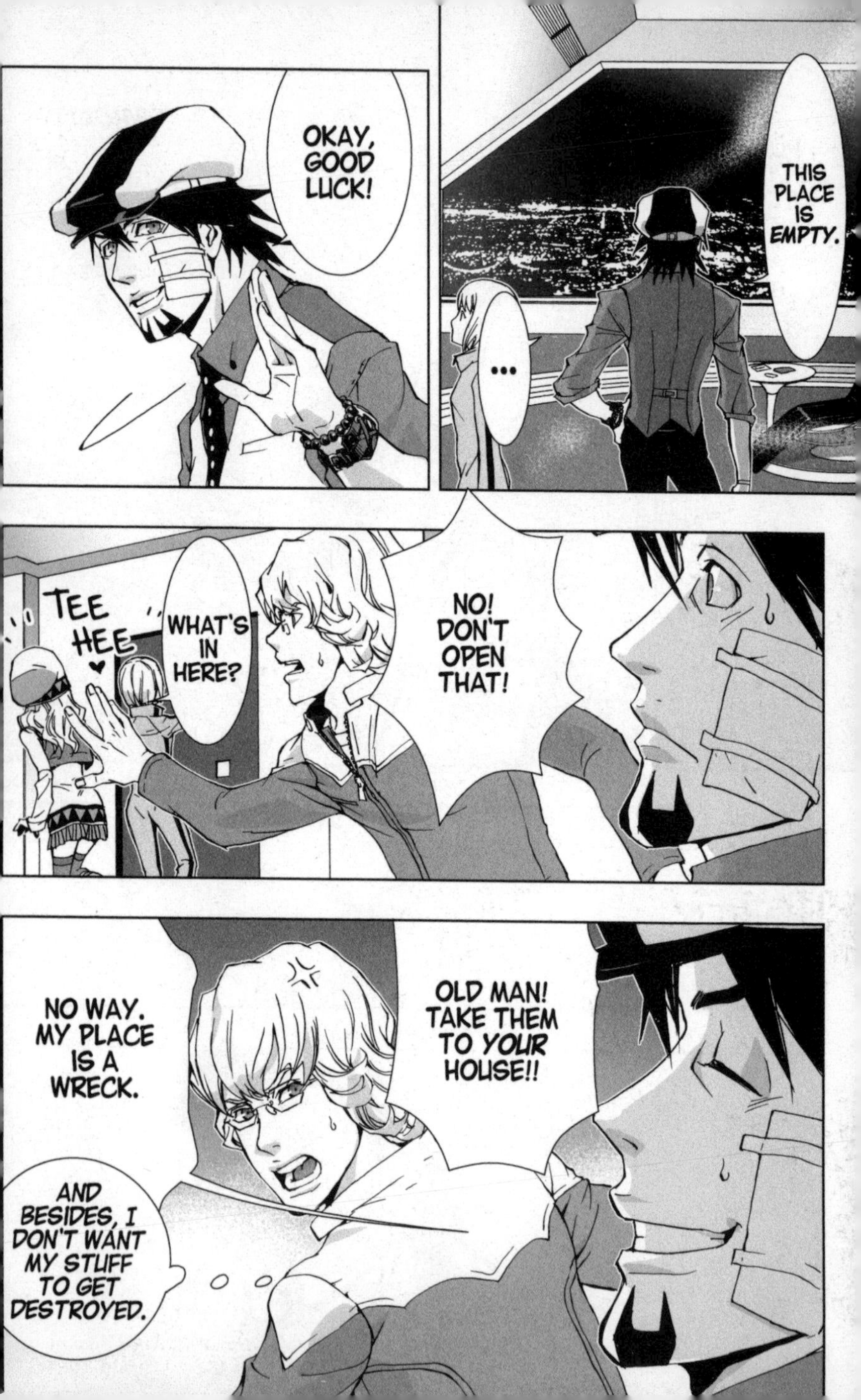
THIS PLACE IS EMPTY.
...
OKAY, GOOD LUCK!
NO! DON'T OPEN THAT!
WHAT'S IN HERE?
TEE HEE ♥
OLD MAN! TAKE THEM TO *YOUR* HOUSE!!
NO WAY. MY PLACE IS A WRECK.
AND BESIDES, I DON'T WANT MY STUFF TO GET DESTROYED.

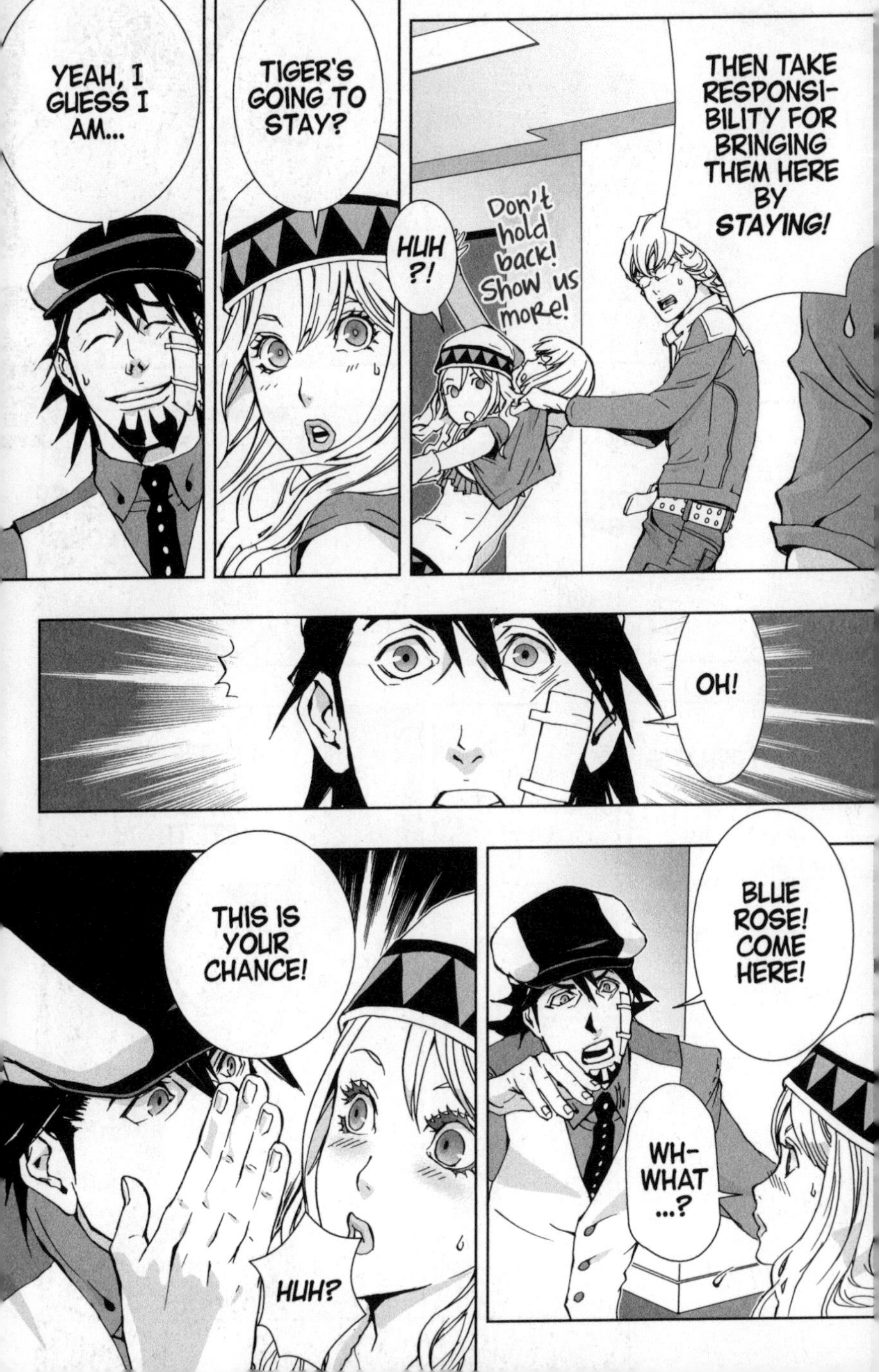
THEN TAKE RESPONSIBILITY FOR BRINGING THEM HERE BY STAYING!
Don't hold back! Show us more!
HUH ?!
TIGER'S GOING TO STAY?
YEAH, I GUESS I AM...
OH!
BLUE ROSE! COME HERE!
WH-WHAT ...?
THIS IS YOUR CHANCE!
HUH?

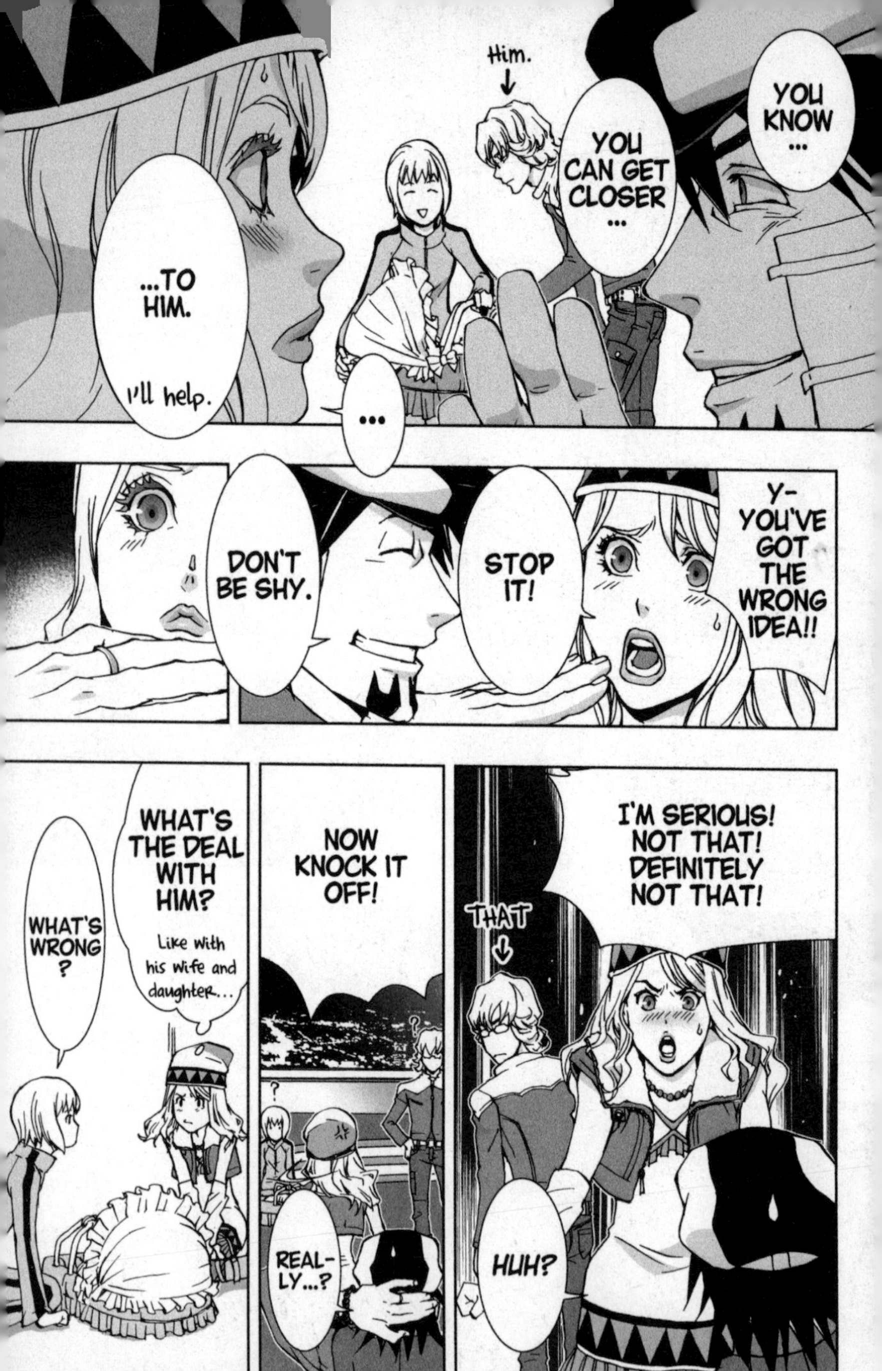
YOU KNOW...
YOU CAN GET CLOSER...
Him.
...TO HIM.
I'll help.
...
Y-YOU'VE GOT THE WRONG IDEA!!
STOP IT!
DON'T BE SHY.
I'M SERIOUS! NOT THAT! DEFINITELY NOT THAT!
THAT
HUH?
NOW KNOCK IT OFF!
REAL-LY...?
WHAT'S THE DEAL WITH HIM?
Like with his wife and daughter...
WHAT'S WRONG?

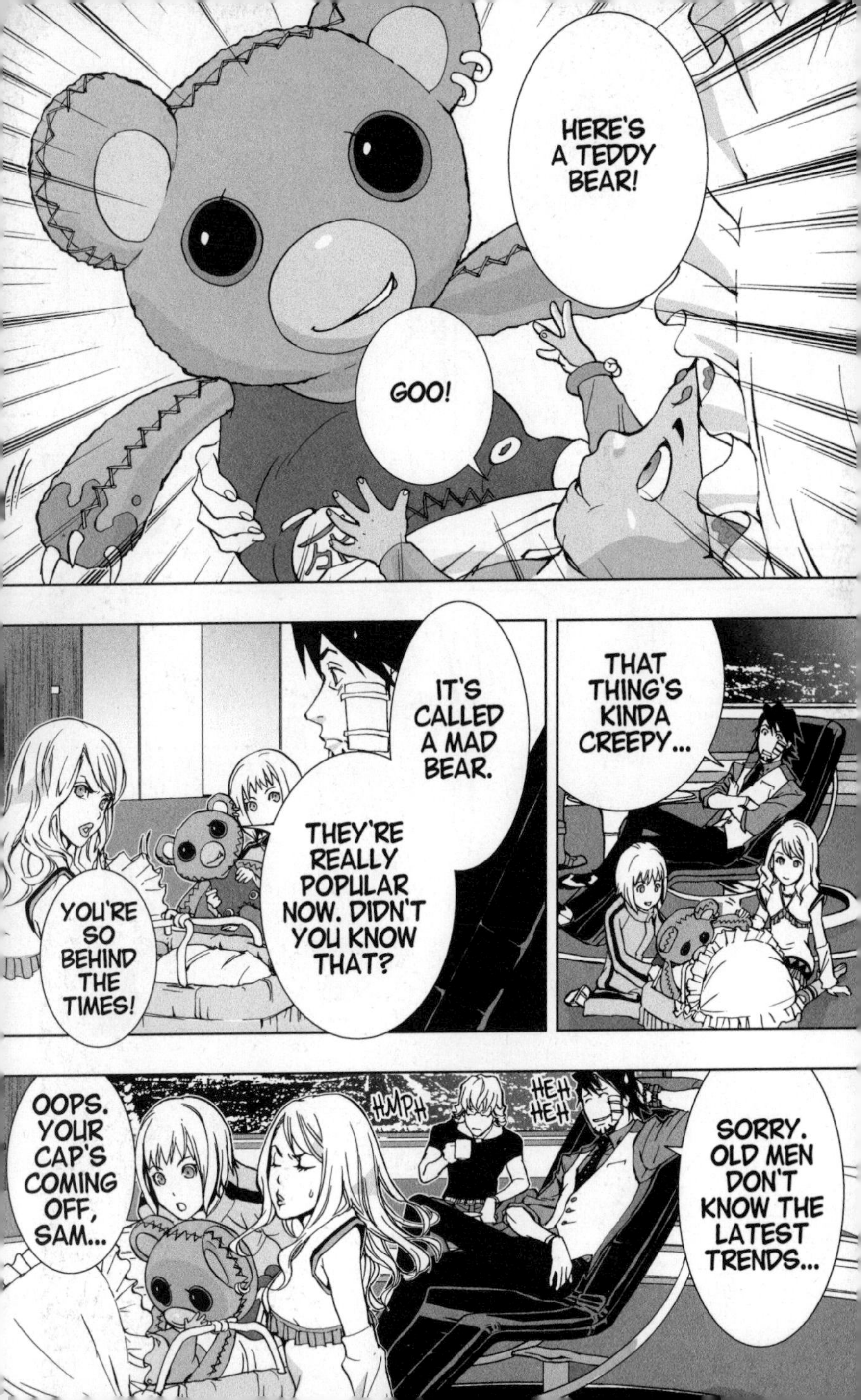
HERE'S A TEDDY BEAR!
GOO!
THAT THING'S KINDA CREEPY...
IT'S CALLED A MAD BEAR.
THEY'RE REALLY POPULAR NOW. DIDN'T YOU KNOW THAT?
YOU'RE SO BEHIND THE TIMES!
SORRY. OLD MEN DON'T KNOW THE LATEST TRENDS...
HEH HEH
HMPH
OOPS. YOUR CAP'S COMING OFF, SAM...

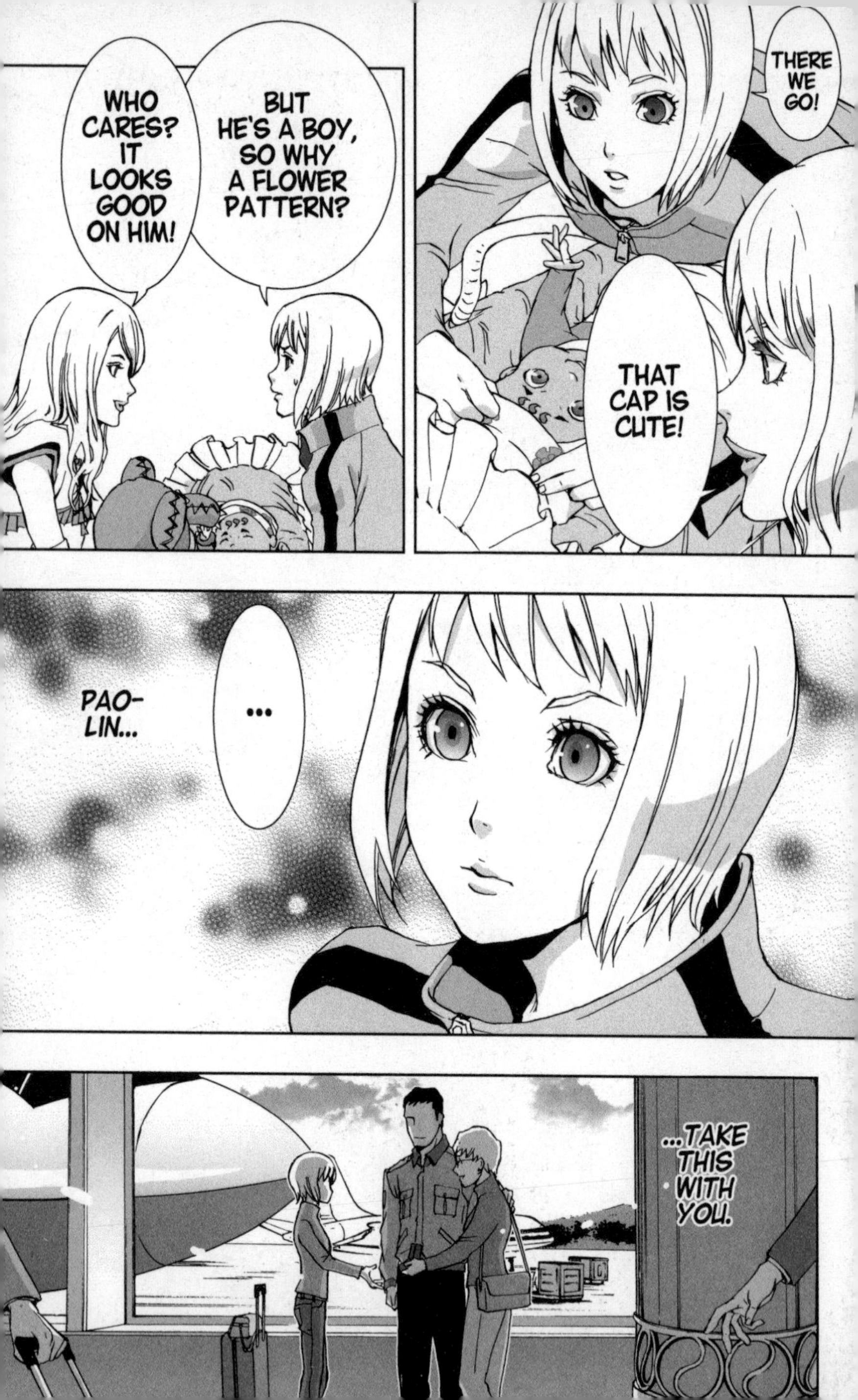
THERE WE GO!
THAT CAP IS CUTE!
BUT HE'S A BOY, SO WHY A FLOWER PATTERN?
WHO CARES? IT LOOKS GOOD ON HIM!
...
PAO-LIN...
...TAKE THIS WITH YOU.

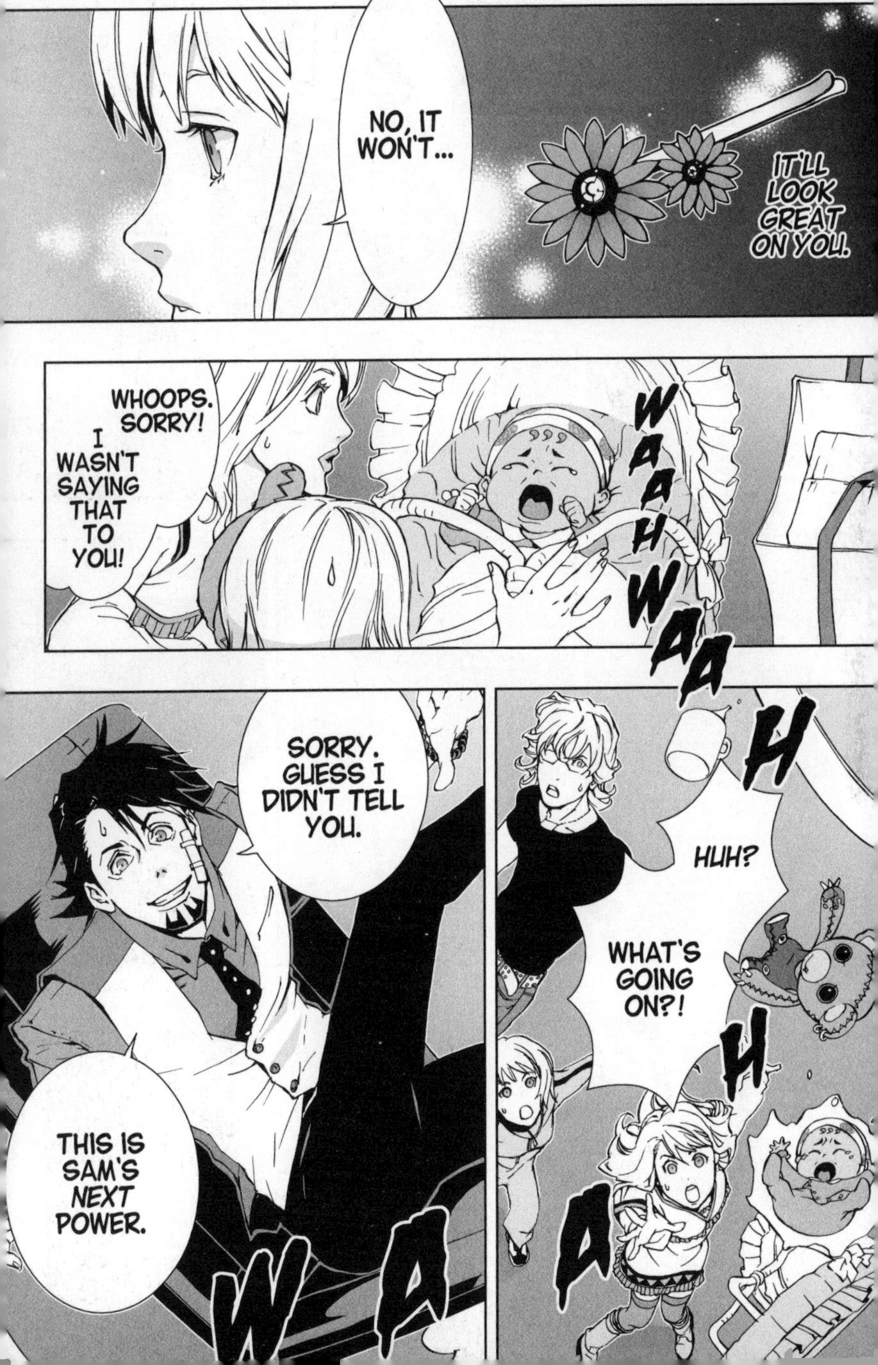
IT'LL LOOK GREAT ON YOU.
NO, IT WON'T...
WAAHWAAH
WHOOPS. SORRY! I WASN'T SAYING THAT TO YOU!
HUH?
WHAT'S GOING ON?!
SORRY. GUESS I DIDN'T TELL YOU.
THIS IS SAM'S NEXT POWER.

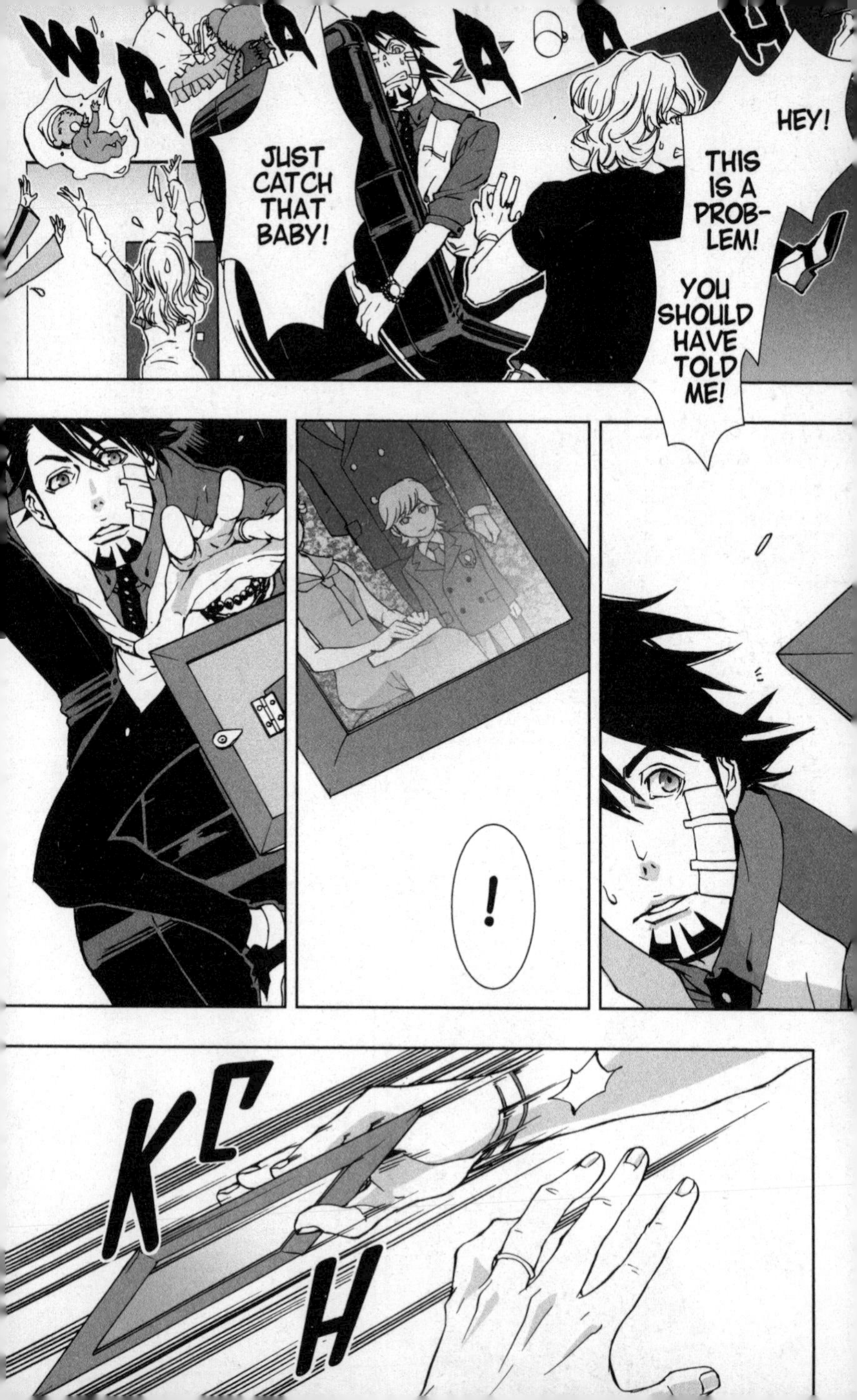
WAAAAAH
HEY!
THIS IS A PROB-LEM!
YOU SHOULD HAVE TOLD ME!
JUST CATCH THAT BABY!
!
KCH

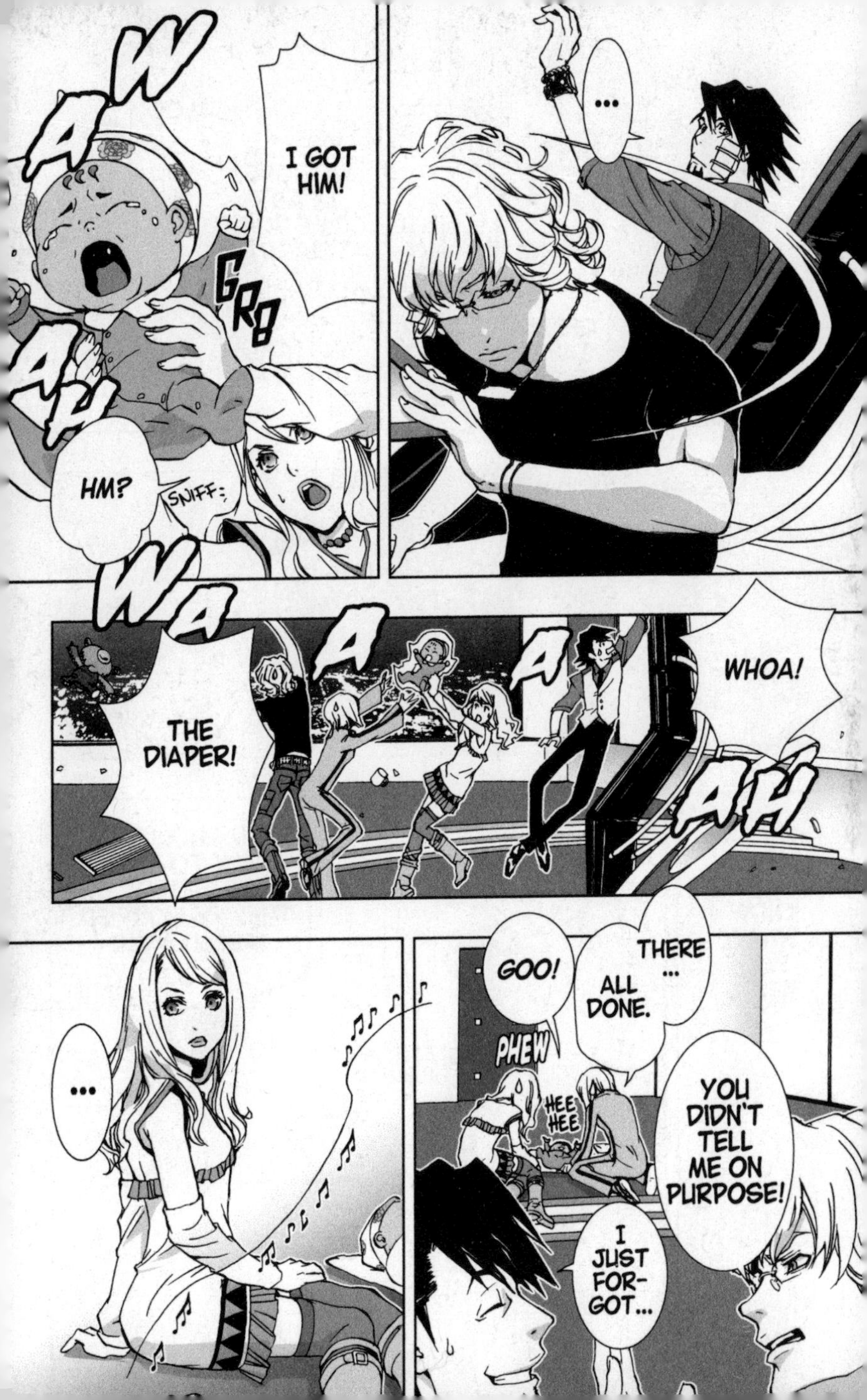
...
I GOT HIM!
AW
A
GRB
AY
HM?
SNIFF
WHOA!
WA
A
A
AH
THE DIAPER!
THERE... ALL DONE.
GOO!
PHEW
HEE HEE
YOU DIDN'T TELL ME ON PURPOSE!
I JUST FOR-GOT...
...

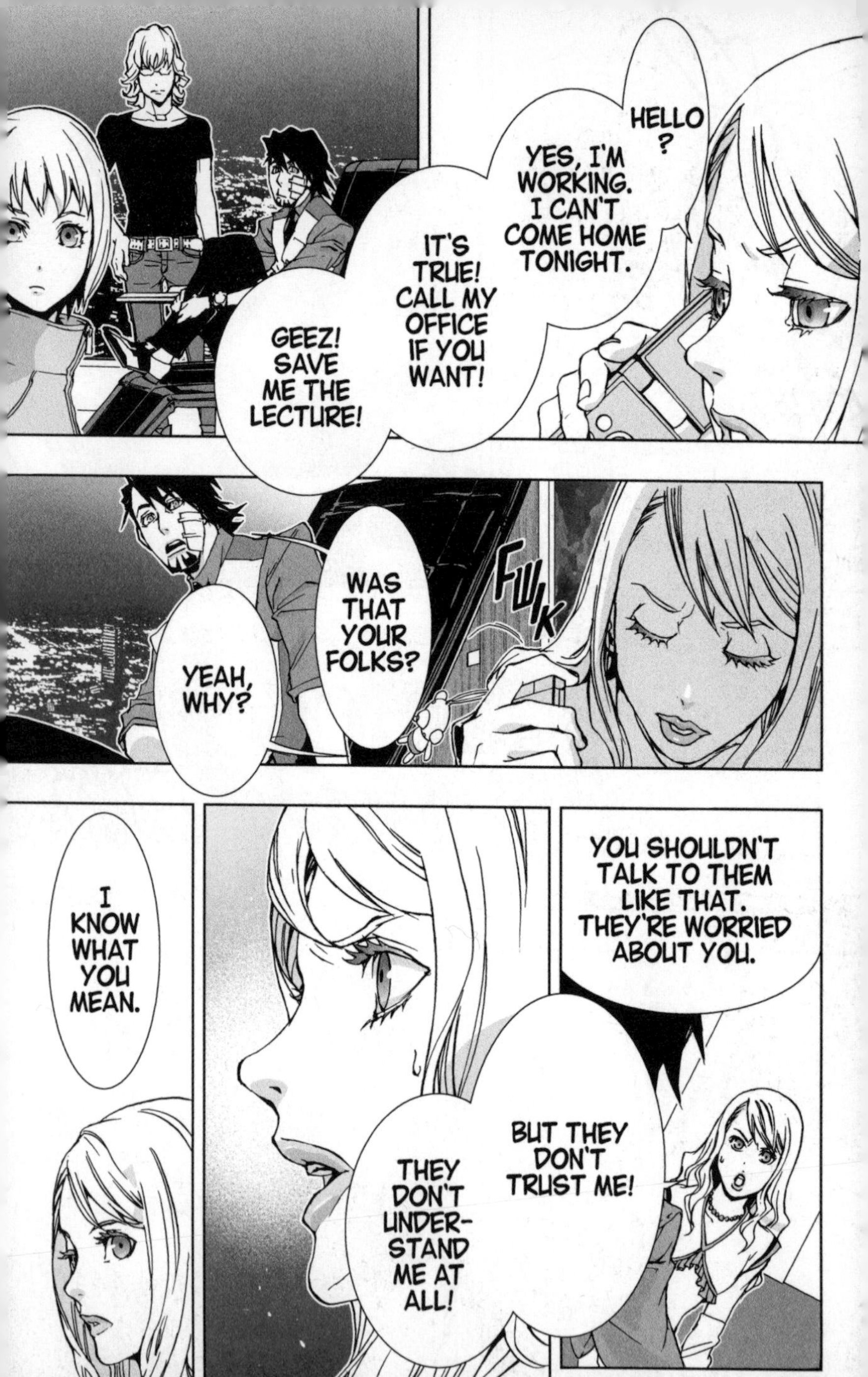
HELLO?
YES, I'M WORKING. I CAN'T COME HOME TONIGHT.
IT'S TRUE! CALL MY OFFICE IF YOU WANT!
GEEZ! SAVE ME THE LECTURE!
FWIK
WAS THAT YOUR FOLKS?
YEAH, WHY?
YOU SHOULDN'T TALK TO THEM LIKE THAT. THEY'RE WORRIED ABOUT YOU.
BUT THEY DON'T TRUST ME!
THEY DON'T UNDER-STAND ME AT ALL!
I KNOW WHAT YOU MEAN.

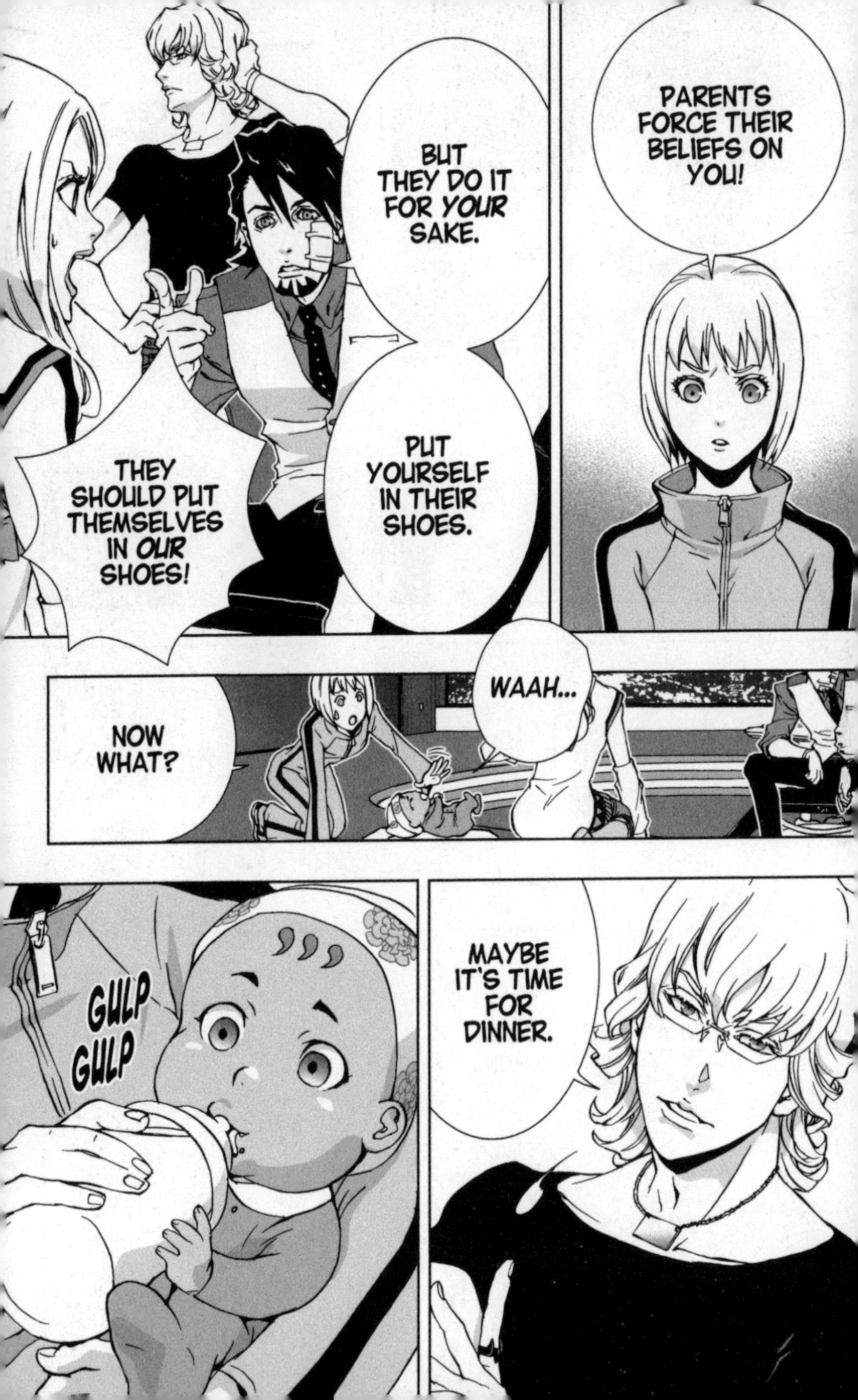
PARENTS FORCE THEIR BELIEFS ON YOU!
BUT THEY DO IT FOR *YOUR* SAKE.
PUT YOURSELF IN THEIR SHOES.
THEY SHOULD PUT THEMSELVES IN *OUR* SHOES!
WAAH...
NOW WHAT?
MAYBE IT'S TIME FOR DINNER.
GULP GULP

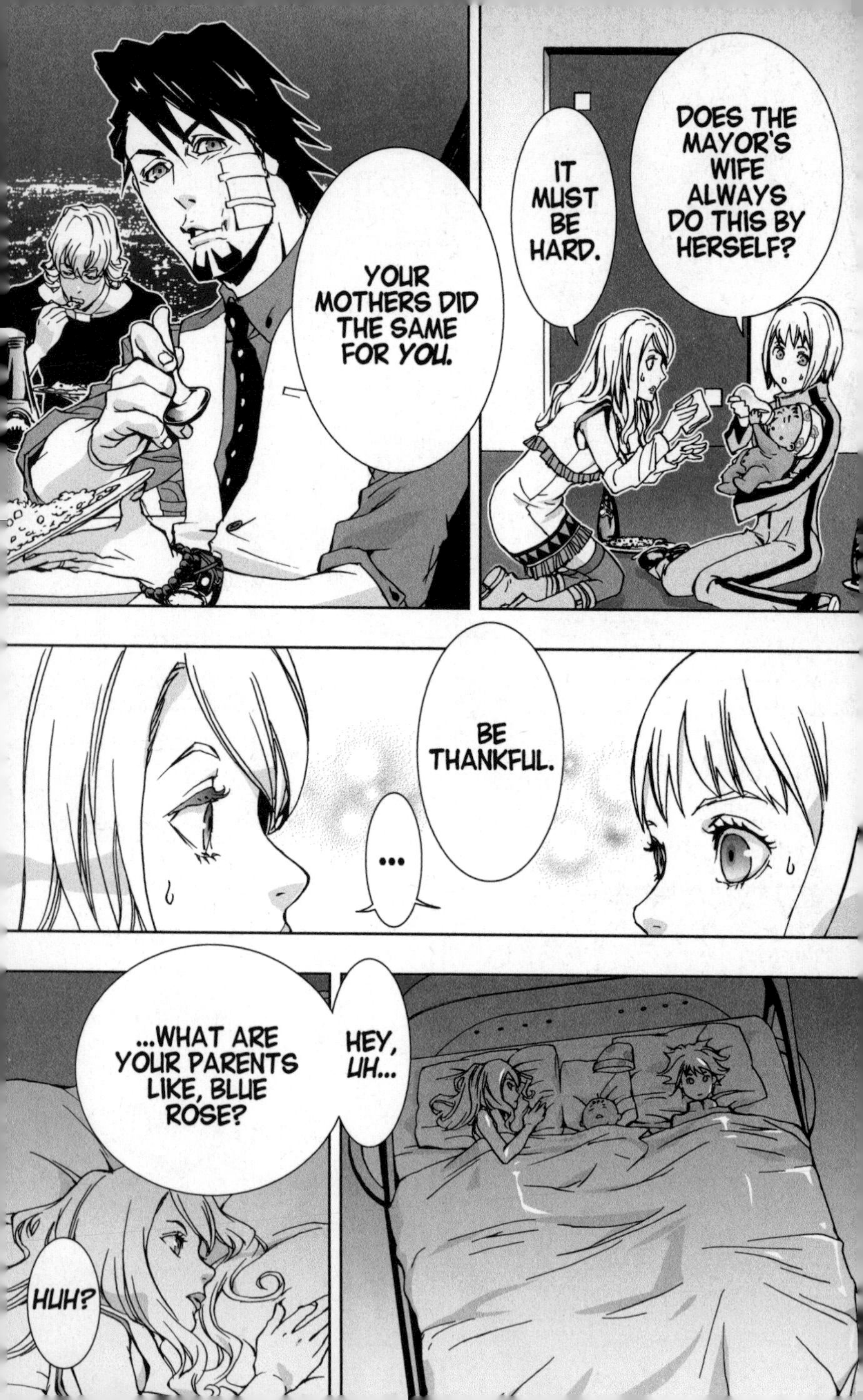
DOES THE MAYOR'S WIFE ALWAYS DO THIS BY HERSELF?
IT MUST BE HARD.
YOUR MOTHERS DID THE SAME FOR *YOU.*
BE THANKFUL.
...
HEY, UH...
...WHAT ARE YOUR PARENTS LIKE, BLUE ROSE?
HUH?

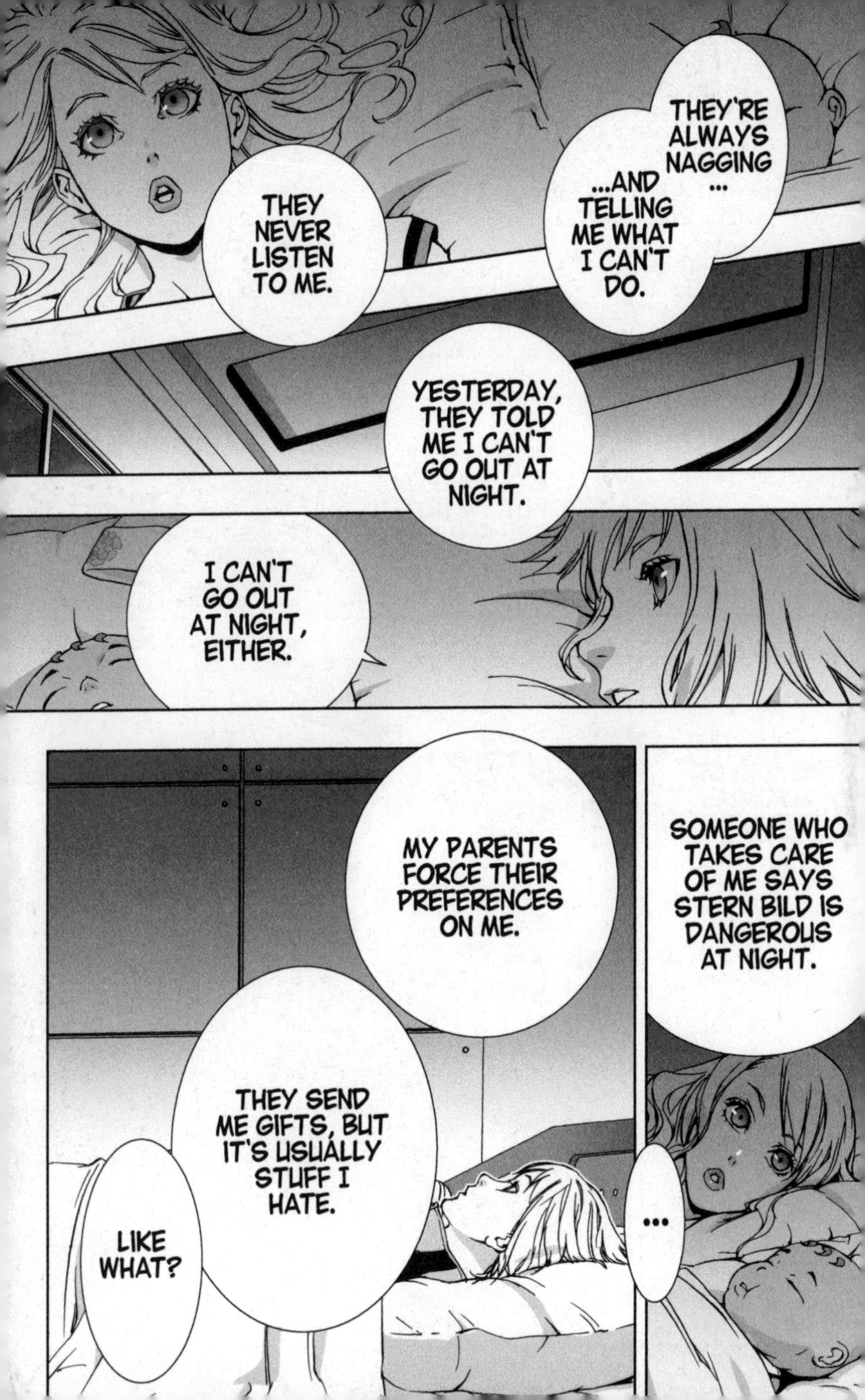
THEY'RE ALWAYS NAGGING ...
...AND TELLING ME WHAT I CAN'T DO.
THEY NEVER LISTEN TO ME.
YESTERDAY, THEY TOLD ME I CAN'T GO OUT AT NIGHT.
I CAN'T GO OUT AT NIGHT, EITHER.
SOMEONE WHO TAKES CARE OF ME SAYS STERN BILD IS DANGEROUS AT NIGHT.
...
MY PARENTS FORCE THEIR PREFERENCES ON ME.
THEY SEND ME GIFTS, BUT IT'S USUALLY STUFF I HATE.
LIKE WHAT?

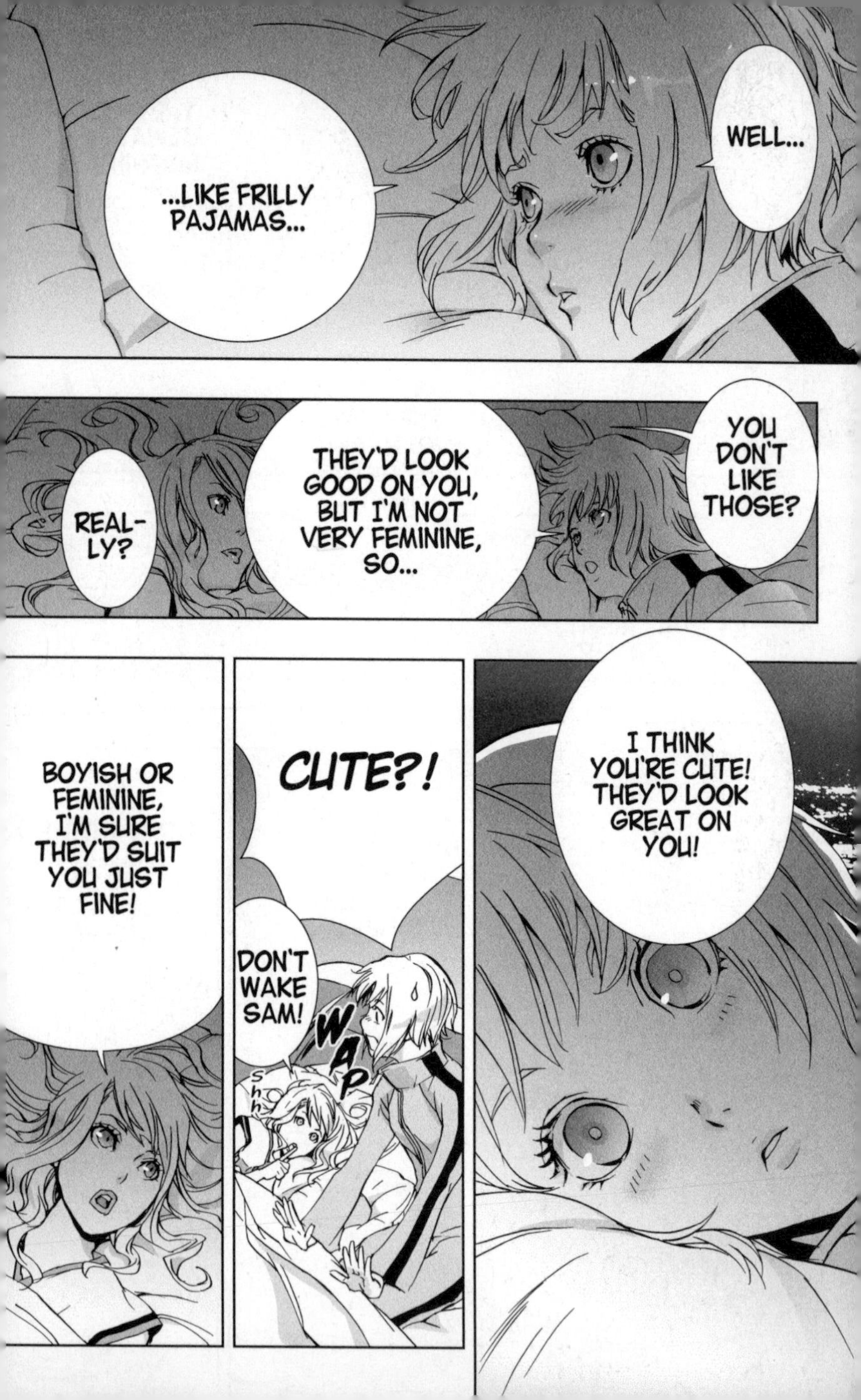
WELL...
...LIKE FRILLY PAJAMAS...
YOU DON'T LIKE THOSE?
THEY'D LOOK GOOD ON YOU, BUT I'M NOT VERY FEMININE, SO...
REAL-LY?
I THINK YOU'RE CUTE! THEY'D LOOK GREAT ON YOU!
CUTE?!
DON'T WAKE SAM!
WAP
Shh
BOYISH OR FEMININE, I'M SURE THEY'D SUIT YOU JUST FINE!

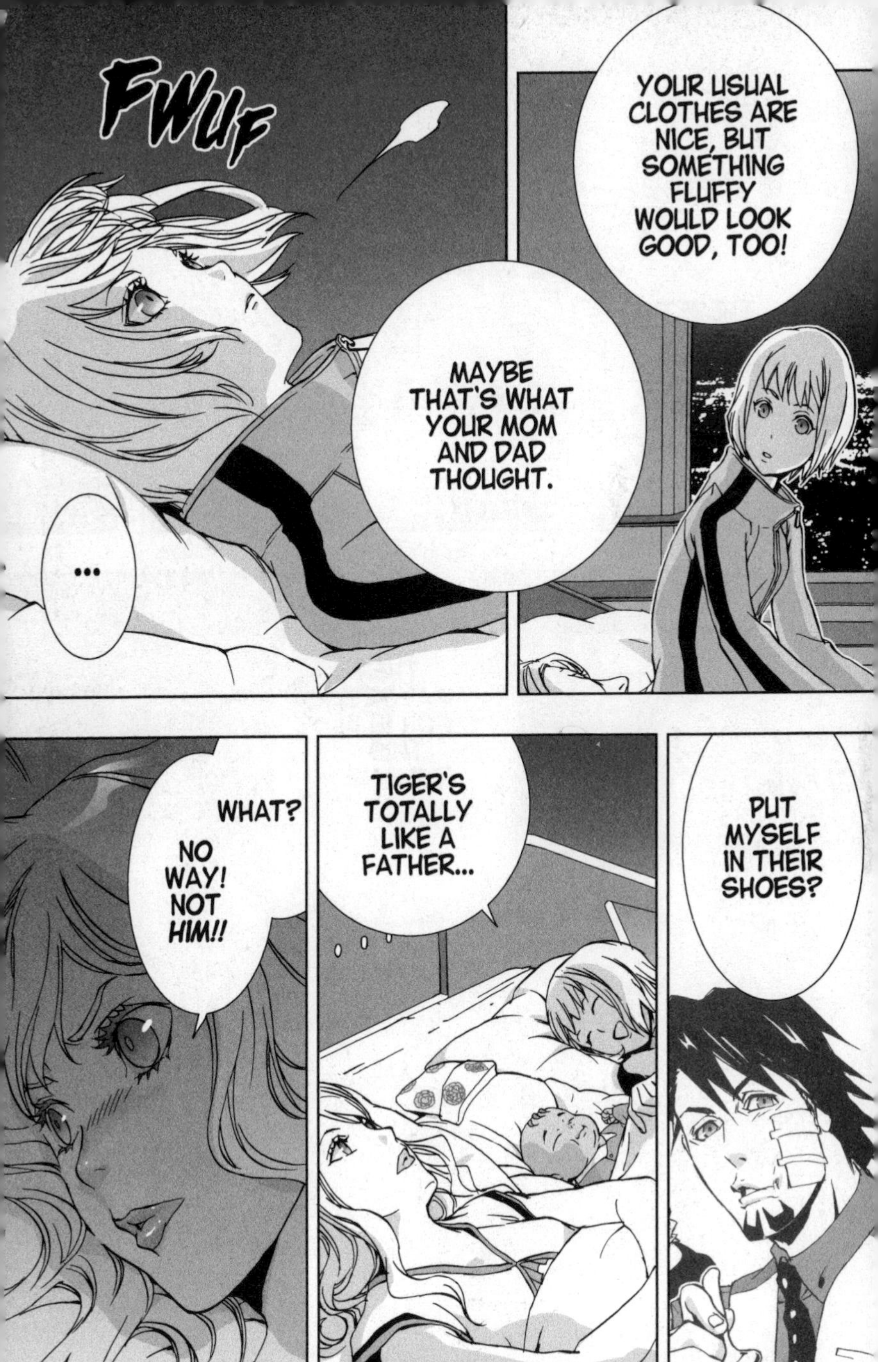
YOUR USUAL CLOTHES ARE NICE, BUT SOMETHING FLUFFY WOULD LOOK GOOD, TOO!
MAYBE THAT'S WHAT YOUR MOM AND DAD THOUGHT.
FWUF
...
PUT MYSELF IN THEIR SHOES?
TIGER'S TOTALLY LIKE A FATHER...
WHAT?
NO WAY! NOT HIM!!

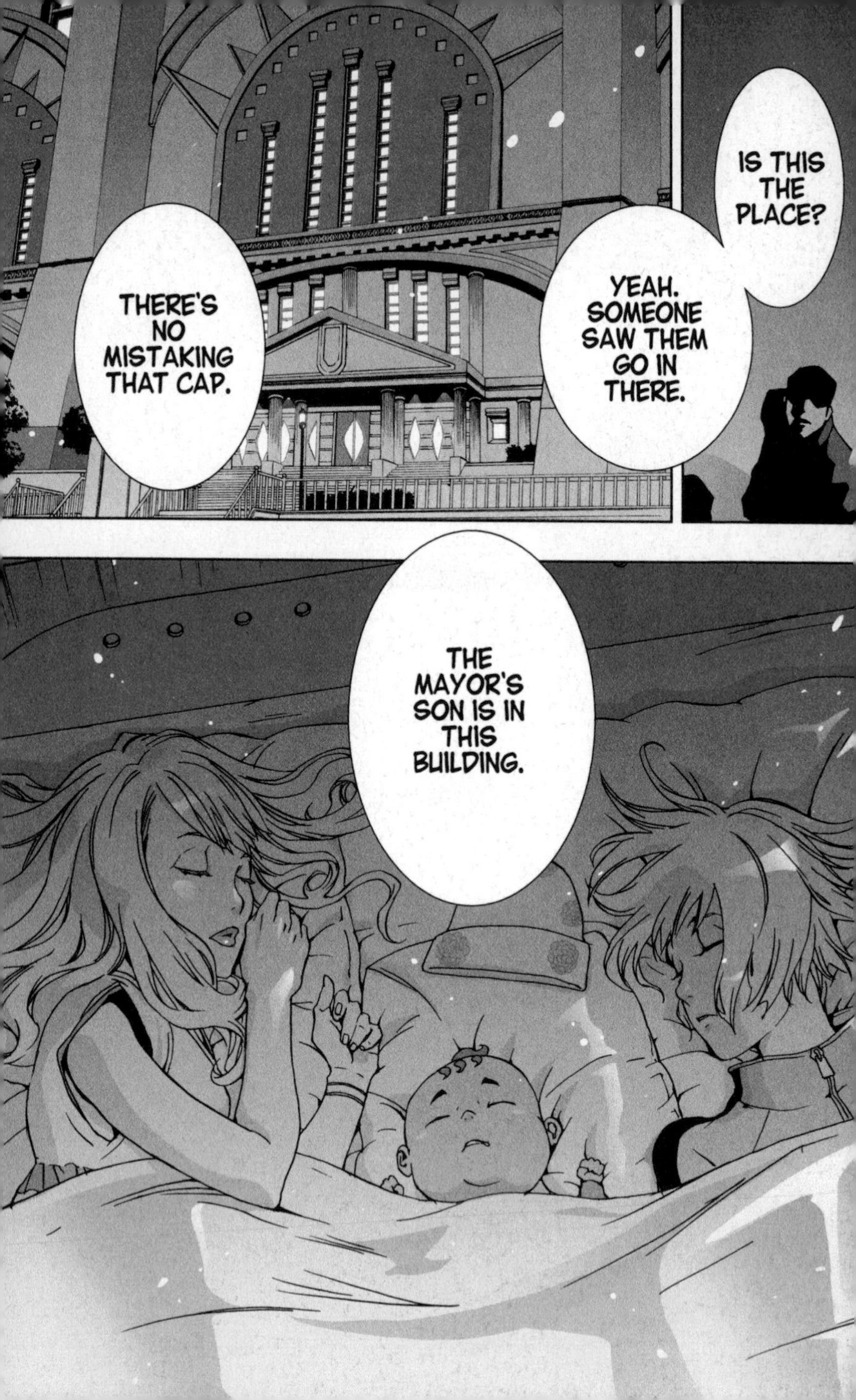
IS THIS THE PLACE?
YEAH. SOMEONE SAW THEM GO IN THERE.
THERE'S NO MISTAKING THAT CAP.
THE MAYOR'S SON IS IN THIS BUILDING.

TIGER&BUNNY
To Be Continued

Mizuki Sakakibara

Assistant
Ayako Mayuzumi
Beth
Eri Saito
Sachiko Ito
Fuku

MIZUKI SAKAKIBARA

Mizuki Sakakibara's American comics debut was Marvel's *Exile* in 2002. Currently, *TIGER & BUNNY* is serialized in *Newtype Ace* magazine by Kadokawa Shoten.

MASAFUMI NISHIDA

Story director. *TIGER & BUNNY* was his first work as a TV animation scriptwriter. He is well known for the movie *Gachi☆Boy* and the Japanese TV dramas *Maoh*, *Kaibutsu-kun*, and *Youkai Ningen Bem*.

MASAKAZU KATSURA

Original character designer. Masakazu Katsura is well known for the manga series *WING MAN*, *Denei Shojo* (*Video Girl Ai*), *I"s*, and *ZETMAN*. Katsura's works have been translated into several languages, including Chinese and French, as well as English.

5

Because of a kidnapping threat, Kotetsu and Barnaby
have their hands full babysitting the mayor's infant
son, who is also a telekinetic NEXT! Unfortunately,
Kotetsu's face just makes the child cry, setting off his
destructive wailing. Pao-Lin and Karina have the right
touch for this job, but sinister forces are lining up
against them!

TIGER&BUNNY 4

VIZ Media Edition

Art **MIZUKI SAKAKIBARA**
Planning / Original Story **SUNRISE**
Original Script **MASAFUMI NISHIDA**
Original Character and Hero Design **MASAKAZU KATSURA**

TIGER & BUNNY Volume 4
© Mizuki SAKAKIBARA 2013
© SUNRISE/T&B PARTNERS, MBS
First published in Japan in 2013 by KADOKAWA CORPORATION, Tokyo.
English translation rights arranged with KADOKAWA CORPORATION, Tokyo.

Translation & English Adaptation **LABAAMEN & JOHN WERRY, HC LANGUAGE SOLUTIONS**
Touch-up Art & Lettering **STEPHEN DUTRO**
Design **FAWN LAU**
Editor **MIKE MONTESA**

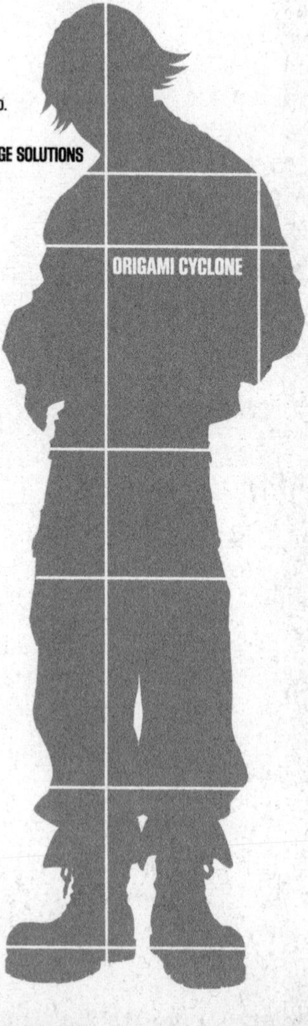

Printed in the U.S.A.

Published by VIZ Media, LLC
P.O. Box 77010
San Francisco, CA 94107

10 9 8 7 6 5 4 3 2 1
First printing, February 2014

ORIGAMI CYCLONE

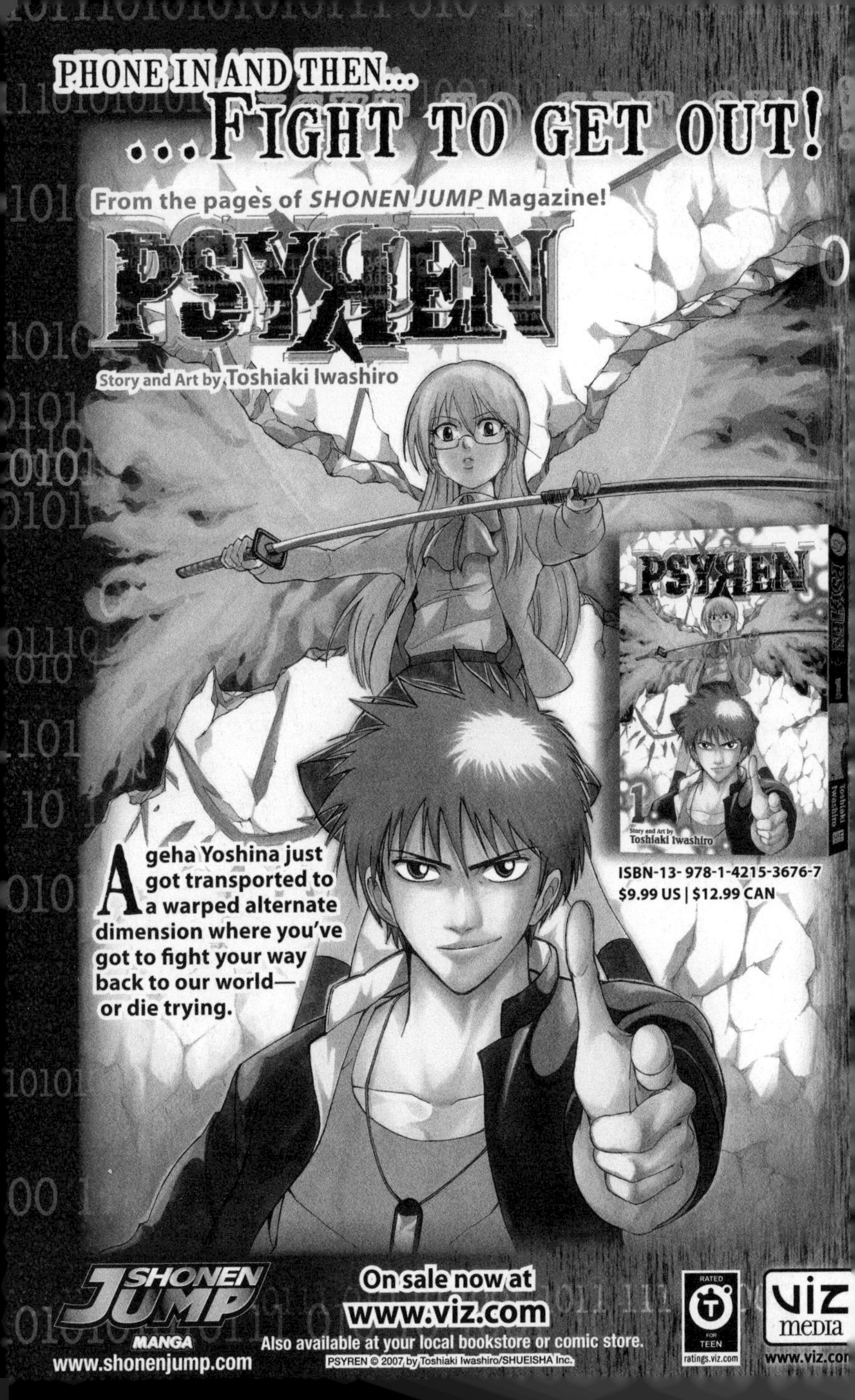
PHONE IN AND THEN...
...FIGHT TO GET OUT!
From the pages of SHONEN JUMP Magazine!
PSYREN
Story and Art by Toshiaki Iwashiro
PSYREN
1
Story and Art by Toshiaki Iwashiro
ISBN-13- 978-1-4215-3676-7
$9.99 US | $12.99 CAN
Ageha Yoshina just got transported to a warped alternate dimension where you've got to fight your way back to our world—or die trying.
SHONEN JUMP
MANGA
www.shonenjump.com
On sale now at
www.viz.com
Also available at your local bookstore or comic store.
PSYREN © 2007 by Toshiaki Iwashiro/SHUEISHA Inc.
RATED
T
FOR
TEEN
ratings.viz.com
viz
media
www.viz.com

Enter_the_world_of_

LOVELESS

story_+_art_by_YUN_KOUGA

2-in-1 EDITIONS

Each 2-in-1 edition includes 6 color pages and 50 pages of never-before-seen BONUS comics, artist commentary and interviews!

only $14.99!
($16.99 CAN / £9.99 UK)

Available at your local book store, comic book shop or library, or online at:
store.viz.com

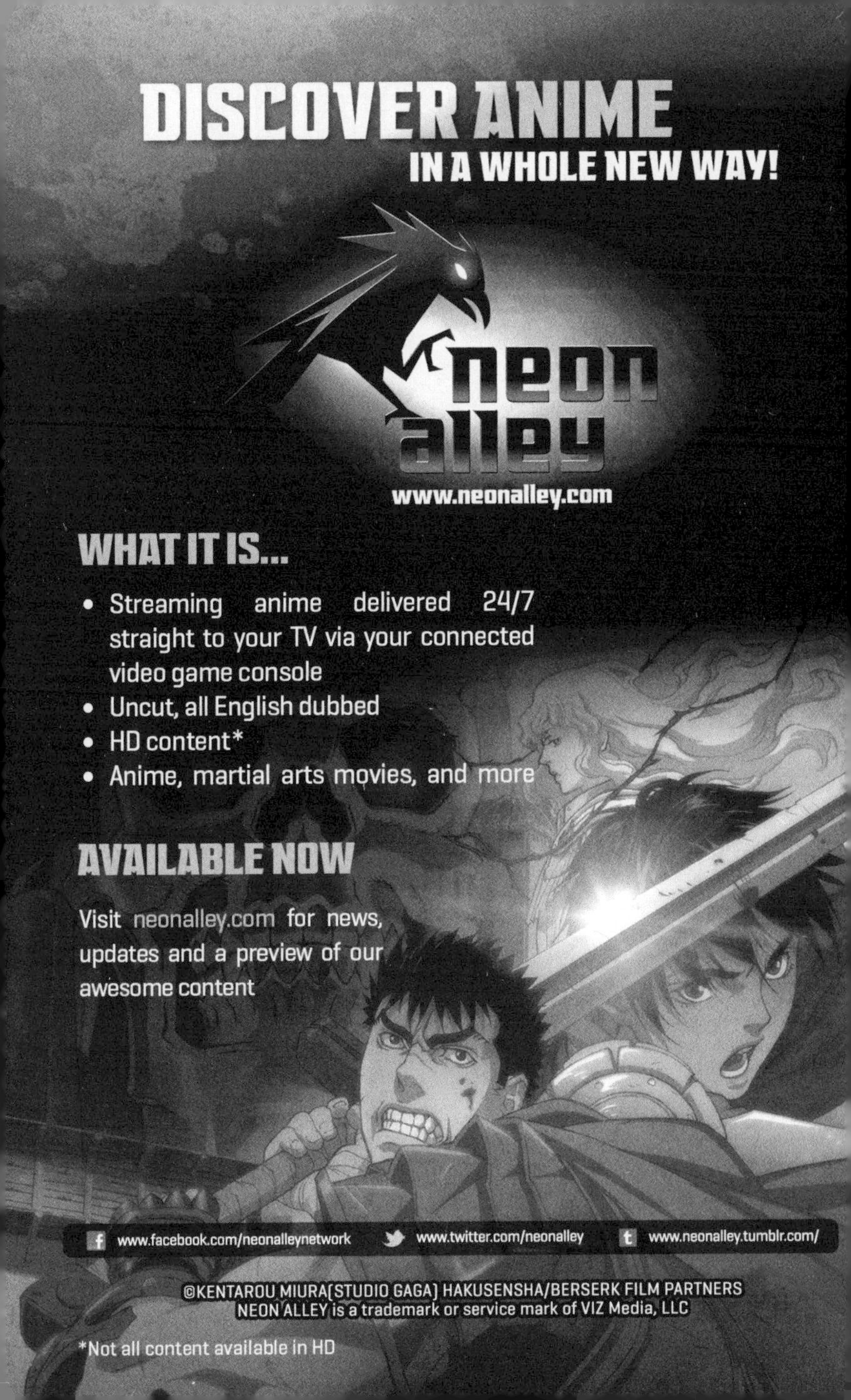
DISCOVER ANIME
IN A WHOLE NEW WAY!
neon alley
www.neonalley.com
WHAT IT IS...
• Streaming anime delivered 24/7 straight to your TV via your connected video game console
• Uncut, all English dubbed
• HD content*
• Anime, martial arts movies, and more
AVAILABLE NOW
Visit neonalley.com for news, updates and a preview of our awesome content
www.facebook.com/neonalleynetwork
www.twitter.com/neonalley
www.neonalley.tumblr.com/
©KENTAROU MIURA(STUDIO GAGA) HAKUSENSHA/BERSERK FILM PARTNERS
NEON ALLEY is a trademark or service mark of VIZ Media, LLC
*Not all content available in HD

YOU'RE READING THE WRONG WAY!

Tiger & Bunny reads from right to left, starting in the upper-right corner. Japanese is read from right to left, meaning that action, sound effects, and word-balloon order are completely reversed from English order.

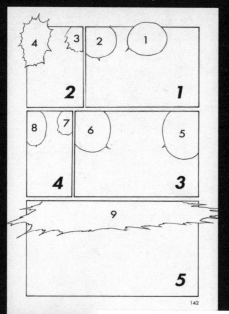